Primitive Mythology

Primitive Mythology

The Mythic World of the Australian and Papuan Natives

LUCIEN LÉVY-BRUHL

Translated by
BRIAN ELLIOTT

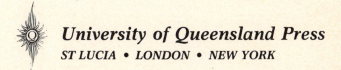

University of Queensland Press
ST LUCIA • LONDON • NEW YORK

La Mythologie Primitive first published in Paris in 1935 by Alcan Publishers

English translation © University of Queensland Press, St Lucia, Queensland 1983

Typeset by University of Queensland Press
Printed and bound by The Dominion Press–Hedges & Bell, Melbourne

Distributed in the United Kingdom, Europe, the Middle East, Africa, and the Caribbean by Prentice-Hall International, International Book Distributors Ltd, 66 Wood Lane End, Hemel Hempstead, Herts., England.

Published with the assistance of the French Minister of Cultural Affairs and the University Presses of France

National Library of Australia
Cataloguing-in-Publication data

Lévy-Bruhl, Lucien, 1857–1939.
 [La mythologie primitive. English].
 Primitive mythology.

 Bibliography.
 Includes index.
 ISBN 0 7022 1667 4.

 [1]. Aborigines, Australian – Religion and mythology. 2. Mythology, Papuan.
 I. Elliott, Brian, 1910–   . II. Title.
 III. Title: La mythologie primitive.

299'.92

Library of Congress Cataloguing in Publication Data

Lévy-Bruhl, Lucien, 1857–1939.
 Primitive mythology.

 Translation of: La mythologie primitive.
 Bibliography: p.
 Includes index.
 1. Mythology, Australian (Aboriginal) 2. Mythology, Papuan. 3. Ethnology – Papua New Guinea. 4. Folklore.
 I. Title.
 BL2610.L413   1983   299'.92   82-17332
 ISBN 0-7022-1667-4

Contents

Translator's Preface

This translation of *La Mythologie primitive* was undertaken for a particular reason, and although it was a quite personal reason (an urge which for a variety of causes I felt in a personal way), I think I ought to explain it. Being myself Australian-born I was very sensitively aware of the strongly prevailing sentiment of guilt which many Australians of European origin feel in regard to the long neglect and disparagement, misinformation and general brutal indifference concerning the Aboriginal natives of the country. Some of them still (though much diminished in number) live in something approximating to their former tribal conditions; others in a state of degradation as neither blacks nor whites but simply as fringe-dwellers, fully admitted to the society of neither the one community nor the other. A few — very few indeed — have made a happy and successful adaptation to the modern western way of life. The rest are simply lost human beings, who meet with no tolerance and can expect to find no welcome anywhere. Two hundred years of white occupation and settlement have brought about this misery in a people who, as we now realize, had been the undisturbed possessors of the land for forty thousand years or more. For a great part of these last two hundred years, no one cared about their distress — indeed, few were even aware of it. Lately it has been more in people's minds; but even now, few have any clear notion of what it means, or of what to do about it.

When, some five or six years ago, I first came across *La Mythologie primitive*, my impulse was to look for an English version of it, with a hope of bringing it to the attention of others. I could not find one. I wrote to the publishers in Paris to ask if they were able to point one out. They were not. It seemed they had understood my enquiry to be a request for permission to translate the book myself. I plucked up the courage to ask myself why not? Since no one else had attempted it, and no one, it seemed, was even offering to attempt it, clearly I had some kind of responsibility to try. I had no doubt whatever of the work's usefulness, even though it was already nearly fifty years old. So I set myself to work. Having in mind the interests of Australian readers — who are not, in the general way, very versatile linguists — I decided to include, as well as Lévy-Bruhl's text, as much as possible of his note material. As for the most part the material was merely indicated by footnotes, giving title and page reference, I found this a daunting complication, but with the resources at hand and some special library assistance, I did manage to assemble and translate the greater part of it. I also, in a number of instances, filled out Lévy-Bruhl's quotations when he had taken them in a reduced form from the originals, and I sometimes extended them a little when the matter was relevant and the content interesting. These additions added bulk to the book; but I hope they were justified, if only because, in comparison with European resources, Australia is but meagrely serviced with libraries of the ample extent that the allusions implied. A student who might be intent on checking and pursuing them could very well be severely frustrated unless he was situated in one of the larger city centres. Even then he would be unlikely to find all of them, as I discovered for myself. Chasing up the references became, however, one of the most interesting and rewarding parts of the undertaking as a whole, and if for that reason only I was happy to be able to include them.

The book itself, as I came increasingly to realize, was a work of major importance — for the world, and not merely for Australia. Lévy-Bruhl is no inconsiderable writer, and this is one of the best of his writings on the subject of primitive man. I am not disinclined to assert it is *the* best. One wonders why *La Mythologie primitive* was not translated nearer to the time when it appeared (1935). But a factor which no doubt had a bearing was a certain decline in regard suffered by the older school of anthropologists, still partly antiquarians, like the English Tylor, Frazer and Lang, in whose steps Lévy-Bruhl followed, though not docilely. They were being set against a vigorous upsurge of new ideas and more systematically scientific enquiry, based more than formerly upon practical field-studies. New theories of mental behaviour at primitive and all levels brought into controversy Lévy-Bruhl's insistent concern with what he had been calling "primitive mentality", and for a long time his opinions appeared to be somewhat discredited. He was obviously troubled by the attack on his terminology, which was taken to be an attempt to undermine his working concepts. He shows some uneasiness on this score at the beginning of *Primitive Mythology*, and even more in the posthumously published *Les Cahiers de Lévy-Bruhl* (1963), entitled in English *The Notebooks on Primitive Mentality* (1975). But the smoke and the smother have now died down, and less energy is nowadays given to fighting that intellectual battle than to understanding what his terms actually mean. The present-day reader of *Primitive Mythology* will not be put to great difficulty in understanding him.

His subject matter in *Primitive Mythology* is by no means limited to the Australian and New Guinea fields promised on the title page. It really is concerned with primitive mythology, in Australia and elsewhere, and hence with the bearing of mythology on all developing thought from primitive to civilized.

Modern Australian readers will be very humbly impressed to discover how much this far-away French scholar had read and digested of Australian (as well as much other) ethnological material, which large labour must have been accomplished at a time when few Australians had any notion what was being published, or for that matter, cared to find out. It was of course not a casual, but a professional interest with him; but it puts most of us to the blush nevertheless. The same humane breadth of concern appears just as clearly in what he has to say of other primitive races, but it is on Australia and New Guinea that his concentrated attention rests. His observations touch on African, North and South American, Eskimo, and other mythologies. His approach to them all, however, is as we might expect – and it is for Australian readers particularly a stimulating perspective – solidly French, or perhaps continentally European would describe it better. I would not wish to make too much of this point; it is not so marked as to convey an impression of foreignness, and yet it does add a freshness. It also entails something else which I would not wish to make too much of, either: there are little shocks here and there which we must have the generosity to weather, because he does not know Australia as well as we do. To complain of them would be parochial; but they may be noticed – I should hope, with understanding and good humour – in passing.

What we have, then, is a scholarly assessment, in which the stress of the author's findings falls mostly on general conclusions rather than on fine detail, although there is no shortage of detail. The valuations are in the last resort philosophical. The work as a whole is a close examination of the "primitive" mind (for which various tribal communities provide the evidence), offered by a highly developed — and, as already emphasized, French — "civilized" one. It is a comment made by intellect on the basic human intelligence, the intelligence, however, out of which all later rational and intellectual progress had to grow. There is a certain irony in this tribute paid by humanity in its finest state of advancement to what an Australian poet has called the "human LCM" — to the humanism of the earth. It is of course never in Lévy-Bruhl's mind to suggest that what he calls "primitive mentality" means for him inferior humanity. Lévy-Bruhl does not ever demean or belittle the primitive mind, but it is plain that he sees it as preliminary to civilized order. The change is spectacular, but also in a sense miraculous: this miracle is always present to his view. Similarly when he considers the particular case of religion (and we must not mistake him here), he sees mythology as anterior to it, not as something incidental.

Primitive Mythology is about primitive mythology and nothing more. But no Australian (and perhaps no citizen of some other countries) can read it without drawing his own political inferences. There is a profound problem before this nation, and it is one which must be faced; and soon rather than later. It may possibly be of some constructive help to all concerned to realize — to school ourselves to realize — that it is really not one, but two problems: two problems that can never be separated, because one is obverse to the other. It has been said often enough that the two causes cannot be reconciled; but we may hope (if perhaps, for the present, only desperately) that in some long and patient prospect there may come a common understanding. There have already appeared a few, if merely nascent, signs of change. It is we — the white aggressors, the destroyers and rapists of black culture — who must accept the greater responsibility and bear the deepest blame. We have nothing but ignorance to plead in mitigation (callousness we dare not advance). But the blacks, who are by *disposition* (the term belongs to Lévy-Bruhl) humane, and basically so, must also eventually accept some responsibility to make an accommodation. Indeed they have already shown such a willingness in various ways, not always to their own advantage; but they must be helped, too, in all possible ways, not least in ways that will protect them, to make the adaptations that time and circumstance force upon them. Change is inevitable, not only for us; for them as well. And this must be so to some considerable extent even in fully tribal centres, so far relatively undisturbed. It must not be too drastic; it must be tolerable. But change is a more integral part of all human tradition than most of us commonly realize, the blacks included. All will not go well until each party acquires enough knowledge and understanding to see and respect the *point of view* of the other. Of the two, it will inevitably be the white party that will be the hardest to move – that is to say, with their hearts, and not merely with their heads. But it must in the long run be both, on both counts: blacks and whites, and hearts and heads, together. It seems particularly relevant to emphasize this point now, as this translation goes to press (early 1983), in view of increasing Aboriginal militancy in the cause of Land Rights.

How is understanding to be achieved? Not easily. But a beginning can be made if all concerned can be brought to *recognize* that the problem is twofold. The blacks are *our* part of it; but equally *we are theirs*. That is the long and the short of the political situation; that being the case, what can *Primitive Mythology* do for either? Not much, of course, and nothing quickly, but in the end, something essential. It can teach us – the whites particularly, but the blacks too, perhaps in the long run; not necessarily through reading it, but as a consequence of the way opinion percolates through society as a whole – it can teach us what we most need to know. And that is not *what* we must think about this two-dimensional problem, but *how*.

* * *

There is no doubt that an interest in the Aboriginal Problem, which began blindly out of conscience, ended up as a symbolic arena for many Australians in search of an identity. Very few had the kind of impartial interest that Elkin, quoting from Kant, put forward as the ideal goal for anthropology: "Man and every reasonable agent exists as an end in himself, and not as a mere mean or instrument to be employed by any will whatsoever, not even by his own, but must in every action regard his existence and that of every other intelligent, as an end in itself." [J.J. Healy, *Literature and the Aborigine in Australia* (St Lucia: University of Queensland Press, 1978)].

I add this extract partly to pay tribute to a very perceptive writer, and partly by way of a reminder that the underlying principles of Lévy-Bruhl's mind are still as vitally acceptable today, in spite of great social changes, as they were in 1935 when *La Mythologie primitive* first appeared.

Acknowledgements

My grateful thanks are due to a number of people who have helped me in various ways: to the University of Adelaide and particularly the Department of English (with several successive and sympathetic chairmen, including Colin Horne, George Turner, Tony Slade and Ken Ruthven), for much more than I can adequately epitomize or express; to the Barr Smith Library of the same university, and particularly the members of its inter-library loans section, for much tedious searching and help with texts I could not have done without; to the South Australian State Library, the Latrobe Library (Melbourne), the Menzies and the National Libraries (Canberra), to other Australian libraries and the National Library of Canada in Ottawa. I owe much gratitude to Graeme Pretty for useful discussion and sympathetic advice, and particularly for helping me to the resources of the anthropological, archaeological and ethnological sections of the South Australian State Museum. I record fond and personal gratitude to Robin Eaden for her painstaking editorial criticism and assistance during the preparation of the manuscript, and to Christine Lecky for typing it. I must not omit my gratitude to George Rude for some trenchant remarks about an early phase of the translation which I hope may now meet with approval!

I must also acknowledge grateful thanks to the Literature Board of the Australia Council, which provided me with generous funds to visit libraries in search of texts and sources.

The French Government, through the Ministry of Cultural Affairs, has assisted with a substantial grant towards the publication of the work.

I must also add a word of gratitude to Mme F. Laye, of the Service de Traductions of the Presses Universitaires de France for her continued encouragement and practical assistance towards the completion and publication of the translation.

As the present work is a republication in translation it makes only minimal demands on copyright material, but I wish to acknowledge the goodwill of all authors and publishers from whom quotations have been used, sometimes in slightly extended form; and in particular to record my thanks to the Societas Scientiarum Fennicae (Helsinki), the Koninglijk Instituut voor Taal-, Land- en Volkenkunde (Translation Series, Leiden), E.J. Brill (Cologne), Macmillan and Co. (London), the editor of *Oceania* (Sydney) and the University of Queensland Press, for material taken from works by Gunnar Landtman, J. van Baal, Paul Wirz, F.E. Williams and other *Oceania* contributors; and to Jack Healy personally for the passage quoted at the end of the Translator's Preface.

Primitive Mythology

Introduction

It will be best to say at once what I hope to accomplish in this book. I have in mind a study of certain, as we say, primitive tribes, particularly the Aborigines of Australia and New Guinea, and to this end I shall make use of a selection of basic mythological examples. It is not my intention to deal formally with the history of religion or of sociology, but only to relate the myths to the natural environment and to the settled orientations of primitive people's minds. Such a study may have its usefulness for a better understanding of the myths themselves, and of the part they play in primitive society.

Since this is the plan, we shall need to begin by asking what myths are. Can we assume that myth and all that goes with it means the same thing for primitive societies as it does for us? In several earlier books I felt it necessary to make a cautious preliminary enquiry about primitive views of causation, the soul and the supernatural: what, if anything at all, existed in the mind of the primitive to correspond with our notions of these things? These were stumbling blocks I had to dispose of before I could possibly concede (however much people generally take it for granted) that primitive people form their ideas of these things in the same way as we do, or that they are able to express them interchangeably with ours. It is the same with myths. I feel quite unable to assume that what the word means for us is the same as what it means to the Australian or Papuan.[1] Unless this point is first cleared up we shall surely run into confusion, and our conclusions can never be better than hazardous.[2]

There are very good reasons, of course, and I do not close my eyes to them, why we use the same word to signify both the myths of primitives and those we are familiar with from the art and literature of classical antiquity. No less than Andrew Lang, I admire the perspicacity of Fontenelle, who pointed out clearly the qualities the two have in common. As he demonstrated, the similarities can at times be striking; what he said was very perceptive and is entitled to be remembered.

But we need more than a recognition of these affinities to assert that anything that is true of classical mythology will apply equally to primitive. In such a comparison how can we possibly forget the enormous distance which separates classical antiquity from the Aborigines of Australia and New Guinea? In those Mediterranean regions where the classical myths took shape, there had long existed formal religions, each set up with its hierarchy of gods and demigods, ritual, temples and priesthood. Moreover in the end the myths became intimately assimilated into poetry and the arts; they settled down as literature as much as they remained part of religion. Nothing like this happened in Australia or New Guinea. There we find neither gods nor hierarchies, no established body of beliefs that we would wish to describe formally as a religion: no priesthood, no temple-worship, no altars.[3] Before differences of this magnitude we cannot with any wisdom take for granted that the two cultural phenomena, even though we agree to call both by the same name of myths, are to be understood in the same sense.

How safely, then, can we apply our notion of myth to the primitive examples? Can we do so at all? It is impossible to be dogmatic; we know too little. The best plan, then, will be to begin by setting all our pre-conceived ideas firmly aside for the time being. We must try to deal with the topic as though we were making a first approach to a mental experience never before analyzed or classified. We must open up our minds. Let us look at these myths in their own setting, but in that setting only. At a later stage it may well be interesting to compare them with less primitive examples, and it may also then be much more rewarding.

And finally, if it be asked why I have concentrated upon the myths of Australia and New Guinea, the simple answer is that these are clear examples of primitive societies, and that the documentation is abundant and of high quality. As will be seen in due course, I shall by no means refuse to look further afield, or reject myths from other sub-civilized cultures. This choice does not, in any case, imply any conviction on my part that the Australians and Papuans must be the most "primitive" or the most "archaic" peoples still surviving in the world today.[4]

The primitive mythology we are in a position to examine is for the most part very fragmented, without systematic organization. Few individuals in tribal communities have a complete knowledge of their legends. All such knowledge is privileged and belongs exclusively to the older men who, having endured the various stages of tribal initiation, have married and acquired paternal status.[5] Any one of these may be acquainted with a number of myths, possibly even a great many different ones; and yet commonly he will not know a single legend in its entirety — that is, the beginning or the end, or some important episodes may be unknown. It is very rare for one person to be able to report the whole narrative.[6]

It is also the case that the myths of a tribe (admittedly there are exceptions) seldom cohere in a consistent scheme. It has frequently been observed that the stories remain external to one another, it might almost be said, unrelated; and rich and resourceful as the myths are, no effort seems to have been made to regularize them. Landtman noticed this particularly with the Kiwai Island Papuans.[7] This is something that surprises us. Doubtless the cause lies in our own minds, however: assumptions drawn from the speculations of former times about mythology. The theorists of the eighteenth and nineteenth centuries looked to find (and therefore did find) in it a concerted effort to explain the origins of everything. The lines were similar, although traced back to remoter ages, to what was being attempted in theology and metaphysics. This approach inspired a philosophy of myth which related effectively only to those traditions which grew up alongside the formal religions they were associated with, or the metaphysical doctrines underlying them. Had those theorists been confronted with mythologies like these of Australia or New Guinea, they could scarcely have failed to see the inconsistencies in them, or notice what they implied.

But such a primitive lack of system is characteristic; it is not restricted to Australia and New Guinea. To cite only one other example, in the Andaman Islands, as we learn from A.R. Radcliffe-Brown, "one feature of the legends that must be pointed out is their unsystematic nature. The same informant may give, on different occasions, two entirely different versions of such a thing as the origin of fire, or the beginning of the human race. The Andamanese, to all appearance, regard each little story as independent, and do not consciously compare one with another. Thus they seem to be entirely unconscious of what are obvious contradictions to the student of the legends."[8]

The effect of this, since individual myths pay no more attention to the rest than if they did not exist, is that contradictions are inevitable. But much as they may startle Europeans, they in no way embarrass the Islanders, who pay no heed to them. This nonchalance is also found elsewhere. In Dutch New Guinea, for example, "it is extraordinarily difficult to adapt oneself to the native way of thinking", says Paul Wirz, "and moreover the Marind constantly contradict themselves in their myths". At Dobu Island (British New Guinea), according to R.F. Fortune, "the combined legends of all the Dobuan totemistic lines make a most illogical system. No Dobuan bothers to institute comparisons, however. So no one ever finds out that the system as a whole is self-contradictory." Later Fortune adds, "in truth, the Dobuan does not push hard upon logic in his account of Creation. He does not notice that one legend conflicts with another. No one Dobuan has ever attempted a composition of the various legends that contain accounts of origins . . . It is tacitly assumed that A precedes B in one connection, although B precedes A in another connection."[9]

Contradictions of the same kind appear in Eskimo mythology. What is more remarkable, persons may be met with among them who are quite capable of recognizing the discrepancies when they are pointed out. Some will even go so far as to defend the assumptions which disconcert us. Knud Rasmussen, who for a time lived among the Iglulik tribe and enjoyed their confidence, reports a conversation he had on this subject with Orulo, the wife of his friend of the shaman Aua.

> At this Orulo laughed and said, "Too much thought only leads to trouble. All this that we are talking about took place in a time so far back that there was no time at all. We Eskimos do not concern ourselves with solving riddles. We repeat the old stories in the way they were told to us, and with the words we ourselves remember. And if there should then seem to be a lack of reason in the story as a whole, there is yet enough remaining in the way of incomprehensible happenings, which our thought cannot grasp. If it were but everyday things, there would be nothing to believe in. How came all the living creatures on earth in the beginning? Can anyone explain that?"
>
> And then, after having thought for a moment, she added the following, which shows in a striking fashion how little the actual logical sequence counts with the Eskimos in their mythology: "You talk about the stormy petrel catching seals before there were any seals. But even if we managed to settle this point so that all worked out as it should, there would still be more than enough remaining which we cannot explain. Can you tell me where the

mother of the caribou got her breeches from: breeches made of caribou skin before there were any caribou? You always want these supernatural things to make sense, but we do not bother about that. We are content not to understand."[10]

This kind of Eskimo *credo quia absurdum* is at one stroke evidence of the robust faith the people place in their myths and the very slight demand made upon their intelligence by rationality in these matters.

It is not only in their mythologies that primitives show themselves impervious to contradictions that to us would appear glaring. As I have had occasion to point out in another connection, with particular reference to the question of *participation*,[11] this indifference to rationality is one of the ways in which the habit of their minds most noticeably contrasts with our own. No doubt the basic framework of the human mind is everywhere the same. Once primitive types become clearly and vividly aware that a contradiction is present, they are nonplussed by it as much as we are. They repudiate it with the same vehemence. But it is a precisely distinguishing facet of the disposition of their minds that, quite often, what appears contradictory to us does not seem so to them. They remain unaffected by it and seem able to adjust to the inconsistency. Their habit of thought, in this sense, would appear to be *prelogical*.[12] This state of mind is narrowly bound up with the mystical conditioning of their whole mentality. It attaches no great importance to either physical or rational explanations of the possibility of things, but on the contrary reflects their general tendency to come to conclusions which show very little reliance upon conceptual thinking. Undoubtedly they make use of concepts to some extent; how could they possibly do without them altogether? But the concepts their minds do formulate occur less frequently than with us, and they are not so systematically integrated. As a result their range of expression is limited; they cannot easily pass from one initial concept to another of either lesser or greater generality — that is to say, from the original to other concepts of more minute particularity embraced within it, or alternatively to any broader one which is general enough to include the first. Primitives like these do not have at command the wonderful resources of logic and language which speed and facilitate so many operations of the civilized intelligence. "The brain-power of the Kanaka", writes Leenhardt, "has scarcely yet managed to classify the data of sense-experience; it has never managed to set up generalizations.

'Tree', 'animal', 'sea', 'bite' do not exist for them as concepts, as they do in our way of thinking."[13]

A special study on this subject was made recently among the Cherokee. Its authors (in the first place, James Mooney) had observed among the children of this extensive tribe of south east North America a very high and lively mental activity, and among its medicine-men — who could be regarded as its intellectual elite — a rich and abundant body of knowledge. But there was a reverse to the medal.

> All this knowledge, however, is far from codified. I have often made a point of it to try and find out in how far it was systematized, or as we would call it, rationally ordered in their minds. This has always brought disappointing though interesting results.
>
> Such a medicine man who was universally acknowledged as being the one who knew most, as Og was, when asked to write down all the different diseases he knew, and when given 5 days to think it over, managed to find only 38 more or less different ones.
>
> Another one, when asked to enumerate them offhand, could not get past a dozen, this in spite of the fact that both of them must have known upward of a hundred, since compilations made by me from oral information obtained from several individuals and gleaned from three manuscripts [named] revealed that some 230 different diseases (that is "different" from a Cherokee point of view) were known.
>
> . . . The same remarks hold for their botanical knowledge, and could even be made to apply to their knowledge of religion and mythology.
>
> . . . Continuing an experiment along the same lines with another medicine man, this time with reference to the religion, afterlife, the spirits he invoked in the formulas, I could not get him by this method to tell me five per cent of what he knew on this score; ultimately I extracted all he knew — and a bulky lot it was — by indirect and roundabout questions.
>
> . . . In spite of their vast amount of erudition, and in some cases, of their superior intelligence, these old fellows do not seem to be any more methodical than their lay congeners . . .
>
> . . . He [Og] was practically the only medicine man of the many I have known who could be said to have a certain perspective in his knowledge, and who was not hopelessly unable to connect two bits of information that came from different branches of his erudition.[14]

Mooney (or his disciple Olbrechts) also remarks that "Although Cherokee words do express such concepts as 'herbs' (in general), or that refer to definite families of plants ('families' to be taken here from the Cherokee point of view, as 'those that grow in the mountains', 'those that are ever green', 'those that grow near the river', etc.), these are but rarely heard, and as a rule the specific names of the plant are used."[15]

This handful of observations throws a glimmer of light on the habitual working of a kind of intelligence which is much less conceptual than ours. The sum of their knowledge, or to use Mooney and Olbrechts' well-chosen term, erudition, may amount to something considerable. But because it is never analyzed it remains structureless; it is simply a wholesale purchase. The intelligence receives, but does not differentiate the information, and so cannot use it profitably. On every fresh occasion it refers back to what it learned in some other, past situation, and unless the resemblance is very obvious the connection is likely to be missed. Points of recognition do not sort themselves out into any kind of order, conceptually, so that some have more, others less meaning; all are simply juxtaposed, higgledy-piggledy. The details merely pile up. In its turn this mass of data, abundant but disorderly, is not conducive to the formation of concepts. The fixed habit therefore develops of using the information simply as it comes to hand. Consequently whatever may be the native vigour and vivacity of their minds, these Indians soon find the rational progress of their thinking blocked because the indispensable mental machinery is not there. The way therefore lies all the more open to precommitments of a mystical kind. And by the same token the chances are so much the more likely that contradictions will pass unnoticed, or if seen, be ignored.

If mental habits like these are still to be seen today among the erudite Cherokee — and that in spite of the fact that they have been living for generations in a settled relationship with whites, from whom they have acquired not only writing, but many other civilized arts — with how much more reason shall we expect to find them dominating communities as primitive as the Australian and Papuan Aborigines! Even so, as I have had previous occasion to remark, tribal and other *representations* which do not take the form of regular concepts are not necessarily for that reason wholly deprived of general significance.[16] An element of common emotion can in some sort substitute for and supply the function of general reference. That in effect is what happens with mythical *representations*, which as a general rule operate through the *affective category of the supernatural*.[17] In this way there is built up between the various myths a kind of relationship which masks their lack of coordination and at the same time ensures that the contradictions are not noticed.

The Aborigines of Australia and New Guinea recognize neither gods, goddesses nor divinities of any graduated order; nothing, in short, which resembles a pantheon.[18] Nor do the legends set out to rehearse the genealogies, exploits or personal attributes of persons treated as divine. Yet they do not on that account carry out functions any less vital and essential. Malinowski has demonstrated this with some examples drawn from the Trobriand Islands. He has very effectively described the mental processes of these Melanesians.[19] It becomes apparent that myths constitute in a very real sense the most precious heritage of this tribe; they are at the heart of all it reveres as sacred.

The most important myths will be known only to the tribal elders, who jealously guard their secrecy. They pass them on to nobody unless there is good reason for doing so, and then only to those (they are few in number) who are fully qualified to receive them.

> But such is their loyalty to their secrets, that they never drop a hint to the white "authority" of the great world of native thought and sanction of which he is really unaware. The old custodians of secret knowledge sit in the camp sphinx-like, watching with eagle eye the effect of white contact on the young men and deciding how much of the knowledge of their fathers they can with safety entrust to them, and just when the imparting of secrets can most effectively be made. If the time is never propitious, then the secrets die with the old men, and though they die in sorrow, knowing that the old rites and myths will pass into oblivion, and that the tribe is doomed to extinction, yet they die triumphantly, having been loyal to their trust.[20]

The truth is, the notion of doing otherwise would never enter their minds. To divulge the myths would be to desecrate them. They would lose the sacredness of their character and at the same time their mystical efficacy would vanish. If this last fails, the tribe itself cannot survive. A.P. Elkin makes it quite clear why: "For the very life of nature and therefore of the human race itself depends on these rites and sites. The Aboriginal totemistic philosophy binds man to nature in a living whole, which is symbolized and maintained by the complex of myths, rites and sacred sites. Unless the myths with their sanctions are preserved, the rites performed and the sites maintained as spirit sanctuaries, that living bond is broken, man and nature are separated, and neither man nor nature has any assurance of life in the future."[21]

We shall see presently how great is the importance given by Australian and Papuan Aborigines to the sacred sites, and realize that the myths and ceremonies are merely different aspects of one and the same mystical reality. Just as the tribe cannot go on existing without performing the ceremonies, so it is no less certainly condemned to decay if, through desecration, the sacred power of the myths is weakened. If need be, the old men will carry their mysteries with them to the grave.

Among the Marind-anim (Dutch New Guinea), Wirz tells us, "The myths provide the real foundation not only of all the open festivals, in which actors wearing masks portray the *Dema*, but of the secret ceremonies also". Wirz, who made the myths the pivot of his study of the Marind-anim, says in plain terms in another passage, that without them he could never have understood either the mental character or the tribal institutions of these people.

> One may arrive at terms of close intimacy with the Marind, understand their language and live among them, but the *Dema-wiel* and likewise the *Majo* ritual will for all that remain unintelligible unless one possesses the key. The mythology supplies it. At any moment, even in the routines of daily life, one comes up against myths of the *Dema*, the ancestors from whom everything came in the first place, and on whom everything still depends: miracles, magic formulas, all ancient customs, festivals, dances, songs, increase ceremonies, secret rituals. Everything rests on mythology, and on the *Dema*.[22]

Since the myths occupy such a position in Marind-anim affairs, both sacred and profane, they cannot be kept as jealously secret as those of which Elkin spoke. Very possibly some, those that are most highly sacred, may be kept hidden from the non-initiated. Or it may be that women and other uninitiated persons are allowed to become acquainted with the superficial meaning of the myths only, while the deeper significance and the mystical content which make them potent are passed on only to such men as are prepared and qualified to receive the instruction. It is the duty and responsibility of these to keep and transmit them, and ultimately to conduct the secret ceremonies which are centred upon them. Such, also, as the Piddingtons have shown us, is the practice of the Karadjeri, a north west Australian tribe. "Karad-jeri myths are of two kinds, those which are known to both sexes and those which are known to men alone. The later . . . are mainly concerned with the cosmogony and with initiation ceremonies."[23]

As might be expected, custom in these matters varies from tribe to tribe. Nevertheless there is a reasonable degree of conformity, of which T.G.H. Strehlow has given an explanation.

> The myths of a tribe are, so to speak, the *personal property* of a small group. The general outlines of a myth may be, and often are, known throughout a very large area; but the little intimate details of the story and the traditional designs proper to the ceremonies are known only to a few old men. Thus, the above story [allusion to the Ankota myth] is the property of a small group (now extinct) of men belonging to the Ngala-Mbitjana sub-sections who once dwelt in the vicinity of Ankota. When the old ancestor was reincarnated in the person of the man who died recently in Alice Springs, the legend, the decorative patterns, and all *tjurunga* became his exclusive property. So long as he lived no one else, except his father or grandfather or father's brother could relate the story to any "outsider".
>
> This makes it difficult to record the longer myths, in which the wanderings of ancestors over the great tracts of country are described. Thus, for instance, all the Aranda men whose totemic centres lie close to the track taken by that group of *tjilpa* [wild cat totem] ancestors which passed over Mount Conway know the various important *tjilpa* places on the route. But the *details* of the happenings along the route – and it is only in these that we get a glimpse of the real significance of this tradition – are all kept secret by the little sub-section groups which dwell along their line of travel. Hence, to get a true account of the tradition one has to question the old headmen of these groups in turn; and this is a lengthy and tiring procedure.[24]

In New Guinea, according to Landtman,

> . . . the Kiwais have an almost inexhaustible treasure of myths and legends, showing the wonderful imagination with which they are gifted. . . . Looked upon from the European point of view, most of the tales contained narratives of events which have happened, and which, consequently, the hearer is expected to believe. Others appear as pure tales of imagination (*Märchen*) related for the sake of entertaining the listener. From the native standpoint this distinction does not exist. To them all kinds of legendary stories are real, and equally true are the stories of their doings. According to the native mind, nearly all the tales are traditions of what has actually taken place. This is even the case with tales in which animals appear behaving as men, for in times past they could speak. In a few instances only my informants set down cer-

tain narratives as pure fiction merely calculated to amuse the people.[25]

Keysser says to the same effect that for the Kai people all their legends are myths; they distinguish no separate class of fairytales or fables. "What we look on as fabulous, are for the Kai authentic myths like all the rest." On the other hand among the Aranda (Spencer's Arunta), as Carl Strehlow reports, "the sacred legends of the tribe are passed on only to those members who have been accepted into the status of manhood, and by these they are believed to be true; but the mere tales are told also to women and children, perhaps with the object of dissuading them from trespassing on the men's secrets or to frighten them with evil spirits who might spy on them. Others again are merely intended to entertain."[26]

Since we are concerned with myth, we can afford for the present to disregard all the mere tales — there are relatively few — which observers agree are not to be taken seriously. In what touches the rest, however, Landtman and Keysser on the one hand, and Carl Strehlow on the other, clearly represent different points of view. Landtman's interest lies professedly in folklore only; he has published an abundant collection of it. All he aims to show is that the Kiwai people appear to be untroubled by any sense of the impossible, and that nothing stops them, therefore, from crediting as real, incidents in the stories that seem highly improbable. But to these tales he never thinks of attributing the vital functions which, as Wirz and Elkin claim, are filled by the sacred myths of the tribes they have studied. Keysser draws no real distinctions between mere folktales and myths whose repetition serves a solemn spiritual purpose. As for Carl Strehlow, it was never any part of his plan to enquire what kind of belief the Aranda and Loritja gave to casual stories. Indeed he was very particular to stress the difference between mere tribal trivia and the myths, which for these people as for those studied by Elkin, were in most cases not merely of enormous importance to the community, but also solemnly sacred and secret. At Dobu, the legends out of which the ritual indispensable for the cultivation of the yam crop is composed are the exclusive property of the families who own them; each family cherishes its own and keeps them rigorously secret.[27]

Malinowski has vividly described the distinguishing differences between various kinds of legendry, as seen in the Trobriand Islands. The native folklore, he says,

. . . that is, the verbal tradition, the store of tales, legends and texts handed on by previous generations, is composed of the following classes: first of all there is what the natives call *libogwo*, "old talk", but which we would call tradition; secondly, *kukwanebu*, fairy tales, recited for amusement, at definite seasons, and relating avowedly untrue events; thirdly, *wosi*, the various songs, and *vinavina*, ditties, chanted at play or under other special circumstances; and last, not least, *megwa* or *yopa*, the magic spells. All these classes are strictly distinguished from one another by name, function, social setting, and by certain formal characteristics . . .

(The *libogwo*), which is believed to be true, consists on the one hand of historical tales, such as the deeds of past chiefs, exploits in the *Koya*, stories of shipwreck, etc. On the other hand, the *libogwo* class also contains what the natives call *lili'u* – myths, narratives deeply believed by them, held by them in reverence, and exercising an active influence on their conduct and tribal life. Now the natives distinguish definitely between myth and historic account, but this distinction is difficult to formulate, and cannot be stated but in a somewhat deliberate manner. [The native, that is, is unable to express his views abstractly.] . . . Indeed, whenever a story is told, any native, even a boy, would be able to say whether this is one of his tribal *lili'u* or not. For the other tales, that is the historical ones, they have no special word, but they would describe the events as happening among "humans like ourselves". Thus tradition, from which the store of tales is received, hands them on labelled as *lili'u*, and the definition of a *lili'u*, is that it is a story transmitted with such a label. And even this definition is contained by the facts themselves, and not explicitly stated by the natives in their current stock of expressions.[28]

In short, in the Trobriands folktale and tribal legend are kept essentially distinct from myth, though here the myths are not secret. Nevertheless people respect them and accept them as a guide; the beings and events of which they speak belong to a past age, which is not part of recorded history.

A remark of A.P. Elkin's helps us to penetrate a little more deeply into the idea the Australian Aborigines have of their secret and sacred mythology. The myths provide the basis asserted by tradition of all that is vital and necessary to them in their natural environment, as also for their ritual institutions. For all these things, Elkin tells us, the tribes have "a term, such as *altjira* (Aranda), *dzjugur* (Aluridja), *bugari* (Karadjeri), *lalan* (Ungarinjin), which has a number of meanings, all of which, however, are summed up in the long-past time when the culture-heroes and ancestors introduced the tribal culture and instituted its rites and laws". "'The same term also means 'dream' (noun or verb). But to the Aborigines this does not signify mere phantasy, but spiritual reality. A man's 'dreaming' is his share of the secret myths and rites, of the historical traditions, of the old or 'eternal dreamtime'."[29]

What M. and R. Piddington say comes to the same thing: "'The Karadjeri have a very extensive mythology, that is, stories of the activities of characters, most of whom have affinities with animals, birds, fish, and so on, in the distant past; the period is known as *bugari*, which is also the term for dreams."[30]

To these terms listed by Elkin, and meaning simultaneously the mythical age or anything belonging to it, and dreaming, one more may be added, *ungud*. This word, according to Elkin himself, has at least as many meanings, seemingly diverse, as those above. Like them it has a bearing essentially on the mythical age and it is not without a relationship to dreams.[31]

If one expression, essentially the same though taking forms appropriate to the various languages, is current in so many separate tribes of the centre and north west of Australia, and in all of them denotes both the mythic past and the experience of dreaming — no doubt, a particular kind of dreaming — this is something which could not have come about by accident or mere coincidence. Clearly, therefore, in the minds of these Aborigines the mythic world and dreams have some important principle in common. Both stand outside and above ordinary day-to-day experience. And both therefore open a prospect upon what, for lack of any more suitable term, we must call the supernatural.[32]

According to the primitive view, what is seen in a dream is no less real than what is perceived in the waking state — it may be even more so, because what is revealed in this way is of a superior order and may exert an influence on the course of events which it will be impossible to resist.[33] Now since the beings and events with which myths concern themselves are supernatural also, what they tell about those matters has the force, as does a dream, of revelation. Both myths and dreams, therefore, are objects of deepest respect. The natives feel that both have about them something compellingly sacred. On hearing the myths they often undergo the same emotional reactions as will move them when the affective category of the supernatural comes into play. Hence the world into which their dreams lead them is hardly, if at all, to be distinguished from the world of the mythic past (Elkin's "eternal dreamtime"): a world of invisible forces and supernatural powers, on which for ever, and from one moment to the next, hangs the happiness and wellbeing, even the continuing existence of the human community. This is what is to be understood from the existence in so many Australian and New Guinea tribes of words like *altjira, dzjugur, bugari, lalan, ungud*. All of these combine the connotations of "dream experience" and "the mythic period and all that it involves".[34]

Unseen forces and supernatural powers may also reveal their presence and make their action felt in another way. Whenever anything is seen, or happens, that is strange and unexpected, whenever something startles and arrests the attention of the native, the event demonstrates to him, *ipso facto*, that one or more of the unseen powers is at work close at hand. Anything habitual or predictable — which conforms, as we would put it, with the ordinary laws of nature — will never disturb his equanimity. More or less automatically, in practice, he puts to good use all such phenomena, and therefore nothing of that sort calls for particular reflection. But whatever is unexpected, he takes for a sign and a warning it would be rash to disregard. It is something he must find the meaning of at once, if he can; for it is an indication that the world of the unseen is intruding into the life of every day.

For such primitive minds as these the supernatural world is ever at hand, ready to shoot up into consciousness at the slightest prompting. Hence their quick tendency to blend together all the separate evidences by which it reveals its presence. For minds thus disposed, dreams constitute one of the modes of supernatural revelation, and are bound to be considered closely related to myths, which constitute another. Some will go so far as to assert, like the Yuma, that as sources of myth dreams provide the most reliable material. But similarly, a connection just as intimate is to be seen between myth and this other revelation; it is apparent whenever the hidden powers show themselves as present in any extraordinary or unexpected circumstance.

This is not simply a guess, it is a fact. We find the basic identity of these two modes of revelation fully appreciated and expressed among the Marind-anim, in a manner which leaves no reason for doubt; and among other tribes of Dutch New Guinea as well. The evidence of Wirz on the subject is positive confirmation of this, all the more convincing because he was in no position to foresee what use we might make of the information. Marind-anim mythology is highly developed and elaborately involved. It supplies the content of a large part of Paul Wirz's elaborate study. Everything turns for the Marind upon the *Dema*, that is, ancestral figures of the mythic past, beings endowed with super-natural powers, to whom is attributed the *creation* of all living species animal and vegetable, of the islands and of the sea, of the dry land, and of the human race and all human institutions: in short, of everything that exists in the world of today. But the word *dema* does not distinguish personal mythical beings only, ancestral figures who are part men and part animals (or plants); its broad use is adjectival, signifying anything strange and unex-pected; *unusual* and therefore *supernatural.* "In the notion of *dema"* — these are Wirz's first words as he begins his account of the myths —

> ... the Marind blends and combines together a series of ideas whose common property is that there is in all of them something strange, exceptional and beyond explanation.
>
> In the first place, *dema* corresponds exactly with the Melanesian *mana.* Every physical object is animated, that is it contains certain psychic powers. But not every such object is itself a *Dema.* Quite the contrary. Those are *Dema,* however, in which the psychic force and energy exist in intense concentration: a native finds a stone, for example, which notably draws attention to itself through its unusual shape — it has the appearance, perhaps, of a betel nut, or a small fish. It occurs to the finder to compare the stone with a real betel nut, or a real fish, and he supposes that the animating powers of both are alike. The native thus comes to believe that the powers contained in the unusual stone must themselves be of an exceptional intensity.[35]

In effect the unexpected appearance of the stone gives it apocalyptic authority. Anything is thus *dema* if the action of an unseen power becomes manifest in it. The animated object in that way acquires the power to act as the focal centre of a myth. Wirz does not make a point of describing this process. But he does sketch out in a few lines the psychological circumstances in which such exotic manifestations lead to the appearance of new myths.

> Everything which is age-old and looks back to the far-distant past is intrinsically rare, and on that account sufficiently extraordinary to be described as *dema*; hence, very suitable to be adopted into the mythological system. It is in this fashion that the true and universally acknowledged *Dema* reveal the continuity which car-

ries their traces back to the most remote ages, so that we may consider ourselves, in their case, firmly on mythological ground.

When some event has occurred which was extraordinary enough for the story to be told over and over again, the repetitions, as they go on, will tend progressively to vary and become exaggerated – and this is something the Marind are particularly prone to. So in no very great time an incident originally of hardly any significance at all may become inflated into a tale of unbelievable impressiveness. After a single generation has passed, for example, a mere idiot may become fixed in the popular memory as a *Dema* and from then on no one will ever think to question his *Dema* nature. It is a fair conjecture that the whole *Dema* mythology has been built up from traditions of tangled causation and wild exaggeration of this kind.[36]

This may be a somewhat sketchy explanation of the emergence of the myths – of some of them, that is – but at any rate it need not detain us. We can at least regard the following point as firmly established. As the Marind-anim see it, the occurrence of something beyond the range of customary expectation is, in the same way as a dream, a special revelation of something belonging to the world of the unseen; and that is the world the myths transport us into. Our analysis of the various meanings of the word *dema* also brings us to the same conclusion, the more convincingly as it is we and not the Marind who formulate the distinctions; for the Marind pass from one sense to another without thinking of it. This complexity – duality or plurality – in the connotations of the word, precisely because the Marind are *not* aware of it, provides us with a valuable insight into the nature and origin of at least some of their myths.[37]

In certain other parts of Dutch New Guinea, where he was one of the earliest European visitors, Wirz discovered an equivalent to the Marind-anim *dema*, there called *kugi*.

The religious ideas of the native of Central New Guinea cluster about a principle I would be willing to consider basic to all primitive portrayal of supernatural objects and events, since it includes all aspects of the native's imaginary world, the world lying beyond his sensory comprehension . . . Complex as may be the various meanings of *kugi*, there seems as yet, at this early stage in the development of religious ideas, to have been no attempt to differentiate them. *Kugi* brings together a whole series of ideas which, if not clearly distinguished one from another, nevertheless cohere uniquely. Thus all is *kugi* which is intimately associated with [I should myself prefer to say, which *participates in*][38] the world of the unseen. As Europeans our first impulse would be to dissect the motives from which such a belief in the extra-sensory world arises. We would certainly place in separate categories the belief in ghosts — that is, spirits of the dead — and that in demon-presences in natural phenomena; or we would certainly enquire what was the common root of both.[39]

But the native does nothing about it. So far as he is concerned it is all simply *kugi*. If he wonders about the existence of supernatural forces and phenomena at all, his notions are confused, obscure, and tangled.

He adds a few pages later, "For the native it is all one single complex of contingent fear and subjection, monolithic and completely resistant to analysis".[40] Seen in this light, the total of ideas, images and emotions which coalesce in the *kugi* principle approaches very closely to the elements which constitute the whole "affective category of the supernatural". The content of fear and subjection in the face of supernatural forces is exactly the same.

Wirz continues to insist upon the undifferentiated general character of what he calls the *kugi*-concept. What he means by this is something neither personal, nor in a strict sense impersonal. It can frequently be both at the same time (as is the case with *dema* and the other similar expressions). "It includes in its broad grasp everything that is supernatural, inexplicable, or (like *dema* in this also) inconceivable; and all that is unremittingly hostile to man."[41]

While for the Marind-anim, *Dema* (taken as a noun) certainly denotes the tribal ancestors, whose exploits and adventures fill many myths, Wirz does not assert that in Central Dutch New Guinea *kugi* is used with exactly the same implications. He does say this, however:

At so very primitive a stage as this, religious ideas are as yet undefined. One cannot point to any distinctly identifiable belief in demonic spirits, and no personification is applied to the forces and phenomena of nature. There is no hierarchy of thinking and feeling, individuated spirit-beings, still less any belief in one single divine creative principle, such as the adherents of monotheism always imagine they can find in any primitive community; no clearly defined cult of ancestor-worship; nothing, on the contrary, but an obscure feeling that certain powers beyond the grasp of one's ordinary human senses, but malicious and utterly capricious, are menacingly present. This, it would seem, is all that is included in the religous thoughts of these aborigines.[42]

In the light of this opinion it is not surprising that Wirz has nothing to say about the myths of these tribes; in this area he did not collect any. Possibly he considered the state of development the people had reached was too early for proper myths to appear. Nevertheless he does refer to *kugi* (using the world as a noun, not merely adjectivally) while at the same time pointing out (by withholding the normal German substantival capital K and carefully printing "kugi") that these *kugi*, though in some sense objectified, are not by any means to be thought of as personal objects, let alone persons.

> No connection seems to exist between the *kugi* and the physical forces which operate in nature, and they are not related to the stars and constellations; as for the personification of such agencies, they know nothing at all of it. I questioned the natives again and again about the origin of thunder and lightning, and never had but one unvarying answer: what causes thunderstorms is a crack in the fabric of the sky, which they suppose to be a solid vault.
> . . . In earthquakes alone, which here are frequent, do they see themselves as haunted by *kugi*; in this case *kugi* clearly signifies the spirits of the dead who dwell in the mountains. These ghosts take sides and fight battles among themselves, or else wage war with mortal men, and this is how an earthquake begins.[43]

If this account of earthquakes is not strictly speaking a formal myth, at any rate it is very like one. The resemblance is strong enough to justify a guess that they probably have others, an assertion all the more plausible because Wirz, to his great surprise, also found among these people some stone *churingas* which had the same functions as those of the Arunta and other Australian tribes.[44] To quote a recent observer, W.E.H. Stanner, "Mythology, of course, brings these *sacra* into an intimate relation with the dream times (Altjira)".[45] The situation is undoubtedly broadly the same in New Guinea. Since we find *churingas* there, the presumption is convincing that there will also be myths associated with them.

On the shores of Lake Sentani, still in Dutch New Guinea, Wirz came across another general term, *uaropo*, which in many ways corresponds closely with the Marind-anim *dema*. However, "there is one essential difference between *uaropo* and *dema*. The *Dema* are conceived to be the ancestors of the various tribal groups and consequently the forefathers of the clans. This is not so in the case of the *Uaropo*". Otherwise, what is understood by the one also applies to the other. Once again it is a question of a more or less obscure sensation of fear and subjection in regard to certain superior forces; and when to this sensation is added the effect of certain traditional mythological observances, the result is likely to take shape as formal, concrete *representations*. "It follows, therefore, that the *Uaropo* are conceived as individuals; that is, as separate persons motivated by intent and purpose, and not merely as allegories of the forces (*mana*) with which the object identified as *uaropo* is endowed." Thus we have to reckon with *Uaropo* (noun), just as with *Dema* (capitalized), and the myths recount their exploits. However, the *Uaropo* are not at the same time credited with the character of totemic ancestors. *Uaropo* (adjective, uncapitalized), like *dema*, can be applied either to personal beings or to impersonal things indiscriminately. The native feels no obligation to distinguish, like us, between things and persons. "Whatever belongs to the category of *imaginary* things (Wirz regularly uses "imaginary" as a synonym for "suprasensible, supernatural, unseen") is *uaropo*. Against this the native sets up in contrast all common, nonsacred, ordinary and practical things, for which he also has a special term, *pujakara*. *Pujakara* is in all points the opposite to *uaropo*."[46]

Taken as a noun, *uaropo* signifies a spirit which, for example, might inhabit a certain stone – or equally, might quit it. If you ask a native what kind of a spirit this could be, you can never expect a plain answer. "Once he has said *uaropo*, he has said all that can be said. He feels no need to reflect further on the matter. In any case it makes no sense whatever to ask questions of this sort of the people of Sentani or Humboldt Bay."[47] Quite so, and Wirz himself gives the reason. Since the natives are incapable of explaining how they use their terms, it is not very likely they will be able to analyze the complex mental and emotional states the terms denote. But there is no reason why we ourselves should not make the attempt, or at least ask what are the elements out of which the complexities arise. First, though, we are bound to do what we can to reconstitute the atmosphere in which they were formed. This means we must also try to grasp the impact produced upon the native intelligence and sensibility by the myths.

There is no opportunity here to show in detail how *uaropo* spirits enter into and possess the minds of certain of the older tribesmen, upon whom they have an effect which becomes increasingly powerful with time. As their years advance they tend to appear more and more intensely mystical in their lifestyle, coming gradually to feel themselves fully identified with the spirits. From the spirits they thus acquire superhuman faculties and thus at the same time become the centre of a cult of their own. I must be content for the moment to point out that many rocks and stones are also gradually entered and become possessed by the *uaropo*; these are recognizable by precisely the same signs as mark the *dema* stones of the Marind-anim. [Wirz here raises the question of the origin of the stones concerned, but then without staying, remarks that the natives themselves have no great curiosity about the matter.]

> More than the question how they got there, the outward shape and form of certain stones awakes in the native intelligence the reflection that it cannot be merely a stone that confronts him, but that he has now to deal with a superior being endowed with magical powers. On this account the stones, whether they are found under water or on the dry land, in the bush or overgrown with grass on the hillside, occupy a special place among the enormous host of *uaropo* spirits . . . Many of these stones have a markedly unusual look about them, or a clear resemblance to some particular fruit or fish, crab, or other creature, or a suggestion of sago, or some other edible substance.[48]

The essential condition is that they have some appearance that is for one reason or another extraordinary: dimension, shape, colour, resemblance to some animal or fruit, etc.

In certain cases the *uaropo* idea becomes mingled with that of *soimi*, but Wirz was unable to decide precisely what were the limits of *soimi*.

> The expression *soimi* is commonly applied to all kinds of objects, by no means only stones, which stand out in contrast with others that are simply usual, hence without any magical properties at all. The idea of *soimi* seems thus identical in certain respects with *uaropo*, but as applying to material objects; while *uaropo* imputes the presence of a personal spirit-being. For example the posts which in former times provided ornaments to the assembly-houses and sacred lodges, carved with figures of men and animals, used to be described as *soimi*; even the carved decorations, wooden fishes and birds, which it was customary to place on the *atap* roof of those houses were, the people said, *soimi*. That these were not objects of an ordinary lay order merely, was obvious; but neither were they connected with any sort of ritual. I went to great trouble to enquire into these human and animal figures, always with negative results.
>
> [All stones which contain spirits are classed as *soimi*; whether or not they are animated, they may still have a benevolent function.]

It is believed that the influence of such a stone is intrinsically of great worth and benefit. The wellbeing of the population as a whole may be dependent upon it. So long as the stone remains in their care and the people do not neglect it the group will suffer no setback, nor will their garden-produce fail, no epidemic will attack them and there will be peace and prosperity . . . But if the stones should not be carefully tended and people were not constantly watchful over them, they would run away into the bush, or at the very least cease to be protective. Food shortages would come about; the people would sicken and die. I was informed at Ifar that if anyone were to strike a *soimi*, a flooding rain would fall and everything would be devastated. Nevertheless no sacrificial offering is ever made to the *soimi* . . . Every stone has its own guardian, who takes care of it and sees to the rituals. As a rule it is the village headman, who in this respect carries out something like the function of a parish priest.

From each *soimi* stone there emanate certain powerful influences which correspond with those of the spirit-being (*uaropo*) intimately dwelling within it. These forces, whether for the benefit of individuals or of the community as a whole, the people seek to turn to profit and advantage . . . [Nevertheless there is nothing in this to resemble what a shaman or medicine-man does.] The main importance of the practices is of another kind. Two rituals must never be neglected: these are the ceremonial smoking of the stones and the formal recitation of spells or prayers. These two formalities constitute a centre for practically all the religious ideas of these Papuans.

It is obvious that we have to reckon here with extremely primitive practices which date from the earliest times and have been carried forward into modern times without change. This would seem to be so in spite of many diverse influences brought to bear on the tribes.[49]

In this account of the Lake Sentani natives Wirz does not discuss the mythic ancestors. But he does refer to "certain mythological traditions, in which the imagination of the people is extraordinarily rich".[50] In any case what he saw was enough to make clear that the Sentani natives, like the Marind-anim and the tribes of Central Dutch New Guinea , draw a distinction between two worlds: there is on the one hand the world of everyday experience, and on the other there is another world which lies beyond the reach of the senses, inhabited by unseen and supernatural powers neither identifiably personal nor unambiguously impersonal. At this rate *uaropo* and *soimi* appear substantially equivalent to *dema* and *kugi*.

In the Kimberley district of north west Australia, among the Ungarinyin, A.P. Elkin recently found a number of interesting rock-paintings. They were of the same kind as those seen by Grey not far from the same place, more than a century earlier, in the neighbourhood of the Glenelg River. He also found there certain ideas similar to some we have been contemplating in Dutch New Guinea. One of these appears in the *Wondjina* figures. *Wondjina* is the name by which the natives call the rock galleries themselves where these painted figures are found; they also apply it to the figures. Like the drawings reproduced by Grey in his *Journal*, these figures have faces but no mouths.[51] The faces appear to be regarding intently the plants and animals painted near them on the same rock-wall, upon whose reproduction and fertility (increase) they have a benevolent influence. Elkin explains that *wondjina* at the same time also has the sense of "the rain, or the rain-power". "The first, and perhaps primary, significance of *wondjina* is that of the power that makes, or is in, the rain. If a *wondjina* head be retouched, if *wondjina* be made 'pretty fellow', rain will fall, even in a dry season." "It is perhaps permissible to regard *wondjina* as the regenerative and reproductive power in nature and man − a power which is especially associated with rain."[52]

Thus *wondjina* does not express any one single idea clearly defined, but rather a complex of symbols and sentiments all of which inhere in one principal mystical fact, the kernel of which − if one may so express it − is contained in the two intimately linked notions of rain and natural regeneration. The Ungarinyin also have another term, *ungud*, which invites comparison here. The natives themselves do not insist on distinguishing it from *wondjina*, though it may seem even more complex. "*Ungud* has a number of meanings," says Elkin, "of which one, especially as used by the western hordes of the tribe, equates it to *wondjina*." Moreover "the name *ungud* is sometimes used as though it referred to a person, sometimes as though it referred to a far-off time, and sometimes, too, for the rainbow-serpent water spirit." *Ungud* also affords a clinching explanation of anything that is outstandingly remarkable (as for example certain arrangements of stones which have obviously been set up by art). To the question, "What is that?" the reply is simply, "It is *ungud*". That is to say, it belongs to the far-off time, the mythic period that is called by the same name. "But sometimes, the term *ungud* is used instead of *wondjina*, and as such it means rain and rainbow, that is, the rainbow serpent." (The rainbow serpent assures the refreshment of rain and brings the birth of children.) "The use of the term *ungud* also connects the paintings with the long past culture-giving epoch . . . *Ungud* carries with it an air of finality. If a thing is *ungud*, or made by *Ungud*, there is either no more to be said, or else no more will be said even if it were possible for the informer to do so. The *wondjina* paintings are therefore efficacious because they are *ungud*, because they were instituted by *Ungud*, or in the *ungud* time."

Elkin writes:

> In conclusion, we can say that the function of the *wondjina* paintings is to ensure the regular recurrence of the wet season, the normal increase of edible animals and plants and possibly also of useful objects like ochre, the influence of the sun, and the availability of the supply of spirit-children. [Spirit-children find their way into women's bodies, to be born at the due conclusion of pregnancy.] Man's part is to retouch, perhaps occasionally to paint anew, the *wondjina* heads and adornments, and to paint pictures of the desired objects and species on the *wondjina-banya* or rock galleries. The efficacy of the special paintings is associated with the fact that they are *ungud*, that is, belong to a far-past, creative time. Preservation of continuity with this period is essential for present prosperity; thus, the form of the head must not vary, and the figure, in theory at least, should only be retouched, not painted afresh.[53]

These last remarks might convey an impression that we possess a clear understanding of the senses of *ungud* and *wondjina*; but the clarity is superficial. All we can grasp with a plain understanding is the general purpose served by the rock-paintings: the natives expect from them a beneficial influence on the animal and vegetable species which are their food. As for *wondjina* and *ungud* regarded as concepts, the impression we are left with is of an impenetrable obscurity. It is as though the words contained something quite unassimilable by our western minds. But I must frankly confess that whenever, after Elkin's example, I speak of the *wondjina* or *ungud* "concept" (or "idea", even "notion"), I find myself embarrassed to realize I am actually de-naturing the very thing I am eager to express. *Wondjina* and *ungud* are not in effect *concepts* or *ideas* at all. They are something different altogether, belonging intrinsically to the primitive habit of thinking, which does not order and classify the data of its thought-processes into categorical groupings, as ours does. A general concept, with us, is a thought that can be resolved by analysis into other concepts subordinate to it. We recognize that the first idea is related to the others in an intelligible way. But mental projections like *wondjina* and *ungud* cannot properly be called concepts in that way. Their meaning floats so free as to range unrestricted between particular spirit-beings and a view of reality so diffuse that it is altogether elusive. They suggest to the mind thoughts of a complexity that cannot be grasped by any of the methodical mental means we are accustomed to. What we have before us are *representations* so broad in their reference that to us they appear to have no general, that is coherently logical, consistency at all. Consequently if we speak about *wondjina* and *ungud* as though they have the generality of our own kind of rational concepts, we are following a misleading trail. Far from bringing the essential meaning closer, to do so drives it further away from our grasp.

What should we do, then? Give up the attempt to grasp them? Certainly, if by grasping we understand forcing them into categories which, in fact, only destroy them. But it may not be beyond us to render them intelligible up to a point. If we are to have any chance of succeeding, we must first (and this is indispensable) try to put ourselves into the state of mind which primitives have always, without exception, found themselves adopting in the presence of mythic and supernatural realities. We need to encounter those complex experiences for what they are in themselves, not to insist on analyzing them; and so come to feel the actual impact, rather than arriving at a mere description of it, of the "affective category of the supernatural".

The Karadjeri are another north west Australian tribe among whom Marjorie and Ralph Piddington have noted a "concept" similar to the foregoing:

> The term *bugari*, like the word *alchera* among the Aranda, possesses several meanings. In the first place it connotes that which has a binding force upon the society; to describe an institution as *bugari* means that that institution has a special sanction which renders it inviolable. This is derived from the fact that all things which are *bugari* were instituted by mythical beings in *bugari* times, that is, in the distant past when the world was created. Thus the most general meaning of the term when applied to a social institution is that it has a sort of categorical imperative associated with it.
>
> Apart from its reference to the world's inception and the sanction for present institutions derived therefrom, the word *bugari* is also used to denote the totem of an individual; the connection is fairly clear when we consider that each totemic group is derived from an ancestor or ancestors who in *bugari* times instituted it,

and thus in Karadjeri totemism the individual is linked, through his membership of the totemic group, not only with the other members of the group and the associated natural species, but also with *bugari* times.

Associated with the last meaning is another use of the word to denote dreams; this again is quite clear in view of the fact that the most important aspect of dreams, in the native mind, is that through a dream a father establishes the patrilineal inheritance of the totem of his children.[54]

The similarity, virtually the identity, of these senses of *bugari* with certain of the meanings of *dema, kugi, uaropo, ungud* is so obvious there is no need to underline it. One element, and that the most important and no doubt also the most definitive, is common to all: the emotive representation of a past age and a world-system lying outside the actuality of what is known now. That world of supernatural beings and powers is seen as the source and origin of all things which exist today. Piddington, like Wirz, says in express terms that the period was that in which the ancient ancestors created or produced everything; and that those archaic ancestors are the ones remembered in the myths. This view is very generally accepted. From the way other observers also speak, even though they may not all be concerned directly with the myths (they do, all the same, allude to the *dema, kugi, ungud, bugari,* and so on), we need by no means hesitate to take for granted that this same supernatural and suprasensible world existed also for the tribes they studied, and we may with similar confidence assume it was peopled equally with mythic beings.

Wirz has adequately shown that for the Marind-anim, and similarly for the other Dutch New Guinea tribes he visited, two worlds exist which remain always distinct yet are never separate: one is the world of everyday sense-experience, the other is the unseen world of supernatural beings, powers and events, which intervenes continually in the former. The spiritual world, the world of mystery, was the world in which the common world had its origin. Myth, Wirz explains very reasonably, is the means whereby the native mind (looking always for first, never second causes) bridges the ineffable distance between the two. It thus supplies the all-embracing – indeed, the only possible – explanation of things unknown, that the enquiring native intelligence can either assimilate or be satisfied by.[55]

At the same time he outlines a psychological interpretation of the explanatory process. Like Tylor[56] and most of Tylor's followers in the English school of anthropologists, Wirz seems to credit the Papuan with a rational philosophy of his own, which, whenever he is moved to ponder on the *raison d'être* of anything, readily supplies him with answers which arrive dressed up in mythological form. If these answers appear to us, more often than not, to be nothing but childish nonsense, the reason is simple: the Papuans have not yet learned how (in the idiom of Descartes) to "lead out their thoughts in systematic order".

> The native perceives the various phenomena, he senses and sorts out the ways in which they act together in harmony, he rationalizes and speculates, he wonders about the persistence of life after death, about the personal existence of the dead and their activity, about the causation of events and of the realities of nature, sickness and death. But his capacity to argue and conclude does not carry him far. At a certain point it fails him, and his whole enquiry into cause and effect goes unanswered, or peters out in contradiction, confusion and obscurity.[57]

It does not occur to Wirz himself – particularly when the question revolves upon the supernatural world and its intervention into common life – to ask whether the natives could perhaps possess mental habits of a different kind from ours; whether, indeed, their minds might possibly be oriented in a different direction. He simply takes for granted that whatever it is that makes them thoughtful, raises for them exactly the same enigmas as it would for us, supposing we were to find ourselves situated just where they are – but carrying with us our present language and traditions, plus all the rules of rational deduction we have learned from Aristotle. As for the contradiction and confusion the natives tolerate so cheerfully, he lays these at the door of their deficiency in certain mental skills, as Tylor had done before him, and as others have done since, when they embraced Tylor's theories.[58] These our modern scholars, confronted with any such phenomena as may take them unaware, seem to speculate and philosophize in something of the same way, until presently there comes a moment when they find themselves astray in a thick mist, hopelessly lost, and stuck irretrievably in a bog.

Such "rationalizing", according to Wirz, leads the natives to "conclude" that, as well as the world they know by experience, there is also (the word is Wirz's own) another *imaginary* one, which exists in order that they may look in it to find explanations for the things they cannot understand in the real one. Thus their belief in this "imaginary" world must itself have been arrived at through an exercise of rational logic, the product of their need to discover the effective cause of this or that particular fact, or of this or that event in the world of their ordinary experience.

But let me ask, is it right and proper to attempt to bring our present and contemporary civilized habits of mind, or the traditions which have orientated them, without change, into the domain of the Aborigines of Australia and New Guinea? On the other hand if, as I have suggested, we are willing to renounce all such expectations derived (at one fell swoop, and with no further question) from Tylor and his disciples, all those confusions and contradictions ascribed to the natives will take on quite another aspect. Their credulous belief in an "imaginary" world will no longer look like a lame proposition in logic. As to that, it becomes evident that that "imaginary" world is imaginary for us only – not for them. In the eyes of the natives it is real; even more profoundly real than the common, everyday one. No less than that one, it is known through actual experience. But such experience is of a supernatural order: that is precisely the reason why it has a higher value.

Wirz and Tylor take the reality that is "above and beyond nature" to be something which must be arrived at with the support of a proper logical "conclusion". To me, on the other hand, it carries the conviction of something completely "given", an unquestioned *datum*. Where Wirz believes he can see the operation of a purely intellectual deduction, I maintain it is rather something that he himself calls (he uses the expression several times) a species of sensory subjectivity (*Gefühl, Furcht- und Abhängigkeitsgefühl*), in other words, an experience directly related to the affective category of the supernatural. Because of this the primitives we are discussing do not waste time trying to *explain* everything that surprises or astonishes them, merely because it is inconsistent with the commonplace; or at least, certainly not in the manner suggested by Wirz and the others. The cause of that particular kind of wonder never leads them to ask abstruse questions, or to ponder, speculate or philosophize. They may well be metaphysicians of their own kind, but that kind is not one marked with any passion for intellectual high-flying. The civilized appetite for pure knowledge is not theirs. Their metaphysics is quite spontaneous; it is the result of the frequent, one might say constant, experience of a reality which goes beyond and dominates all common nature, and yet is present and active in it at all times.

"All belief in the *Dema*", Wirz tells us, "springs on the one hand from the myths, and on the other from forces and phenomena that are strange and exceptional, but nevertheless still to be seen today."[59] This is perfectly true. But one may go a little further, to add that mythology itself springs from the same insights or perceptions. It arises out of the whole elaborate complex of visions, dreams, images, impressions and emotions which, after the experience of centuries, is invariably aroused in their bosoms with every fresh awareness of things strange, rare and unaccustomed. Wirz himself has brought us the conclusive proof of this origin. The words *dema* and *kugi*, like the corresponding terms in the other native languages, are significantly double in their meaning, serving at the same time to denote whatever is unusual or extraordinary, and also anything that has to do with dreams and the world of supernature. Among the Marind-anim, for example, *dema* is applied to anything unfamiliar or especially striking in appearance, and *Dema* signifies the great mythic ancestors from whom proceeds all life and substance that is in existence at the present day.[60] These *Dema*, nearly all of them animal-men or men-animals, have emerged and, so to speak, crystallized out into individuals and formed personalities during the course of the ages; what they came out of, in the first place, was that vague, dim, impersonal but suprasensible, super-natural, pervading presence that is always felt in strange circumstances and situations, the original mythic magic.

I would not for a moment dream of suggesting that no Australian or Papuan would ever ask himself a question such as, "Why does such and such an odd or peculiar thing happen? — What is the reason for this or that strange detail, for example the colour of this bird's feathers, the shape of that one's beak?" But neither do I doubt that when he finds the answer, it will take the form of a myth. If he looks to find it, as a matter of course, not where it would be our impulse to search — in a context of antecedent cause and effect — but somewhere in the world of invisible powers and mythic beings, that will be merely for the simple reason that that is for him the world that is given. His experience of it is immediate, and therefore, as he sees it, entirely decisive. It is through such perceptions as these that he obeys and expresses the innate mysticism of his mind. The supernatural beings and the unseen powers by which he is forever enclosed and surrounded, furnish him at all times with an ever-ready answer to any question, no matter how crucial, that it may occur to him to pose. They will also, at the same time and by the same token, completely fill his soul with a complex blend of fearful emotions — dread, humility, self-obliteration, submission and holy awe — with which, whatever may be the task he is engaged upon, and however little it may have to do with things mystical or supernatural, his spirit will nevertheless be deeply and permanently imbued.[61]

Chapter I

The Mythic World

The constant reappearance of terms like *alchera, ungud, wondjina, bugari, dema, kugi, uaropo* and the rest is a plain indication that certain Australian and Papuan tribes keep a clear distinction between the two worlds of common and of supernatural experience, though they do not hold them, for all that, to be separate. The natives feel as much concern about the supernatural as they do about the common world. What they believe in respect of beings and objects belonging to the supernatural world is expressed in the myths.

But before we make any attempt to analyze any of the myths one at a time, it will be as well to begin with a preliminary observation. Here as in any other study of a primitive society we could find ourselves running a risk of grave error if we were to make an inept use of concepts of a kind the people themselves would be unlikely to understand.

Even the word world, for example – natural or supernatural, it makes no difference – for us means a *kosmos*. Such a metaphor carries certain implications – of order, hierarchy, a rational arrangement of the elements out of which it is built up. In short it conveys the idea of an organized whole, whose systematic unity recalls the complete consensus of agreement we see in the innumerable cohering cells of a living body. However (to say nothing of the world we refer to as "natural"), the *supernatural* world of these Papuans or Australians is not like that at all. The powers and forces that they are aware of as present in that world all act independently, each for itself alone. Each influence they exert makes itself felt in isolation from the rest; no principle functions in any way so as to bind one to another. They simply coexist. Scrupulous and conscientious observers like Spencer and Gillen in Australia, Landtman and Wirz in New Guinea – to name only these – are in complete agreement on this point, namely that no subordination is ever seen of minor powers to major ones, nor of the general powers as a whole to any one single supreme being. When the powers or personalities make their appearance in any myth, it is always separately and dispersedly.

In view of this fact, should a study of such a mythic world remain fragmentary, and aim at a piecemeal impression instead of looking for system where apparently no system exists? Should we perhaps pass on from one myth to the next, or from cycle to cycle, without any attempt to establish any cohesion between them, or any consistency even of an external kind? Should we make no attempt to set aside even the most crudely obvious contradictions, since the natives themselves are not troubled by them and indeed never actually seem to notice them? Apart from the fact that such a policy would go against the grain of all our own studious habits and our settled inclination always to look for evidence of method in anything we are investigating, the probability is that all our findings would themselves turn out to be as chaotic as the matter we have been examining. Such a result would involve a misconstruction of just those very elements of generalized perception which, as we have noted already, never fail to appear in the myths, such as, for example, the broad sense of kinship which pervades them from their common origin, the homogeneity of tone which they express, the constant recurrence of certain themes, frequent similarities between narrative episodes, and above all the powerfully common emotion which is stimulated by them whenever they set in action the affective category of the supernatural.

But in any case, these Australian and Papuan myths conform to certain generalizing perceptions governing the interpretation of time and place. This is yet another element of community consciousness, which may conveniently be looked into before we begin upon the mythic world itself.

All the names used to describe the mythic age – *alchera* (*altjira*), *ungud*, *kugi*, *dema*, etc. – imply the idea and image of an epoch or period of time long past, when certain beings existed and certain events were taking place of a kind no longer seen in the world we know. Spencer and Gillen tell us that the most usual sense of *alchera* is simply "the far distant past". This far distant past belonged so far back that, as a part of time, it had a dimension of reality quite unlike the kind of reality which is familiar to us today. Preuss refers to it as *die Urzeit*, or pre-time.[1]

Certainly one may seriously doubt how far the existence of these names implies any idea in the primitive mind of an actual period of history (even if we define history quite loosely) — that is, any identifiable tract of time which ran its course in the measurable long-ago. To us the background of time past which we call history is an institution of the mind so familiar, it is almost impossible to imagine any human intelligence lacking it. For all that, it would appear that what the Australian and Papuan Aborigines understand by "long ago" is, on the evidence we possess, something which only remotely resembles what the expression means for us. Malinowski, for example, points out that

> . . . these natives do not conceive of a past as of a lengthy duration, unrolling itself in successive stages of time. They have no idea of a long vista of historical occurrences, narrowing down and dimming as they recede towards a distant background of legend and myth, which stands out as something entirely different from the earlier planes. This view, so characteristic of the naive, historical thinking among ourselves, is entirely foreign to the natives. Whenever they speak of some event of the past, they distinguish whether it happened within their own memory or that of their fathers, or not. But, once beyond this line of demarcation, all the past events are placed by them on one plane, and there are no gradations of "long ago" and "very long ago". Any idea of epochs in time is absent from their mind; the past is one vast storehouse of events, and the line of demarcation between myth and history does not coincide with any division into definite and distinct periods of time.
>
> Again, they have no idea of what could be called the evolution of the world towards a series of successive changes, which happened in nature or in humanity, as we do. We, in our religious and scientific outlook alike, know that earth ages and that humanity ages, and we think of both in these terms; for them, both are eternally the same, eternally youthful. Thus, in judging the remoteness of traditional events, they cannot use the coordinates of a social setting constantly in change and divided into epochs . . . The mythical personages of the natives' legends . . . live in the same houses, eat the same food, handle the same weapons and implements as those in use at present.[2]

In spite of this they do in their way recognize that myths are different from historical record. "In the mythical world, although surrounding conditions were similar, all sorts of events happened which do not happen nowadays, and people were endowed with powers such as present men and their historical ancestors do not possess. In mythical times, human beings come out of the ground, they change into animals, and these become people again; men and women rejuvenate and slough their skins; flying canoes speed through the air, and things are transformed into stone."³

Malinowski goes on presently to remark on the entire absence of any notion of developmental progress.

> It is important to realize that, though natives do speak about times when humanity was not upon the earth, of times when there were no gardens, etc., yet all these things arrive ready-made; they do not change or evolve. The first people, who came from underground, came up adorned with the same familiar trinkets, carrying their lime pot and chewing their betel nut. The event, the emergence from the earth was mythical, that is, such as does not happen now; but the human beings and the country which received them were such as exist today.⁴

Hence the mythic world does not for them stand as the point of departure for a long course of historical development to follow; that is a concept of which the native in any case has not any remote notion. The past whose memory they cherish does not go very far back. Beyond what is thus remembered suddenly looms the mythic age. The Dobu Islanders say without hesitation that four or five generations ago their island was inhabited by mythical personages and all events of that time were mythic. The age when those things took place had nothing in common with the people and their modern way of life. It was a period, as another writer neatly expressed it, "so far back, there was yet no time at all".⁵

Like Malinowski, R.F. Fortune also demonstrates that the Dobu Islanders have no notion of any kind of historical evolution. He finds some expressive phrases to describe the period: "Kasabweibweileta, Bunelada, Nemwadole, Wanoge and many other characters among the first ancestors still exist, and exert the same influence that legend vouches for their having exerted some five generations ago when existence first came into being and natural history began."⁶ His language is sophisticated, but apposite. It is unlikely that the Dobuans themselves would have been accustomed to a terminology so abstruse. But like many other primitives they are very well aware of the qualitative differences between experience of the mythic world and that of the world of every day, differences that are reflected clearly in the mood and colour of both. We shall be given a number of proofs of this awareness presently.

In his studies of the African Bushman, some traits of whose mental life invite comparison with Australian and Papuan

Aborigines, H. Vedder draws attention to their complete lack of interest in the past as such.[7] What is over is done with; it no longer matters. There is no need even to think about it. And so the Bushmen preserve nothing that even distantly resembles history. They live entirely in the present and for its present demands. Yet they possess a multitudinous stock of myths and legends. Moreover the events they report take place in a setting of ancient time. But this is not to assert that the age in question possesses any kind of measurable perspective. Really it is not time at all in any rational sense; it is a special kind of time, itself as mythical as the events it embraces or the beings who have their existence in it.

That is what appears to us to be so strange: instead of the myths fitting into a certain epoch of historical time, the epoch itself participates actively in the identity of the world of the myths. To say the same thing in another way, objects and beings which have their existence within that world possess a certain kind of contemporaneity which relates and unites them. It is difficult for us to grasp this time-relationship, which is also a mystical identification. It is our habit to think of the past as though it were a vast, coloured stage-set against which our present life acts itself out; it is the great panorama against which we trace the outlines of our perceptions and formulate our thoughts. It provides for us the very proportions of space and time. We need not dispute that some such background may be present in the minds of primitives; but what we do need to recognize is that for them the truly impressive reality, the reality which seizes and holds their attention, is not of that abstract kind but rather something more tangible. Their minds naturally fasten upon a solidly objective picture of reality, space reduced to its plainly visible dimensions, points of direction, and a sense of place or location defined for them by their close identification — their *participation* — with certain spiritual beings which inhabit the sacred sites; and in a similar way their definition of time is determined for them, not physically but qualitatively, by those same participatory associations.[8]

The natives thus have a vivid sense of the difference between the mythic age and the present (including such actual history as the present age implies). This they express in their own fashion, not, as we would, by means of historical analysis and comparison, but simply by referring to the characteristics of both. According to Carl Strehlow, the Aranda refer to their mythic ancestors as *altjirangamitjina*, which means "the eternal uncreated". These "eternal" spirit-beings are often present today, though in altered form, not perceptible to ordinary human sense. To point this out is not to deny their actuality; their existence continues, precisely because it is not temporally limited. Elkin writes, "*Dzugur* must not merely be thought of as past time, but as present and future, and a state as well as a period".[9]

It follows thus that when natives declare the mythic world is the beginning of all things, this does not mean only that it is of a transcendent or metahistorical antiquity; it signifies as well, and above all, that everything that now exists is derived from it. In other words, to use Elkin's phrase, it was the "Creation Time". When regarded in this light, Wirz observes, the myths are equivalent to a Book of Genesis. The natives themselves treat them with a reverential respect no less than we give to Scripture. Malinowski says the same: "Myth as it exists in a savage community . . . is not merely a story told but a reality lived . . . [It] is to the savage what, to a fully believing Christian, is the Biblical story of the Creation, of the Fall, of the Redemption by Christ's sacrifice on the Cross." Preuss too has amply demonstrated the religious authority of the myths. He also confirms the point that primitives do not form any concept of the historical duration of time. When he declares they place their mythic period in the very remote past, or *Urzeit*, it is not upon *Zeit* that he lays his stress, but upon *Ur-*.[10]

Once we have clarified this distinction between mythic and historic time it becomes easier to avoid a possible misconception. When we use the word ancestor, sometimes we may be referring to one of the mythic beings from whom a human group originally descended, and sometimes to a relatively recent forebear (or forefather) of the present generation. Plainly these two meanings need to be kept distinct.

The *forefathers* who, for example in tribes like the Zuñi or certain Bantu peoples, hold a position of very high prestige and veneration, were in fact in their own living day persons exactly like their modern descendants. They were born, they lived their lives in just the same way. They died precisely as those now living will die. Some stand out for personal reasons, some for their noble character, some for what they achieved. Even the obscure, those of whom no particular recollection remains, are nevertheless carefully kept in mind. Pains are taken to see that their spirits are not offended by neglect in the ceremonies and sacrifices. For the present generation is convinced that its well-being, indeed its very life, is in certain respects dependent upon the benevolence of the spirits of the dead. If they were displeased it could bring down dire calamities: rampant sickness, sterility in women, drought or famine. Therefore everything possible must be done to appease them. The offerings and sacrifices which are their due will therefore never be omitted. It was on account of the high ritual respect accorded to the spirits of their forefathers by the Tongalanders (Bantu), that H.A. Junod asserted that they had the status of gods. But even though they seem thus to be deified, and no one would be so rash as to set out on any new project without assuring himself of their favour (they are consulted by divination), they are nevertheless invariably understood to be human ghosts. They really did live in the past at a definite time. They were the real fathers and grandfathers of the men of today.

The *ancestors* of whom the myths speak are, on the contrary, quite distinct from these. No historical connection that can be traced attaches them to any generation immediately past. They belong to that extra-temporal phase of time which goes so far back there was yet no time at all. In that remote age they created or brought forth all that now exists, each spirit being responsible for the particular group whose ancestor he became. How did he create them? Was it by some act of physiological generation in the sense that we understand? In the context of mythic thinking this question simply does not arise, at least not in such terms. Caring not at all, in the ordinary way, for the automatic logic of cause and effect, the myths pay attention only to the kind of creation which is also metamorphosis.

Elkin, in a discussion of Australian totemism in relation to sexuality, points to the existence of a native belief that birth is not dependent upon physical paternity. "The great central idea of Kurnai society", he writes, "is community of descent", and he cites a passage from L. Fison and A.W. Howitt: "Every descendant of Yeerung is a brother, every descendant of Djeetgun is a sister; all else are Brajerak, aliens to their blood." Elkin adds, "The belief that all the women of a community have a different ancestral source from the men may seem strange to us, but the associated Aboriginal belief in pre-existence of spirits makes it logical enough to the native mind." It is the spirits who make new births possible by becoming reincarnated. In the first instance it was a mythic being who brought them into existence. By doing so he also became the ancestor of the generations which afterwards followed.[11]

But the mythic ancestors in their own persons never suffered the limiting conditions of human life. As the "eternal uncreated" there was no need for them to be born or to experience death. "In the beginning," an Aranda legend says, "there was living at Ankota a man who had sprung from the earth without father or mother . . .".[12] The exploits of such marvellous beings take place outside of time and therefore do not bring them to any mortal end. Their continued presence in the landscape is still plainly to be read in its contours, after they have assumed some ultimate metamorphic shape, fixed as a tree or a rock, etc. No offerings or sacrifices are offered to them. But tribal ceremonies, mostly in the form of ritual representations of the legends, are celebrated in their honour. These ceremonies serve to bring about a sense of participation and intimate communion with the beings. They are thus equivalent to religious rituals, though it is true they take a form unlike the religious ceremonies we are accustomed to, and are not addressed to what we would regard as gods.

Spencer and Gillen have shown that among the Arunta and Luritcha (Strehlow's Aranda and Loritja), ancestor-worship as we usually interpret the expression is not known. The same is true, broadly speaking, of all the Australian and New Guinea tribes we are concerned with. On the other hand, in other places where it is practised, and has been treated as important, the primitive original mythic or totemic ancestors themselves (if any are still recognized) are seldom or never given prominence; they play a part that by no means compares with the social and religious significance they have in Australia. What happens, it would seem, is that the greater the importance the (human-type) forefathers come to assume in the lives of their descendants, the further back the (mythic-type) ancestors seem to be forced into the shadow. Or they may even be forgotten altogether.

Nevertheless if we may think of tribes like the Aranda or the Marind-anim as having an earlier origin, and of others like the Zuñi or the Bantu as relatively later − as, in effect, their cultural successors − perhaps something of the spirit of the mythic ancestors belonging to the more primitive cultures may be thought of as passing down to the later ones by a sort of historical carry-over, dim as its contained memories might have become. This may well be the reason at bottom why the "ancestors" of the more and the less primitive tribes can both be called by the same name. Reasoning on probability, we may assume that the emotions of hope and fear shown by the more recent peoples towards their own human-type ancestors must simply have developed as a continuity out of the corresponding emotions of the older cultures they had superseded. We have observed a good deal that may point in this direction among a number of later primitives. And yet the explanation is not a wholly satisfying one. Perhaps the veneration and awe commanded by those earliest human-type ancestors, together with the weight of tradition — never-challenged, sacred, according to which every departure from established precedent, unless seen as approved by the ancestors, is a sacrilegious crime — constitutes a surviving, living vestige of the ancient self-created, self-defining mode of spiritual awareness. As such it recalls the deep emotions experienced by the more primitive foregoers, as for example the Aranda or the Marind-anim, whenever they allowed their thoughts to dwell on the mythic world and all that had been brought to pass through its agency. The tremendous authoritarian prestige of the forms and precedents laid down by the early human-type founding fathers, indeed the very cults of which they were themselves to become the venerated centres, may thus be viewed as having derived originally from those same emotions. Over the course of centuries these cults have been, first kindled, then fostered, by that mystical modality of thought itself. With it then ensued all the variously evolving culture heroes — creators, discovers, transformers and mythic figures generally — who were to shape and people the legends.

Nor should we forget that these human forefathers, the same as all the other dead, are part of the world of unseen powers. That world lies very close to the mythic world, if indeed the two are not identical. Viewed in this light the venerated forefathers and the mythic creators do not stand far apart. They become the subject of beliefs of the same kind. Whether it is a question of the one or the other, the way a man relates to them will be decided by the aspect of primitive experience which, to make sure of distinguishing it from material issues, I have called mystical. In other words, they evoke the affective category of the supernatural. This is explanation enough why any mythic being, the creator of a human group, can properly be called an "ancestor" without having literally engendered it; and why, on the other hand, forefathers of the human sort can often be invested with a sacred prestige similar to, if not exactly identical with, the authority accorded to mythic beings.[13]

From the earliest times observers of the Australian Aborigines have remarked on their highly developed sense of location, and on their extraordinary ability to put it to practical use. "I have often been struck", wrote an early settler, "with the exact position each tribe takes in the general encampment, precisely in the position from each other their country lies according to the compass (of which they have a perfect notion). I have found this invariably the case, and latterly could form an idea, on the arrival of blacks, what part they came from."[14]

When different communities occupy contiguous sites, the fact is not without interest; indeed contiguity plays so important a part that it may amount to something like actual kinship. "Without belonging to the same group, men who inhabit localities close to one another are more closely associated than men living at a distance from one another, and, as a matter of fact, this local bond is strongly marked – indeed, so marked was it during the performance of their sacred ceremonies, that we constantly found it necessary to use the term 'local relationship'."[15]

The sense of kinship between two such neighbour-groups comes from their equal *participation* in the mystical presences which emanate from the land itself throughout the territory they share. Any incursion by outsiders on whatever grows or lives there is resented by all as an injury threatening the very life of one group or the other. I have demonstrated this kind of participation in another work, but I throw in here a few more instances gathered from various Australian locations.[16] In the Boulia district (north west central Queensland), "whenever . . . a big flood comes up, it brings Karnmari, the nature-spirit in the form of a huge water-snake, so that suppose our traveller wants to effect a crossing, he will only venture in up to the waist: if the water be warm he will get across either there or at some other spot; but if too cold and he persists in the attempt, he is sure to be caught by the snake, i.e., drowned, when nothing can cure him or bring back animation. If about to swim any big stream or river which he suspects or fears, the native will speak to Karnmari, expressing himself somewhat as follows: 'Do not touch me. I belong to this country'. But were he to cross even his own country's river with a stranger to the district, it is possible that evil might befall him."[17] The presence of a stranger brings a risk of weakening the intimate participation between the native and his local river spirits.

In this part of Queensland not only does every tribe occupy its own territory, with exclusive right of movement over it and of hunting as it wishes, but within it every family has its own particular domain. Its members know in detail how the country lies, what plants grow in it, the spots where various animals abound, and so on.

> In the same way as a European knows what vegetables, shrubs or flowers are growing in his garden, so do the natives have a very fair idea of the amount and whereabouts of any special growth or edible roots, fruits and seeds, as well as of the particular haunts of the various animals and birds found on their own particular piece of ground. For one family or individual to obtain vegetable, fowl or meat without permission upon the land belonging to another family, constitutes trespass and merits punishment. This, however, is usually not of a very serious character, unless a non-tribesman is concerned: a slanging match with both parties indulging in obscene epithets (Bloomfield River), or a spearing in the leg (Cape Bedford). Trespass is, after all, but rarely committed, considering that, on account of their very hospitality, when one family experiences a superabundance of food of any description, its friends and neighbours are generally invited to partake of it. For a non-tribesman to trespass means death, and the risks run on occasion are enormous.[18]

Such reactions are instinctive, since the assault is upon the sources of the tribe's existence. The land and its people are one; animals and plants, all belong together in a unity, and this in a literal sense, not just metaphorically.

This "local relationship", or *participation*, between a limited area of country and the creatures, human and other, which live in it, is particularly striking in what are called totemic centres. Radcliffe-Brown writes:

> As regards many of the totems, it would seem that the totemic centre or ceremonial ground is in a part of the country where the totem species is naturally plentiful . . . In a number of cases . . . I was able to satisfy myself that the totem animal or plant is actually more abundant near the ceremonial ground belonging to it than in other parts of the country. In a large proportion of cases the place where the ceremony is performed is called by a name formed by adding the suffix -*na* to the name of the totem. Thus there are two centres for *murumbari* [a beetle], and in both cases the name of the totem centre is Murumbarina.[19]

Local totemic centres, the animal or vegetable species and the human groups which frequent them, all similarly owe their existence to the mythic ancestors. This is the belief asserted by Spencer and Gillen in Central and Northern Australia, and by Elkin and Radcliffe-Brown in a number of tribes of the North

West. "The ceremony at a given centre," Radcliffe-Brown writes in a later article, "is the possession of the clan to which that centre belongs and is performed by the men of that clan. There is a system of myths which recount how the various totem-centres came into existence as a result of the doings of certain mythical ancestors. It may be noted that a totem-centre is usually a spot in the neighbourhood of which the totem species is very plentiful.[20]

The intimacy of the bond between, on the one hand, the totemic ceremonies, the local centre where they must be celebrated, and the totemic animal or plant, and on the other, the mythic ancestor from whom they all descend, has been stressed by a number of observers. All have insisted upon its capital importance in the native view. Elkin, for example, says, "The cult-totems are always local, that is, each is associated with a definite portion of tribal territory, and therefore each totemic clan is custodian of the myths and rites which describe the doings of the heroes of old in its particular locality." Again, in even clearer terms:

> . . . this totem has not only historical and heroic reference, but also local reference; that is, it is associated with a definite area of tribal territory. Thus a person's cult-totem (kangaroo, black snake, etc.) links him to the locality in which the culture-hero or ancestor of that totem travelled, performed certain actions and it may be, instituted rites and customs . . . Thus the totemite's own personal share of the heroic period is associated with a definite area of country. He must preserve and hand on that share. More especial-ly in this connection is he concerned with the definite sites within the area which are particularly associated with the creative and more important acts of the hero. When he visits these he is deeply affected — his reaction is one of reverence, awe and faith.[21]

The consequences of such a participation are not hard to appreciate. "The bond between a person and his (or her) country is not merely geographical or fortuitous, but living and spiritual and sacred. His country . . . is the symbol of, and gateway to, the great unseen world of heroes, ancestors, and life-giving powers which avail for man and nature."[22] Consequently to remove the native from his totemic centres is not a simple matter of throwing him into exile, putting him merely in a position of disadvantage; it is strictly and literally, to deprive him of the means of life. Plainly,

> . . . it is inequitable and unsatisfactory to expect Aborigines to live their normal lives when removed from their ancestral lands. Not only do they then lack the highly specialized knowledge of the

natural resources of their own country, but more important still, they are deprived at one stroke of all that they hold most dear in their religious and ceremonial life. As Dr Elkin and others show, Aboriginal beliefs and ritual practices tend to be always localized, to centre in the lands of their forebears, the particular trees, stones and waterholes of which are the abiding places of the spiritual beings or supernatural forces on which, to the native mind, his sustenance and protection depend. He cannot perform the rites which, he thinks, give him his food and certainly give him a sense of social well-being . . . Take a native away from his tribal territory and he can no longer carry out the major part of his ritual; he pines for his own country . . .[23]

In New Guinea among the Marind-anim, once again we find almost exactly the same form of participation between the mythic ancestors and local places. These were the scene of their activities; totem-centres, which are also features of notable physical interest in the landscape.

The places to which the *Dema* returned, and where they still linger, are known as the *Dema-mirav*, i.e., *Dema*-sites. In most cases such spots have a striking outward appearance in consequence of some strange or unexpected aspect. In them occur unusual land formations, chasms, uplands, swamps with sandbanks or gravel deposits fresh or salt. Curious noises may be heard in them. In the rivers the *Dema* cause unpredictable currents and eddies, in the sea they raise waves which are dangerous for canoes. Occasionally people catch sight of strange apparitions, the *Dema* themselves, rising out of the earth, though mostly such visions are but fleeting and uncertain . . . For the most part, however, belief in the *Dema-mirav* turns upon certain events and happenings which have come to pass at those places. The native considers all these factors together and constructs from them long chains of cause and effect which mesh together like a net. Moreover no native will ever accept any event at face value, but always wants to know what led to it; hence he will bring up other incidents which, either at the same time or before, possibly long before, have taken place at the same spot. But no explanation has any force for him without the *Dema*, for all strange and unusual things may invariably be traced back to the *Dema*. Moreover everything which proceeds from the *Dema* in the first place is itself *dema*.[24]

His imagination, permanently filled if not altogether obsessed with what he takes, or perhaps rather feels, to be *dema* matters, wavers between the two senses in which he understands the word, notwithstanding he never draws any distinction between them. For him *dema* means, on the one hand, everything that is strange, unaccustomed and extraordinary, including the impersonal force which has the same impact; and on the other, the *Dema*,[25] the personal culture heroes, the mythic ancestors, always human and animal at the same time. He shifts between the two senses without noticing the differences; or it might be better to suggest that his mind accepts only one meaning. All the contributing evidences – the general character of the region, outstanding and remarkable features of the landscape, etc. – are for him indications, as they are for the Australians, of the presence and the activity (in the past and now) of the mythic ancestors. In short the native cannot look around him anywhere without feeling in a very vivid way that here, there and everywhere some supernatural power, some mythic being, has at some time made his presence felt, and indeed may still be present in the place. Earth and sea are to him as living books in which the myths are inscribed.

"Another characteristic of the *Dema-mirav*: they are very often totemic centres. That is to say, they are places where the species descended from the original creatures produced by the *Dema* exist in large numbers. The myths themselves also fairly often relate closely to the presence in the area of certain particular animals, plants, or other natural objects." We see here again, evidently, the same kind of participation in action as we have already observed in Australia, between a certain site (a local totemic centre), the mythic hero who was the creator or introducer of some particular species, the present-day representatives of that species, and the ceremonies established by the ancestor, now performed by the clan at that site. Wirz adds:

> It can hardly be simply by chance, that species descended from the same ancestors as, according to the myths, a totemic clan itself, should be found in abundance in its territory. Such myths have a grain of plausibility. Every detail in the configuration of a landscape, as well as the presence in the clan territory of a particular animal or plant, has contributed something to the formation of the tribal mythology and to the development of totemic relationships between the tribe and its ancestors, the *Dema*, who were in some manner already from the first in some sort of accord with the landscape and with the presence in it of the creatures.[26]

In this way we find intimately blended together, or even fully identified in the minds of the Marind-anim, certain trends of thought which, though connected, are habitually regarded by us as quite distinct. They involve the relationships between causes and effects, connections which reflect sources or origins or methods of production; or which may be due to kinship, or to the disposition of things in space or time. No matter how closely such ideas are brought together, we ourselves would never be capable of fusing them into one concept, because from the beginning we have always seen them as separate, and formulated an abstract view of them. But with the Marind-anim the fusion takes place at one stroke and without prompting. The result is a state of mind quite complex and highly coloured with emotion, of a kind it may well be possible for us to conceive as existing, but which we ourselves could never arrive at by any mental exercise of our own. Here everything is dependent upon the *Dema*.

> Whatever may happen, the native is forever aware of an intimate relationship between any event, the *Dema* who is its inevitable cause, and man, who however plays a passive role. Incidentally every *Dema* who has his dwelling in a known spot close to any village will become identified similarly with the village and treated as a near relation; he will be deemed to be its oldest inhabitant.
>
> Just as the villages, with the sago or coconut plantations attached to them, have always been looked upon as the proper domain of the forefathers by whose enterprise they were originally, it would seem, established, so every detail and all the outstanding features of the whole tribal territory are regarded as proceeding from the most venerably ancient ancestors of all, the *Dema*, whose shaping power is still perceived in every incident that occurs, and in every appearance of any unusual or unaccountable circumstance that is encountered in the area. This is all testimony to the closeness of the bond of union between the Marind-anim and their tribal country.[27]

In this intimacy we recognize plainly the phenomenon I have called participation. Every single feature of the region has for the Marind-anim a mystical significance. For this reason they feel themselves to be totally involved with the mythic ancestors. They owe their own very existence to those ancestors, who created not only the broad landscape itself, but every detail within it, down to the animals and plants.

At Kiwai Island, "almost every conspicuous place in the landscape is thought to be the abode of some mythical being. In certain cases the existence of such local beings seems to be taken as a matter of course, although hardly anything can be told of them except the name, which is generally that of the place with the word *abera* (father) or *nogere* (old man) affixed. Certain of these local spirits are akin to human beings, others are mythical animals, and occasionally we meet with trees with miraculous properties."[28]

Malinowski observes similar beliefs in the Trobriand Islands. He describes them vividly, especially in showing how the myths add life to the landscape.

> Here it must be noted that the mythically changed features of the landscape bear testimony in the native's mind to the truth of the myth. The mythical world receives its substance in rock and hill, in the changes in land and sea. The pierced sea-passages, the cleft boulders, the petrified human beings, all these bring the mythological world close to the natives, make it tangible and permanent. On the other hand, the story thus powerfully illustrated reacts on the landscape, fills it with dramatic happenings, which, fixed there forever, give it a definite meaning.[29]

In this way a legend is captured in the very outlines of the landscape in which it is at home. Something in the shape of the terrain, some particular local physical feature, has provided the occasion for a story. And similarly, what the myths tell brings clearly to the eye the ancient work of the ancestors as it affected the physiognomy of the landscape.

Even in country now occupied by whites, as long as the natives have not forgotten their myths altogether, they continue to sense their presence in the very earth. The configuration of the landscape preserves for them its old spiritual implications. In central Australia, for instance, hardly two years ago, Olive Pink made an exploratory investigation in a northern Aranda area. She was accompanied by an elder, or headman[30] of the region, and reports that this man of authority offered to point out to her the "old men" (mythic ancestors) of the tribe who could be seen in features of the landscape about them. The figures were *arumba arunga* of both sexes — literally "spirit-doubles" or paternal grandparents of mythical status — visible monuments recalling the beings' former presence at this place in the *altjira* time. The landmarks he indicated to her were "the two singing boys", "the left-handed boomerang" (tossed there by one of the tribal heroes from a crow-flight distance of something like 120 miles away!), and the "old man porcupine". By "old man" I suppose he meant "belonging to the mythic period".[31]

> These are all *arumba arunga*; that is, they are material evidence of the earlier earthly life of their spirit-ancestors, or evidence of their actions, and so, by implication, of *them*, that is, of the eternal part of them. There was also the "mother and baby blue kangaroo". I am not certain whether this was [a] human mother and her baby,

called "Blue Kangaroo" as their totem name, or a blue kangaroo and her young one.

The stones pointed out as "that mother and baby blue kangaroo" were two pieces of bluestone, a larger and a smaller, protruding from the gravelly bed of the creek (then dry).

The first *arumba arunga* we saw as the *thera aragutja* [glossed as *tjurunga* = sacred]. To the spiritually blind eyes of a non-native, this was simply a low hill, though remarkable because of its isolated white limestone cap on the bronze country . . . When one's spiritual eyes had been opened by the totemite's explanation one could quite well imagine it as the decorated heads of two *altjira* women.

Here they settled down, decorating their heads with lime and white rats' tails . . .

Then about a mile further on, we saw the top of the head of one of the same women, but only the lime-painted top and no hair-string headbands showing. Here she had "gone into the ground".

[Some days later, at another site.] People of the *altjira*, in the guise of trees and natural features, were pointed out all around us. It was then that the spiritual "value" of the site began to grip one, its reality to the native and his vivid narration of the myths connected with it making it "real" to me also.

Two gum trees were described as "wild dogs" . . . Several bloodwood trees were the same old bandicoot headman — commanding the wildcat men to "go away" back to their "own country". The stark limbs of a dead tree were indicated as his arms outstretched in command. These intruders were seen in the form of gum trees (mallees, I think), bordering the creek some distance away. A beefwood tree was where the *tjurunga* had originally been stored, on a "shelf" placed in its branches, in the *altjira*, and continued until the arrival of "whites" in his horde country. So, although it had long been a place desecrated by people of our own culture, nevertheless, in the company of the present reincarnation of its first headman, it retained its feeling of sanctity, a feeling which was expressed in the ritual performed in approaching it, and in this recital of the myths of historical basis connected with it.[32]

It would not be hard to instance other participations of the same nature as these in a great many other tribes whose place in the scale of civilization is much the same as that of the Australians and Papuans. I shall refer to only one or two more examples. In the Andaman Islands, according to Radcliffe-Brown,

We may say, briefly, that the local motives of the legends serve to express the social values of the localities. In general each locality has its own version of the legends, in which the events related are supposed to have taken place at some spot or other of the neighbourhood. Thus all the more prominent features of a locality are associated with the events of the legends . . . The effect of these associations between the places with which he is familiar and the events of the legendary epoch in the mind of the Andaman Islander probably is similar to the effect on ourselves of the historical associations of our own country; they serve to make him aware of his attachment to his country or to express his sense of that attachment.[33]

Leenhardt in New Caledonia remarks similarly, "All the topographical details [i.e., local references in a legend] are strictly correct. Moreover this precision is an explanation why the Kanaka will refuse to tell any story if he is in doubt about the names of the places referred to in it. It would seem the native needs to be able to fix it on firm local supports to retain it in his memory or imagination." In the geographical allusions he finds incorporated living traces of the legendary heroes. Leenhardt himself points this out in another context: "Finally we should not forget that the prayer to topographical places, which, at Houailoo, preceded the prayer to the ancestors, . . . was addressed to places identified with the totem, or the ancestor. These places were part of a total participative experience in which the heroic person and his environment were mingled indistinguishably together."[34]

Thus in that very distant past, the time which was "so far back there was not yet any time at all", before even the landscape itself looked as it now does, everything was very different from what we experience today. It was the world the myths depict. For the native mind and imagination, it was the focus of a passionate and inexhaustible interest. They recognized in the picture the myths presented, the source and origin of all the known and present world, which would not now exist but by virtue of that beginning; and which is able to continue, as we shall presently see, only through a constant − or rather periodic − renewal of the same creative process. How effectively do the myths present this idea? Is it possible for us to express it in civilized language without excessively distorting its nature?

If we attempt to express it as a clearly articulated concept, or even to speak about it with any precision, we can hardly expect to arrive at a really faithful impression, because the world we wish to describe is too elusive. There are two reasons: in the first place, it is not an ordered world, with elements which all fit together in the style our minds approve; in the second, many of the elements which do characterize it, and this includes the most essential of them, undoubtedly spring directly from primitive experience itself. Now that kind of experience, though it gives to primitives their insights into the supernatural and is in that respect more rich and ample than our own, is quite incapable of being reduced to a conceptual framework. We may try, but anything we are likely to achieve will fall short of rendering the mythic world really intelligible. (Rather, the nearer we come to categorizing it rationally, the further we shall be from really knowing it!) Nevertheless the effort may help us, as far as it is possible at all, to enter into the spirit of the experience and appreciate the closeness of the contact which primitives feel with the supernatural powers and mythic presences.

The fact is, they have a constant feeling of being in the presence of a countless multitude of invisible beings and powers, which have always existed since the mythic age. But in that age the invisible was often quite visible; the beings wandered over the land in various tangible shapes. Moreover this picture of such individual figures freely moving about does not exclude the coexistent presence of another force of almost universal immanence, but which is impersonal; a spirit that is present in all individuals and all objects, more concentrated and powerful here, more rarefied or weaker there. Among the Marind-anim, for example, anything odd, unusual or remarkable noticed in any object or creature will immediately arouse suspicion that some supernatural force is causing it. The striking appearance of a rock, a waterspout at sea, something peculiar in an animal's behaviour, will result in their being described as *dema*. But in the same breath the Marind will also speak of *Demas*, referring to personalized and individual mythic beings to whom they can give names; the natives are quite aware of their supernatural powers, the exploits they have accomplished, the sites they are associated with, the traces they have left behind them and so forth. It is therefore a matter of surprise only to persons whose minds are conditioned as ours are, that the same word can be used to describe both what is indicated in the strange or unusual aspects of things observed in the common world today, and what pertains to the mythic heroes.

Other Australian and New Guinea tribes use terms analogous to *dema* with a similar flexibility. We have, for example, already noted the diversity of interpretations placed upon *wondjina* by the Ungarinyin (north west Australia). Elkin explains further:

Wondjina . . . may be a life-giving power which is symbolized by the special *wondjina* paintings in each gallery. On the other hand, the *Wondjina* at the gallery of each *tambun* may be a different culture-hero of the *ungud*, to be compared with the different *mura-mura* heroes of the mythical age of the Dieri tribe, or the *altjira* heroes of the Aranda *altjirunga*. The natives speak of the *Wondjina* of this centre, and the *Wondjina* of that centre, and so on, and even compare them with one another with regard to their responses to man's requests. The point has yet to be definitely settled, but according to Love's interpretation of the Warara mythology, the "*Wondjuna*" were the first men who wandered over the earth, making many of the natural features and going into the earth in spots where the pictures remained and where the spirits abide for ever.[35]

What is there to prevent our seeing in these *Wondjina* the mythic ancestors of the Arunta or the *Dema* of the Marind-anim?

As Preuss reflects (it is an arresting thought), we habitually attribute to the distinction between personal and impersonal an importance which to the primitive mind means nothing at all. There is only one reality, and it is felt with the same force, in the same way, whether the experience comes at one time in *dema* style, or at another as *Dema* (that is, in the form of a personal or *Dema* spirit, a mythic hero). There is nothing in this to embarrass the primitive mind. As for ourselves, adds Preuss, when we are attempting to visualize the creation of the world, do we not just as spontaneously call up our image of the Power behind it in personal terms?[36]

All the mythical personages of the Australian and New Guinea tribes under review preserve a remarkably even homogeneous character. They are not born, they do not die; they are the "eternal uncreated" (Strehlow's *altjirangamatjina*). Spencer and Gillen call them *numbakulla*. The word means "always existing" and "out of nothing".[37] They all possess in a high degree the power of transformation, whether it is themselves or something else they transform. They are as likely to be met with in the form of a plant or animal, as in human form. And in fine it is they who have brought into existence (the word "created" could perhaps have some out-of-context associations) everything the present world contains: all the features of the landscape which make up its physical appearance, all the animal and vegetable species which live in it, all the institutions of the tribes by which they survive, and so on. It almost always happens that a tribe or clan and the animal or vegetable species whose name it bears (and which it names as its totem) have for their common ancestor one of these mythic personages.

Thus in an Arunta example, the *numbakulla* ancestor of the important *Achilpa* group, "while traversing the country . . . not only created mountains, rivers, flats and sandhills, but also brought into existence all kinds of animals and plants".[38] He also fixed the sites for local centres of the various groups: *Achilpa* (wild cat), *Erlia* (emu), *Arura* (kangaroo), *Emora* (possum), etc. Carl Strehlow says similarly of the mythic personages of the Aranda legend:

> After the sea had withdrawn from the solid land, the *altirangamat-jina* everywhere arose from the underground hollows where they had dwelt hitherto. They mostly emerged in human form but also possessed superhuman powers and could bring forth animals of the kind whose name they themselves bore . . . They could change themselves into those animals at any moment and many by choice continued to move about the land in that shape – for example, the kangaroos (*ara*), the emus (*ilia*), the eagles (*eritja*) and some others – and when they make their appearance in the myths it is by that animal name they are known.

The Loritja version differs slightly:

> The *tukutita* (that is, the "eternal uncreated") came out of the earth at various places. In the beginning they were human in form, but one day there came out of the west a malicious creature in the form of a huge black and white striped dog. Its name was Tutururu (that is, "he with the white stripe along his head"). This wretch harried and pestered the *tukutita* until they ran away, taking on animal form. Some became kangaroos, others emus, others again changed into eagles, etc. After this two *tukutita* arrived from the east, called Guranguna ("the good"). When they saw the evil dog they attacked it and drove it off as far as Wottatari in the distant west. There Tutururu disappeared in a great cave of the earth which in that country is where evil spirits dwell. However the two *tukutita* fetched a great heap of spinifex grass and piled it at the entrance of the cave and set it alight, so that in the dense smoke Tutururu and many more bad spirits choked. Then the two Guranguna returned to the east and at Untu, a place to the south of Merina, transformed themselves into two craggy rocks. After Tutururu ceased to attack them most of the *tukutita* resumed their human shapes, but always retained the ability to take on at will the forms of the animals whose name they bore. After a great deal of wandering which is the subject of their special totemic tradition, the *tukutita* eventually became changed, some into trees (*nganaringuta*), some into rocks (*puliringuta*), and a very few individuals into wooden or stone *tjurunga* (*kuntanka*).[39]

What is the real sense, in the minds of the Australian Aborigines, of that remarkable phrase, "the eternal uncreated"? It does not for them carry any of the metaphysical implications it does for us. It expresses essentially what the Ungarinyin intend by *ungud* and the natives of Central Dutch New Guinea by *kugi*. Elkin and Wirz interpret these two words in exactly the same way. *Ungud, kugi*, both signify the time beyond which enquiry cannot go, with all that that implies. Never ask a native what was the cause or origin of anything: it is a question they never put to themselves! If you raise it, they will not trouble about an answer. Once they have told you a creature is *ungud* or *kugi* they have told you everything possible. The limit has been reached. Or rather, perhaps, we pass on to a higher plane of thought, as when in our own theological speculations we discover that eternity stands outside of time.

When the curious, who cannot be content with such an explanation, insist on pushing their enquiries further, their tenacity appears to the native ill-mannered and misplaced. He may even view it as a form of blasphemy, if such a word can be used in this context. A.C. Haddon reports from the Torres Straits Islands:

> Mr Bruce, in a written communication, first called my attention to the fact that in the legends and folk-lore the principal personages, both male and female, are rarely married, "and when anyone is recounting", he goes on to say, "the deeds and adventures of any of them, and you ask if they were married or who their parents were, he looks at you and replies as if you had committed an act of desecration in asking such a question: "Certainly not! He comes in his own manner without a mother or a father."
>
> It is very amusing to hear the mamoose Harry scorning the idea of these people marrying or having parents. These great personages are as real to him as are his own wife and children.[40]

We need not stop to concern ourselves about the marriage issue; what is of interest is to see that Mr Bruce, asking about the parentage of the heroes, realizes he is committing a kind of sacrilege, at which the native headman is as shocked as he is surprised. But clearly the white man does not understand what is passing through the mind of the native, for whom the reality of the heroic personages is not only not in doubt, but lies beyond and outside the limits of time. Like the mythic ancestors of the Aranda and Loritja, they are "the eternal uncreated". Without having been themselves physically engendered, they have brought forth the rest of the creation. They belong to the *altjira*, *ungud, kugi*, etc., period, and to ask what was their parentage is grossly to misconstrue the most important aspect of their identity. Even children are aware of that! – who but a stupid white man could ask so ridiculous a question?

On the subject of the *Dema* in the Marind mythology, Wirz lays stress on the same essential attributes. "They exist everywhere: as well in the depths as on the surface of the earth, in the air, in all lakes and rivers, in the sea. They can transform themselves into any animal or object, they can reveal their presence through any kind of strange activity, or through any unusual happening in nature." Seen in this light they have a range that wavers between complete impersonality and full individuality. In a more narrowly restricted sense they can be considered like forefathers. Briefly, insofar as mankind is descended from them, the *Dema* "were beings in human form, endowed with the power to transform and reproduce themselves, and from whom there sprang every kind of object or thing". But here follows a more detailed account:

> The ancestors of the Marind-anim, as of all other men and all other living creatures in general, were, very long ago, the *Dema* . . .
>
> The *Dema* (they are also called *Amai*, that is, grandfathers, forebears) were beings of double (human and animal) form, endowed with unusual and extraordinary powers, which were supernatural. In addition to everything else they possessed the power of self-transformation and could perform all sorts of very strange actions which are no longer possible for men who live now. All that existed then was *dema*; real men, plants and animals (that is to say, as we know them today) were not yet present on earth. On the contrary, all creatures and all things in nature then existing still possessed powers which, in the course of succeeding generations, they lost. Thus they became the men, animals and plants familiar to us today. Whatever now exists came first from the *Dema*. In some cases the *Dema* transformed themselves directly into animals, plants and other things; in others they bred, engendered, or in some other fashion brought them into existence. (This no longer happens.)

Thus the fact is explained that all the creatures and objects in nature are akin to the various clans, since they and the clans all trace their ancestry back to a common source in the *Dema*. This is Marind-anim totemism, or at any rate one aspect of it.[41] With unremitting emphasis the myths draw the outlines of this age, one whose character was both uniform and protean: a diversity inexhaustible in detail yet almost perfectly consistent in the main drift. In every primitive community the ancestors or culture heroes are, like the *Dema* of the Marind-anim, at the same time human and animal (or human and vegetable). In all instances they are possessed, among a number of other faculties, of the two basic powers of transforming at will either themselves or their surroundings, and of "bringing forth", "creating", "inventing" and "founding". In any case the world through which they once moved (the myths seem to delight in following their peregrinations) was, like themselves, supernatural. In it everything, both living beings and inanimate objects – between which the primitive mind does not draw the clear distinction we do – was *dema*. Hence in that mythic age nature and supernature were the same. Whenever the legends are repeated or ceremonies performed, so as to bring the supernatural world vividly before his eyes, primitive man experiences the feeling of being in very close communion with the superior, transcendent but yet familiar powers of that other reality.

Radcliffe-Brown, in *The Andaman Islanders*, observed, "It is obvious that the Andaman Islander cannot regard ancestors as being persons exactly like himself, for they were responsible for the establishment of the social order to which he merely conforms, and of which he has the advantage. He says, therefore, that they were bigger men than himself, meaning by this that they were bigger mentally or spiritually, rather than physically, that they were endowed with powers much greater than those even of the medicine men of the present time." Similarly at Kiwai Island, Landtman tells us, "In former [that is, mythic] times the dogs were different to what they are now, for they were like people, except that they had four legs. They used to help their master to work in the gardens, and would speak as men do."[42]

It is normal in the myths for animals and men to be placed upon the same footing. This assimilation is so far taken for granted that it often simply remains implicit. The story has been speaking of men when suddenly, at a fresh turn of the narrative, we see they are not human beings but kangaroos – or *vice versa*. To quote only one example among thousands – "'There were once'", says a Loritja legend, "two eagles who lived at Kalbi . . . They had built their nest on a lofty cliff, and in it were two young eagles which the old ones fed with wallaby meat. One day the old eagles flew far away from their dwelling-place and came to Eritjakwata, where they speared a grey kangaroo and, as it was nightfall, they lay down to sleep."[43] Were they eagles or men? The myths sees no need to be specific.

The following is a Marind myth.

> Piakor gave birth to a series of offspring as follows. First a bird (*a mokmok*) which had a human face. The second child was once again a bird (*a ruas*), the third a fish (*kimu*), the fourth another fish (*ongajab*). Geb was vexed: "They are all downright *Dema!*" he said. The fifth was a human child. Geb was happy at having a boy at last, and named him Lanua. The sixth was another boy who was called Mangis. The seventh was a girl named Belewil. The children who came after were once again *Dema*-birds, including an owl (*nomohu*) and another bird (*kirkue*).[44]

Here we see among the numerous progeny of one mother some who were human children, of both sexes, and others who were animal creatures belonging to either air or water. Piakor's husband seems more annoyed than surprised.

Stories of this kind are legion among myths (it is hard to draw a rigid line between myth and folklore). To us they seem quite fantastic, in no way credible. But that is because we lack the natives' sense of the close and immediate reality of the mythic world and all that it involves. The conviction they feel on this point is so firm it colours their view even of the natural world about them. The natives know as well as we do that their wives will not become mothers of birds or fish. But it does not follow on that account that such a birth must seem to them, as to us, an utter impossibility. If someone were to inform them that something of the kind had just happened in the neighbourhood, they would not automatically disbelieve the message. It must of course be a *dema* child; it could be no other. And they would at once become absorbed in speculation as to what so strange a birth might portend. What misfortunate consequence must now be looked for, and how might it be averted?

Happenings of this kind and others no less apparently astonishing, though unlikely in the present world, were not remarkable in the mythic age. The most improbable transformations were accomplished with complete ease and in the twinkling of an eye, thanks to the powers possessed by the *Dema*. The motley brood of Piakor were nothing to excite comment in a world where, *a priori*, nothing at all, however extraordinary, was ever regarded as impossible.

The natives themselves, obviously, come nowhere near to formulating abstract generalizations like this. They do, nevertheless, effectively enough make clear the tendencies that come uninhibited into their minds. They are few myths relating to the mythic age in which a whole variety of beings and things do not undergo instantaneous interchanges one with another. A *Dema* ancestor transforms himself into a rock, and thereafter remains a rock forever. A more or less long and narrow scrap of wood turns into a crocodile. And so on. In less time than it takes to say so, a new form has been substituted for the one we were looking at. This characteristic of the mythic world has been given a name: we call it "fluidity". It has the effect of bringing out the contrast between the mythical "supernature" and nature as we understand it. Nowadays we expect all natural phenomena to follow regular sequences of cause and effect, even though such a course may not be so unalterably fixed as we see in the representations believed in by primitives. The mythic world recognizes no law at all in nature, not even of this flexible kind. The "fluidity" of the mythic world consists simply in the fact that the shapes and forms of the very species themselves, the plants and animals, appear to be as variable, as malleable as are the "laws" governing their existence. Hence anything at all can happen, and at any moment. Similarly, at any instant any one living being may change into the form of any other, whether this is done by the effect of its own individual power, or by the *Dema*. It all depends on what power may be available, and it depends on that alone.

In the world of our common experience, when we set out to educate a child from babyhood to manhood, we are obliged to take pains in many different ways and over a period of many years; a long course of mental and physical training is needed. In the myths, however, infant prodigies are always shooting ahead. Although as a rule native women continue to nurse their babies for two or even three years at the breast, in the myths we often find a child is no sooner born but he can do without it. At a few days of age only, he can walk and talk and fashion weapons of war. Soon he has the strength of a grown man and no one can match him. The same miraculous speed appears in the growth of mythic animals and plants. "The (palm) tree grew so rapidly that on the same day it bore ripe nuts, which in a very short time had sprouted again, so that soon around Javi's grave a whole coconut grove had sprung up, which people came from everywhere to see." "Just where the blood of the cassowary had dripped drop by drop into the earth there sprang up a fruit tree (*objara*) which the next morning was already bearing its crop." And in another

Marind myth, "And out of the grave next day an areca palm had sprung up, a beautiful, slender tree, whose nuts were already ripe; up till then it had been unknown. Everybody came along to admire the tree and sample the nuts."[45]

The fluid versatility associated with the mythic world has been neatly epitomized in Fortune's description:

> Creation in Dobu is explained by the metamorphosis of some natural thing into another. Language is specialized to express the conception of metamorphosis. Thus *gurewa* means a stone, *egurewa* to become a stone by metamorphosis from something else, *manua* means a bird, *emanua* to become a bird by metamorphosis . . . In the beginning of time various human persons *emanua nidi*, changed into birds. Thus birds came to be. Inconsistently enough, various birds hatched eggs from which issued the first human beings upon earth . . . Yams came and grew from humans in metamorphosis.[46]

According to these Dobuan myths not only does everything that exists today proceed from the ancestors "in the beginning of time", or else was "created" by them, but the method of their creation was by means of metamorphosis. In that age the vital principle of all beings was that they should transform or be transformed.

Fortune also insists on a point we have already drawn attention to: the fact that the so-remote past of the myths is at once both past and present.

> The occurrences of Creation do not live in legend alone, however, as events divided strictly from the present by an intervening gulf of time. There is a firm belief in continuity. Although a legendary scene is laid in the time of Creation, its actors still live, their influences still prevail. Thus, an underwater moving rock called Nuakekepaki still menaces and often overturns canoes on the open seas. Legend tells how Nuakekepaki is a deep-sea moving rock-man, who, to pay for a wife taken from the land-dwellers, overturned canoes to obtain the valuables they contained, which he duly paid to his mothers-in-law and their brothers as the *kwesi* or bride-price. All that can be made of this character is that he is a rock in one aspect, a man in another, and that as a rock he had supernatural qualities. He still overturns canoes to obtain the valuables they contain, apart from his former duty to his parents-in-law in the time of the first ancestors.

Similarly, "In accordance with all Dobuan theory the heroes or villains of legends still are alive, living supernaturals still capable of producing effects whether of themselves or under magical compulsion".[47]

The belief that the mythic beings, in particular the mythic ancestors (who never die), still continue to make their presence felt in the world of today, explains an important aspect of the social life of these primitives, and at the same time also a good deal about their conditioned habit of thought. As to the first, we are well aware of the importance they place upon their ceremonies and rituals (whether of the secret kind, or other), in which the mythic ancestors are given pride of place, and which are celebrated solely on their account. The records of Spencer and Gillen, Strehlow, Wirz, Landtman and many more, all leave no doubt on this point. The presence and the action taken by the ancestors amounts to an imperative need. They represent the root and stem of every living creature, of life itself, the source of all being in which it is necessary for all to participate while they continue to exist. The enormous amount of labour and effort devoted, through the ceremonies and rituals, to persuading the mythic ancestors to continue to assure for them all that is indispensable for the community's well-being, is evidence that the matter is one of wholly vital consequence.

In the second place, we must not forget that what I have called "supernature", something which the natives never separate in their minds from the world they know in dreams and in the myths, intervenes constantly in the ordinary daily course of their lives. Because of that the regular order is subject to frequent interruptions and exceptions. Those irregularities make an even stronger impression on their customary thoughts than does the regular course of nature. Not that they actually fail to take note of the normal and predictable order of the phenomena; various skills that they have developed, and in some cases carried to a high degree of perfection, prove very convincingly that they are able to observe and profit by certain particular trains of cause and effect, and turn them to good advantage. But they recognize no reason why they need to reflect analytically about such chains of consequence in nature, since they are always so regular and invariable. They exist; one makes use of them; and that is all there is to it.

Here we have a kind of explanation why, as Auguste Comte pointed out, there appears nowhere in the records of mythology a god of Gravity. Quite apart from the fact that gravity is an abstraction such as no primitive mind has ever formulated (or therefore, *a fortiori*, discovered a name for), why should anybody trouble to question an action which is so ordinary and unfailing? Where is the excitement in observing how weights, left to their own devices, invariably fall as low as they can? An effect which never varies can hold no interesting surprises. Neither does it prompt any enquiries. But supposing some solid body were to hang suspended in mid air, or float up higher instead of dropping to earth, *then* might be the time to open one's eyes and gape! "What supernatural power is intervening here?" everyone will ask.

Here let us refresh our recollection a little concerning the mystical emphasis in the orientation of the primitive mind. For such intelligences the mythic world, which has never ceased to exist and operate, still at every instant brings its influence to bear upon the world of present fact. Its impact is felt constantly in, for instance, every sudden appearance of some strange, unusual or otherwise extraordinary fact or effect − what the Marind-anim speak of as *dema*. According to our own style of thinking, the very existence of physical nature is itself a demonstration of system and order operating within an immutable framework of law: that is to say, we insist upon a determinist view of the phenomena and on a categorical invariability of specific form (i.e., the recognized forms of the various species) throughout all living nature. We therefore refuse to give any countenance to the existence of magical beings or miraculous events, and banish them relentlessly to the realm of fiction and fable. But the primitive mind has a quite different attitude. For it the mythic world, which is both *supernature* and *prenature* at the same time, comes first of all to consideration and is the prime reality; it is reality of the highest possible degree. It is, in short, the foundation on which nature in general must rest. It must be so, because it was the heroes, the ancestors, of the mythic age who brought forth (or "created") every creature that is alive today. In order that they may all continue to survive it is essential that the goodwill and concurrent favour of the mythic heroes should be retained. Therefore from time to time efforts must be made to make sure of them by performing the ceremonies they themselves instituted in the beginning.

Men, animals and plants today no doubt preserve little more than a remote resemblance to their ancestors of the mythic age. They have lost most of the powers their prototypes possessed. Nevertheless there are a few survivals. Certain animals, and in particular certain men, retain the privilege of *participating* more actively than do others in the supernatural world. A little of the old mythic "fluidity" still works in them. Sorcerers, medicine-men and shamans still enjoy to a greater or lesser extent the ability to change their form and reappear in some other shape according to their wish, and this power, as we realize, is one of the distinguishing properties of mythic beings.

To claim that in all these primitive tribes the people believe in the existence – past, yet also nevertheless still present – of their mythic ancestors, culture heroes or *Dema*, comes to the same thing as recognizing that their minds are mystically directed towards them – that, in effect, they are always ready to perceive in any incident, no matter how slight its variance from the expected course, the presence and action of the supernatural. And similarly there will always be found among them some who will be sorcerers or medicine-men; for the unusual powers belonging to these are themselves only one more proof, among many, of the intervention of supernature in the common world. And so these two beliefs – in the myths as such, and in the special powers of certain individual animals or men (that is, in sorcery and magic) – in the last analysis both spring from the same source. Both are as vitally alive at present as that fountainhead is itself inexhaustible.

It was earlier observed that to such primitive tribes as these, the idea of an evolving process of history was quite foreign. It must stand to reason, therefore, that they can have no notion of progress in general. The very formulation of such an idea presupposes there has already been some kind of advance in the knowledge of nature and the applications to which it can be put. In fact, among these primitive communities, if there can be said to be any such advance at all, it is for the most part exceedingly slow; moreoever even when there is, nobody attaches any importance to it. What would be the use of finding out how the various phenomena regularly modify one another, when at any instant their expected pattern of continuity can be perverted or stopped by the intervention of some supranatural force? Minds thus constituted will always be bound to turn by preference to the mythic world for their bearings, because it is there that the powers reside who are in control of their good or evil fortune, and whose concurrence and favour it is indispensable to have before setting out upon any enterprise. Thus, to cite only a single example, among the Cuna Indians (Isthmus of Panama) studied by Erland Nordenskiöld, no sickness can be cured with physical medicine alone; the proper accompanying spell or rigmarole must be recited also. Nothing prompts these Indians to reflect how the effectiveness of the medicine may vary according to the dose, the age of the patient, or any other circumstance; much less to undertake any kind of experimental investigation. What would be the good of it? What is important (and nothing else is), is simply to make sure that at the right moment the right ritual words are uttered.[48]

Facts of this nature are beyond counting. In all similar circumstances the mental stand of our Australian and New Guinea primitives is very much the same. Any enquiry in which they feel no spiritual involvement is automatically brushed aside, since it is certain to be fruitless. Their attention remains wholly concentrated upon the world of supernatural powers and mythic beings, which are for them a well-spring of sensations compounded of quasi-religious fear, reverence, awe and submission. If they go so far as to form any value-judgements on such matters at all, the "fluidity" of the mythic world must certainly seem to them a criterion superior to the commonplace fixity of the world of every day. For similar reasons the *Dema*, with their power instantly to transform themselves into anything, must seem to the Marind-anim incomparably more impressive beings than any human personalities at large upon the earth today, whose special powers, however impressive they may have been long ago, have now been reduced to so few, they have dwindled almost to nothing.

So long as minds exist which are oriented in such a fashion, whatever stage of development their culture has reached, the idea of progress and change will hardly touch them even lightly. The noblest of their ideals and their profoundest ambitions will remain wholly bound up in an endless *participation* with their own understood tribal "supernature". That is to say, they will seek an indefinitely prolonged communion with the mythic spirits to whom, as an established tribal group, they owe their origin in the remote past, and their continuing existence in the present; and to whom they must look for all assurance of survival in the future.

Chapter II

Mythical Beings, Half Human, Half Animal

Many Australian and Papuan myths are concerned with the actions and exploits of ancestors or culture heroes. These were the beings who, through the extraordinary powers with which they were gifted, created and brought to pass everything that the present world contains: living creatures, inanimate objects, the landscape itself with its lakes, rivers, mountains, rocks and everything else. They founded the institutions of human society and invented the instruments which made society itself possible. At the same time they possessed the special power of metamorphosis: they could transform themselves at will into whatever shape or form they pleased.

The myths almost always (there are exceptions, but they are rare) show the ancestors and culture heroes as beings with both a human and an animal identity. On this point evidence is abundant and very consistent. With regard to the Aboriginal tribes of central Australia Spencer and Gillen tell us so repeatedly. In the texts collected by Carl Strehlow it amounts to a *leit-motiv*. Among the Marind-anim the *Dema* are sometimes represented as having human form, and sometimes animal or vegetable. They pass from one to the other with complete ease.

This faculty of changing their form, possessed by the mythological personages of the Australian and Papuan tribes we are directly concerned with, is also characteristic of their neighbours and of primitive tribes generally. It has been pointed out by Ehrenreich in the most ancient of South American Indian myths, and is no less common in North America, particularly among the Plains Indians and those of the north west (British Columbia). Among black African tribes it turns up with the same regularity. In short, it is not by any means simply a product of special tribal circumstances in Australia and New Guinea (where the cultures are in any case far from conforming to a single pattern), nor is it derived from any merely local condition-ing factor. In virtually every place where myths of a comparable sort have been collected, the ancestors and culture heroes are presented as having both human and animal form simultaneous-ly. What can account for a feature so very widespread, yet to us so astonishing? Can we find any explanation for the duality of nature that appears in these magically endowed mythical beings?

There is no question but that they are so endowed. Not only do they possess the power to transform themselves at will into other forms, but they are not slow to use it. Nothing is easier for them than, at the appropriate time, to turn themselves into some animal or whatever they choose. But quite apart from magical transformations of this kind, we have still to enquire how it is possible for an ancestor to be intrinsically, that is, in himself and by nature, both man and beast at the same time: one is a man-kangaroo, another a man-frog, or a man-duck, or a man-wildcat, and so on; among the Marind-anim, this *Dema* is also a coconut palm, that one a crocodile or even a rocky outcrop. The problem has two faces, or at least we can look at it in two ways: 1. What kind of an idea of animals and plants can be represented by such a manner of portraying the mythic ancestors and tribal heroes? 2. What is this duality of nature (human and animal), found in one and the same individual?

Any attempt to answer these questions is doomed to be checkmated, unless we make the effort to look at the facts, and to feel about them, as far as possible in the way the natives do. To these Australians, Papuans, or Red Indians, half human, half animal mythic beings like these are no mere fictions designed for entertainment, or to thrill or captivate the imagination. They are beings who have really existed in the past and who still exist; their reality is deeper and more essential than that of any of the beings in whose midst we find ourselves in the world of today. What the myths relate of them is imbued with a character of quasi-religious seriousness. With rare exceptions, no impulse to doubt their existence ever enters the native mind. If the doubt were suggested to them it would be poorly received and prompt-ly set aside. Such a doubt would be incompatible with the nor-mal habit of their thought. Given the characteristic "fluidity" of the mythic world, nothing in it can be ruled out as impossible. However unlikely the story it tells, no myth will ever be rejected merely on that account. Rasmussen recalls hearing his Eskimo friends affirm their faith in the myths, explaining why they so completely satisfied them: "That is what tradition reports," they said, "so it must be true."[1]

It is not easy to imagine confidence like this being shaken. An Aranda myth reported by Carl Strehlow tells how the man-wildcat ancestor Mulbanka travelled in the company of his two wives and a band of young novices. At the conclusion of a ceremony, "Mulbanka arose, place all the young men inside a dillybag made of kangaroo skin, which he carried under his arm . . . and wandered towards the north. He came to Toppata, . . . where he saw a mob of wallabies on the hillside, so he opened the bag and let the young men out." Strehlow adds, "As the blacks see it, this sleight-of-hand in putting a number of young men into a small bag involved no difficulty. At the moment when Mulbanka puts the young men in the bag they are transformed into *tjurungas* the size of a *namatuna* [a small bull-roarer, a few centimetres long]. The moment he took them out again they resumed their original shape. In the same way he carried the two women in the form of *tjurungas* under his other arm."[2]

Observers have sometimes been baffled to discover what they see as a wholly unconvincing credulousness among people who, like these, are in other respects capable of reflection and criticism. But properly speaking, credulity is not the point. Minds which, orientated in mysticism, are traditionally dominated by the representation of a mythic universe in which all things are "fluid", naturally come to accept and preserve this attitude without questioning it. It excludes in advance all reason for doubting anything that may happen in such a universe.

And again, these myths seldom fail to remind us how all objects and all creatures belonging to that mythical time, particularly the animals, were bigger and stronger, and possessed wider powers than those of today. All could speak and reason, make plans and carry them out in the expected way, just as human beings do. Why, then, should we be surprised to find that the myths place men and animals on an equal footing? The ancestor or culture hero who makes his appearance in the form of a kangaroo, or bird, or snake, loses nothing by abandoning his human shape. He is still himself; still capable of the same heroic exploits. He is diminished neither in power nor dignity.

There is no need to urge the point further; it is enough to recall the atmosphere in which the natives respond to the myths and to see that they find themselves completely at ease in it. But these are only preliminary considerations, and do not go to the heart of the problem. What sort of an idea do the people really have of animals? And how does their acceptance of that idea lead them to look upon their culture heroes and mythic ancestors as men and beasts, both at the same time?

To begin with, the idea incorporates certain data of objective experience, assimiliated over thousands of years. The Australian Aborigines, for instance, could never, with the few weapons and implements at their disposal, have developed their mastery over the animals which provide their diet — kangaroos, emus, possums, small marsupials, birds, fish — without becoming very minutely informed about their habitat, their pattern of behaviour, their seasonal migrations, and in general, everything about the way they live. Knowledge of these things may often be a matter of life or death. They set about acquiring it by patient observation, with an extraordinary fineness of perception and a memory that is altogether prodigious.

> The tracking powers of the native are well known, but it is difficult to realise the skill which they display unless one has seen them at work. Not only does the native know the track of every beast and bird, but after examining any burrow, he will at once, from the direction in which the last track runs, or even after smelling the earth at the burrow entrance, tell you whether the animal is at home or not. From earliest childhood boys and girls alike are trained to take note of every track made by every living thing. With the women especially it is a frequent amusement to imitate on the sandy ground the tracks of various animals, which they do with wonderful accuracy with their hands.[3]

Wirz speaks similarly of the Marind-anim: "Their knowledge of plants and the uses to which they can be put is truly amazing. The native, wherever he may be in his own area, can always survive trouble, whereas a stranger might perish from starvation in those savannas which stretch further than the eye can reach."[4] There is no need to insist further on what has been said so often before. We need to remember only this: that the native retains an exact and detailed picture in his mind of every plant and every animal that is of importance to him, more minute and precise than the most observant of white hunters or colonists.

The sheer fullness of minute and particular detail in this picture has, simply on that account, an inhibiting effect which makes it quite uncomfortable for the native to move mentally from small and limited but concrete images to ideas of any breadth, as we are able so easily to do. This difference in our mental habits is reflected in the use of language, as I have attempted to demonstrate in another place.[5] The vocabulary of many primitive languages, luxuriantly prodigal with terms for denoting all the various creatures on which their interests concentrate, is by the same token a sure indication that, in that field at least, the habitual thought-processes of the people are deficient in conceptual flexibility; it is, moreover, in itself an obstacle to any further development in that field. Primitive minds for this reason have little urge to compare and classify things, or to replace images and notions of a narrowly (and precisely so-called) "specific" character with others that are more broadly abstract or general, less rich perhaps in detail but a great deal more profitably viable in real use. Admirably well instructed, indeed learned, from their own point of view, they are certainly far better informed about the plants and animals of their own proper region than any of our rural workers would be about their own neighbourhood at home. But all this knowledge and wisdom remains restricted to small and particular local facts, and as a consequence, lacks any organized system or structure and appears laxly fragmentary. When the Australian Aborigine is confronted with local tracks and traces, signs and pointers which he has learned how to interpret, the conclusions he draws from them are as a rule not to be faulted. But this extraordinary skill has been acquired only at a price. He pays for it with an almost complete absence of general ideas: ideas which might have become a basis and foundation for the exercise and development of his mind; and which, once incorporated into his linguistic competence in the form of concepts, might have provided for following generations a patrimony of inestimable value. If it had not been for the Aborigines' amazing success in their adaptation to their arid native environment, it would have been difficult indeed, if not impossible, for them actually to survive in it. But precisely because they achieved that adaptation so perfectly, their intellectual life became, so to speak, caught up in its own cogs; it was held back and arrested in order to preserve the race itself.

However that may be, there is a common saying that "All things visible have also their invisible counterparts", which may be applied to plants and animals as reasonably as it may to all living creatures generally. Certainly in their mental attitude towards those creatures of which they have so expert a knowledge, the Aborigines reveal a predominating regard for their essentially mystical orientations. Hence it follows that the size of an animal, or its physical strength, its means of attack and defence, its obvious and tangible characteristics generally, all mean less to the native than the hidden powers and faculties with which the creature is endowed. These are the things he is concerned about first, whenever he sees, or even merely imagines, a member of the species. These are the questions of first importance that he must take into consideration when planning the surest and least dangerous way to overcome it. He will never trust to his skill and experience as a hunter alone. If an animal is to be stalked and killed, the first tactic will be to concentrate effectively on an exploitation of its *disposition*.[6] To that end he will make use of certain spells and charms to slow down the pace of the creature, to paralyze its defences, and render it passive and submissive to his aim to capture it. The same kind of preliminary preparation is required for all the other means that are employed in the hunt: magic to help his weapons, his dogs, his snares, his canoes and so forth to play their part effectively. Tabus that are sometimes quite severe and very complex will need to be observed before, during and after the period in which the hunt or the fishing excursion takes place, both by the men who take part in it and also those who remain at home, in particular by the wives. In short, all is conducted in a fashion which assumes that, in the animals which are being hunted, there are mystical forces which must be appeased or mastered by means of other forces of the same mystical nature.

This is illustrated in a document of 1879, concerning the Aborigines of Port Lincoln in South Australia. We are informed that they have "a number of distiches, handed down to them by their ancestors, and known only to the grown-up men, which are rapidly pronounced when they are going to pursue or spear an animal. The literal meaning of these charms, or imprecations, as the natives term them, is probably unknown to themselves, since they are unable to explain it; but the object and confidently believed effect of them is, to throw the animal off its guard, so that it may not observe its enemy, or to weaken it, that it may not be able to escape from its pursuers."[7] To cite an example or two from more recent times, Landtman's study of the Kiwai Papuans (British New Guinea) lists a large number of magical formulas which the natives make use of in order to procure success in fishing for dugong, or to make the plants in their gardens grow. From the Trobriand Islands, Malinowski has provided us with a detailed description of the special requirements associated with fishing for shark.

At the beginning of each shark-fishing season new canoes are built, and the old ones overhauled. The bulk of the shark-magic is performed with this activity. When the season approaches, the owners of canoes needing repair, and the intended owners of new ones, consult with the magician and offer him presents. On an appointed day, the magician performs a rite in his house, offering some food to ancestral spirits and reciting a spell. During the rite the presents he has received are exposed in his hut. After that, the men get the timber into the village and proceed to work at the canoes for a couple of weeks. This is the period of the strictest taboos observed by the whole community. No noise is allowed in the village, no hammering of wood against wood, or working with implements, no noisy playing or games. Neither men nor women adorn their bodies or comb their hair, nor do they anoint themselves with coconut oil. Women are not allowed to make any "grass petticoats". The whole village have to keep the sex taboo, and all strangers are strictly forbidden access to the village. These two last prohibitions last only during the short period of building and overhauling the canoes. The remainder are kept throughout the shark fishing season, though less rigorously after the work on the boats is finished.

When all the boats are ready the magician utters charms over certain herbs, with which the canoes are rubbed. The fishing implements also have incantations chanted over them, and the fishermen proceed ceremonially on the first fishing excursion. The greater part of the quarry caught during the first outing is sent to the main chief in the village of Omarakana.

During the whole season of shark fishing, which lasts for about two moons, the magician keeps certain special observances and performs certain rites. Thus he has to abstain from sexual intercourse, and, in fact, his wife and family move away from the house, in which he remains alone, keeping the interior and the surrounds of his hut clean and tidy. He must keep to the village, as he is forbidden to hear the sound of drums or of song. When the fishermen go out on an expedition, he opens wide the door of his house and sits on the platform without his pubic covering, keeping the legs apart. This is said to make the shark keep his mouth wide open and catch on to the bait. Sometimes the magician sits in the same attitude and condition on the beach, singing a song of magical import to attract the shark.[8]

The mystical powers of animals, as also the charms and spells used for overcoming them, are kept alive by tradition; that is to say, for the most part, through myths and legends, which as occasion arises will always spring at once to mind; and their authority is unquestioned. They are a never-failing resource. Whenever a native sees an emu, a kangaroo, or any bird, insect, fish or fruit, or when some particular feature of the landscape suddenly comes into view, certain legends or scraps of legend will come immediately into his mind. Nature all about him is peopled with spirit-beings who fill his world with much more variety and meaning than we ourselves ever see when we look around, limited as our vision is to the objectively verifiable data. The difference shows vividly in what Catherine Stow says: "How interesting the blacks made my bush walks for me! Every ridge, plain and bend had its name and probably legend; each bird a past, every excrescence of nature a reason for its being. Those walks certainly at least modified my conceit. I was always the dunce of the party – the smallest [black] child knew more of woodcraft [that is bushmanship] than I did, and had something to tell of everything."[9]

In particular, these Australian natives will insist – but so will almost all primitives – that some certain animal is more cunning than any man, and able to achieve more. The knowledge and skill in question are of course to be understood in the natives' way. The learning they aspire to for themselves is not of the kind that ransacks the nature of things and then explicates the laws by which it operates; but rather the ability to forecast what happy or unhappy fortune lies ahead, to discover whether an enterprise will succeed or fail, and above all to recognize the *dispositions* (whether or not favourable) of such beings or creatures, visible or invisible, as are everywhere about them. It is because of what certain animals "know" that in various tribes they are eagerly consulted. Omens and auguries are expected of them. As to their special "cunning", the abilities which make the liveliest impression on the Aboriginal mind are not the same as normally excite our own special wonder and admiration: for example, the power of flight in birds, agility in fishes, and the like. Those are matters merely taken for granted; routine phenomena, which call for no particular remark, like the ordinary light of day or the familiar progression of the seasons. Certainly the native can be envious of such skills; he would acquire them for himself if he could. Sometimes he even persuades himself he may attain them if, for instance, he eats the flesh of the animal, just as a warrior may hope to absorb the strength and valour of his enemy by eating his heart, liver or brain. A number of myths exist in which we see the hero attach wings to his shoulders, or swallow the feather of some bird, in order to acquire the power of flight. But generally speaking, it is not these obvious faculties, but the subtle mystical potency of the animal, its unknown and invisible powers, that the native looks upon as having the most impressive importance.

Myths, legends and stories in this last category are countless. The few examples which follow will no doubt suffice. Formerly the tribes inhabiting southern Australia maintained a special respect for bears as sharp and knowing creatures. (We are aware that bears are similarly respectfully regarded in northern Asia also, among the Aino, and in many parts of northern America.)[10] An Australian pioneer remarked:

> The bear is a privileged animal, and is often consulted in very great undertakings. I was out with a celebrated Western Port black tracking five other blacks. The tracks had been lost some days at a part of the country where we expected they must pass. We ran down a creek; after going some miles a bear made a noise as we passed. The black stopped, and a parley commenced. I stood gazing alternately at the black and the bear. At length my black came to me and said, "Me big one stupid; bear tell me no you go that way". We immediately crossed the creek, and took a different track. Strange as it may appear, we had not altered our course above one and a half miles before we came upon the tracks of the five blacks and never lost them after.[11]

One should never skin a bear, this writer adds; the effect would be to prevent rain from falling. I add testimony from another witness to the same intent:

> I can vouch for their superstition on this head. I sadly wanted a bear's skin to make a cap, but I could never get it. One day a black of the Yarra tribe, who had brought in a bear early, before the rest of the blacks had returned to the encampment, was importuned by me to skin it. He refused to skin it; but at length, by giving him presents, and showing him that no harm could come of the act, because all the sorcerers and all the blacks who could communicate with the sorcerers and other chief men were absent, he took off the skin and gave it to me. I took the skin to my tent, and meant to make it into a cap; but the young man became very restless. Remorse overtook him . . . He said, "Poor blacks lose 'em all water now", and he became so much alarmed, and exhibited such contrition and terror, that the old doctors came to enquire into the cause. He told all. Much excitement followed. I said that the blacks had nothing to fear. I laughed at their terrors; but at length I was obliged to give them the skin. The skin and the bear were buried in the same manner in which a black man is buried. Though the bear was actually roasting, his body was taken away and buried with the skin. This ceremony they all believed would propitiate the bears, and avert the calamity of a loss of water.[12]

Birds, snakes, certain insects, fish, etc., similarly have their own particular powers. They are attributed to them on a sort of *a priori* basis. It is not obvious, in any case, that whatever the creatures need in order to live, they are always able to find? Do they not always know where to look for their prey, and how to escape their enemies? Clearly therefore they are well in posession of what the Aborigines consider wisdom. They can communicate with one another. It is true, no one can understand what they say (only a few shamans and medicine men can do that); but nobody doubts they can talk among themselves. The Aranda assert that there are many different birds which *laugh*; for example, certain young parrots. There are other birds which *weep* or *groan* — such as numerous owls. As for the animals brought in by white men, they say much the same of those: horses *laugh*, cows *weep*, sheep and poultry *gabble*.[13] But these are universal fancies. They turn up in myths and legends everywhere, and nobody questions them. In former times all animals were in all points equal to men. They conversed and argued with men and in the same manner. Of these once-upon-a-time skills not every vestige has been lost. Though they no longer hob-nob with humanity, at least they can chatter away among themselves.[14]

After this it is easy enough to credit that in the mythic age animals and men were much the same. Such a belief was almost universally accepted. Undoubtedly, according to W.E. Roth, it is current among blacks in the northern part of Queensland, "so much so that when a native wishes to speak of the earliest conceivable eras, he usually expresses himself somewhat in the form of 'When the animals and birds were all blackfellows' ". In the Bloomfield River region dogs are considered to have thinking powers — that is to say, a spiritual principle known as *wau-wu* — "and bear a sort of relationship to their masters, who will speak of them as their mother, son, brother, etc., in addition to mentioning them by their proper names". Similarly at Kiwai, "In ancient times animals could talk. This is still to a certain extent true of birds, who 'half he pick up talk belong people, what place he (the bird) stop, half he got yarn belong self'."[15]

If in the mythic period animals were taken to be also human beings, or at any rate equal to human beings in the corresponding faculties and powers, many surviving beliefs which at first sight seem to us childishly improbable can be explained with complete simplicity. There is nothing monstrous about a talking animal; it has simply managed to retain one special faculty which its mythic ancestors enjoyed, though other modern contemporaries of its kind have lost it. And so if you say something to an Australian or Papuan native about Balaam and his talking she-ass, it will be a matter of no surprise to him. In the same spirit, a *Dema* wife like Piakor could give birth to a succession of offspring, some animal and others human. Nor, in this way, will anybody be much astonished at the following Arunta attitude of mind, reported by Spencer and Gillen: "The native always has a dread of anything which appears strange and out of the common. In connection with this it may be noted that on the very rare occasions when the child is born at a very premature stage as the result of an accident, nothing will persuade them that it is an undeveloped human being; they are perfectly convinced that it is the young of some other species, such as a kangaroo, which has by mistake got inside the woman."[16]

The natives will mistake animals they have never seen before for human beings. And by the same token, men whose appearance is unfamiliar to them may be supposed animals. Taplin reports, in reference to the Narrinyeri, a tribe in South Australia: "The natives told me that some twenty years before I came to Point McLeay they first saw white men on horseback, and thought the horses were their visitors' mothers, because they carried them on their backs! I also heard that another tribe regarded the first pack-bullocks they saw as the whitefellows' wives, because they carried the luggage!" Similarly the Burdekin blacks asked the explorer Leichhardt if his oxen were his wives, no doubt for much the same reason. Among the Cape Bedford blacks Roth tells us that the first time they saw Europeans, they called them *berangobadi* (the name of a kind of shark with a light coloured skin). In New Zealand the arrival of the first horse produced a grand sensation. (The animals of New Zealand up to that time had never included any large quadruped.) E.J. Wakefield wrote:

> With two or three vigorous plunges the horse suddenly emerged from the water, and bore me into the middle of them. Such a complete panic can hardly be imagined. They fled yelling in all directions without looking behind them; and as fast as I galloped past those who were running across the sandy flat and up the steep path leading to the *pa* [village] of Tihoe, they fairly lay down on their faces, and gave themselves up for lost. Half-way up the hill I dismounted, and they plucked up courage to come and look at the *kari nui*, or "large dog". The most amusing questions were put to me as to its habits and disposition. "Can he talk?" said one; "Does

he like boiled potatoes?" said another; and a third, "Musn't he have a blanket to lie down upon at night?" . . . The horse was taken into the central courtyard of the *pa*; a dozen hands were always offering him Indian corn, and grass, and sow-thistle, when they had learned what he really did eat; and a wooden bowl full of water was kept constantly replenished close to him. And little knots of curious observers sat around the circle of his tether-rope, remarking, and conjecturing, and disputing, about the meaning and intention of every whisk of his tail or shake of his ears.[17]

Other descriptions are to be found elsewhere of reactions no less naive and amusing. That is how they strike us, at any rate; but it is only because, without stopping to think, we attribute to these primitive people a generalized notion of animals that is scarcely any different from our own. But they, in fact, and unlike us, do not interpose any insuperable distinguishing barrier between themselves and animals, even of a speculative kind. It thus follows that the reactions just described were not those of idiots or simpletons, but absolutely what one might reasonably expect from a first sight of living creatures whose like they had never in their lives seen before.[18]

Our classifications of living animals are based upon comparative analyses of their physical build and bodily functions. This approach seems to us so reasonable we find it inconceivable that anybody could consider using any other. For all that we must acknowledge, firstly, that Australian and Papuan Aborigines (and various other primitives) use classifications that do not in the least resemble ours. (We have already seen why not. The zoological classification of animals, the botanical of plants, has barely any presence in their minds.)[19] And secondly, we must acknowledge that on the other hand there will often be some particular plant or animal which, usually for inexplicable mystical reasons which have nothing to do with its visible characteristics, occupies an exceptionally important place in their estimation.

Dr Roth was never the man to overstate the intellectual refinement of the Queensland Aborigines he studied for so many years, and at such close range. Nevertheless he was struck by some singular features in their classificatory system, or what passed for one. It is a subject to which he repeatedly returns.

Divisions of inanimate nature have been occasionally met with between animals and plants, but really satisfactory explanations have not been forthcoming. Thus at Cape Grafton in 1897, I came across a local account of a binary division of *Kuragulu* and *Kurabanna* (*banna* = water), that is to say of things on land generally distinguished from those on water. The former, indicative of red earth, includes everything relating to the land, e.g., red clay, grass, sun, wind, rock, star, fire and land animals such as kangaroo, bandicoot, black iguana, yellow iguana, emu and pelican; the latter comprises water, and white or light coloured things and includes mud, cloud, rain, thunder, fresh and salt water, eels, wild duck, shark, alligator, water-snake, and all white timbers.

On the Tully River the respective grouping is more certain. Thus plants (wherein sex is not recognized) are divisible into four groups . . . [examples given] . . . Grasses and small shrubs are not put into groups or divisions . . . These same Tully River natives do not classify the animals like the plants into groups, but anything extra big, large, etc., anything out of the common, is spoken of by a different name.[20]

Among the Mullanpara blacks (Lower Tully River) there is thus one word for ordinary eels and another for particularly big ones; and the same is true of snakes, tortoises, wallabies, dogs, etc.[21] Whatever is out of the ordinary, as we remember, is evidence of the presence of unseen powers. It is hardly to be doubted, therefore, that this very elementary attempt at a classification of the animals by the Queensland tribes is made according to some secret innate property they must have – a property which has exceptional importance in native eyes, as in the case Captain Rattray has pointed out among the Ashanti.[22]

An item gathered by Dr Fortune shows how, in the minds of the Dobu Papuans, certain participation-relationships between the creatures in some measure act in the same way as classifications which our style of thinking would define by way of concepts. And at the same time they throw a curious light on the natives' view of man himself.

The Dobu language possesses a word, *tomot*, which denotes "what belongs to man, what is human". And yet this word is not used of white men. It follows that white men are not included in the regular category of human beings. Naturally the Dobuans are not so foolish as not to see the many ways in which white men are the same as themselves. Why should they not widen the application of *tomot* so as to make room for these hitherto unknown members of the species, notwithstanding their skin was of an unexpected colour and their language unrecognizable in Dobu? But it never occurred to anyone to do so. The range of *tomot* remained exactly what it had always been before the whites appeared. There would have been some occasion for surprise in this only if *tomot* had been a broadly comprehensive term like one of ours. In fact it was nothing of the kind. The word connotes an understood totality of *participations* shared by the people of Dobu but no one else: their common attachment to the island soil and the blue skies above it, their general inheritance from ancient mythic time, the native institutions and culture – all of this as well as the mere obvious possession of a human body. As to being human in form, it was not so hard to concede at a pinch that the whites were that, though the colour of their skin might put the matter in some minor doubt. (It is well known that among a number of Australian and some Pacific tribes white people were at first, on account of their paleness, taken to be not living men but ghosts.) Primitives, moreover, generally speaking make no distinction between body and skin; hence, since the skin was different, white men therefore must have different bodies also. And in any case the multifarious participations mentioned above did not have any existence for them. So all in all *tomot* could not properly apply to them.[23]

In the language of the Iglulik Eskimos, as Rasmussen tells us, white men are similarly referred to by the shamans as "beings almost human".[24] What is it they lack in order to become wholly so? Nothing, it would seem, in point of outward form, unless it were the pallor of their complexions. But since they possess no intimate share, as all Eskimos do, in the known earth, the sea and the sky of the land in which their Eskimo parents and grandparents have always lived, and in which the Eskimo mythic ancestors created and founded everything that gives life to and has meaning for the tribe, so they remain for ever strangers. This means they are permanently alien. Most primitives feel this difference strongly. I have referred elsewhere to the heated mood of protest very often stirred up by missionaries when, in their sermons, they allude to the Almighty Judge before whom all men of whatever race or colour shall be arraigned together at the day of Judgement. Native peoples do not easily accept the idea that an identical destiny can await both themselves and Europeans. The life to come is a continuation of life here and now. But here and now there is little that whites share in common with natives. Born elsewhere, they have their own kind of *participations* with a far-off and unknown land, a remote heaven, and completely unfamiliar gods. Everything in their past life, indeed everything they are and have at present, places white men apart from the native-born. How then can the life to come be expected to bring them together?

There is another consideration, and not a trifling one: this word *tomot*, which does not include white men, does include yam tubers! What, from our point of view, could be more absurd, or more ridiculously incomprehensible? That a mere vegetable, cultivated only to be swallowed as food, should be accepted as part of a complex "human" community from which white men are shut out! Nevertheless if we make an effort to put ourselves into the frame of mind of the Dobuans, we can perhaps acquire some insight into what leads them to support such a paradox. They have no notion whatever of our classification of living creatures. They are even less acquainted with anything as systemic as our concepts of genera and species. What does engage their attention is participation. The intimate relationships between the various beings and creatures, and the mystical powers operating among them, are of much greater importance in their view than physical form, the mere visible externals. Now between the Dobuans and their yams there exist traditionally many such intimate participations. Like the Dobuans themselves, the yams have their pride of heritage. A given family stock of yams is fully integral – we ought rather to say, looks upon itself as wholly integrated – with a human family ("family" being taken, of course, in the special sense in which the Papuans of Dobu use the word). Yams belonging to this stock will agree to grow only in ground owned by that family and cultivated with the aid of the proper secret spells, which likewise are the family's exclusive property. Plant them anywhere else and no matter what trouble you go to, the tubers will never come to anything. They will refuse to sprout or grow!

This family solidarity will appear less strange once we accept that, in Dobuan eyes, these vegetables are also persons. "If then," Fortune remarks, "we come upon a ritual addressed to seed yams, let it not be supposed that a man is muttering (spells must be recited in a quiet voice) a form of words to yams merely. He is addressing a personal being as truly as we are when we address God. For the yams are personal beings in metamorphosed form."[25]

Fortune found his curiosity keenly aroused by this strange belief and was determined to throw as much light on it as he could. It may not come amiss to record here, though with some abridgement, the gist of his enquiry.

> Once when Magile (the woman who did the woman's ritual in my garden) was charming over a bundle of smouldering green leaves her son said to me: "The Trobrianders charm out loud. Here, on

the contrary, we murmur underneath. The yams hear. They say among themselves, This is our language – not loud like everyday talk. You must understand that yams are persons. Alo recently told you of it. If you call aloud the yams say, How is this – are they fighting among themselves? But when we charm softly they listen to our speech attentively. They grow big for our calling on them."

Alo had recently told me a story in which the yams figured as persons. I had not known whether this was a figurative device of legend or a fact of literal belief. The statement of Magile's son, Kinosi, pointed to the latter alternative. Some nights later I said to Alo: "Kinosi said in the garden yams are persons. How is this?"

"Yams are persons," said Alo, " – what else? Like women, they give birth to children. As my grandmother gave birth to children, among them my mother, as she gave birth to me and as my daughter will bear children, and they my grandchildren, when I am dead – such is also the way of yams."

"But," I said, "how is it yams are persons? Do persons stay still always?"

Alo had his counterstatement.

"At night they come forth from the earth and roam about. For this reason, if we approach a garden at night we tread very quietly . . . We do not dig the harvest when the sun is low in the morning (the usual time for garden work). We wait till the sun has mounted. Then we know they are back. If we dig in the early morning, how should we find yams? Nothing would be there. . . ."

This statement proved to be no spontaneous argument, but a direct statement of traditional belief. I enquired if the vine and the root tubers walked about at nights entire. My enquiry was cast in all seriousness and received with all seriousness.

"No! The vines remain. You may see them steadfast any night in the garden. The tubers alone emerge from the ground and walk the bush tracks in the night."[26]

Taking the question up again later, under changed circumstances, Fortune still met with the same response. Hence his conclusion that:

Yams are treated as highly personal beings. The word *tomot* is used freely of them. *Tomot* is the only word that covers man, woman and child, irrespective of age and sex. It also connotes native as opposed to belonging to the white man, when used adjectivally. This latter usage contains the prevalent idea that the white man is "another kind", not really a human being in the native sense, but a being with different qualities from the native. The Dobuan will class yams with his own people as personal beings, but he excludes white men. In fact, he has indeed the more friendly feeling for the yams.[27]

If anything still remains doubtful on this point, we might glance at a myth of which Fortune gives us a short version.

> A woman of the time of the first ancestors whose name was Anabuyueta bore a many-armed son (who subsequently turned out to be an octopus). She set him in fresh water when he curled up and very nearly died. Accordingly he was set in the salt water. There he swam away and made his home in a rock cave of the deep sea floor. Anabuyueta went out to the deep sea to visit him, taking with her some seed yams. There on the sea floor she planted them and charmed them so that they grew. "Today if we plant in the sea they die. But the seed of the yams grown by Anabuyueta in the sea is the seed we of the Green Parrot totem use today — and it is indeed no ordinary seed — but descends from the sea garden of the Murus Octopus."[28]

These yam ancestors are clearly also persons.

Since we are here concerned with tubers which are also persons, does this amount to anthropomorphism? It depends on how we interpret the word; there is some risk of misunderstanding. As it is usually interpreted, anthropomorphism implies that we attribute to creatures unlike ourselves, or even to inanimate objects, the outward form, moral attributes, even the actions and manners of men. The plastic arts, poetry and folklore all make a liberal use of this convention. We have animal tales in which the beasts talk, quarrel, cheat one another and fight among themselves, dressed up, so to speak, in human virtues and vices: scheming and spitefulness, mischief, cruelty, lewdness, revenge, anger, folly, ingenuousness, tenderness, maternal affection, self-sacrifice, and so on. It is done in a spirit of burlesque or travesty, as when the illustrator Grandville depicts cats, dogs, wolves, birds, crocodiles, hippopotamuses etc., wearing boots, trousers and hats.[29] It is sheer nonsense, all meant for fun. Primitive people too have stories of this kind, intended as jokes. But mostly when animals and plants make an appearance in serious myths it is a different matter; they have then nothing in common with this sort of free-and-easy anthropomorphism. Primitives do not ever, according to some kind of preconceived plan, simply transfer to such beings (or objects) as those, qualities and faculties which belong to man alone. Why indeed should they? Their own culture tells them already that those faculties and qualities are not exclusive to man; other beings possess them equally, as a full right, and as part of their nature.

Thus, distantly removed as animals are from ourselves in form and appearance, the myths need use no fiction or contrivance to bring out their spiritual equality. That was present from the beginning; no one ever pretended otherwise. This explains or at any rate helps to explain, the *dispositions* which all primitive people attribute to animals and regard as so important.[30] Before the spirit of anthropomorphism can thrive, a certain perspective of remoteness must have developed about the animal, to create a sense of opposition to the human. That of course is the way we see animals. But primitives do not see them in that way at all. "We and the animals", said Perez, the Indian Nordenskiöld brought back with him from his last expedition to Panama, "are alike. The Cuna Indians do not believe, as Christian people do, that any deep gulf exists between man and the animals . . . You never speak of animals transforming themselves into men, because animals always were men to begin with, underneath their animal form."[31]

It is an easy step from the mental attitude here described to the full duality of nature seen in the ancient mythic ancestors, who are men and animals simultaneously. "Going back to this far-away time," says Spencer, "we find ourselves in the midst of semi-human creatures endowed with powers not possessed by their living descendants and inhabiting the same country which is now inhabited by the tribe, but which was then devoid of many of its most marked features, the origin of which, such as the gaps and gorges in the MacDonnell Ranges, is attributed to the mythical Alchera ancestors." And further, "In the Alchera lived ancestors who, in the native mind, are so intimately associated with the animals or plants the name of which they bear that an Alchera man of, say, the kangaroo totem may sometimes be spoken of as a man-kangaroo or as a kangaroo-man. The identity of the human individual is often sunk in that of the animal or plant from which he is supposed to have originated. It is useless to try to get further back than the Alchera; the history of the tribe as known to the natives commences then." Elsewhere Spencer refers to the Alchera tradition as "evidently a crude attempt to describe the origin of human beings out of non-human creatures who were of various forms; some of them were representatives of animals, others of plants, but in all cases they are to be regarded as intermediate stages in the transition of an animal or a plant ancestor into a human individual who bore its name as that of his totem."[32]

Carl Strehlow speaks even more positively. Whether he is

translating (into German) and commentating the texts of the legends, or describing Aranda and Loritja ceremonies, the mythic-ancestral duality of all nature is affirmed on every page. Sometimes it becomes naively obvious because of the coexistence in one individual of certain features belonging to the human form and others belonging to plant or animal nature. Thus Altjira, the ancestor to whom Strehlow refers as the Supreme Being of the Aranda, is depicted as a big, strong man with a reddish skin colour, and long fair hair falling to his shoulders. But he has the feet of an emu . . . Of his many sons and daughters, the sons too have emu-feet, the daughters the feet of dogs.[33]

"Two large *renina* snakes who had long fed on roots of grass and reed at Iloara . . . travelled east and arrived at a place called Labara . . . where a gathering of *renina* men had assembled. These set out in pursuit of the two snakes, who angrily tied on their headbands, fixed their shields to their backs, and fled away." "In Iwopataka, a place between Alice and Owens Springs, there once lived many *ngapa-* or crow-men, who lived on *manna latjia* (an edible root). One day . . . the headman of the *ngapa-*people said to his camp companions, 'You stay here, I'll just go along and see if I can find out where this feather-down comes from.' He took the form of a crow and flew off to the west, coming to earth again at Ariljarilja, a spot to the north of Gosse's Range."[34] It is scarcely necessary to continue the long list of mythic ancestors who are like these. All are half human, half animal (or vegetable). Quite often their changes from form to form are accomplished without any overt mention in the story: suddenly the animal is a man, or the man an animal, or the individual may partake of both identities at the same moment. No warning is given except by what happens in the narrative and its changes of direction.

The same kind of man-animal or man-vegetable ancestors exist in other Australian tribes; also in New Guinea, for example in the Marind-anim. The evidences are typically similar. Thus, "its tracks (that is, of the *Dema*-cassowary) are curious to look at; one footprint is like a man's, the other seems to be that of a different and quite unknown creature (in this region the *Dema*-cassowary is represented as a double-natured, half-human being)". "Another *Dema*, Iano, who in the myth was half man, half kangaroo, was the parent of human children as well as of true kangaroos. He is therefore on the one hand the creator-ancestor of the kangaroo as a native animal, and on the other of the human clan which has the kangaroo for its totem." Finally, to put paid to this long string of instances which could easily go on forever, "Mahu is often called a *Dema*-dog (*Ngat Dema*), and when he is described it is in the character of a man with a dog-nature. (He has an especially large development of the genital organs.) It followed that when he fathered the race of dogs, they in their turn were not 'true' dogs, but on the contrary had in them a great deal of human nature still; especially as they could talk and had the power to change their form. They were therefore dog-*Demas* (*Dema-ngat*). It was from these that dogs properly so-called were descended. This is related in a separate myth."[35]

This radical duality expresses itself in various ways. Sometimes both natures appear together, of which there may even be ocular proof: one of the ancestor's feet is human while the other is animal, etc. At other times, instead of coexisting, the two natures appear by turns. At a given moment one yields to the other; but that may disappear in due course, and then the other is back again. Thus:

> A *Dema*-pig, whose name was Sapi, came from Habee Island to Uambi, where he made havoc in the people's plantations and stole the yam tubers. By day he appeared simply to be an ordinary young man (*miakim*), wearing his ornaments, combing his hair carefully, and carrying his club — that is, he was all that a *miakim* should be. But by night, while the people slept, he would sneak across to the plantations, climb over the hedges and, transforming himself into a hog, would wreck the gardens hunting for yams and taro. Towards dawn he would transform himself back into a young man and slip back quietly to the village.

Dema plants, and even stones, possess the same ability to move about. "These stones have an extraordinary potency and for that reason their shape is not immutably fixed; *Demas* of this kind can at any time change their form. It is believed indeed that if you leave one of these stones unprotected and exposed, it will suddenly sprout legs and run away. The natives therefore are always careful when carrying these stones to keep them in a little plaited bag which they hang round their neck."[36]

Here again we are reminded of the "fluidity" of the mythic world, and we see, too, how tightly it conforms with the mental background of the native culture, out of which such myths emerge. What principally impress the minds of these people are the magical unknowns, mystical powers and faculties with which beings are endowed, but which remain unseen. Outward form is regarded as having only a secondary importance;

therefore it hardly calls for notice. People pay attention to it only if there is a particular practical reason. We could almost go so far as to assert that *supernature* (meaning, beings with such mythical powers) can do whatever it will with what we understand by *nature*, and turn it to any desired end. It meets with no resistance from the làws governing natural phenomena and is equally untroubled by the physical form of the creatures. No metamorphosis, however ridiculous it might appear to us, is therefore ruled out simply as physically impossible. There are no *a priori* impossibilities; these primitives know no obligation to take account of any conditional limits upon possibility. What the myths provide them with examples of, they accept as true. It is a simple argument *ab actu ad posse* – anything that has happened before, may happen again. Who will stop to question whether men-animals, or men-vegetables even, are possible, since the myths make it certain that they existed in the past and still do?

But we should remember that for the native mind, this duality and its associated interchangeability of form does not imply the same logical consequences as would seem necessary to us. According to our way of thinking, if we could suppose it possible for a man to change himself into a dog, we should not expect the change to stop at a substitution of one kind of outward and visible appearance for another – from smooth-skinned biped to shaggy quadruped. Certainly something more than that would seem to be involved: the new dog would seem scarcely likely to have much in common, mentally speaking, with the former man. More, we are so convinced of this incongruity that any such change is necessarily considered by us to be possible only in the realm of fancy; nothing will ever persuade us that in sober reality a man could turn into a dog, or a dog into a man.[37]

But with the Australian Aborigines the case is different. From their earliest infancy they have been accustomed to hear about beings who are at the same time both animals and men and can change with complete ease from the one form to the other. When as a fully adult man, initiated, married and socially responsible,[38] the Aborigine is entrusted by the elders with the sacred and secret lore of the tribe, he discovers in the myths and legends (tribal epics)[39] scriptural authority for what the ancestors (the "eternal uncreated") performed; and they were always beings of that half human, half animal kind. He sees them brought to life again in the persons of elaborately decorated actors in tribal ceremonies.[40] The ritual dancing and chanting may move him to a point of deep and intimate communion, a state of absorption and entrancement in which he loses his own sense of individual identity to become mystically reunited with the animal-ancestor. From what source, then, should there spring any impulse to doubt those interchanges? The tribesman's attitude is a product of collective emotion, necessarily accompanied by unquestioning faith. Such faith forestalls all possible criticism. As for any anatomical, physiological or psychological impossibilities, crucial as they appear to our way of thinking, he simply has no awareness of them. In any case he knows with confident certainty that nothing at all is so improbably or extraordinarily strange that it cannot be brought to pass, provided only that the mystical power which comes into play is of sufficient strength.[41]

Paul Ehrenreich, who towards the end of the last century made a study of the myths of some very primitive South American tribes, has drawn attention to certain figures among them which quite remarkably recall the half human, half animal ancestors we have been discussing.

> The culture heroes [corresponding to the creation-ancestors of the Aranda, Loritja, Marind-anim, etc.] are not necessarily human. They are just as likely to be animals, or beings of a mixed nature who by slow degrees come to assume a human form – as for example, Abaangui among the Guarayo, or Keri and Kame among the Bakairi ... Theriomorphism is most marked in North America: there the coyote, the mink, the crow and the hare[42] all play heroic or demiurgic roles. However, all such myths, concerned with hero-figures, and springing from identical ideas, exhibit a remarkably close inter-relationship throughout the world.
>   Of course it follows in any mythical system that the same phenomenon may find expression just as well in a personification as in a simple theriomorph, or a merely inanimate, externally activated object.[43]

Ehrenreich in 1905 had had no real opportunity to examine the Australian and Papuan myths which are the special concern of this present study; the important researches of Spencer and Gillen, and then Carl Strehlow, appeared later,[44] and by the same token the work of Wirz and Landtman and, more recently, of Radcliffe-Brown, Elkin, Malinowski and Fortune, were all inaccessible to him. But had he seen them, he would have found in them striking corroboration of his opinion, just quoted, touching the resemblances and intimate inter-relationships between myths about culture-heroes in all parts of the world. As to the

Australian and New Guinea tribes we are considering, the correspondences are more than evident.

Culture heroes and creation figures, the *Dema* of the Marind-anim, the "eternal uncreated" of the Aranda and Loritja, the *Uaropo* in Central Dutch New Guinea, etc., all exhibit the same uniform and basic lines, with differences in detail sometimes more, sometimes less marked. They are the same as Ehrenreich notices in his South American mythical heroes. In referring to these beings he makes use of the same term *Urheber* (ancient and ancestral founder, creator, author of all things) as Wirz uses. This *creator* is presented as the great originator of the tribe, or of mankind in general: he it was who "brought them forth", whether by transforming already existing beings of mixed nature from animal to human form, or by producing them out of the earth. Primitive tradition thus assumes at the very beginning a personal hero whose posterity peoples the world.[45]

It is of no particular significance that in the South American examples this myth-hero stands out in lonely eminence – or there may exist two of them only, brothers or twins – while the Australian and New Guinea legends relate the feats of a multitude of animal ancestors or *Dema*. It comes to the same thing in both cases: both traditions account for the beginnings of all human communities, all living species, and even of the appearances of the landscape, far back in the original mythic period beyond which history does not look. Like the Australian and New Guinea culture heroes, the mythic ancestors of the South American tribes are in the main half human, half animal beings possessing extraordinary and magical powers. No metamorphosis is beyond their power. They can at will transform either other creatures or themselves. Hence in the north west they come to be known as "the great converters".[46] It is from these ancestors also, in South America as in the South Pacific, that the tribal festivals and ceremonies descend. On this point, indeed, Ehrenreich anticipated both Spencer and Gillen, and Wirz. "Festivals and ceremonial dances, with other important customs and usages, were set up by the culture heroes, and that is the reason why they are kept up by all succeeding generations, who look upon themselves as their descendants. This is a very firmly established American idea, of which we possess some detailed information, especially as touching the Indians of the prairies (North America). In South America we find similar notions among the Bakairi, the Uaupe and the Ticuna."[47] But it is not only an American notion, it is Pacific and Oceanian also, as

Ehrenreich might himself have been able to add, had he been able to look further abroad for his terms of comparison.

In point of fact, when he comes to interpret these myths he does not shrink from an even bolder generalization. He regards all myths as alike, in all parts of the world, wherever they appear to spring from like causes:

> That simple nature-myths may arise, indeed have done so in all places, only stands to reason; it is an obvious rational postulate which follows from the generally identical organization of the human brain, which, as von den Steinen suggests, offers perhaps the only practical proof we have that all mankind constitutes a single biological species.
>
> That the instances of similarity in so many old and primitive stories occur at widely separated points is no refutation. The most closely corresponding of them are indeed those which have the widest distribution in the world and rest upon a perception and interpretation of the same basic phenomena, of a regular and recurrent kind, or a character likely to capture attention; such, for example, as the movements of the sun and moon, eclipses, waxing and waning, and the like.[48]

Ehrenreich accepted as proven the "naturist" theory of mythology. It is now abandoned, or at least is no longer regarded as universally valid. We no longer believe that the myths were all generated by gazing at the spectacle of the great periodic phenomena, in particular the motions of the stars and planets, or that they derive from the attempt to conceptualize these phenomena; or that at their root lies anything in the nature of an obvious rational postulate. The undeniable resemblance between myths from different parts of the world, their seeming uniformity (on which Ehrenreich insists, and reasonably), cannot any longer pass for proof that they have arisen from a universally felt need for rational explanations, or what we may call *intellectual* satisfaction; or that there exists any natural, innately philosophical appetite which they serve. The hypothesis was an attractive one, and even had something in it very compelling, as long as one remained convinced (as Ehrenreich was) that the minds of primitive persons functioned exactly like our own. It assumed their understanding was ordered in precisely the same manner as ours, and that they would ask just the same questions as we would, supposing ourselves to be in their place and supposing also that we could have been, at that time, exactly the same kind of thinkers as we are today. This indeed was the underlying postulate that supported the animism of Tylor and his disciples. Experience has proved it untenable. The primitive mind, which rests upon foundations so very different from ours, is above all an intensely mystical one. Were we to ascribe to its origins any "rational" or "logical postulate", we should be following an altogether false trail.

To try to solve such a problem of origin in a way that would fit all the world at once was no doubt too hopeful. Nor need we suppose all myths must arise from any one single, however well-defined, human impulse; what seems more likely is a complex of many separate motivations, among which not a few may be more emotional than rational. Of course there may also be present an interest in finding an acceptable "reason" for what in the first place excites the imagination only. But the very explanation that seems to the primitive most reasonable is available at once, without any search. They already possess it in advance – in principle, if not in detail. The moment the affective category of the supernatural appears in action, the explanation is effectively understood. Mysteries and enigmas in the processes of nature never daunt them, never even suggest to them any need for intellectual effort. Conditioned as they are by their mystical orientations, minds like theirs are prompt to recognize, at the back of every creature or object in the natural world, the operation of invisible supernatural forces. They perceive their intervention whenever anything strikes them as unusual or strangely unaccountable. As they see the world, it is wholly surrounded and enveloped in the *supernature* which in its turn penetrates and sustains all *nature*. Hence the "fluid" qualities which nature even today can still display. The myths were not created with any intended aim to explain this fluid versatility. What they do is simply to reflect the immanence of the supernatural mysteries. From those spring up the mythological themes which give so much puzzlement to our modern civilized minds, but which remain nevertheless so curiously and consistently alike in all parts of the world: animals endowed with miraculous powers, and placed on an equal footing with man; ancestral personages who are at once both men and animals (or plants), whether themselves "uncreated" or creators; culture heroes, metamorphs, etc.

Hence through the medium of the myths, primitive man manages to retain familiar contact with the mystical world of powers unseen and beyond the range of nature – powers as deeply real, or indeed more real than those of common sense-experience. The transcendent inspiration thus resident in the myths, their at once living and life-giving virtuosity, the power and force contained in them, derived from the animal ancestors and from the great culture heroes, together constitute a revelation which we who are modern and civilized, no matter what efforts we might make, never can possibly absorb into our experience as can the Australian or Papuan natives. During the performance of their sacred rituals, at certain moments at any rate, they certainly and profoundly experience the real presence of the mythic beings, and are able to identify with them. For us the myths can never amount to anything more than subjects for research — too often they seem like nothing more than exhibits in glass cases, museum pieces to be compared with the same primitives' craft objects and works of native art. But at least such a subject of study, if we are careful at the outset not to vitiate it through misconceptions of the true nature of the primitive mind, may be very helpful to us if we wish to understand something of the *participation* phenomena on which all such tribal peoples depend, not merely for their simple well-being, but even for their very existence.

Chapter III

Myths, Totemism and Kinship

Radcliffe-Brown categorizes the essential points of totemism in Western and Eastern Australia as follows: "the association between a *local group* − termed here a horde; a *natural species*; a *local centre for increase rites*, and a *mythical being* . . . The problem of totemism is part of the wider problem of the relation of man to nature in ritual and myth."[1] But these problems should not be separated. We must show how the first fits into the second. If we are to understand the Australian Aborigine's behaviour in regard to his totem, we must first consider what the myths and ceremonies tell him about it, since it is from them he receives instruction and learns what are his obligations. Both are equally sacred.

Totemism is a very broad term. Under it have been brought together a great many facts and even institutions. Some are very diverse, and there are, indeed − in Africa, America, Oceania − several different kinds of totemism. Here, as in previous chapters, we shall confine attention to the Australian and Papuan variety. This has already been the subject of a close study by Durkheim in *The Elementary Forms of the Religious Life.*[2]

Arunta and Luritcha (Aranda and Loritja) totemism has received much notice since detailed descriptions were first made available by Spencer and Gillen, and by Carl Strehlow.[3] I can here do no more than draw upon the resources provided by these celebrated studies. Nor is it any part of my design to explain again what they have already made clear, or to repeat the analyses available in Durkheim. I wish only to show, in entire agreement with Radcliffe-Brown, how these things may become more readily comprehensible if, as we come to them, we take adequately into account the determining mystical orientations of the Aboriginal mind. In point of fact, that mysticism appears nowhere more clearly than in the myths and ceremonies. There is nowhere better to look if we hope to understand the light in which the Aborigines regard animals and plants, and especially if we are to form a competent idea of the relationship that exists for them between certain living species and the particular human groups associated with them. According to Spencer,

> The totemic system of the Arunta and other Central Australian tribes is based upon the idea of the reincarnation of the Alchera ancestors, who were in many cases regarded as the actual transformations of animals and plants, or such inanimate objects as water, fire, wind, sun, moon and stars. To the Australian native there is no difficulty in the assumption that an animal or plant could be transformed directly into a human being, or that the spirit part which he supposes it to possess, just as he does in his own case, could remain, on the death of the animal, associated with such an object as a Churinga, and at some future time arise in the form of a human being.[4]

It would be difficult to imagine a more complete *participatory* identification. Every Arunta tribesman is the reborn, reincarnated spirit of a mythic-age ("dreamtime") spirit-being. Throughout all intervening time he has continued to exist in the form of a *churinga*.[5] Much as he may at present be a natural, human man, he also as a matter of course participates in the nature of the animal identified as his totem. "The relationship between a man and his totem", Spencer explains in another publication, "may well be exemplified by a remark made by an Arunta man when we had taken his photograph. We were asking him about the matter, and he said, pointing to the photograph, 'That one is just the same as me; so is a kangaroo.' " No doubt Spencer was as much astonished when he first heard this, as was von den Steinen when the Bororo bragged to him that they were red araras.[6] Assertions like these, which appear so extravagant to our way of thinking, are brought out by primitives in a perfectly calm tone. They see nothing surprising, or even worthy of particular note, in them, so long as the idea they hold of the animal in question, heavily charged as it is with mystical overtones, remains in control. As we have seen, they place animals on an equal footing with men. The key to this enigma, if enigma it be, is to be found in the myths, more particularly in those of them which represent the tribal heroes and ancestors as half human, half animal beings, or as we might also express it, beings which participate in both natures equally and simultaneously. When a modern man *participates* in the identity of his totem (which he does with the fullest consciousness and sense of commitment), he is following a pattern which carries back to that controlling idea and is derived from it.

It is that, too, which determines his attitude toward the totem animal. The idea of behaving towards it as though it were simply any casual animal or plant, should that ever occur to him, would certainly be distasteful, and even at times fill him with horror. Does he not sense it as an intimate part of his own identity? Carl Strehlow says:

> This totem, whether animal or plant, he looks upon as though it were his elder brother (*kalja*), and it becomes his duty to treat it with the greatest respect. Either wholly or with certain understood restrictions, he is forbidden to eat the totem. A man belonging to the kangaroo totem must never strike the animal brutally on the muzzle so that the blood gushes out; he may kill it only with blows on the back of the neck. Thus he may hunt his totem, but kill it only with decorous consideration. Of the game he may eat nothing but the head, the feet and the liver; the rest of the meat he is obliged to give to his companions.[7]

Spencer and Gillen have drawn attention to a considerable number of Arunta and Luritcha totems. The list (some hundreds) fills several pages. How does it come about that a particular animal, plant or object is included or rejected? We do not know, and perhaps the Aborigines themselves would not know how to answer the question. A curious remark of Strehlow's may point to something, at least in regard to animals and plants.

> Among those which are not totemic, only pelicans and a certain lizard are eaten. If the pelican does not provide a totem, evidently it is because it is seen only as a bird of passage in rainy years. As for the lizard *buljinkana*, the explanation given is that in the mythic age no *buljinkana* ancestor appeared. Most animals and plants which do not belong to totems are regarded as bedevilled. One, a small marsupial, is a reputed animal-sorcerer; . . . poisonous plants are plants of the evil one. Other animals and plants, not totemic, have a bad taste or smell . . .[8]

Is there any rational conclusion to be drawn from these hints? It is hard to decide. This kind of logic, even if the natives offer it spontaneously and without having first been asked leading questions, is bound to be hazardous; it calls for considerable caution. Nevertheless it may be that in certain instances – not in our power, certainly, to predict – the presence or absence of beneficial or malign qualities in an animal or plant could have a bearing upon totemic participation, and determine whether it is to exist or not. That might give some support to the very widely held view that the myths of primitive tribes relate directly to their common experience of life.

Like most other observers, as for example Radcliffe-Brown, Elkin, Ursula McConnel, Ralph and Marjorie Piddington, Raymond Firth and many more, Spencer and Gillen emphasize the close association of any tribal group and its totem with some particular site or "local centre".

> If we now turn to the traditions [that is, the myths] and examine those relating to certain totems which may be taken as illustrative of the whole series, we find that they are concerned almost entirely with the way in which what we may call the Alchera members of the various totems came to be located in various spots scattered over the country now occupied by the tribe the members of which are regarded as their descendants, or, to speak more precisely, as their reincarnations [instances given: i.e., wild cat, hakea flower, frog, witchetty grub ancestors and their dreamtime wanderings] . . . At each of these spots – and they are all well known to the old men, who pass the knowledge on from generation to generation – a certain number of the Alchera ancestors went into the ground, each leaving his Churinga behind. His body died, but some natural feature, such as a rock or tree, arose to mark the spot, while his spirit part remained in the Churinga. These Churinga, as well as others that the wandering parties left behind them, were stored in *Pertalchera*, or sacred storehouses, that usually had the form of small caves and fissures in the rocks, or even a hollow tree or a carefully concealed hole in a sandbank. The result is that, as we follow their wanderings, we find the whole country is dotted over with *Knanikilla*, or local totem centres at each of which are deposited a number of Churinga, with *Kuruna*, or spirit individuals, associated with them. Each *Knanikilla* is, of course, connected with one totem.[9]

The important role of local centres in the ceremonies will be considered later.

In other Central Australian tribes, over a vast area extending from Spencer's Gulf in South Australia as far north as latitude 25, according to Howitt, forms of totemism have been observed, closely resembling, if not identical with, the Arunta and Luritcha system described by Spencer and Gillen. For example, in the Lake Eyre region there are legends concerning the Mura-muras, predecessors and prototypes of the present-day blacks. The natives believe in the former and even the present existence of these ancestors. Their wanderings over Central Australia, the origins of the present native race and the institution of the sacred ceremonies, are all embodied in the myths and preserved by oral tradition. Among the Kurnai particularly the legendary ancestors are clearly at once men and animals (man-pelican, man-duck, man-heron).[10] Howitt's word for these mixed beings is "composite". He compares them with the figures which people the Arunta and Luritcha myths, and explains the closeness of the tie between the tribesmen and their totems.

> With them [the Kurnai] certain animals, birds and reptiles have each its own individual name, but all are known collectively as *Muk-jiak*, that is, "excellent flesh (or meat)"; while other creatures used for food are merely *Jiak*. Now in all these tales, in which a bird-man or reptile-man or animal-man takes part, in a twofold character, it is a *Muk-kurnai*. This may be translated as "eminent man or men", the Kurnai of the legend being thus distinguished from the Kurnai of the present time. The whole term may be fairly interpreted as "eminent ancestors", for they were not only the predecessors of the tribe but also in one sense the *Wehntwin*, that is, the Grandfathers. It may be added that there are not only *Muk-kurnai* but also *Muk-rukut* (rukut being woman) . . . The *Muk-kurnai* and the *Muk-jiak* animals are therefore the same as the ancestors, and a suggestion naturally arises that these latter are also the totems . . . The Mura-muras, Alcheringa ancestors and Muk-kurnai are all somewhat on the same level . . .[11]

From this comparison a conclusion seems to follow which Howitt has already formulated, though cautiously:

> The three types of belief represented by the Alcheringa ancestors, the Mura-muras and the Muk-kurnai have certain features in common. They recognize a primitive time before man existed, and when the earth was inhabited by beings, the prototypes of, but more powerful in magic than the native tribes. Those beings, if they did not create man, at least perfected him from some unformed and scarcely human creatures. Although this appears when one looks at the subject broadly, there are yet differences which distinguish the several types of belief from each other.[12]

This illuminates both the general uniformity of all that is essential in the characteristics of the mythic ancestors in diverse Australian tribes, and the very close affinity which unites the totemic institutions with the myths. Howitt also very perceptively points out the ambiguity which lurks in the word "ancestor". He writes:

> It seems to be usually assumed from the evidences, for instance, of tribes like those of Fiji that ancestor worship has been at the root of primitive religions; but Australian evidence seems to carry us back to a stage before ancestors came to be worshipped,

although they were looked upon as having been greater and wiser than their descendants, the present race. This is very evident from the account given by Spencer and Gillen of the Arunta and other tribes having kindred beliefs. I find that among the Lake Eyre tribes it was not the ancestors but a supernatural human race, antecedent to them, who are seen in myth and tradition to have been similarly superior to their successors. Here there is even less of a possible approach to ancestor worship than with the Aruntas. In the tribes of South-East Australia the ancestors appear in the guise of totems or theriomorphic human beings, in some respects resembling both the Alcheringa ancestors and the Mura-muras.[13]

There is reason, then, as we see here, for keeping in mind Howitt's distinction between the kind of ancestors who were unambiguously human beings like their modern descendants, and those who, living in the mythic period, belonged to a category of supernaturals, and were of "composite" animal and human form. Among the tribes he refers to, the facts are exactly the same as among the Arunta and Luritcha: totemic beliefs and institutions are expressed directly in the myths, and every individual looks on himself as descended from a ["dreamtime"] theriomorphic progenitor. It is the same again with the Wik-munkan, a tribe investigated by Ursula McConnel:

> The Wik-munkan word for totem is *pulwaiya*. *Pul* or *pola* is the term used to distinguish the father's father or forebear in the male line. *Waiya* is sometimes used with kinship terms to signify "old", e.g., *mukwaiya* is the term used for the mother's older sister when she is no longer young. There is an intimate personal link between a *pulwaiya* and its clan people. On leaving the totemic centre of the cuscus a child was told to say, "Apo! polia!" i.e., "Goodbye, grandfather", as if speaking to a real person.[14]

Wirz has analyzed the connections between totemic institutions and myths among the Marind-anim. His conclusions possess admirable clarity.

> The ways in which the Marind regard their totems derive directly from the myths of the *Dema* (ancestors) and the belief in their supernatural powers and faculties. It was in consequence of these powers that they had been able in the first place to transform themselves, bring forth various natural objects, and fill the role of creators for the whole universe. In addition they also created a manlike progeny who, after a few generations, gradually lost their original special supernatural powers and so became ordinary mortals. Thus men, animals, plants and other created things may all trace their origin back to an identical ancestor, and so may all be interrelated through ties of blood. Remembering this the

Marind speak of the *Dema* as their Amai, that is, forebears or grandfathers.

Thus Marind totemic relationships stem directly from their belief in the *Dema* as ancestors. Whatever object a *Dema* had the power to transform himself into, or had himself brought into existence, it thus became in some sense symbolic of the clan as a whole or even its principal totem; therefore the clan came to be named from it. Any mythological-totemic community which takes its name in this way from a major totem is called by the Marind a *boan*. A *boan* may be made up of one or more lesser groups along with their common mythological tradition; hence any one of the groups finds itself involved in a close relationship with all the totemic objects in the myths of the whole *boan*.[15]

Again Wirz refers in terms equally plain to numerous myths which, taken all together, amount to a kind of Genesis. Indeed they go beyond that, to make clear the basis of totemic relationships generally. Without a knowledge of the myths this would remain incomprehensible . . . The clan totemism of the Marind and neighbouring tribes consequently forms a broadly universal totemic system in the truest sense, embracing everything that exists. This must clearly be accounted the result of mythological speculation.[16]

As much, therefore, and possibly more than the Arunta totemic institutions, those of the Marind-anim throw light upon the capital importance of the myths in the lives of the natives. It is from this source that the individual derives the very notion of his own identity, as also of his ties with all the other beings and objects surrounding him – animals, plants, rivers, the sea, etc. It is by no means a firmly rigid image and in fact is essentially mystical; but neither is it elusively abstract. It is quite concrete, in effect, and where a personal totem is involved, highly emotional. Mythology, too, is what tells him all he can know about the *Dema*, those half-human, half-animal and at the same time superhuman beings of the far-away mythic age when all nature was supernature; about how they brought forth or created the outstanding features of the landscape and everything that is found in it today, including plants, animals and men; and about how they first discovered all things that were needful for life, and established ceremonies and other institutions.

When a human group and an animal species have both been produced in the mythic age by the same *Dema* creator, whether by natural generation or any other process, they are fraternally related in a full and literal sense. They have both sprung from the same double, animal-and-human source. Their community of origin establishes between them the strongest imaginable bond. Since both participate in the same original essence, they are therefore *participators* in each other; and their quasi-identity in substance is recognized in the name they both bear. As formerly the kangaroo *Dema* could at will take either the human or the animal form, just so nowadays his human descendants possess as much right as the animals, since he is the ancestor of both equally, to be called by the name of kangaroos. This is simply another way of saying, what rests upon the faith and authority of the myths, that the group has the kangaroo for its totem.

Whether the totem, as in this example, is an animal or a plant — or, as happens more rarely, an object; or maybe a heavenly body, or rain, or fire (all these can be endowed with life and take form as persons) — is of little importance. What the native mind fixes upon is nothing tangible, nothing that can be seen, scented, tasted or touched; but is rather a mystical essence, the presence in both at the same time of the common ancestor, which becomes for him the object of a veneration and respect of quasi-religious intensity.

Thanks to this mystical quality, out of which the myths spring in the first place, but which they also contribute to sustain, the native mind passes untroubled over what would appear to be the most forbidding obstacles. Certain characteristics distinguish with self-evident clarity between vegetable or mineral (not to speak of animal) entities and a being like man who can think and act. The native is as aware of these as we are. That is, he sees them in a general way, though his idea of them will be far from precise. But the myths (and nobody doubts the myths; their effect has been deeply imprinted since childhood) have taught him to believe firmly that those other entities are related to him, they are his brothers. What seems to us the unbridgeable distance between man and the rest simply fades out; it vanishes away before the feeling he has (or one might as well call it straight out, his awareness) of their common identity in essential being. The coconut is a tree which in the ordinary way the Marind knows how to cultivate and protect against its predators. He gathers the nuts and eats them. But considering it in another light, this same tree is the descendant of a *Dema* whose emergence and destiny is related in one of the most famous myths of the Marind. This *Dema* was at the same time a man and a coconut palm. Through the special powers with which he was endowed he brought into existence on the one hand a particular variety of palm tree, and on the other, a particular human group or clan; and they were naturally both closely identifiable with himself. Every member of the Marind tribe who belongs to that clan is conscious of being intimately related to that particular kind of palm tree because of their essential common identity with the ancestor. A complex tissue of myth, custom and emotion which for the native has great importance, thus establishes a kind of "totemic atmosphere". From the day he first comes to have any consciousness of his own existence, the native has breathed that atmosphere. He moves in it as his natural ambient.

It is not conceivable to him that anyone could exist except as belonging to a clan, or that any clan could exist without a totemic relationship with at least one species of beings or objects. Whenever he may chance to meet anybody he does not already know, the first question he is bound to ask will be, "What is your totem?"

To say all this in another way, the action of the myths upon the minds of these people is so strong and goes so deep that the entire representation of nature is impregnated with it. The myths lay down the basis for every relationship between the human groups and the creatures about them. Without the myths, as Wirz shows, the tribal institutions of the people, and totemism itself, above all, would have no chance of becoming understood. "Everything", Wirz explains, "turns upon the facts of mythological-totemic kinship. That is the footing upon which the whole structure of social life is built. On every occasion – festivals, ceremonies and the like – everything depends upon just one factor: what is your *boan*, or to what group of boans do you belong? This mythological-totemic system of grouping is additional to and separate from any natural classification by age and family."[17]

Like Spencer and Gillen, like Strehlow and also Elkin, though with less insistence, Wirz lays stress on the local associations of the totemic clans. "In places where a pure clan totemism is seen, the totems themselves are as a rule quite local in character, in agreement with the region, whether limited or extensive, which the clan inhabits." Especially among the Marind-anim,

> . . . there is no doubt at all that their system of mythological-totemic relationships was developed in the territory which they now occupy. Everywhere we find that the groups or clans stand in a certain relationship to animals and plants, geographical and other phenomena which give their character to the area or con-

note a reference to past local events, incidents involving the foundation-fathers of the clan or group. The essential distinguishing mark of all such totems is the presence of *Dema* as founders of the clan and as the creators of all the totemic posterity of the region. The *Dema* always appear in a close bond with the territory occupied by the clan, still in modern as in ancient times; as also with its flora and fauna, and certain salient features which form the natural landscape.[18]

When a tribe finds itself in frequent and longstanding contact with a neighbouring group, new myths evolve, and these tie in with older ones. At the same time the totemic relationship between them becomes more complex and is enriched.

The common origin of a clan and its totem implies also certain other natural affinities. These show in everyday life, in certain facts which the natives point to as further confirmation, if any were needed, of what is shared. "Characteristics and properties of quite a wide diversity belonging to a certain species are attributed also to the members of the corresponding totemic clan. Similarly it is believed that the talents possessed by a totemic clan, its idiosyncrasies and even certain of its technical skills can be traced back to its totemic ancestors. For all the totemic animals, and all members of the corresponding clan, are related to one another, are in other words natural kin, and therefore each *participates* in the life of the rest." This comes out in the whole pattern of behaviour of the natives, even in their habits of thinking. "Thus at Mabuiag Island (Torres Straits) members of the crocodile clan are said to be of a cruel disposition, those of the cassowary clan are reputed to be fast runners, and those belonging to the dog clan are supposed to be good-natured and fond of company."[19] Landtman found similar beliefs at Kiwai Island.

In all places where an ingrained belief in this totemic relationship is established, the implied sharing of natural traits between a man and his totemic animal or plant has to be extended to points of supposed resemblance so extreme, it would seem to us they could hardly appear more unlike.

Not even outward form is expected. Admittedly external appearance has not the same importance for these native peoples as it has for us. Any creature, they believe, whether man or animal, is potentially capable of changing from whatever may be its usual form to some other that is quite different, and then of returning to the first, without for a single instant ceasing to be its true self. In modern times none but tribal sorcerers still retain this ability, but in the mythic age when all existing identities were still *dema*, all possessed it equally.[20] Nowadays, with some exceptions, it is lost. The "fluidity" of the ancient world has been followed by the idea of fixity in all created forms. But that does not in any way prevent creatures dissimilar in outward shape from being in real essentials alike; nor in spite of visible differences (by which we can tell a man from a bird, say) does it stand in the way of the likeness being admitted to be present. This represents one of the deeper aspects of totemic faith: modes of being, affinities, relationships and *participations* laid down in the mythic past, though not still obvious today, remain none the less real for all that.

What I am here struggling to reduce to abstract and general terms, the Marind-anim express concretely in the following manner: "Every object necessarily contains within itself the image of the *Dema* who originated it (whether by generation or transformation). By this we must [almost] always understand either human or animal form, for above all else a *Dema* needs to be provided with sense-experience. The three holes in the coconut's shell (where it sprouts) survive today because they represent the eyes and mouth of the *Dema* who created the first palm."[21] In another place Wirz again points out that in all the descendants of any totem there is always present the original form of the *Dema* who was its first founder (i.e., his basic human identity); and that, in spite of what we might suppose, this is also no less true of its animal or vegetable descendants than of the men and women. So far as the animals are concerned, the point can be taken without great difficulty because it is easy enough to imagine a man being transformed into a beast. But all other objects and creatures also are, just as much as men, reflecting images of the *Dema* who created them. So they too, at least in a certain measure, are possessed of human form, just as man is. Thus, reverting to the example of the coconut, not merely do the three holes in the shell stand for the eyes and mouth of the *Dema*, but his legs are seen as the stem of the palm and his hair as its leaves. In the rustling of the tops one can imagine hearing the *Dema*'s voice. "That was how, long ago, the *Dema* used to speak," the Marind-anim would say.

It is the same with all other creatures and objects whose beginnings, according to the myths, go back to the *Dema* as their creators. In the mythic age, however, "they were different from their modern counterparts, in the sense that there still attached to them a colour of the strange and wonderful. They were all at that stage still in some measure *dema*, although already a good deal more like the creatures of today than they had been at first."[22] Even objects fabricated by the hand of man provide no exception to this. The Marind see nothing astonishing, or even paradoxical, in their claim that "the bow itself has human form fundamentally; because it, too, was created by a *Dema*". There exists in fact a fully developed myth in connection with the bow-*Dema*, including his involvement with a wife and children, his adventures, and much more. It thus follows naturally that in bows fabricated by the Marind-anim today, the presence of human form is necessarily found repeated. The bow-wood itself, in which they distinguish between the forward extremity, which they call the nose, and the rear, called the foot, is what represents the mythical *Dema* himself. The bowstring, with its two loops, is the *Dema's* wife — she clings passionately about his neck — and so on.[23]

Here let me repeat something I have already said in another work; that is, that primitives seldom hesitate to assert resemblances between beings or objects where we see no such thing.[24] We may at once recall certain Australian Aboriginal designs, drawings or patterns in which no, or scarcely any, pretence is made at a representational likeness. It suffices that the lines, to the natives' way of thinking, have an understood reference to the objects, whose image they carry independently in their minds. The circumstances here among the Marind-anim are comparable. The bow owes its origin to a *Dema* who, like all the others, possessed two forms at the same time: the form of a bow and also the form of a man; and could pass without the slightest difficulty from one to the other. True enough, bows of modern times have none of this *dema* "fluidity" left. They no longer enjoy the supernatural powers of the bow-*Dema* and in particular they do not have his capacity for metamorphosis. Nevertheless, human form still subsists in them. Traces of it can still be recognized. True, the signs are slight, but what matter? Even were they not visible at all, still one need never hesitate to affirm it is really there. Evidence of the senses can never prevail over a well established collective belief; even less if it is a merely negative one. That a form remains unseen is by no means proof of its absence. Thus the Australian Aborigine whose kidney fat has been spirited away by an enemy sorcerer will continue to believe himself doomed, even after it is pointed out to him that no wound is visible on his skin to show where it could have been taken out.[25]

We here touch upon an attitude of mind found very frequently among primitives and bound up with the mystical composition of their minds. It leads them to accept as self-evident certain propositions which to our eyes appear, to say the least, curious, or even palpably absurd. The Marind myths speak of palm trees or bows which have their own and also human form. We have seen that the Dobuans seriously maintained that yams are persons. They also say the same of a certain rock under the sea, and about the wind. How can they have come to this? Can they not see, as we do, that yams are plants which grow and mature? That the rock is simply a mass of inert substance lying motionless in the water? and that the wind which whips up the waves possesses neither head nor limbs? – Of course! These mere outward appearances are as obvious to them as to us. But for them nothing, neither beings nor objects, is ever a monomorph; it always has more forms than one. Nor will such things fit, *ne varietur*, into the inflexible categories of an ordered, rationally disposed system of nature. Quite the contrary! For the myths have conditioned the primitive mind to accept a view of nature as "fluid" and to regard the beings and objects within it as passing coolly from one form to another; or else (what comes to the same thing) as possessing two distinct forms, *one* of which is human. In the way they see it, the outward form of a thing (the expression is Sir E.F. Im Thurn's) is merely an "accident" – which is to say, it does not constitute any part of the *real* identity of the being concerned. Let it change its form, let it even have several forms, no importance attaches to the fact; the mystical *essence* of the being remains intact. This is a mental stand we cannot adopt without very great difficulty, and certainly cannot sustain for more than a brief moment.[26]

Moreover when we speak of a being's having human form, what is in our mind is an image which, if not absolutely and minutely complete, is in effect roundly total – not every detail may be filled in, but we have an impression of the picture as a whole. We would not be content to rest with a visualization only of some fragment: the trunk, perhaps, or the lower limbs, or only the head of a man; "human form" for us carries no conviction unless it implies the entire man. Here again the primitive attitude of mind stands apart from ours. As we have seen, for the native intelligence every *appurtenance* of a creature is identical with the whole creature. No appurtenance could be more intimately allied to it than the various parts of its body, particularly indeed the bones and the skull, since they do not decompose after death as do the flesh and softer tissues. Thus many societies look upon the skull of a man as equivalent to the man himself. It is evident, therefore, that in order to suggest primitively the presence of human form, total representation of a man is not necessary; the presence of only one or perhaps a few fragments of his body is adequate to project the whole. In the cave paintings of the Australian Aborigines, or the drawings made by the natives of New Guinea, as also in many still surviving prehistoric drawings, the head may stand for the entire body; and similarly the eye alone may stand for the whole head. In this way the native is moved by an ever-active tendency to look beyond mere physical and literal perception to something else which that perception opens up and initiates for him. Objects and phenomena may often interest him, therefore, not so much for what they visibly are, as for what is to be revealed *through* them. When images are placed before his eyes, he looks not at the picture itself, but at what he can find to interpret in it. Every image is above all a sign, a symbol.

Hence it follows that a single detail, quite by itself, may stand for an entire form. Therefore if one is already convinced for some existing reason that a being or thing, independently of what it actually looks like, possesses human form – or at least if one believes that, because of its origin, it already enjoys some *participation* in humanity – then one simple detail pointing in the human direction will be sufficient to evoke the whole impression. The three holes in the coconut will be the eyes and mouth of the coconut palm *Dema*, the two extremes of the bow-wood will be the nose and foot of the bow-*Dema*. Since it is granted that the coconut-*Dema* and the bow-*Dema* are really persons, such simple points of correspondence in detail, slight and far-fetched as they may seem to us, are sufficient evidence to establish the presence of human form in any object derived from them.

Such a habit of mind is not restricted to Australian and New Guinea natives only. We meet it, sometimes more, sometimes less marked, among a number of other primitive types. To refer to one example only, according to Bushman belief rain is a person (as is the wind at Dobu, and also in several other places). Among the invaluable items of information collected more than sixty years ago by Bleek and Lloyd directly from a group of !Xam Bushmen, the dual idea of rain (dual, that is, for us; not for them) comes out very clearly. They know quite well that rain consists of water in precipitation. Before rain can fall (and they know this quite well also) clouds of a certain kind must build up and then descend suitably low. But they are none the less persuaded that it depends also on the *disposition* of the rain – thus the rain has human form and personality.

Suppose a prolonged drought is desolating the countryside – the threat of famine hangs over man and beast alike. The people consult the rainmaker. He reveals what has gone wrong. The clouds came up and rain was ready to fall, but then someone unpropitiously lit a fire. The fire frightened and offended the rain, so that it went away. So now the rainmaker is requested to call it back, using tactics that will make sure of a *feminine* rain – one that is quiet and steady, a slow, soaking rain that will penetrate the soil and moisten it deeply; not a rough, violent masculine kind, a *buck* rain, which will cause floods without refreshing or fertilizing the earth, devastating it like a hurricane. Thus rain may be male or female – sometimes buck, sometimes doe; and presently the rainmaker will also refer to it in human terminology. The clouds are its hair, the threads of water trickling down from the sky are its limbs. The rain must be a person; the visible details (hair, limbs) imply the rest that is not seen. It is not necessary actually to see it, to know that it exists![27]

It may be that here we have the key to several kinds of primitive symbolism. The Marind-anim, like many others, regularly ornament their artifacts with designs derived from human faces and bodies. They take such trouble and devote so much ingenuity to this that the mere desire to give the object a pleasing appearance is hardly enough to explain it. There is no doubt at all that the impulse goes well beyond any mere need to gratify an artistic feeling. What they are in most cases trying to do in this way is to bring the artifact into closer contact with its mystical prototype, *viz.*, the *Dema* from whom it is descended, and who had human as well as non-human form. What we take for ornament is thus a mnemonic of that mystical form. Its purpose is to express and strengthen the bond or participation between the fabricated object and its human-form *Dema*. For this purpose a single aspect of the body, as has been shown, can symbolize the whole.

Like animals and plants, Wirz tells us, so tools and musical instruments, furniture, and weapons also relate to *Dema* ancestors. This conveys the suggestion that such objects also, once, in the mythic age, were living beings; that is why it is still possible to recognize in them traces of human face and form.

Hence, really, there scarcely exists any useful article which the native does not provide artistically with ornamental eyes or nose, even a whole human shape; or in which such figures cannot be either totally or partially picked out.

They give human form to their canoes, as is expressly stated in their myth about the invention of canoes. The oars are almost always provided with patterns of ornament – spiral lines – which are their eyes; and similarly with certain arrows, clubs, baskets and other objects of plaited work, betel-spatulas or drums. On these last, for good measure, you will also see the mouth (the open part of the drum) and the teeth (these are drops of resin on the membrane). Without these it could not become what it needs to be: an instrument capable of proper resonance.[28]

Taken in the rigid sense indicated, totemism for the Marind-anim thus implies the closest conceivable bonding between beings or groups of beings. It involves not only common origins, but a real identity of inherited substance.

But Wirz employs the word also in another sense which is a great deal broader. In this connection there is no longer any question of consubstantial identity but only of a simple, possibly quite loose, link through some outward similarity, often enough nothing more than a mere analogy, or some purely superficial resemblance. Taken in this relaxed sense totemism seems no longer to insist on all the conditions we have just seen treated as essential.

Any quite accidental circumstance, or anything at all that is simply held in common by the beings concerned can become the occasion of a totemic identification between them, as a recent example illustrates. A clan called the Sapi-ze [*ze* signifies "people", members of a group], whose name harks back to their mythic ancestor Sapi, some little time ago acquired a fresh totemic association. The new connection was with horned cattle. It happened thus, simply because in Malay (Indonesian) the beast was called *sepi*, and it was under this name that the cattle had been introduced to the Marind in the neighbourhood of Merauke. A more elementary reason for a totemic affiliation is hardly imaginable![29]

True indeed, and there are plenty of analogous instances to support this one, which, if it stood alone, would not look very convincing. But names, among the Marind-anim, as among primitives in general, are far from counting as "accidental circumstances". They are *appurtenances* of the beings who bear them, and among the most important. His name is a part of any being's proper substance; in a certain sense it is the being himself. Anything that affects his name affects him. A person's true name may often be kept secret. Hence what happened in the minds of these Marind people is easily enough explained. Seeing horned cattle for the first time, and being told then that their name was *sepi*, they were bound to jump to the conclusion that there must be some sort of common substance between them and the clan which had Sapi for its totem and was called the Sapi-*ze*. The cattle therefore had every right to be regarded as part of the clan. It was not the Marind-anim who admitted them to it. The totemic tie already pre-existed; the Marind had only to confirm it. If the Marind had still been living in the same style and circumstances as before the fatal contact with white men, a new entire myth centred on these animals would not have been long in appearing, so as to account plausibly for their relationship to the Sapi-*ze*.

Two further examples of this sort:

To the fire *boan*, with status as a new member (since the Marind have not been very long acquainted with it) belongs the barndoor fowl, for this simple and plausible reason, that in the crowing of the cock they imagine they hear the cry *Ta-kav-a!* — a fair sample of the simple fashion in which totemic associations can more or less playfully arise. Other instances parallel this. Many things of a red colour, for example, are allotted to the fire *boan*. An ornamental tree recently introduced and planted in the Merauke district has been accepted by the Marind into their mythologic-totemic system and, because its flowers are flame-coloured, given to the fire *boan*. For those flowers, they say, have the redness of fire.

The people of Bangu, since the remotest time, have built their houses along a coast where mangroves spring up out of the mud. Fishing in muddy water and wading in ooze here are things which from time immemorial have entered into their blood and bone. So in the end they came to see animating spirits at work in all the mud and slush: the *Dema* were responsible for every change along that clay-featured littoral as the mud gradually built up or leached away. What could be simpler, then, than for the people to identify themselves completely with the environment and call themselves by its name? Thus as time went on the closest possible bond was forged between the people of Bangu and the world of nature all about them. To be a man of Bangu and to be descended from mud came to mean practically the same thing.

No instance could more effectively prompt the conclusion that, as the Marind see totemism, it is really nothing more nor less than a mere complex of associations, even quite loose ones, between families or clans, or between certain beings and objects in nature, carried along with various facts, events and other data relating to the territory where the people live. These are all matters that the natives have assimiliated into their mythological beliefs in terms of the activity of the animistic *Dema* who are everywhere at work.[30]

In these words Wirz himself suggests a formula for reconciling the two apparently discrepant senses he gives to totemism. If the Marind-anim assign the newly introduced tree to the fire totem, that is because there undoubtedly already exists a reason why its flowers must be of a bright and burning colour. For it cannot be mere chance. The primitive mind, as we realize, gives scarcely any countenance to the existence of mere chance. No matter how insignificant a thing may appear, it must nevertheless contain a meaning or revelation of some kind. So what may seem to us a simply accidental circumstance is in reality a cover for the activity of some *Dema*, begun long ago in the mythic age, and still in force today. By this reasoning totemism as understood in Wirz's second sense can be brought round to a harmony with his first – and in fact provides a convincing foundation for it.

To say that the *Dema* are "everywhere at work" comes to much the same thing, as Wirz repeatedly insists, as attributing to the broad pattern of Marind mythological faith a kind of remote succedaneum for reason. Reason, for us, is what gives unity, consistency and coherence to the world – we think of it as the basis of all system and stability in the laws of nature. Totemic affinities are, to be sure, rather felt than argued, and rest often enough on notions of similarity, as in the instance of the bow, which we are likely to consider extravagant. But they nevertheless do constitute in their own way, as the myths do in theirs, a repository of infinite scope, in which are brought together all the beings and all the objects it is given to the people to encounter in their common experience of life. When a plant or animal, hitherto unknown, is introduced into their region, the Marind will at once concern themselves to determine to what *boan* it belongs. Some resemblance in a detail, such as to us could seem trivial or irrelevant, will nevertheless decide the issue. They will see it as providing the key to an intimate relationship, by virtue of which the new arrival will certainly fall into the place designed for it among the vast array of possible totemic affinities. Henceforward its standing will be clear, not merely in regard to the members of its own *boan* but also to other clans more or less closely allied. Whatever relationship exists between their various *Dema* regulates the harmony between the clans.

Wirz has supplied many instances of this. Creatures and objects of the natural world, therefore (at the cost of a few contradictions, no doubt, but then these pass unnoticed) all find their place in a system which bristles with mythological and totemic complexities, the product, as are the myths themselves, of an intensely mystical mentality. In that the mind of the Marind finds a satisfaction which leaves all further enquiry completely unnecessary and undesired.

It may be opportune to attempt at this point a more exact distinction between what the Marind-anim understand by mythological-totemic relationships and ordinary kinship.

We are happily able, for this purpose, to draw upon an instance which seems to be placed ready-made in our hands – a crucial test-case – on which Wirz has already laid great stress, although, it is true, for reasons of another nature. I refer to the myth of the bow which we have just been discussing. The bow-*Dema* figures in a great many legends, since every *boan* (group of clans) lays claim to its own version of the myth. In all of them, though, the *Dema* associated with the bow is of the same double nature, possessing at the same time both bow-form and human form. His mixed identity is unmistakably revealed in the imagery that has been built up around him: he is portrayed as having a nose, feet and a neck about which his wife clings tightly, etc. The Marind go beyond this, indeed: they give him a mouth (slots between the nodes), eyes (studs above the slots) and a beard (fine root-like lines underneath them). Every part of the bow is given its name.[31]

Since this is so, the question naturally arises as to how the native regards a bow he has actually made himself, with his own hands, and which he uses in the ordinary course of life for hunting, fishing or for warfare. What does he take to be the relationship of this artifact to the mythic original bow which had both human form and bow-form at one and the same time? Wirz assures us

Even though the bow is man-made, the Marind for all that sees in it the image of its *Dema*-creator. Because of this a kind of "soul" passes from the primitive *Dema*-creation to the modern weapon, just as by and large every imitation of a natural object incorporates in itself a "soul" derived from what it imitates (this is also how images representing ancestral personages are *animated*). Since the strength and elasticity of the bow, when bent, project forth an arrow and enable it to kill the enemy, or the animal which has been aimed at, these are for the Marind manifest signs of the "soul" that is present in the bow; they are properties and functions which come to it from the *Dema*. They occur again as a matter of course in every new bow which is manufactured on the model of the first one, that of the bow-Dema, in exactly the same way as every animal possesses properties and characteristics which display themselves in its customary deportment, and have been inherited from its ancestors, the *Dema*. The Marind are accustomed to express this notion by saying, "That comes from the *Dema*", or "That was a custom of the *Dema*". For example, I still remember very clearly how the Marind-anim, referring to the characteristic motion of the giant stork, would cry out as they shook their heads, "See there what it was once the *Dema's* habit to do!"

Again,

Once the myth of the bow had become known, the Marind, as though in a spirit of amusement, extended their conclusions. They traced the resilience and kinetic energy of the drawn bow back to its creator, although they were perfectly well able to distinguish them from an animal psyche, just as though these properties had been transmitted down to their bows through generations of heredity, in the way that the psychic faculties of animals are inherited.[32]

This is a very curious belief, and if we are to understand (supposing understanding to be at all possible) how the lifeless modern bow can be regarded as the true inheritor of the *Dema's* mythic power – and no metaphor is intended – we need to reflect with some care on what the Marind-anim believe about the way heredity functions in creatures that do have life. It may be that if we can grasp that, we shall discover a key to what we find so enigmatic in their belief concerning the bow. Like ourselves they do not fail to observe that the young of animals resemble their parents, and are similar in general form, often repeating quite small physical details, and that at an equivalent stage of maturity they will behave in exactly the same manner. But because these facts are routine and invariable, they of course do not strike the native as remarkable. So his curiosity is not aroused. Explanation is called for only in cases where expectation breaks down: as for example, when a woman gives birth to twins; or when, as happens occasionally in the myths, an animal produces offspring of a species different from itself – sometimes, for example, even a human child. In such a case it will of course at once be recognized that a supernatural power has intervened. But as for the reason why an ordinary child should resemble its parents, or an animal should have the same form as the pair whose coupling preceded its birth, no one gives it a thought.

No more in this connection than in any other, do second causes seem to primitives real causes. If by any chance they should feel a need to account for a particularly striking resemblance, they can do so easily enough. The explanation is always at hand, laid down firmly in advance; it needs no searching. Everybody knows that parents and children alike owe everything they possess — outward form or other characteristics, patterns of behaviour, anything at all, in effect, which distinguishes them — to the fact that both generations *participate* equally in the same essential identity of being ("type" or "archetype"), which is named after their common *Dema*, and belongs to the mythic world. Just as, by our own abstract style of reasoning, any two quantities which are equal to a third are *ipso facto* taken to be equal to each other (a self-evident truth requiring no proof), so, according to the native point of view, all beings which participate in the same *Dema*-identity participate in each other. They must resemble one another, because they all resemble the *Dema*. Modern storks shake their heads exactly as the *Dema* stork did, and as all other storks have done since the mythic age. There is no need to prove or explain this: it is axiomatic.

We are not entitled, for all that, to assume that primitives know nothing at all of the physiological conditions which control the transmission of hereditary characteristics. Even in areas where, before the arrival of white men, the people were ignorant (as it is asserted) of the link between the act of copulation and the birth of children, they always understand about the reproductive procedures of animals. But there is no need here to raise problems which, once we have succeeded in viewing them with a native eye, often turn out not to exist.[33] That a male and a female must have joined before resembling offspring can be produced was not, assuredly, something they had to be taught. However the coupling is not regarded as in itself the cause of life. As they see it, it is a condition which must be fulfilled; necessarily, but not worth stopping to consider separately. The real cause lies elsewhere, in a mystical participation.

When we understand this, what the Marind-anim believe in regard to the bow makes sense. The properties of the bow are the legacy of the *Dema* (and it is of course the same with other man-made artifacts). Everyone knows that bows do not reproduce in the same manner as animals or plants; if a new one is desired, it must be made. But that is not what matters. Bows made today are constructed in the image of the original bow of the *Dema*; all bows have been so made since the mythic age, and that is the whole point. Even if not physiologically, the properties of the original bow are still carried forward from generation to generation. Though the conditions are different, that difference does nothing to prevent the consummation of the same kind of mystical participation, in the case of hunting bows, as takes place between creatures that live.

Nevertheless, and let me repeat it yet again, every Marind knows very well that young animals are produced from gravid females, while no one bow was ever born naturally from another. This is an undeniable fact, and the distinction cannot fail to come home to him. It is a characteristic of his way of thinking that he does not deduce from it the conclusions we would judge to be inevitable. He is inclined, on the contrary, to cast a tolerant eye upon certain analogies we would regard as remote. For just as there are certain conditions which must be met before animal reproduction can take place, so there are others determining what must happen before a new bow can be created. For example, a certain kind of tree must be selected for the wood; certain procedures must be followed in preparing the string; the task must be attacked in a certain way; certain tabus must be strictly observed for as long as the work continues, and so on. In the one case as in the other, it is true, the part played by all these conditions is merely subordinate; for what is of prime importance is to achieve *participation* with the mythic ancestor – participation, that is, between the kangaroo and the kangaroo-*Dema*; participation between the bow made today and the bow-*Dema*.

So it is not at all surprising if the Marind looks to discover in his bow traces of the human form which the bow-*Dema* was able to assume, and also some of his original skill and efficacy, albeit on a diminished scale. Nor is there anything strange in the need he feels to assure himself of the *Dema*'s favourable *disposition* towards him. Bows do not all inherit equal powers: some are well, others not so well fortified. In almost every place, as we realize, primitives who hope for success in some particular venture or undertaking experience considerable anxiety about the *disposition* (or goodwill) towards them of spirits, creatures or even objects which might feel any concern about the matter, or whose co-operation they design to enlist, and they take whatever steps they can to gain their favour. For example, in West Africa the witch-doctor called to conduct a trial-by-poison addresses the judicial poison with an appeal to cause the death of the accused if he is guilty, but to leave him unharmed if he is not. The Djagga when preparing to make a beehive implores the favour of the tree which provided him with wood for his axe, of the cord with which he will hoist up his hive, of the string he will use to tie it in place, and then of the bees who will work in it. At Kiwai Island the Papuans carry offerings to the harpoon which has killed a dugong for them, in order to show their gratitude, and also with hope of persuading it to be helpful to them again at some time in the future. In other places various kinds of requests are directed to tools and implements, weapons or canoes. What I have have been trying to show is that in spite of appearances there really is no need, in order to explain such practices, for supposing that any particular *individual* ghost or demon must dwell within these objects or creatures. Once, no doubt, that seemed a simple and attractive hypothesis, and circumstantially plausible. But on closer examination the facts fail to confirm it. Wirz quite positively rejects this kind of *animism* as an explanation, though it is true he does use the word himself in a different sense. This could be a possible source of confusion.[34] What he really does demonstrate convincingly is how the powers and properties attributed to the bow, notwithstanding they may have some superficial appearance of being derived from a spirit dwelling in the substance of the weapon and possessing a separate will of its own, are not in fact due to anything of the sort, or to any other kind of "soul" present in it, but, according to the Marind view, simply to the effective *participation* that the bow enjoys with the bow-*Dema*.

Chapter IV

The Power of Myth and its Effects

In Australian tribes the possession of certain myths is a privilege reserved to men who have passed through the ordeals of initiation, up to and including the final rituals, who are married and have children of their own; who, in short, take their full place in the corporate life of the group.[1] Not all the myths are secret and restricted to these elders. There are many which could be called public property; even women and children know them. Moreover, here as elsewhere, the line of demarcation between myths properly so-called and what may be regarded as legends or tales is not always easy to trace.

What is important in a myth is its esoteric meaning. It is possible that the mere words could be heard from the lips of an uninitiated person, who knew nothing of the secret content. As von Leonhardi points out, "Certainly many of those (Aranda) who chant these Songs do so without understanding them at all, any more than do the women and children who are permitted to be present at the ceremonies and dances. But the elders, who are the guardians of the traditions, know exactly and in detail what each myth is about and can explain them."[2] The Karadjeri make the same distinction.

> Of the many Karadjeri myths of *bugari* times, the majority are totemic, that is to say, they describe the activities of beings who were neither men nor animals, but exhibited alternately the characters of both these types of creature . . . Some of the myths, however, concern mythical beings who are not identified with any natural species, and hence cannot be described as totemic. But one must remember that in the minds of the natives the two types of myth form part of an integrated whole – the legendary history of the Aborigines. The sacred myths, which may not be told to women, are mainly concerned with cosmogony, and especially with the institution of initiation ceremonies.[3]

The reason why the full meaning of the myths has to be kept secret, even when the text is known, is not in doubt. Possession of them is not merely acquired knowledge, it actually confers a power which will be destroyed if it is profaned. Such a loss would be fatal to the tribe. This power is what enables it to remain in contact with the mythic ancestors and maintain *participation* with them. It is the means whereby their presence is made real and ensures that their activity will from time to time be renewed. The ceremonial representation of such myths is far more than a repetition of mere formalities; it is more like an *auto da fé*. It involves in the highest degree the very life of the tribe. If there should be no men of mature age and authority left, no guardians of the sacred traditions competent to recite the myths at proper times, the tribe itself would be doomed to extinction.[4] For then the younger men could never be instructed in their turn. The animal and vegetable species on which the natives live would be doomed to perish.

The beneficial effect of the sacred myths follows simply from their being ceremonially performed. It does not happen merely because those who are present (whether seen or unseen, including representatives of the species concerned) hear what is said. Every single word, every formulated phrase, as it is uttered, acts as a force, a power; the more sacred the myth, naturally, the more powerful the force. The myth sung or recited deals with the significant deeds and wanderings of the ancestors and creators of all living species, the founders of all tribal institutions.

As a rule the ceremonies can take place only at appropriately determined times or during the period of a ritual festival, and only certain individuals may perform them. The favourable effect looked for cannot follow unless all the proper conditions are scrupulously met. For example, among the Bukaua of former German New Guinea, as Lehner reports,

> . . . the legends are narrated in the evenings at a time when the yams and taro grow mature. The performance is concluded with an invocation embracing all crops, and takes place beside the storehouse in which either the harvested fruits or the seedling tubers are kept. The invocation follows the recital (Lehner gives, without translating, the Bukaua text); it entreats the spirits of the ancestors (whom it addresses coaxingly in picturesque phrases as "man" or "cricket" or "grasshopper") to put a thriving vigour into countless seedlings, to make the already large tubers fill out even fatter, to encourage the sugarcane to flourish even more hand-

somely and induce the bananas to produce quite monstrously huge bunches. But it is also clear that the narration has another purpose, and that is to indicate to the ancestors, whose spirits are believed to be actually present, through the repetition of myths and stories partly of their original creation, partly received from tradition, that they are always kept in mind; and to remind them that they ought on that account to be benevolent towards their present-day descendants, and above all towards the seedlings ready for planting, or those already planted, in accordance with the hopeful wishes expressed in the invocation.[5]

Similarly among the Marind-anim, "the magical incantations addressed to the planting slips, to the planted tubers and the growing plants show that it is really a matter of directing primitive prayers or charms to the *Dema* as the creators of the plants in question; these charms derive directly from the myths, without which they cannot be understood at all."[6]

It is possible to make a comparison between these Australian or Papuan beliefs and those of the Cuna Indians of the Isthmus of Panama, Nordenskiöld learned about these from Perez, the intelligent Indian he brought back with him to Göteborg. What the Indians believe is that the magical power of the charms derives from what they convey concerning the origins of the various beings, things, cures, or the like; that is, from the fact that they relate to the myths in just the same way as Wirz describes among the Marind-anim. "Every magical incantation", Nordenskiöld tells us, "must be preceded by a certain formula which specifies the origin of the cure that is being applied, otherwise it will have no effect."[7]

A few pages later he adds still more precisely: "If the medicine, or the charm that goes with it, is to take effect, it is absolutely needful to know the origin of the herb, and how it was brought into existence by the first mother." Another instance declares that "First the singer must take into account the original creation of the *nuchus*" (these are spirits associated with certain little wooden figurines) "and how God made them. Unless he knows all that, his incantation will have no effect."

Man's power over animals depends upon the same indispensable knowledge, as the following story bears out.

Once in the forest there was a Cuna Indian who was never successful in finding game. He sat down on the branch of a tree. A *nia* or *pila* came up to him and asked him what he was doing there. So he said he was hunting . . . The demon put a pinch of some drug on the man's tongue to enable him to learn quickly, then he taught him how to attract animals. It depended, predictably, on an incantation recalling the origin of the beast . . . Long ago, and perhaps even still, the *nèles* (medicine men) used to receive visits from the beasts of the forest. They would talk to them just as though they were people. The *nèle* went into one of the rooms into which his hut was divided, and would concentrate his thoughts on the origin of the animals; then he began his chant. It was because he knew the secret of the beasts' creation that he could make them tame.[8]

Finally, among the same Cuna Indians, knowing about the origin of fire is a strong protection against being attacked by it. "There are certain persons who can hold a red hot iron in their hand, or grasp in their fist a venomous snake, and so on, provided only that they know about the origin of fire or snakes. In the Cuna Village of Tientiki there is a fourteen-year-old boy who can walk unharmed into a fire, merely because he knows the charm which tells how fire was created. Perez often saw people pick up red hot irons, and others who tamed serpents."[9]

Thus, knowing the origin of animals, of iron, fire, etc., confers a reliable power on the knower, which can be applied by means of charms and incantations. Naturally it is the myths which provide this knowledge. All these evidences therefore attest their potency.

The same belief obtains among native farmers in Timor. "When the plants in one field look poorly or simply don't flourish, someone who knows well the myths and traditions associated with the rice goes to that plot. He passes the night there, in the hut on the plantation, repeating the legends which tell how the people came to possess the rice (that is, they are myths of origin) . . . Those who do this are not priests . . . They hope by this means to entice back the rice spirit, who, they think, must have gone far away."[10]

Let us come back to Australia and New Guinea. There are times when the presence of the ancestors is too vital, their assent and approval too necessary, for a simple repetition of the stories to be deemed an adequate means of securing their interest. But other means are also available. For the Arunta it is never sufficient merely to recapitulate the exploits of the mythic heroes; something positive must be done to make sure they are truly and immediately present. They must therefore be individually and specifically called up. This is the purpose underlying a number of different festive and ceremonial activities, which are virtually dramatic performances. We are not to suppose, nevertheless, that the native's reaction on these occasions is the same as ours is at the theatre. He does not attend them only to be amused and distracted, or to rest his mind after matters more serious. On the contrary, actors and spectators alike follow the unfolding episodes of these representations with a fervid attention and quasi-religious veneration.[11] (Certainly there are also a few comic interludes which relieve tension from time to time.) What is enacted is of vital concern to the very life of the tribe, and in consequence to every individual member of it; no one ever conceives of himself as separate from or unrelated to the rest, even in death. In order to make sure the ceremonies are performed properly, no expense of time, labour or energy is ever thought too much. Some of the festivals extend for weeks or even months. Spencer and Gillen describe examples among the Arunta.

Wirz, expressing a personal opinion, remarks:

> It is curious to see the Marind, who as a rule are so lively and impulsive in their ways, behaving on these high occasions with such stiff decorum and circumspection. They stick to the customary forms with incredible rigidity; the cermonial itself is quite immutable. It would never occur to anyone to introduce the least modification, or to lighten the solemn mood of the gathering with a quip or a joke. Quite the contrary; the whole is conducted with a formidable gravity. This may well be the reason why most Marind festivals seem to a stranger to take on aspects that are thoroughly unintelligible and indeed mystifying.[12]

Nowhere more clearly than among the Marind-anim, however, does the principal purpose appear for which the most important of these festivals and ceremonies are designed. "The entire secret *mayo* ritual rests on a dual motivation: first, the symbolic repetition of the myths (in particular the myth of the coconut palm), for the instruction of the novices; second, orgiastic sex for the pleasure of the older initiates. Both of these are expected to encourage the fecundity of the palms and it would be hard to say which was the more ancient or fundamental rite."[13] The *mayo* cult includes fertility rituals properly so described. Among these may be considered the ceremonial representations of myths which accompany the ritual giving of food to the novices (the *mayo-anim*). Wirz tells us presently that as part of this ritual, from the moment they enter the *mayo-mirav* (*mirav* here is "secret site"), the novices behave as though they were absolutely blank-minded, as though just new-born. They know nothing at all. All ornament and decoration is removed from them. They are unaware even of food. There is nothing they know how to do. Everything is before them to be learned. Their instruction about all things must come from the ancestors, the *Dema*, personified by the *mitwar-anim* (that is to say, the ceremonial performers), who will inform them about everything, and do so in the order according to which mythology relates the creation of the plants and animals by the *Dema*. Thus, in point of fact, the *mayo* ceremonies constitute a rapid recapitulation of the whole mythological and legendary tradition. They include representations of what the *Dema* did in ancient times and explanations of the origins of plants and animals, also of the discovery of implements, tools and working practices. All of these matters without exception must be traced back to the mythic ancestors.[14]

It would plainly appear, then, that with the Marind-anim both initiation ceremonies and increase rituals rest essentially and almost entirely upon the authority of the myths. Both take the form of dramatic representations. Wirz is therefore quite justified in suggesting that anybody unfamiliar with the myths could be present from one end of the ceremonies to the other and make nothing of them at all. The two kinds of ritual in fact differ more in their intention than in their content. The substance of both is invariably mythological; the myths supply everything that is presented by the actors or symbolized in the masks, costumes, ornaments and gestures, the singing and dancing, etc. In the increase ceremonies the object is to bring about an assured fecundity and abundance in nature, while the initiation rituals are more particularly concerned with educating the novices. Uninitiated men are presumed to be as ignorant as a baby; they therefore have everything to learn. Especially they are required to learn about matters which constitute the most necessary elements in the life of the tribe: that is, they must learn what the ancestors performed in the mythic past, and what their activity is still. The ceremonies put all this knowledge visually before their eyes. In the performances they actually see the ancestral figures create the life of nature, establish the cultural institutions of the tribe and lay down precedents for everything from which the tribe to this day still draws its benefits.

Since this is so it is therefore understandable that in the mythic age, as Carl Strehlow avers, the two kinds of ceremony were really the same.

In the beginning the *altjirangamatjina* (the mythic ancestors) wandered over the country with their novices and carried out certain ceremonies, not only at their "eternal sites" (that is to say, their local totemic centres), but also along the way as they journeyed. The purpose of the ceremonies was to initiate the young men into the religious customs and at the same time magnify the strength and abundance of the ancestors' totem animal or plant. Each individual ancestor was associated with only one natural species and had power to increase and fortify that one kind only. The modern Aranda and Loritja still carry out regularly the ceremonies instituted by the *altjirangamatjina*. But there is an essential distinction to make clear. In the *Urzeit* a twofold end was designed and accomplished with but a single ceremony. Nowadays two separate ceremonies are conducted, each with a purpose distinct from the other.[15]

Strehlow goes on to emphasize that in the two ceremonies the content is substantially the same.

While the young men are passing through the various initiation rites, a number of ceremonies will be shown to them, exactly, except for a few sacred particulars, as they will be performed on authentic occasions. However, these are not intended to promote the health and increase of the totem concerned, but only to show those who have been, or are about to be, admitted to the rank of men, how such ceremonies ought to be conducted ... When, however, these same ceremonies are carried out at the prescribed totem sites, where in the *Urzeit* the *altjirangamatjina* dwelt, or where they paused in the course of their journeying, and when they are intended to foster the vigour and abundance of the totem, they are then called *mbatjalkatiuma* (Loritja *kutinjingani*); the word means "bring forth, make fruitful, put into prime condition".[16]

We should be quite wrong, moreover (still according to Strehlow) to interpret the ceremonies in a purely utilitarian sense. They are not performed merely for the tribe's material benefit. Such an attitude suits ill with the outlook of the Aborigines in general. The actual reason for the celebration of the rituals, Strehlow was invariably assured, was simply "because the ancestors created the precedent".[17] The material advantages following from the performances only come in as a secondary consideration. Nor is it to be understood that the objective is always in itself desirable (though mostly it is); hardly so in the case of the ceremony for the increase of blowflies! — and there are others.[18] In fact, however, and with exceptions excepted, when the Aborigine performs a totemic ceremony he does not doubt that the vegetable or animal species concerned will reproduce more plentifully and grow to a larger size. His trust in this result is complete and no doubt his zeal follows in proportion to his faith. But Strehlow is none the less justified in claiming that such material gain is not the only, and not even the principal motive for the ceremonies. They are above all of a quasi-religious character. The ancestors, who themselves in the first place carried out these increase rituals, set the precedent for their descendants to continue. The descendants therefore have an absolute responsibility to obey the prescription. Many scientific observers, particularly of more recent date, have emphasized the strict obligation felt by all the natives to perform the rites. It is for them a categorical imperative. No doubt they do look for practical benefits from doing so, but even if the consequences must be disastrous, they would still regard their responsibility as impossible to avoid.

In Carl Strehlow's study, thanks to the texts he reproduces, translates and comments on, we are able to follow step by step the presentation of certain myths in ceremonies. In them we see the ancestors represented by human actors, but still in their double character of animal and man. Their costumes (where they have one), their decoration and ornament, their dances, and above all their miming, reproduce the demeanour of the totem animal. They imitate its habitual movements while a chorus chants the main matter of the myths.[19] For example in the mouse ceremony, two actors belonging to the totem represent mice, one an ancestor-mouse of the *ntena* variety, the other a *lukara*, and they frisk about together. "On the clayey surface of the damp ground they gnaw some bushes, then with their teeth pull off the top twigs of a shrub known by the whites as cotton-bush; these they carry off to their spacious mousehole and tear it to shreds. The *altjirangamitjina*-mouse keeps watch in his hole, a boomerang in his hand."[20]

Two emu-rituals are included, one to be performed by day, the other at night. In the night ceremony only one performer appears. "He is decorated with a broad black band which runs from his knees to his forehead, outlined with a line of down. Round his middle there is a broad black band, also outlined with down. On his head he wears a *tonka* with a long emu feather stuck in it . . . The actor stands in the performing area with his hands placed on his back, bending the upper part of the body a little forward, mimicking an old emu just arrived at a drinking place — the imitation is carried off to perfection, as only the blacks can do it."[21] Similar miming is seen, a similar representation of half-human, half-animal ancestors, the same kind of pantomime, in the totemic ceremonies of the crow, the frog, the duck, the honey-ant, "sugar-bag" (bee), and all the rest.

Spencer and Gillen, who also describe the ceremonies, add this reflection: "At the first glance it looks much as if all that they were intended to represent were the behaviour of certain animals, but in reality they have a much deeper meaning, for each performer represents an ancestral individual who lived in the Alchera . . . It is as a reincarnation of the never-dying spirit part of one of these ancestors that every member of the tribe is born, and therefore, when born, he, or she, bears of necessity the name of the animal or plant associated with the Alchera ancestor."[22] Spencer and Gillen here are at one with Strehlow in seeing these pantomimic representations as a translation of the totemic traditions into visible form, exactly as in the secret rituals of the Marind-anim. But their account of the material differs insofar as they hardly mention the myths at all. They are more interested in investigating the way tribesmen as individuals relate to their totems. But in any case that relationship, as may be seen from the passage just quoted, implies the existence in the *alcheringa* of mythic ancestors who were half-human, half-animal. The exploits and adventures of these ancestors, their wanderings, the ceremonies instituted by them and the transformations related of them provide material for several chapters in Spencer and Gillen's monumental book, *The Arunta*, which are indispensable to any scholar who wishes to understand the ceremonies.

Thus the ceremonies, although Spencer and Gillen do not say so as forcefully as Strehlow or Wirz, carry performers and spectators alike back into the true mythic atmosphere. They bring to life before the natives' eyes the "eternal uncreated", with whom it is essential for the tribe to maintain communion. To render this *participation* effective is the principal reason for the existence of the rituals. *Intichiuma* ceremonies, Spencer and Gillen explain — *intichiuma* is the word they use for what Strehlow calls *mbat-jalkatiuma* — "have for their sole object the purpose of increasing the number of the animal or plant after which their totem is called; and thus, taking the tribe as a whole, the object of these ceremonies is that of increasing the total food supply". Further: "At the present day each totem has its own ceremony, and no two of them are alike; but although they differ to a great extent as far as the actual performance is concerned, the important point is that one and all" serve the same end. In this passage and others like it, it would appear that Spencer and Gillen do not claim any more for the ceremonies they call *intichiuma* than that one single purpose; and it is a merely utilitarian one. But in other contexts and especially in regard to other ceremonies they acknowledge the presence of mystical – indeed they do not hesitate to affirm, religious – elements among the complex of motives obeyed by the natives. They do, however, from the outset, make this express reservation: ". . . their performance is not associated, in the native mind, with the idea of appealing to the assistance of any Supernatural Being".[23]

A more recent observer, A.P. Elkin, places his emphasis firmly on the "secret life" (the tribal rituals) of the Australian Aborigines, the capital importance of which did not escape Spencer and Gillen, though for them, as we have noticed, it tended usually to remain in the background. Elkin brings it well forward. It is here that he looks for an explanation of the way the natives experience mentally, and also react physically to, all contact with what is considered sacred:

> These rites and the *talu* sites are an integral part of the secret life of the tribe . . . the existence of fully initiated men is essential for the performance and perpetuation of the rites and the care of the sites. Nor is this all, for the very life of nature and therefore of the human race itself depends on these rites and sites. The Aboriginal totemistic philosophy binds man to nature in a living whole, which is symbolized and maintained by the complex of myths, rites and sacred sites. Unless the myths with their sanctions are preserved, the rites performed and the sites maintained as spirit sanctuaries, that living bond is broken, man and nature are separated, and neither man nor nature has any assurance of life in the future. This does not mean that man thinks he has magical control over natural species, but that he has a sanctified method of expressing that mutual need which man and nature have, the one of the other. And he does his part at the appropriate seasons towards maintaining the life and regularity of nature by means of ritual which is standardized and sanctioned by myth, and by preserving continuity with the past through these same rites and sacred sites and symbols.
>
> It should be obvious that where such increase ceremonies are part of tribal life (that is, or was, over the northern half or rather two-thirds of Australia), man's confidence and hope is intimately bound up with them. That is, they are of positive social value. Indeed their performance seems to be essential for the persistence of the tribe; at least, that is the opinion of the native informants, who seem to be justified by the sad results which accompany the breaking down of this aspect of secret life. One informant said with reference to the desecration by whites of a *talu* site, "We cannot perform *talu*, so we must die." The bond with nature and continuity with the *dzugur* or heroic age were broken. Therefore,

there could not be confidence in the present, nor hope for the future.[24]

On Elkin's no less than Wirz's testimony the ceremonies would thus remain unintelligible without the myths.

These rites are almost always performed at secret sites which have been sanctified by mythology and are therefore definitely associated with the great culture-heroes or ancestors. These sites are believed to be the homes of the spirits of the particular species concerned, either because the hero or ancestor performed *talu* there or because he or a great representative of the totem left part or all of his body at the spot. In other words, the belief in the pre-existence of spirits expresses the Aboriginal philosophy of nature and natural species as well as of man, and lies at the base of the increase rites. The pre-existent spirits live at the sacred sites, and the purpose of the rites is to send them out into, or make them available for, the various totemic species or even man himself. The actions and words frequently make this quite obvious. The performers actually throw dust or stones from the spirit-home, mentioning as they do so the name of the species, along with words to the effect that it is to increase or grow in various places referred to by name. This is recognizably what we may recall Spencer and Gillen describing as reincarnation.[25]

Something similar has been observed by Ralph Piddington among the Karadjeri in north-west Australia.

Increase ceremonies are generally located at places where the natural species in question is plentiful. Thus, for example, Birdinapa Point, which forms the northern edge of Lagrange Bay is the best place on the coast for any kind of fishing, and here are located a number of fish increase centres.

Increase ceremonies are usually performed once a year, and when a natural species appears at one season only, the ceremony associated with that species is performed just before it becomes plentiful; on the other hand the increase ceremonies associated with those foods which are perennial may be carried out at any time.

An invariable accompaniment to Karadjeri increase ceremonies is a series of instructions uttered by the performers as they carry out the ritual; these are of one general pattern, and consist of instructions to the species to become plentiful. They are continued throughout the ceremonies, various *ngura* (districts) being named in succession as places where the totem in question should become plentiful. It should be noted that in reciting these lists of *ngura* the natives name only those places in which the species is actually to be found; at the cockle increase ceremony a performer was corrected by his fellows for naming a part of the coast where cockles are not found. These instructions are associated with the belief that all increase centres were instituted in *bugari* times, when a number of spirit members of the species were left at the centres; and these come out under the influence of the ritual and so ensure the increase of the natural species. Sometimes a song associated with the mythological origin of the ceremony is sung.[26]

Here are present together all the essential elements of the pattern: ceremony, local totemic site, the seasonal factor if it is involved, myth. These are accompanied by the "instructions" addressed to the species in which increase is desired. In the example which now follows we trace both the ceremony, as instituted by the half human, half bird ancestor, and the myth it relates to, belonging to the cockle totem:

> The ceremony was instituted in *bugari* times by Djui (bower bird) who, together with his wife (who was also a *djui*) came from the district north of Broome. Djui made a nest in a tree and a playground; his diet consisted solely of fish and shellfish; the former he killed with a *djambi* [Piddington's footnote: wooden instrument used by the Karadjeri for this purpose] which he carried. He made a small yard of stones and one day, on looking into it, saw a number of fish. He then travelled down the coast making the present native fish traps, semicircular rows of stones in which fish are caught as the tide recedes. He killed a mullet, the body of which became a stone, which is now the mullet increase centre on the northern shore of Lagrange Bay, and he also instituted the cockle increase centre at Lagrange Bay.
>
> After a while the exclusively fish diet began to disagree with Djui and his wife. They became very sick and finally died, leaving the fish traps, and instructing people not to live on fish alone but to eat *nalgoo* and other fruits as well.
>
> They also gave the tradition that men obtain fish (because the male *djui* did so) while women collect and cook cockles because the female *djui* performed these duties.[27]

The role of the mythic ancestor is here spelled out quite clearly. But on the other hand there are also many ceremonies in which the ancestor is not presented in person. This does not imply he is not involved. Take, for example, the *goanna* (monitor lizard) ceremony which Piddington describes. He reports simply that "the performers decorate themselves with stripes of *tabula* representing goannas. They then clean out a hole in the ground, making pathways along which the goannas are to go to the various districts where they will subsequently be caught. Finally vines are coiled up inside the hole and dragged out along the pathway, thus, it is said, dragging out goannas".[28] This is clearly an instance of sympathetic magic. Perhaps the proper comparison is with the "instructions" given in other cases to the species for its increase. We shall need to come back in due course to the function of sympathetic magic in ceremonies of this kind.

Finally, at Dobu, there is a certain ceremony which comes before the yam-planting. Fortune comments: "I think that this ritual which precedes planting is self-explanatory. It recalls the early history of yams that have descended in the Green Parrot totem from their first birth from human beings, in the time of the ancestors (Samuela, daughter of Bulelala, being cut up and planted as a red yam). It is believed that the yams are personal beings who hear the spells directed towards them and must needs respond . . ."[29] Among the islanders, as in Australia, and with the Marind-anim, the increase ritual is itself meaningful only in so far as it reflects the meaning of the myth. It is from the power of the myth alone that it derives its efficacy.

Some short time since, Elkin discovered in the Kimberley District of north west Australia a number of rock paintings. The natives who were with him were quite open with him about their utility. Their material function was quite like the "instructions" embodied in increase ceremonies. In general the paintings appear to represent human figures, similar to those Grey saw in the same area a hundred years earlier, and reproduced in his *Journal*: faces with no mouth, surrounded with a kind of broad headband in a horseshoe shape.[30] The Karadjeri call them *wondjina*, or sometimes *ungud*. We have already been made acquainted with the varying senses of these two words, and with the importance of the place they occupy in the beliefs and practices of the Aborigines.[31] The paintings are located on the walls of caves, cliffs and rock-galleries.

No attempt, however, is made to restore any of these, though in some cases, especially in those of the large *wondjina* and his children, the head, head-paint, hair, eyebrows and eyes are certainly retouched and kept renewed.[32] This operation should only be done at the beginning of the wet season, for the retouching causes rain to fall. As a matter of fact, a blackfellow who was with me retouched the eyes of the large *wondjina* with some charcoal while I was visiting the picture, and, strangely enough, some light showers fell a few days later in the midst of the dry season. This did much to strengthen the Aborigines' faith, and they did not fail to draw my attention to the cause of this unprecedented rain.[33]

Thus the retouching of the paintings at a suitable time produces the same kind of result as the chanting of the myths and the celebration of increase rites. It brings beneficial rains and favours the growth and reproduction of the animal and vegetable species the Aborigines need. Hence, Elkin remarks,

> Two of the heads, at least, are kept "touched up" and can be seen at a distance of about fifty yards. Two others in less conspicuous places also appear to be fairly fresh. The heads are said by the Aborigines to represent *wondjina* women. If they are retouched, with ochre, charcoal or pipeclay, women will have babies. In two places near some of these heads there are a number of more or less round marks, about an inch in diameter. These represent the green, plum-like fruit called *nalgo*. The regular supply of this fruit is maintained by painting or repainting representations of it on a wondjina gallery during the wet season. Indeed even the "baby-increase" female *wondjina* are supposed to be retouched only during the same season, when the productive power of nature is at its height.[34]

Let us suppose an increase is desired in the kangaroo population. "Just inside, on the roof of the tunnel are two outline paintings of large female kangaroos with young in the pouch. Two *wondjina* heads are painted so as to look at the kangaroos. The latter appear to have been fairly recently painted or retouched. This is said to be done during the wet season to ensure the natural increase of the species." The increase is thus brought about in two ways at once, through the power of the *wondjina* heads acting upon the images of the members of the species concerned which are depicted on the wall, and also through the power the heads have to cause rain to fall. The two operations are not clearly distinct because rain is on its own account a factor in the increase of plants and animals.

> Mr W.R. Easton, who has explored in the Kimberley District, told me that a certain blackfellow at Walcott Inlet was pointed out to him as a rain maker. After a great deal of persuasion, this important individual was prevailed upon to explain how he made the rain. The process, so far as Mr Easton could see and understand, was that the man painted one of the mouthless pictures on a rock. This would suggest that the present-day blacks paint these pictures afresh, and not merely retouch them, as many say. I really think that they must do so sometimes. New heads have been painted over the old ones, and are not merely retouched figures. But as the incident witnessed by Mr Easton was by arrangement only a "gammon", the rain-maker probably did not make a proper

wondjina, complete in all details. But Mr Easton's experience does corroborate the function of the paintings as rainmaking.[35]

Among these faces (other parts of the body may or may not also be lightly indicated but the head is the only part that is important), there is none with a mouth. This feature – or rather, the absence of it – aroused Elkin's curiosity. He asked the natives what the reason was. "The natives say that a mouth cannot be made. Apparently the efficacy of the painting is associated with its absence." But in all probability they were simply unable to find a reply to a question no one had ever asked them before. They evaded the issue politely by referring to established custom. Elkin's evaluation of their answer amounts to no more than guesswork and seems not much to the point. He would probably not have put it forward at all if it had occurred to him to recall that a great many prehistoric paintings, drawings and other surviving monuments of the Mediterranean region, quite commonly exhibit mouthless faces. As for the paintings and drawings of the Marind-anim, on the evidence of Father P. Vertenten that deficiency is perfectly usual.[36]

We may also notice that certain heads among them are surrounded, like the Australian rock paintings, with a broad headband in the shape of a horseshoe. The natives told Vertenten what it denoted. It was not in fact a headband at all, but a structure called a *gari* which the performers carry or wear on their heads during certain ceremonies. It is still in use today among the Marind-anim.

> The *gari* is an artifact which, in the Merauke area, is semi-circular in shape. Near Merauke itself it is larger, but here it is almost a metre and a half tall (and I am not speaking of the ribs, which are longer in proportion). The *gari* is constructed of thin strips made of sago-palm pith, all sewn together and fixed upon a framework formed from three rods and a curved length of rattan, brown in colour.
>
> The *gari* is mounted on the head. The lower part of one of the rods passes through the lengthened hair-ornamentation and is fastened firmly on at the shoulders. The painted section rests on the hair-binding, held fast on each side with a pin thrust obliquely through it. In this way the apparatus is held firm. It is not a heavy object (it can easily be lifted with one hand), but it catches a great deal of wind and as the wearer has to carry out many movements over a lengthy period, it puts him into a regular sweat-bath.[37]

Looking at the illustrations provided by Vertenten, one may easily believe that.

Wirz, in his great work on the Marind-anim, includes other similar pictures. Not content with merely describing this large apparatus, he sought also to define its meaning and use.

> The *gari* is a large semi-circular structure, three or four metres across; though west of the Bian, appreciably smaller. It is brought out by the adherents of the *mayo* cult at their great initiation festival, and on some other occasions. The actor who assumes it — often there may be more than one — carries the *gari* on the back of his neck, or rather, supported between his shoulders, so that his head appears through its inner circular opening . . .
>
> But what the real significance of the *gari* is, can only be conjectured, since no matter what questions are put to the natives, they invariably answer "yes" to whatever is suggested..
>
> Nevertheless conjecture is given support by both the myth itself and information gathered from observation of the recent *mayo* ceremony [witnessed by Wirz]. It is evident that the *gari* carries a direct allusion to the sexual orgies which take place during the *mayo* initiations; and it also functions in some other way, as a signal conveying an indication for the common understanding of the older initiates, it may be, from the number of *garis* seen, of the number of female victims expected to be made available in due course . . .[38]
>
> The actor bearing the *gari* thus represents in the *mayo* ceremony the mythological Opeko-anim (man from Opeko), who brings with him his *mayo-iwag* (*mayo* woman). The latter is represented by a man dressed as a woman (that is, wearing a woman's pubic apron). The two are tied together with a spear linking them, in such a way as to suggest that the woman is completely in the power of the *gari*-performer and can never escape him. At the same time the entrance of the *gari* serves also to give notice to the initiates that the orgies are shortly to begin. That is the reason why it is so large.[39]

A drawing made by a native, reproduced by Wirz, shows a person wearing a *gari*. [It represents the *Dema* Yorma.] The face is without any mouth.[40] It presents a striking resemblance to the paintings recorded by Grey and Elkin.

Finally, a recent publication enables us to trace the *gari* as far as to the Papuans of Kiwai. A form of headgear illustrated by Landtman and called by him *dori* undoubtedly recalls the object described by Wirz among the Marind-anim.[41] Moreover the Marind tribe before settling in the territory it occupies today, must certainly have lived in a region to the east of it, and thus would have been a close neighbour to, and possibly even in close contact with, the Kiwai Papuans.

Putting together the evidence we have just examined, and comparing the different figures, it seems possible to draw several conclusions.

Wirz on a number of occasions refers to a singular resemblance between certain customs of the Marind-anim and those of Central Australian tribes, though without dwelling on them insistently. No doubt he hesitated because there was nothing in Marind society which recalled the marriage system of the Aranda, Loritja and other Central Australian tribes. If he had known the facts since observed by Elkin, and especially those relating to the rock paintings Elkin describes and reproduces (unfortunately without their colours), most likely he would have felt able to say even more.[42] The heads in these paintings are as a rule provided with a decoration very like the *gari*, still worn in the fertility rituals of the Marind-anim and the Kiwai Papuans. It is hard to see in this resemblance merely a fortuitous coincidence, and equally hard to believe that the natives encountered by Grey in the Glenelg River region, Kimberley District, in 1837 and reported on again recently by Elkin and Piddington, spontaneously invented that headgear, while in New Guinea the Papuans spontaneously invented another virtually identical with it.

What are we to think? The anthropological history, even relatively recent, of the Australian tribes is obscure. Of the Marind-anim and the Kiwai Islanders we know nothing more. All that we can positively say today is that there are differences between the institutions of all of them, and they are more numerous than the similarities. Since we know so little of the past, this weighty truth imposes considerable reservations. The survival of very similar artifacts in both Australia and New Guinea today gives us authority for nothing more than a mere guess at the existence, at some very remote former time, of a contact between the peoples, for all that their present separation from one another is very distant. Alternatively we might guess at some sort of transmission of the ornaments through and past the borders of intervening tribes; but of any such movement we have no actual evidence. Possibly in a time to come, when more is known concerning both the Australian tribal people of the north west and the Papuans generally, this enigma may find some solution not at present to be anticipated.

Nevertheless we may remark, while on this topic, that in another of his writings Wirz refers to the use by Torres Strait Islanders of dance ornaments very similar to the *gari*, worn on the head in the same way, which are called by them *deri* or *dari*. The likeness between the names can hardly be a matter of casual chance any more than that between the articles they denote. A.C. Haddon, after describing them in some detail (the British Museum possesses specimens), comes to this conclusion: "I believe all these headdresses are imported from New Guinea, and I am under the impression that they are definitely war accoutrements in the districts where they are made." This conjecture is notably out of agreement with what seems to be their function among the Marind-anim, and I dare say also with their use in Australia. But, according to an observation made by Wirz in reference to just this question, "The merest chance may have the effect of encouraging the fabrication of such objects in quite widely separated regions. We know well that nothing creates as much interest or lends itself so readily to imitation as articles used in dances and festivals, and this happens without the least heed being paid to their original tribal use, in which, in other places, no one takes the slightest interest." If, as would seem plausible, the *gari* made its way down from New Guinea to Australia, we have here an inference that it no doubt passed across by way of Torres Strait.[43]

The *gari* is worn, in New Guinea fertility ceremonies, by performers who portray a particular kind of role. Can we deduce anything from this about the figures in the rock paintings of north west Australia who wear ornaments with some resemblance to the *gari*? Such a speculation is altogether hazardous. Yet we have a little more information to draw upon now than earlier. In the first place, in the numerous photographs reproduced in the various great works by Spencer and Gillen, illustrating Arunta ceremonies equivalent to the Marind fertility rituals, we frequently see that the performers are wearing enormous structures on their heads. They are certainly not very much like *gari*. But there is no reason to doubt that they are artifacts of a comparable kind, and have a comparable purpose.[44] Moreover the Karadjeri and their neighbours, no less than the Arunta and the Marind-anim, possess local totemic centres where the natural species on which the people are most dependent appear particularly abundant. So far no one has shown that they carry out special rituals in those places.[45] Elkin himself, to whom we owe practically all we know of these people, admits there is a great deal still to be learned about them. But such rituals, if they do exist, are likely to be secret ones. It would be surprising if a closer acquaintance with the tribal life did not point them out. If in fact the Karadjeri do possess such ceremonies, it is reasonable to assume the performers would wear head ornaments more or less along the same lines as the Arunta or the Marind-anim. If so the head ornamentation seen in the recently discovered rock paintings, with their similarity to the *gari*, would seem to be of a likely kind.

In support of this guess we may draw on the explanations brought forward by the Karadjeri themselves. It was they who told Elkin that at the beginning of the wet season it would be necessary to retouch and freshen the *wondjina* heads. That was the way to make sure of getting an adequate quantity of rain, and, as would naturally follow, a proper increase in the animal and vegetable species which were the tribe's food supplies – not to mention, also, a gratifying increase in human births. This retouching of the paintings thus came to have the same effect as fertility and increase rituals. What the natives say is quite explicit on that head. So we are quite justified in assuming that characters wearing a *gari*, or a comparable head ornament, whether in Australia or New Guinea, may all have a similar power to exert some beneficial influence on the increase of local animals and plants.

It may be possible to carry this interpretation of the rock paintings – of some of them, that is – just a little further. Take for example the lightly, even somewhat offhandedly drawn figure, his head decorated with a *gari*-like ornament, who is watching a kangaroo placed below him on the rock; or the one (another similar personage) who is staring in much the same way at the *nalgoo* fruits. From all one can gather, the Karadjeri believe firmly that these particular *wondjina* are able to act beneficially on those animals and plants alone so as to bring about their increase. This, then, is information at first hand. The people directly concerned have themselves told us what is the purpose, or at least one of the purposes, of this rock art. But that is all we know. Who the mythical characters are that are represented, or what the *wondjina* heads themselves stand for, Elkin cannot tell us. No doubt these were secret matters and his informants were unwilling to reveal them.

We can diminish this obscurity a little if we remember what was said in the early part of this chapter, where we saw that the natives, wishing to promote the increase of native animals and plants necessary to them, believed the best way was to recite, sing or otherwise represent the myths that were proper to the season and the need. But if, instead of ceremonial performances, they aim to obtain the same result by covering the walls and ceilings of rock galleries with paintings, will we not be justified in assuming that the subjects depicted in them are supplied by the myths? Surely this is simply another way of appealing to the mythic powers. If we take the rock paintings to be representations of mythic material in graphic terms, as the ritual recitations are vocal, and as the ceremonies are mimetic, we can hardly be very far wrong.

No doubt different styles of presentation imply some differences in content. In a dramatic unfolding of a myth, the events follow in order; the performers *become* the personages in the fullest sense, giving expression through word and gesture to all the character's thoughts and feelings. Painting, being essentially static, can only render a single moment of the action. It is therefore quite impossible for any pictorial representation to convey all that is contained in a myth. But it is enough if the image brings the personage, or the animal, effectively to the viewer's mind. Since everybody knows the stories, the heroic characters about whom they are told leap into the imagination. No doubt it is also quite clear as a rule what myth is being presented in a given ceremony, whereas so far we remain ignorant of the personalities depicted in these paintings. But this poses no obstacle to our presuming the *wondjina* heads were intended to give graphic expression to some myth, at any rate to evoke the myth by visually representing one of its heroic characters. The word *wondjina* is frequently used synonymously with *ungud*. That term invariably implicates the mythic period. Hence although we are not yet in any position to say what the subjects are that are depicted in the rock paintings, the grounds are firm enough to assert in principle that they are founded on myth. For their beneficial action on various species of plants and animals, like that of the ceremonies, springs directly from the inherent potency of the myths.

Since the early years of the present century our knowledge of prehistoric art has become much wider and deeper. Sensational discoveries in France, Spain, north and south Africa, and in other places also, along with the use by pre-historians of increasingly reliable techniques of research, have made possible a progress earlier investigators could not have dared to hope for. We have become able to classify these ancient art works, and even at times trace their evolution. But what was the purpose they served, and what their deeper significance? These problems remain still almost untouched. As to the spiritual archaeology of such primitive art, we have nothing to go on beyond the art itself, that is to say, the actual surviving monuments.

So we have had to make guesses, and that is never reliable. The field lay wide open to speculation. The hypothesis that found most favour and gathered the most enduring support nearly always was one which attributed some magical function to the representation of plants and animals. The usual idea was that those who made the pictures must have believed that by drawing them they could magically bring the animals to the hunter's hand. This was a variant of a widespread belief thought to underlie the practice of voodoo: anyone who could manipulate the image could thereby control the original. Thus by scratching lines on a stone, or drawing or painting an animal, palaeolithic man could master it magically.

This theory seems to rest on assumptions of a certain plausible colour, at any rate in certain instances of superstitious beliefs of which some few survive even today. For all that it is hardly a satisfactory explanation. Those who defended it – Salomon Reinach was one – invariably attributed to the primitive artists a wholly material motive.[46] Man needed to defend himself against some animals which could attack him, and to take others for food. Hence he made images which gave him power to dominate them. There is no need to deny categorically the existence of such motives, but they seem hardly adequate to explain the whole origin and function of such art-works, of which so many survive, some of excellent quality.

If we may trust analogy to give us some idea of how prehistoric man thought and felt, obviously it will be best to turn for examples to primitive cultures that still survive intact. The most profitable comparisons are likely to come from those who, until the coming of white men, remained still in a Neolithic, or better still, Palaeolithic state of development: Tasmanians, Australians, Papuans, certain South and North American tribes, etc.[47] The mental world of these people, we are by now well aware, was (or is) intensely mystical. We may therefore conclude that the minds of prehistoric peoples were in general no less so. It follows therefore that the works of art we are concerned with are not very likely to have drawn their inspiration from preoccupations wholly, or even predominantly, pragmatical, materialist or utilitarian. Like the modes of primitive activity with which we are more closely acquainted, it is sound to assume they must have been based upon some fundamental kind of mysticism. As long as we continue to argue along analogical lines in this way, we must of course make allowance for an ever-present possibility of error. But in this present instance the risk does not seem excessive. Certainly it never daunted the pre-historians. "We will have little hesitation", say Emile Cartailhac and the Abbé Breuil, "in concluding upon the basis of ideas currently held by present-day primitives, what must have been the mental attitude which prevailed among our own western hunters in Quaternary times."[48] Cartailhac and Breuil therefore look for an *Open Sesame* to the enigma of Palaeolithic art in the beliefs, customs and ceremonies of the Bushmen, the Eskimos, the Red Indians and the Australian Aborigines.

Before we look at their speculations more closely we may remind ourselves that since Elkin's recent discoveries we are no longer reduced to sheer guesswork when we call upon analogical reasoning to help us out.[49] We have available certain direct and well-authenticated evidence. We know in effect, and without having to guess, exactly what is the point and purpose of the rock paintings made by the Karadjeri. They themselves make no mystery of it. Like the myth-ceremonies and the fertility rituals, the paintings are meant to promote the increase of the animal and vegetable species on which the tribe is dependent. If this object is to be attained, the ancestors – those mythic beings, half-animal, half-human, from whom all, men and animals alike, are descended – must absolutely be actively present. It is the legends and the ceremonies which assure this. According to the Karadjeri the rock paintings have just the same effect, provided they are retouched at the beginning of each wet season. Every one of these methods of representing the mythic beings brings about a *participation*; the tribe enters into communion with the creation-heroes of the mythic age, and from this follows an increase in vigour in the plants, the animals and even the tribe itself.

If then, analogical comparisons are to be made between prehistoric painting, drawing and sculpture and the rock paintings of north west Australia, is it not an extremely valuable advantage for the interpreter to have learned from the lips of the Karadjeri themselves the meaning and function they attribute to their art? Undoubtedly a utilitarian purpose forms some part of their motivation and they pursue it with a clear awareness. But this motive is bound up with, or, more truly, subordinated to the mystical participation of the human group with the ancestors, which the pictorial representation of the mythic personages renders actual and effective. It may well therefore be true, as the current theory contends, that prehistoric man believed the images he created by drawing, painting or carving to be of some magical efficacy. But it is not in any way certain that he believed that by doing so he could directly cause animals to fall into his grasp. As the Karadjeri tell us, the mystical influence of the pictures is of the same kind as the influence of ceremonies and rituals. It brings assurance of the fertility, growth and perpetuity of the animal and vegetable species with the presence and aid of their mythic creators. Because of these the tribe will, from season to season, regularly find its food and sustenance. This will happen as a material result of the influence exerted by the paintings. But such is not the sole and basic purpose. The mystical function anticipates, modifies and finally supersedes the utilitarian function. It is not to be identified with it and must not be confused with it.

We should be careful, moreover, not to attribute to prehistoric man the same way of looking at animals as we have ourselves. The occasionally striking naturalism of Neolithic art may tempt us to suppose the artists had the same mental attitude as artists have now. As long as this relates merely to their observation of shapes and forms, their impressions of animal motion or their general aptitude for depicting such things, there is not too much difficulty in conceding the point. But for the rest? If the way primitives react even under modern conditions can be taken as any indication, it was never the physical strength of the creature, or any of its visual attributes, which came most insistently into his mind when prehistoric man encountered an animal; rather it was its unknown, unseen, most deeply mystical powers.[50] If, to tangle with impossibilities, the idea he entertained of any particular animal could now somehow be revealed to us just as he saw it then, it would no doubt strike us, not as surprising merely, but as altogether inconceivable.

Bearing in mind the explanation that has been advanced of the dual identity of mythic beings, we may now perhaps press a little harder upon a minor problem which has puzzled the prehistorians. From time to time they have come across outline drawings, composite figures, which are neither wholly animal nor precisely human. Saint-Périer has drawn attention to some outstanding examples in two recent articles:

> A rock-graffito from Isturitz shows a round face with an indication of teeth, and with long ears attached suggesting those of a

monkey or hare-like creature . . . We are reminded of the celebrated graffito at the Trois-Frères cave, where the antlers and ears of a deer-like animal have been added to a figure or face with a long beard, certainly human (of that the feet and hands leave no room for doubt).[51]

. . . These latter figures, to which a few animal details would seem to have been added as a caprice, lead us to further designs of forms unmistakably half-human, half-animal, though without hinting at any possibility of a decision as to what species they might belong to . . . Although in most of the figures the forehead is prominent, the cranium globose and the eye is sometimes furnished with an eyebrow, the nose, chin and mouth nevertheless lose all human appearance and are combined into a more or less projecting snout. This is also the case in many graffiti at Les Combarelles (Mas d'Azil), in the roundel referred to as the "Bear-headed Dancer", and at La Madeleine in the equally well-known figure of the "Man with a staff over his shoulder". Others exist which are wholly animal or else appear to be human bodies, as at Altamira. And finally we may recall the "goblins" (*diablotins*) at Teyjat, which must still be placed in the same category because of their composite character, though they provide a unique example of perfectly zoologically recognizable heads (of chamois) mounted on human bodies.[52]

What can these figures all mean? The prehistorians are in complete agreement. "It is no longer to be doubted nowadays," Saint-Périer goes on, "in the light of such an abundance of ethnographical data as we now have, that these half-human, half-animal forms must represent one or other of two things: either they depict ceremonial masks, whether of the kind worn by sorcerers or simply to symbolize the spirits; or they show us hunting-disguises (for stalking game)."

Such, in effect, is the triple-horned hypothesis to which Cartailhac and the Abbé Breuil have boiled it all down; and Salomon Reinach also accepts it. It is a product of analogical rationalization. At the outset, "we see that among the Eskimos, the Red Indians and the Bushmen certain very clever disguises are used to give the hunter an advantage. The man covers himself over with the skin of an animal so he may approach the game without alarming it . . . Sometimes the disguise is total. In these graffiti, then, is it not possible that we see human figures wearing hunting masks?"

A hard proposition to prove! And hardly very satisfying in any case. Outlines like these are not often found representing hunting scenes, neither do we discover near at hand, or even in the same general locality, animals of the species to which the composite figures would seem to belong. Furthermore none of the disguises could be described as "total". The head of a chamois, or a bear, or a horse, fixed on to a human trunk, does not afford a combination one can imagine was ever of much use to a hunter who hoped to deceive or decoy animals in the wild. Perhaps it might be better not to dwell any longer on this branch of the hypothesis.

The authors next recall "masked dances, in which every performer assumes a mask to represent the head of his totem-animal . . .". (This among Bushmen and Red Indians.) Among the Eskimos, they tell us, "the bear-headed shamanic dance venerated the totem in order to obtain a greater abundance of game".

And for their third proposition they speak of "sorcerers' masks", since they reason those were in customary use more or less everywhere in America and Africa.

"With all these examples in mind we come back to our Altamira and other graffiti, strongly disinclined to find anything astonishing in what they convey. It only stands to reason that masks were from the earliest times familiar to our Paleolithic artists, and so was masked dancing."[53]

These last two branches of the hypothesis seem somewhat less questionable than the first, certainly if we take them in a very broad sense. It appears likely enough that Paleolithic man knew how to make masks, and how to use them in his dances and ceremonies. But it by no means follows convincingly that the graffiti (including the half-human, half-animal figures) were actually meant to depict either sorcerers (a vague term) or masked dancers.

It will be enough here, I imagine, to recall what has been said in earlier chapters (especially chapter II), "Mythic Beings, Half-Human, Half-Animal"), to enable us to take in at once what these drawings and graffiti do signify. They were undoubtedly intended to be representations in visual form of beings of dual or mixed identity – the animal ancestors and mythic heroes who play so important a part still in the mystical life of the primitives of today. These are the men-kangaroos, men-wildcats, men-ducks, and the rest, of whom it is impossible to say whether they are more animal than human, or more human than animal. It is true that, in ceremonies and dances, they are often impersonated by actors who wear costumes or masks.[54] Such persons could well have served as models for the graffiti and the composite drawings; Paleolithic artists may so have drawn them. But there was never any need to borrow them from "masked dances". No idea could have been more familiar to the artists than one recalling the mixed beings whose exploits and adventures the myths relate; such images will have been very constantly present in their minds.

So it does not follow that these drawings and engravings, half-human and half-animal though they appear, must necessarily reproduce actual masks and costumes as used in ceremonies and dances. Like the fabricated masks themselves, and for the same reasons, it is more probable they amount to direct representations of mythic beings. For without doubt they rest upon the same purpose for existing as do the dances and the ceremonies themselves; to bring assurance of the real presence and involvement of the mythic beings concerned, so as to foster communion between the totemic group and the particular ancestors whose name it bears, and in whose essential identity it participates.

We can verify from the life, so to speak, an interesting resemblance between these fossil art-works and masks used by certain dancers. In the region of Bering Strait there are Eskimos who make use of a kind of mask with flaps, which conveys very effectively, and with realistic conviction, an impression of the dual identity of the mythic being it represents. At a predetermined moment during the ceremony the mechanism, which is shaped to resemble the head of a bird, opens out like a shutter, with two side-pieces which fold back. A human face now appears: an ingenious method of expressing, very strikingly, the consubstantial unity of the mythic man and bird. In similar fashion, "At La Madeleine," Saint-Périer tells us, "underneath one of the animal-heads, one can plainly see, as through a transparency, suggestions of a human face".[55] This superpositioning of the images carried out by Paleolithic man is exactly equivalent to the shutter-mask invented by the Eskimos. Are we not bound to conclude it was designed with the same end in view?

If this is a sound conjecture – if, that is to say, these outlines and composites made by Paleolithic artists are really and effectively translations into a plastic medium of half-human, half-animal subjects like the beings in Australian and Papuan myths – then certain important conclusions at once suggest themselves. Here we can point them out only briefly.

First, these men of the Later Quaternary period must have possessed a mythology – or something very like one, depending upon the resources of mental versatility permitted them by their command of language. And further, any such body of legend, like the myths of modern primitives, must have dealt with the adventures and exploits, no doubt also the creative innovations, of superior beings who were part-human, part-animal. Perhaps these beings may at times even have been regarded as ancestors – if so, the myths would then have been totemic.

Again, but to speak rather more generally, in view of the fact that Paleolithic man does seem to have possessed myths, and since he went to the trouble of making representations of some of the personages, we are also surely justified in supposing he was steeped in the same kind of atmosphere of mysticism as are present-day primitives. We can therefore presume he had the same belief in a multitude of supernatural powers ever-present all about him, and the same awareness of an enveloping *super-nature*, at once distinct yet also inseparable from *nature*; the same formal notion of a mythic period like *alchera*, *ungud*, *bugari*, and so on. Or in a nutshell, that he was equally responsive to the af-fective category of the supernatural.

"We have had the satisfaction", Cartailhac and the Abbé Breuil wrote in 1906 in the conclusion of their splendid study of the Altamira Cave, "of actually seeing, in a manner we might never have hoped to see, the thought and culture of our troglodytes brought back to real life."[56] We may perhaps venture to suggest that since the mentality of primitives is even better understood today, this restoration has now become still more complete and exact. Because it is no longer assumed that there is no difference between the ways in which primitive and modern minds func-tion, because we are able now to make allowance for the part played by *participation*, and since in general the mystical orienta-tion of the primitive intelligence can now be taken into account, we are in a position at last to understand much more effectively than formerly how that earlier mentality could find an ex-pressive outlet through myths and through various representa-tions made of them in visual or other creative forms. We are thus today much better situated than scholars have been in the past to reconstruct something, at least, of the mind of Paleolithic man. We can reasonably hope to recover the broad aspects of the world as he saw it; and along with the visible prospect, also the world of the powers unseen which was no less constantly present to his mind.

The reason — that is to say, one of the main reasons — for reciting the myths or representing them ceremonially or visually as in the Karadjeri rock-art, is in order to bring about what is called *increase* (Wirz in German uses the word *Vermehrung*) — in other words, to ensure that at the proper season, when animals of a certain species usually breed, or certain fruits, tubers, etc., mature in nature, the supply will be both plentiful and of good quality. (The natives show anxiety about both.) By carrying out the procedures we have described, they aspire to make certain of both. If, however, something in the situation is unpropitious — if, for example, the ceremony is carried out at an improper place or an unsuitable time — it can be expected that the animal in question will appear in fewer numbers than usual, and will be small and sickly; or there may simply not be any at all. The well-being, indeed the whole fate of the tribes, is thus bound up very intimately indeed with the "sacred sites". If these last are desecrated by white men, or cut off from the blacks by any means, the evil is irremediable. Nothing remains for the tribes but to vanish from the land.

The continuity and abundance of the natural species thus do not depend to any dominating extent on factors we would consider to be the crucial ones. The natives do not regard as matters of first importance such considerations as the condition of the land, the number or noxiousness of predators, or even the biological mating of the females or the healthy development of the offspring. It is not that they do not know about these things; for the most part they are well aware of them. But they do not look on them as matters of strict necessity, they are not in themselves adequate causes. As always, they deem the real causes of things to lie elsewhere, in a quarter where what we think of as the proper succession of cause and effect in nature does not apply. The Aranda and Loritja, for example, maintain that before a new human generation can appear it is necessary that spirit-beings (Strehlow calls them *ratapa*) must first of all find their way into the bodies of women. It is not doubted that these spirits will have lived before, possibly a number of times; they will have been waiting in the spirit-place of the totem for an opportunity to return to human life (to be "reincarnated", as Spencer and Gillen express it). Each one of them finds its way into the body of a woman of the correct totem.[57] Pregnancy then follows and develops, and finally the child is born. The physical fecundation of the woman is a necessary condition for pregnancy, but is not the actual cause.

In animals, reproduction is the same process as it is in man; nor do animals, any more than men, when they die, cease utterly to exist. They too continue their existence in some kind of spirit form. After an interval, which may be short or long, they once again return to the bodies of females whose offspring they will become. This is why it is an almost universal belief among primitives that no matter how ruthlessly a species is hunted, it can never become extinct. Some Eskimos even believe a seal may develop an affection for a particular hunter and come back time after time to be killed by him.

For reasons like these also it will follow that various physical and physiological conditions which, to our way of thinking, are the main indispensable factors that the normal progress of any young animal must depend upon, are not considered to be sufficient for the purpose − the suckling of the young by their mothers, their introduction to proper foods after that stage, factors of suitable temperature, and so on. The true cause of growth, as of "incarnation", is mystical. Indeed instances are known − in exceptional circumstances, certainly − in which adult maturity has been attained in a matter of mere days, or hours, even moments. In the Marind myth of the coconut, the next day after a palm first appears it bears nuts, which are ripe immediately.[58] Many myths and legends talk of prodigious rates of growth in the childhood of certain heroes. They are no sooner born than they can talk, walk and fashion weapons for themselves. In a few days they have shot up to a man's full height and strength. There is a Basuto story about a woman, the sole survivor of a massacre, who gives birth to a boy-child in a cattle shed. "She laid him down on the ground and left him for a moment or two, while she looked for something to make a bed for him. When she came back she found a grown man sitting there, with two or three spears in his hand and a string of divining-bones (*ditaola*) round his neck. She said, 'Hallo, man! Where is my child?' and he answered, "It is I, Mother!' Then he asked what had become of the people, and the cattle, and the dogs, and she told him."[59]

For the primitive mind there is nothing here that is beyond belief. Miraculous, even instantaneous growth, is perfectly easily accounted for. The prodigious child demonstrates, merely by what happens, that he possesses a magical power strong enough to transform him in a trice to a fully grown man. The case is most unusual, but not impossible: it is merely an extreme instance. The growing process which in all common cases appears so slow and gradual is not any the less, for that, a product of mystical forces. Their effects are weaker, obviously, than in the case of the Basuto hero, but they are still of the same kind. Speeding up the operation does not change its nature. Miraculous, as compared to routine, progress is merely the same thing raised to a superlative power. And therefore it is not just because they breathe and eat and drink that the human baby and the young animal grow little by little to adult stature. The first and most necessary condition for that to happen is that the supernatural powers must be at work both in them and all about them. That is the reason for all the charms and spells and nonsense rhymes one hears everywhere, meant to promote the health and growth of children or animals. It is also the reason for the wild abundance of old wives' tricks and gabble that pass in so many places for rural magic.

The Australian Aborigines, entirely dependent on hunting and gathering for their subsistence, and being without any tillage of the soil at all, apparently recognize no other way to assure themselves of the production and growth of the various species of animals or plants which make up their food supply, except through the regular repetition of the myths, the proper performance of the totemic ceremonial rituals, or the retouching of rock paintings. If we are to comprehend the sense in which they conceive these procedures to be effectual, it may be of some help to approach the question by way of a comparison with other primitives who, by contrast, do practise some agricultural arts: for example the Kiwai Papuans, or the Tami, Bukaua or the Kai and some others, in what was formerly German New Guinea: for these are active cultivators.

In almost all cases their methods consist in forms of sympathetic magic. At Kiwai Island, for example, they find a variety of ways to touch the plantation grounds and the young plants with spermatic juices, taken from the genital organs of women, in a notion that its fertilizing effect will be transferred to the plants.[60] Another Papuan practice is, at planting time, to bury in the soil large stones shaped like tubers: these, which are carefully lifted and stored after each harvest, are supposed to act by suggestion upon the young yams to persuade them to emulate their bulk and weight. The expression used by Landtman in explaining this is a vivid one: the natives, he says, plant the stones in the earth because they believe they will *teach* the yams or taro to swell.[61] Here "teach" has two meanings: it signifies at the same time to provide an encouraging example, and to exert a mystical force which obliges the plant to obey instruction. That is to say, psychologically there is cajolery; but there is also peremptory compulsion. Or more to the point, it is not really either the one or the other, but a blend of the two. It is a property of primitive minds that they do not clearly distinguish between constraint and cajolery, although in our own case, we might try and yet never succeed in confusing the two. The presence of the stones in the earth has the effect of conditioning the yam tubers to accept the stones as models for emulation. How is this to be explained? It is not to be explained; the natives see no need for enlightenment on such problems. Their trust in the magical power of the stones is strong enough to make all such questions superfluous. Matters proceed exactly as though the tubers were at one and the same time both wheedled and bullied into taking their cue from the stones, and growing until they reach the same size; while by the same token, the bulk of the magic models communicates itself to them automatically. For the native this is a simple matter of *participation*, while we rebel at its cool indifference to our habit of rational analysis. It disconcerts our ingrown need to know the proper reasons for everything.

Whenever the Australian Aborigines repeat or dramatize or act out the myths, or depict them in plastic or visual form, they too are practising a kind of sympathetic magic. The myth in which the half-human, half-animal kangaroo ancestor is portrayed as the creator of the kangaroo species, and is shown, accompanied by his novices, as instituting the formal rituals which his human totemic descendants still faithfully carry out today, itself becomes the *"teacher"* of the kangaroos, from which they *learn* to increase and multiply. It does for them what the stones do for the yam: it encourages them, it helps them and it conditions them to do exactly what they must do, and does so in precisely the same way.

Thus when they are represented vocally, dramatically or visually, the myths give an assurance that the ancestor will really be present, and by the same token also disposed to bring efficacious assistance. Thanks to this real presence his accomplishments in the mythic period will now be repeated in the present. If the ritual is carried out scrupulously, no essential detail being omitted, it can be expected that kangaroos will appear in ample numbers, and of a good size. The good example, if it may be so called, of what took place in the mythic age will then provide the species with a model or precedent, which they will follow to ensure that the present generation of their kind will not fall below the preceding ones. In short there is built up in the minds of the natives, whether they take part in the ceremonies or merely look on, a customary mood of great complexity into which a great many different elements enter, all of them however more or less clearly defined: their belief in the sacred supernatural character of both the myths themselves and the beings whose great deeds and creative achievements they celebrate; their confident trust in the power the myth holds when it is presented in performance or in visual or plastic form, and the power also of the mythical beings when they are invoked and respond with their true presence; the intense sensations they experience of being in communion and spiritual participation with the ancestors thus portrayed and felt to be present with the most vivid force of their belief; their certain faith in the effective outcome of the magical formula they are putting to work, and so on. There is not one of these components of their minds into which, directly or indirectly, the myths do not deeply enter. What more convincing proof could be found of the importance of the myths in the lives, whether secret and ceremonial, or open and public, of these primitive tribesmen?

Chapter V

Participation-Imitation in the Myths

It is the broad belief of the Australian and New Guinea Tribes we have been considering that the increase and fertility rituals must be performed or the tribes will not survive. These ceremonies, in fact, reproduce – that is, *imitate* – those performed by the mythic ancestor (in the case of the Marind-anim, by the *Dema*). He performed it in the presence of the novices at the same time as he "created" the natural species with whose origin the myth deals. The power of the ceremony arises from this imitation. Wirz expresses this effectively. "The coconut palm, as the myth teaches, was brought into existence in consequence of the *mayo* ceremony. Hence the *mayo* ceremony brings fruitfulness to the palms. For this reason, were this ceremony to be omitted it would anger the *Dema* and the palms and other fruiting trees would bear no fruit, and men would become ill and die."[1] There is another passage in which he refers in one breath to the origin and the function of the ceremonies. "It is likely, speaking very generally, that all increase rituals derive their existence from the myths. The *Dema*, when they instituted their erotic rites, created all the useful plants, and it follows as a consequence that it must be possible, even now, though perhaps in a less potent way than formerly, to increase their productivity by performing similar ceremonies." The sexual orgies, clearly, which form an important element in the Marind rituals (as also in the *horiomu* rite at Kiwai Island), are necessary not only for reasons of sympathetic magic in order to coax the plants to become more productive, but because the Marind, by imitating the *Dema*, in some way share or participate in their creative power. True, they do not actually create the plants themselves. But they do, by means of this ritual activity, make it possible for them to grow naturally and reach their normal development.[2]

It is difficult – and better, perhaps, not to succeed too well! – to visualize precisely what such a *participation* entails. But at any rate it seems that in the minds of the Marind-anim present at any such rite, the participation that is desired is effected basically through imitation. The *Dema* in the course of their erotic orgies in the mythic time were able to create various plants and animals. When modern man imitates these particular sexual extravagances he thereby participates in the powers of the *Dema* and so assists the fertility of the species.

Comparable beliefs are also found in other parts of New Guinea. For example among the Elema, in the Gulf of Papua, F.E. Williams has drawn attention to the important part played by the myths in most forms of magic, as well as in the imitative practices they lead to. "The myths of the Elema", he informs us, "are numerous and longwinded. The greater part of each is public; but nearly all of them, I think, contain esoteric passages which have a magical value. These in open narration are always omitted."[3] Further,

> . . . the myths are respectively associated in a broad sense with some one or other of the ten totemic classes of the Elema . . . And they tell of the exploits and particularly the wide travels of various individuals in some sense belonging to the clans. Not a few of the myths deal with long voyages with a successful issue, and thus they provide examples for the modern voyagers [who will thus also arrive happily at the desired haven, since they will be imitating what, according to the myths, was done by the ancestors]. The myths provide magic not only for *bevaia*, but for all sorts of other undertakings, whether of love, or war, or rain-making, or fishing or whatever else. The magician must know the relevant parts of the appropriate myths . . .[4]

A series of examples follows to illustrate this function of the myths. After an account of a myth describing the voyage of Evarapu to Lavau, Williams goes on to explain that the myth lays down "precedents" applying to different stages of the building of canoes, with the associated sexual prohibitions, and so on. These precepts decreed by the mythic ancestors are peremptory; it is absolutely requisite to conform. To follow established precedent, that is to *imitate* the ancestors, is the only way to obtain their favour and at the same time participate in their power.[5]

The myth of Aori and Iviri follows:

> The *bevaia haera* who told me this story made it quite plain that when he set forth in his *bevaia*, which was named *Heava*, he was impersonating Aori himself. He wears the costume which Aori is

supposed to have worn, with a blackened face (and in a way prematurely) the same kind of *love* in his hair which Aori plucked from Iviri's head. As he boards the *bevaia* he thinks, as he puts it, to himself, "I want to pluck the *love* from Iviri's head". He dances on the platform and extends his arms like Aori's wings.[6]

This is a re-enactment of the myth much in the manner of the ceremonies described by Spencer and Gillen, Strehlow, Landtman, Wirz and others. Through this dramatic representation the *bevaia*-man is transformed, for the time being, into the mythic hero whose dress and ornaments he is wearing, whose headdress he has put on, and whose gestures he mimes. By imitating him in this fashion he enters into so intimate a participation with him that he no longer makes any personal distinction: he *is* Aori. The identification is all the more complete and effective because he also bears the name of the hero — the name itself is secret and potent, like the myth.

Everything depends, therefore, as Williams realizes, not so much on the complaisance of the mythic ancestor as on being in possession of the myth: on possessing the name (in which the potency resides), and on performing an imitation of the hero and his actions which is as exact and perfect as possible.

> When a man thus employs a name to help him in his purpose we might at first sight be inclined to think he was actually calling on the bearer of the name for help. I am not at present prepared to state that such an idea is entirely absent from Elema culture, but it does not represent the construction which the magician himself here places upon his action. As a number of definite cases show, he is rather applying the mythical names to himself or to this or that feature of his undertaking. In short, he is himself impersonating a mythical character, or identifying some feature of his undertaking with a corresponding feature of a mythical undertaking which reached a successful close. He apparently feels more confident of success himself by pretending to be the great man of the long-ago, and by making his present undertaking, so to speak, a reproduction of the great man's exploit. Such pretence or impersonation is helped out by the details of costume and action and by such extras as that of the model bird fixed in the rigging.
>
> The same general method, and with it the same explanation, is applicable to other phases of magic as well as to *bevaia maho*. When a man goes a-wooing, for instance, he will, if he knows it, employ the name of *Marai*, a highly secret synonym for the moon (*papare*). In the myth the moon, as a person, is peculiarly attractive to women; and for the time being the lover actually impersonates him. He does not whisper to himself, "Marai, help me to

win this woman", but he thinks without even whispering, "I am
Marai himself, and I will get her".

> A man who knew this *maho charo* (the reference is to a fishing
> myth) told me that when he went fish shooting he pretended to be
> Kivavia himself, and as he took down his arrows he addressed
> them or thought of them as Berari Kapip and Kiwai Kapipi
> (characters in the myth).[7]

He did not beg the mythic hero for favour and assistance; he
assumed identity with him.

These Australian and New Guinea tribes are not the only ones
who are accustomed to look to their mythic ancestors for
precedents like these, models whose imitation will bring success
to any present undertaking. The same kind of assimilation of
mythic precedent to present action is also found in other places,
for example, as far away as in California, among the Karuk.[8]
There are many ways in which Karuk tradition and mythology
differ from what we have been observing, but we do find among
them half-human and half-animal (or vegetable) ancestors who
have ended by becoming incorporated (one could hardly say in-
carnated) in outstanding features and landmarks of the landscape. They also function as models and precedents, in certain
instances, for what modern men must do.

> Everything that the Karuk did was enacted because the Ikx-
> areyavs were believed to have set the example in story times. The
> Ikxareyavs were the people who were in America before the In-
> dians came. Modern Karuks, in a quandary how to render the
> word, volunteered such translations as "the princes", "the chiefs",
> "the angels". These Ikxareyavs were the old-time people, who
> turned into animals, plants, rocks, mountains, plots of ground,
> and even parts of the house, dances and abstractions, when the
> Karuk came to the country, remaining with the Karuk only long
> enough to state and start all customs, telling them in every in-
> stance, "Human will do the same". These doings and sayings are
> still related and quoted in the medicine formulae of the Karuk . . .
> The period of the Ikxareyavs is supposed to lie only a few genera-
> tions back.

As an example, when the Karuk sow tobacco, they speak to the
seed, thus: "Where art thou, Ikxareyav of the Middle of the
World? Thou wast wont to sow thy tobacco. I know about thee.
'Growing mayst thou grow to the sky', thou saidest it. 'Human
will sow with these words, if he knows about me.' " If the crop is
to be successful, the Karuk – like the Marind or the Elema –

must go along with the relevant myth and must imitate what was done by the ancestor or hero, and pronounce the same spells.[9]

In primitive societies the potency of *imitation* is revealed in more situations than simply those in which man exerts himself to some end that is consciously desired. Quite outside the scope of any human advantage, whatever happens or exists in the world about us – the moral as well as the physical qualities of the creatures which inhabit it, even of those elements we call inanimate, such as stones, rocks, rivers, the sea, etc., with their peculiar tendencies and dispositions, their habitual ways of doing whatever they do – everything in short, which makes up our daily experience of life, is and must be what it is, because of its participatory involvement in the origins of life, in the events and beings of the mythic beginnings of time.

This participatory involvement is accomplished through imitation. It finds expression and proceeds to action through similarities and correspondences. Resemblance thus becomes for the primitive mind a kind of broadly guiding principle to explain the character and origin of everything material and spiritual that exists about it. Since such minds never reflect on their own processes, and still less, if that is possible, on the conditioning factors that activate them, they are fully convinced that if everything – beings, objects and facts – is what it appears to be, that is because there existed in the mythic age models and precedents for them, and they were all created in the image of these. How far the functioning of the myths extends in all this is plain to see. It not only teaches man how to succeed in his enterprises by imitating the ancestors and heroes; it reveals the reason for the existence of all the actualities of nature. For these also imitate the primordial facts from which they draw their essential being. Mythology demonstrates the ways in which they participate in those origins.

The tribal elders, therefore, who are the guardians in trust of the sacred myths, and to whom the deep meaning of them has been revealed, know also that all beings and objects in the present world are modern copies – reproductions – of those which existed formerly in the mythic age, and in many cases have continued to exist from the beginning. Take for example the Marind myth of the *Dema* Mahu. Like the other *Dema*, Mahu possessed remarkable powers. He was at the same time man and dog. He was the ancestor of the human clan which bears his name (the Mahu-ze) and also created the race of dogs. They were *dema* dogs to begin with − that is to say, they possessed faculties which dogs today no longer have. Later other dogs descended from them, and these became gradually more like the animals we know. Now the natural qualities and shortcomings of present-day dogs, their physical build, their appetite, their temper which is sometimes mild, sometimes savage, and so on, all repeat and re-express, though with diminished force, the characteristics of those *dema* dogs which themselves imitated the original ancestor the *Dema* Mahu. Exactly the same thing might be said of his human descendants, the Mahu-ze. If from time to time these should display propensities and habits which call to mind those of canines, it is simply because their nature, like that of the canines themselves, imitates the character of the ancestor who is common to both. In tribes like this the whole idea of clan totemism rests upon this participation.

A myth which turns up frequently in this part of the world − and is in any case quite widely distributed elsewhere − explains the origin of death as a consequence of disobedience, or a failure in compliance, or through some weakness. For example, an enfeebled grandmother gives up the attempt to change her skin because her grandchild objects to taking trouble. (As everyone knows, there is scarcely any distinction between the body and the skin. To put on a new skin, as snakes and certain crustaceans do, is equivalent to acquiring a new body − a means to become young again and so escape death indefinitely.) Here is a version of this myth:

> A good old woman had died, but by her own effort she dug her way out of the grave into which she had been put. Thereupon she said to a child: "Bring me a little fire, so that I can warm myself." But the child refused to go; he would not listen to the old woman, who pleaded with him in vain. So the old woman died a second time. Had that child taken notice of her we would not now suffer final death. Even though we should be buried, we would dig ourselves out by our own efforts and reawaken to life, because we should have warmed ourselves at the fire. But as it is, since that child paid no attention to the old woman, we do not reawaken to life but die once for all.[10]

What is the meaning of this story for the native? There seems not to be much doubt. Final death came into the world because of disobedience − a possible reading, certainly. And yet they will not interpret it in just the way we do. As they see it, because everything that happens nowadays has an imitative correspondence with what took place in the mythic age, if the old woman had not, through the fault of the disobliging child, died irrecoverably, we too should today have been spared definitive death. The true cause of death today is therefore not the disobedience of the child (though certainly that was how the old woman came to hers), but rather the *participation-correspondence* between present and past, by the agency of which our modern way of dying imitates the death of that old woman in the mythic age. The meaning of the myth derives from this participation phenomenon alone, and the Melanesian intellect demands no explanation beyond this.

There is a Marind myth in which Amaremb, a *Dema*, gives to a snake a "medicine" which causes him to change his skin. "Since that day snakes no longer die. When they are ill, or feel poorly, all they do is cast their skins. If Amaremb had been able to give some of that same medicine to Yawi, Yawi would not have died; and thus men would not die either. They would simply change skins like the snakes."[11] So, for lack of the correct medicine, Yawi died. As this event took place in the mythic age, the consequence follows that man today is subject to death. If, on the other hand, Yawi had been saved by means of the medicine which saved the snakes, requiring them merely to change skins, man too would now escape death. Such is the power of participation-imitation to regulate what happens in the present through its parallels with events of the mythic period.

In the Gazelle Peninsula, Meier records a series of tales, the principal characters of which are two brothers, To Kabinana and To Karvuvu. The one is sensible and thoughtful, the other stupid and clumsy.

> To Karvuvu was roasting breadfruit. To Kabinana as he was walking by stopped and said to him, "Are you cooking something?" "Yes, I am." "Why are you keeping it dark from our mother? Take her a half-breadfruit!" To Karvuvu went to their mother and took her the food. But she had become a young girl once again, for she had cast her skin. To Karvuvu asked her: "Where is my mother, then?" "I am she." He answered, "But you can't be my mother!" "No (= you are deceived), I am she." "But you don't look like her." "No (= you are deceived), I have cast my skin." Thereupon he continued obstinately to weep for his mother's former skin, for now he no longer recognized her. "I don't want to know about your changed look, whatever it may be. Where did you leave your own proper skin?" She answered, "I threw it in the river and the stream carried it off." To Karvuvu went on grieving. "I can't bear this new skin of

yours, I will go and look for your old one." With that he got up and went away. He looked and looked and in the end he found it caught up in a bush; the water had carried it there. He picked it up and went back with it. He put it on his mother again. To Kabinana came and found them both at home. He asked him, "Why did you put our mother's old skin on again, that she had cast off? You are a numskull for sure! Now all our descendants will die eternally, while all great and little snakes will merely cast their skins!"[12]

The correct interpretation of the myth is underlined by To Kabinana's reproaches. To Karvuvu is responsible through his stupidity for what happens to his mother, and hence indirectly for what happens to all mankind. But if his mother's death is the eventuality awaiting all of man's descendants, that is so because what took place in the mythic world determines all related events that happen in the world today.

The reproach To Kabinana hurls at To Karvuvu turns up like a refrain at the end of many stories. If a man today is guilty of improper relations with his sister-in-law, it is in consequence of the fact that To Karvuvu pigheadedly insisted on marrying his own brother's wife. To Kabinana spoke in disapproval of this marriage, saying, "What you are doing is only bringing corruption on all our future descendants." In other words, when this misdemeanour comes to light in modern times it merely repeats and imitates the wilful fault of To Karvuvu.[13] Every time he is guilty of some fresh folly or iniquity his brother never fails to exclaim, "Oh, what an idiot! You are bringing all our posterity to disgrace!" For example, To Karvuvu made a carving of a shark: "Oh, what shocking folly! You are bringing all our mortal race to misery. This fish will swallow all the others in the sea, and then will attack mankind!" And again: "Did you see that? That bird you have made is a thief. You are bringing despair upon all our mortal descendants. They will become thieves too!" In another situation: "You really are the limit! Now we shall all starve, and our posterity will starve too!" Finally, "You do nothing but bring wretchedness upon our children and our children's children!"[14]

In several North American Indian tribes similar beliefs have been noted. As in Australia and New Guinea, repeating the myth will exert a beneficial influence and assist the success of an undertaking. G.A. Dorsey writes,

Certain Skidi tales are called Coyote tales, not because they are about Coyote, but because he was "full of wild conceits and . . . very tricky" . . . and rarely ever finally vanquished. Therefore, when, for example, a story is told in which Coyote, or some culture-hero overcomes his enemy, the teller thereby indicates his desire that he also may be equally successful in some venture which he had in hand.

The reason the Indians tell about Coyote is that he is lucky. Coyote wanders over the prairies, not knowing where to get anything to eat; but all at once he comes to a dead buffalo, or some other carcass . . . Sometimes he is attacked by many buffalo and gets away from them . . . For the above reasons the Indians believe that by talking about the doings of the Coyote, the tribe as a whole may be given the same luck that Coyote had in wandering over the prairie.[15]

In a similar way errors committed or feelings experienced in modern times are lined up with *precedents* from the mythic period. A boy stole some corn from his sister. She noticed what was missing and begged her brother to own up. At first he refused. Then in the end the boy said, "Yes, I have eaten them" . . . "Since that time the Indian children are in the habit of stealing other people's corn, and when they are caught they will lie about it." Another story speaks of a young woman who was disturbed by the absence of her brother. "All this time the sister was very anxious about her brother. She thought about him, nor would she eat anything. She was sick for him, and she also had lost her senses, and was dying from longing for her brother." In the end he returns, and when he arrives finds his sister in bed, ill. "He went up to her and said, 'My sister.' And she said, "That is the way my brother used to come to me. Now it is all a dream. I cannot tell what has become of my brother.' But the boy said, 'Sister, I am here.' The boy held his sister." She then began to get better and soon quite recovered.[16] "So they were happy, and ever since that time people, if they have brothers or sisters, or if they like any one who is absent, get sick through longing for them." No doubt without such a mythical model people today can still experience anxiety in that situation. But if their heart-sickness makes them gravely ill, there lies the mythic precedent of a sister who almost died of tenderness for a brother who went away and seemed never to be coming back.

A last example, in a myth of the Nez-Percés. Coyote's wife left him. That night she came nowhere near him; and then she went off with somebody else. "Coyote felt very badly over this and said, 'Well, I feel pretty badly. Still the thing cannot be helped. Others will feel as badly as I when they go to the Buffalo country and their wives run away from them.' Sadly he went back to his former home, and since that time wives have often run away from their husbands in the Buffalo country."[17] The myth does not pretend to excuse them or to disregard the moral responsibility of Coyote's wife. But the *precedent* is hers; she created it. Without her this delinquent propensity would never have arisen in wives. The myth says distinctly that no such lapse had ever occurred before the instance related.

Very many "explanatory" (etiological) myths exist which fall back on one precedent or another to account for some peculiar feature in an animal or plant, it might be the colour of a bird's plumage, the shape of its beak, the length of its tail or something of the kind. Here is a typical example. The crow and another bird had agreed to tattoo each other. The crow was the first to carry out his part of the contract. The other bird, finding the job long and tedious, upended the paint pot once and for all over the crow's wings. Since that time crows have been black all over.[18] In the Andaman Islands Radcliffe-Brown collected some similar legends, for example this from the Akbar Bale tribe: "The people had no fire. *Dim-dori* (a fish) went and fetched fire from *Jereg-l'ar-mugu* (the place of departed spirits). He came back and threw the fire at the people and burnt them, and marked them all. The people ran into the sea and became fishes. *Dim-dori* went to shoot them with his bow and arrows, and he also became a fish . . ." Radcliffe-Brown follows this with another tale of the same nature and adds:

> The story serves as an explanation of the markings on birds and fishes, these being where the ancestor who became the species was burnt by the fire. Thus the legend is of the kind that is often called etiological. The common method of explaining such legends is to say that they are crude attempts on the part of primitive man to explain the natural phenomena with which they deal, in this case the bright colours of birds and fishes. Such an explanation cannot be regarded as adequate. Why should the Andaman Islanders want to explain the markings of animals? Why should they explain them in the form of a legend, and why should the legend take this particular form?[19]

Radcliffe-Brown's questions invite an answer, but before we attempt one we should look into another problem on which those myths depend. Does the word *explain* designate the same kind of mental operation when it is applied to ourselves, to the Andamanese, the Papuans and the Australian Aborigines? As we regard them, the phenomena of nature appear to us to be bound by certain conditions which are themselves phenomenal. Some are more, some less, easily recognizable. But it will never occur to us to doubt that they exist, even though we may not always be in a position to describe them in detail (unless in the field of microphysics). To explain a fact, therefore, is somehow to assign it to an already existing frame of reference which we understand, and then to show what its place there is.

Now as we realize, the primitive mind makes very little use of such categorical analyses, indispensable to our way of thinking. Primitive thinking is scarcely at all conceptual. It therefore does not embrace our ideas of the laws of nature or of established specific forms (except that in practice they always know one animal or plant from another; but that is hardly abstract thinking). Even though primitives may grasp and make use of what they see of the casual connections between things, this is not the same as seeing the schematic logic of them. Thus, unless the circumstances are exceptional, the kind of explanation we look for, and can understand, has no interest for them. That is why we scarcely ever observe them, not even the most active-minded of them, to make any systematic study of phenomenal cause and effect. While it frequently happens that they know a great deal about the creatures inhabiting their region, they are not philosophers of the wildwood as Tylor believed, still less are they instinctive natural scientists or physicists. As long as the events of nature follow their expected courses they see no need to dissect them. Why should they? Their concern is only and simply to derive from nature the best possible practical advantage.

But let something unexpected and extraordinary appear, and at once the native pricks up his ears. He is on tenterhooks; now he does require an explanation. Moreover he knows in advance in what direction to look for it. What is unexpected and extraordinary never comes about merely by accident; nor will it have any connection with regular secondary causes. On the contrary it is in itself simple evidence of the fact that some supernatural agency is at work. His thoughts are suddenly struck with a complex of highly emotional possibilities as the affective category of the supernatural comes into play. In this situation, explanation does not connote the satisfaction of a merely intellectual curiosity; it implies the acknowledgement of a mystical intervention. A supernatural force, though it may not be visible, is nevertheless present and active within the scheme of common cause and effect. The short and the long of it is that where we, thinking of the facts in the way we do, look to find our explanation always in terms of natural causes, the constitution of primitive minds enables them to look for theirs outside or above the usual limits.

When we speak of etiological myths, we are therefore using an expression that is both ambiguous and inconsistent. We confuse two kinds of explanation: one satisfies us, and the other the primitives. "Etiological" signifies "revealing the cause" (that is, as a rule, the cause that makes sense to us); but "myth" implies that we knew already that it had a supernatural source. To look towards mythology is *ipso facto* to turn away from phenomenal logic. If we wish to avoid that kind of contradiction, we might do well to cease attaching the epithet etiological to myths, or at least keep well in mind that the 'causes' they reveal are of a different order from those we associate with ordinary secondary causality.

Even as we make this point the second of Radcliffe-Brown's objections — "why should the Islanders explain the animal markings in the form of a legend?" — is already answered. This might seem a surprising reply if in fact an explanation after our own style had been what was looked for; but in such a case we should have to suppose the native wanted to find his answer within nature. The native's curiosity directs itself, however, to quite a different quarter. Since he already recognizes in the matter to be explained the presence and activity of supernatural powers, is there any other form he could possibly look to, to provide expression for the kind of explanation that will satisfy him, unless it were some kind of narrative — in effect, myth? For minds which have been shaped by a centuries-old tradition of intellectual criticism and scientific enquiry, all experience — in respect, that is, of all questions but what touches religion — is homogeneous and unequivocal. It gathers all the whole vast and vague body of factual data which, whether directly or indirectly, it lies within our power to grasp, check, and sometimes to measure. That, but no more. The total experience of primitives, incomparably weaker than that of the civilized in respect of all that concerns the phenomena of nature, would seem on the other hand to be very much richer in some other ways. It includes frequent access to the world of the supernatural, with which it makes contact through dreams, omens, prophecy, trances, shamanism, and through the kind of revelation which is constantly met with in the effects of strange and unexpected things. All these items of mystical experience have an inestimable value. The primitive intelligence prizes them at least as highly as we do science and philosophy. It devotes to them a degree of interest before which everything else pales into insignificance, and whose intensity, however sincerely we may try, we shall be quite unable to evaluate as primitives do. This form of knowledge, if such it may be called, takes up nothing at all from our broad schematic system of linked causality – we have just seen why. It finds its expression and is preserved in the repetition and representation of the myths and in traditional institutions, of which the impact is rather collective than systematic. Any value these things may have as explanation – and they do have some – is achieved by representing how the modern copy relates to the mythical model, how the repetition reproduces the precedent; in short, by invoking the spiritual phenomenon of imitation-participation.

These experiences of the world of supernatural powers appear in forms so diverse that it is difficult, without offering them violence, to reduce them to order. Order – or it might be more fitting to say, uniformity – is present, but simply as an emotional tone; as such it never varies and is never lost. The myths themselves vary in a range between the merely anecdotal (explaining the colouring of a fish or the shape of a bird's beak) and those which solemnly preserve the life-giving traditions of the mythic past, knowledge accessible only to the elders. Such myths cannot be recited or heard without arousing deep and powerful emotions. In either case the affective category of the supernatural comes into play and modern man experiences communion and participation with the ancients.

To recapitulate, we remember that the Marind-anim use the term *dema* in two ways. As an adjective it denotes something awe-inspiring and calls up the affective category of the supernatural. As a substantive (capitalized) it signifies a mythic ancestor. The *Dema* are theriomorphs who can transform themselves at will, and possess supernatural powers. It was they who in the mythic age created or engendered whatever exists today, men, animals, plants, rocks, implements, institutions. All this provided the matter out of which the myths emerged. Hence this distinction: the affective category of the supernatural on one hand, and the actual form and substance of the legends on the other, stand in the same close relationship one to the other, as do the general, non-specific sense of *dema* (adjective) and the specific individualized *Dema*. What the myths *explain*, therefore, is this relationship. The clearest light can no doubt be thrown on the myths if we regard them as objectifications of the elusive reality of supernatural truth.

To have done with this point, we may recall what was decided in our analysis of the expressions *ungud, wondjina, kugi* and others like them. When a native has told us that something (or some institution) is *ungud* or *kugi*, he has said all there is to say. Beyond that there is nothing further to be known. As primitives see it, the matter is now explained as fully and adequately as it possibly could be.

We, on the other hand, by holding so tenaciously (as do our experimental or empiric sciences) to the linked logic of cause and effect, only find that the rational sequence is blurred at both the top and the bottom. There is nothing particularly difficult about tracing the second cause of a second cause. But when a myth demonstrates how something now existing reproduces something which already existed in "the time before time began", and presents this as a true explanation of the present imitation-participation, what more is there to ask for? "Legend", R.F. Fortune observes, "validates magic".[20] That expresses it admirably. By putting modern people and events into line with precedents or models — "archetypes" — in the world of the supernatural, the myths achieve much more than merely determining a nexus of causal connections. They reveal a reason for them which we describe as metaphysical or transcendental. But naturally this reason is never expressed by them in any but concrete and objective terms, and in legendary form.

That such is the function, or one of the main functions, of a certain number of myths described as etiological, is shown by the following instance, observed by Captain Rattray among the Ashanti. He is speaking of the derivation of an Ashanti word (*abusua* = mother), in a proverb which translated runs: "Bent stick in the spirit grove, when your mother is dead that is the end of your family".

They derive it from *sua*, to imitate, the reason being given as follows. "There lived in former times a King of Adanse who had a 'linguist' named Abu. This Abu incurred the king's anger and was heavily fined. Now, at that time children used to inherit from their father. Abu asked his children to assist him to pay the fine imposed by the king, but they refused and all went off *to their mother's relatives*. But Abu's sister's children rendered him assistance to pay off his debts, and Abu, therefore, when he died left all his belongings to them. Other people copied him and willed their property to the sister's children." (*Abu-sua*, literally, copying Abu.) The above is a literal translation of the account given by a native.

Rattray continues, "This is an excellent example of an etiological myth. The Ashantis, who now notice that other nations trace descent through the father, have invented this myth to explain the fact that with them descent is traced through the mother, which now strikes them as curious.

It is amusing to notice that the inventor of this myth has not been able to entirely adapt his mental attitude even to the imaginary setting of his tale, for he quite naturally pictures the children, under the supposed former father-right, running off *to the mother's relatives*[21]

This is an etiological myth, says Captain Rattray — maybe, if we take "etiological" in the special sense just indicated. That is to say, it relates some present-day personality or thing to a precedent which it imitates. But speaking generally, we have no idea when, or how, such myths have sprung up. This generation has accepted them from the last without asking how they arose. In this particular instance reported by Rattray we are witnesses to a myth in process of formation. It is visibly contrived in all its parts — clumsily put together, what is more — for the sake of an invented explanation. Many another of the same sort, it is more than possible, arose when some custom observed from time immemorial came at last to be regarded as in some way discrepant and in need rectification.

Often, too, myths of the kind called etiological may be reflections of tribal institutions. Thus: a clan becomes committed to a special totemic relationship with animals of a certain species. All its members abstain from eating the animal, if not actually from hunting it. When they come across one that has died, they accord it funeral honours as though it were a near relation. In return they expect help and protection in case of need from the animals. This pattern occurs frequently in various places throughout the world, and from it develop a number of myths of very diverse character; for example, the two kinds which follow. Sometimes, as is usual with the Marind-anim and a good many other New Guinea tribes, and also in Australia, Africa and elsewhere, there is a human-animal ancestor common to both the animal species and the human group which takes it for its totem. In certain of these instances the ancestor is even said to have produced twins, one animal, the other human, from whom are descended respectively the animal species and the totemic

clan.[22] Instances also occur, as for example in a number of East
African tribes, of myths which relate how at a time of great
danger an animal came to the rescue of some ancestor or clan
chieftain and brought him to safety. Suppose him to be in flight
from enemies who are close behind and on the point of striking
him down: a helpful crocodile suddenly materializes, takes him
on his back, and lands him safe and sound on the other bank of
the river. Hence the high respect and regard which members of
that particular clan entertain for crocodiles.

Karl von den Steinen reports that most of the myths he collected among the Bakairi in Brazil were of this sort: "They seek
an explanation for some particular phenomenon. Its origin must
always be looked for in something which happened in the
remote past. And since there is no way to account for it but by
supposing something out of the ordinary must have occurred,
the idea was therefore bound to suggest itself that, in the past, a
time existed when the extraordinary was the rule . . ." This con-
venient thesis happily corresponds with the theory we ourselves
arrived at earlier when we remarked (chapter I, pp. 55, 60) that
nature in the mythic age was the same as supernature. Similarly
it corresponds with the no less challenging formula of Fortune
concerning "the time when natural history had not yet begun". It
is easy to see, von den Steinen remarks further, how such myths
came to exist. "Clearly the fact requiring explanation could not
be tacked on to the story. Quite the contrary, it was the story that
was tacked on to the fact."[23]

In this way it often happens that myths, even the most important ones, may come into being through back-projection of some
everyday fact of life (an institutional custom, the relationship
between a human group and an animal or vegetable species, an
outstanding feature of the landscape, or the like) into the remote
past – into the *Alchera*, or the age of the *Dema*; in other words,
into the world of the supernatural where "the extraordinary is
the rule". The myth takes these data as its point of departure but
transfigures them. In the process they emerge as *creations* of the
superhuman ancestors, the culture heroes or *Dema*. In this
altered form they come to be capable of inspiring a quasi-
religious awe[24] and to contain in themselves the basic substance
of their own explanation. In the example reported by Rattray the
precedent which is supposed to explain the custom in fact does
no more, literally, than make a copy of it and offer the copy as
though it were original and belonged to the heroic age. But need

we look far to find other people less primitive than these, ador-
ing gods made largely in their own image?

What renders this process of back-formation plausible and
prevents the mundane facts which are the foundation of legend
from becoming too apparent, what indeed imprints upon the
myth its sacred character and gives it in the end its effect of
mystical authority and potency, is the quality Wirz singles out
among the Marind-anim and which is called by them *dema*. It is
essentially the impression made by whatever is strange beyond
ordinary nature, a product of supernatural influences. It signifies
an uninterrupted continuity of communion with the world of unseen but immanent and indwelling powers; that is to say, with
the very beings whose exploits and adventures provide the
myths with their content. It is this mystical experience which is
the salient point. On it all the rest depend: the whole affective
category of the supernatural, and along with it the general
imitation-participation schema and consequently the myths
themselves.

> Legend in Dobu, while it refers to a historic past, does not refer
> to the past only . . . There is no sharp distinction between past and
> present in Dobuan legend. We have seen how . . . a span of about
> four generations only divides the Dobuan from the time of the first
> ancestors, the time of legend . . . this gulf is not stressed, so that a
> continuity of legend-like performances is still expected and firmly
> believed in, read into the facts of nature.[25]

This is probably the point at which we find the greatest difficulty
when we try sincerely to put ourselves into the mental attitude
of a primitive. With the best will in the world we can never suc-
cessfully persuade ourselves the myths are really "true". That
they fulfil an essential function in the social life of the natives,
that the ceremonies, rituals and carved or painted images which
are all kept up with such assiduous care express a sacred reality
which articulates itself by means of the vehicles they provide, is
something we are able to comprehend. But it would be hopeless
for us ever to attempt to repress our inclination to classify the
myths, even the most barely primitive of them, as anything but
folklore — by which we mean legends, fables and fairy-tales; formulas, in effect, in which, we are convinced, the element of fantastic make-believe plays the dominating part.

Nevertheless if it ever did become possible for us to disabuse
ourselves of the fixed ideas implanted by our long familiarity
with the classical habit of thought, we should find ourselves

obliged to take an altogether opposite stand. We should then have to give over explaining the myths in the reflected light of folklore — as simply mere current inventions, tales or fictions of the folk — and instead look closely into the myths themselves (particularly the more primitive ones, which would hold the key) to discover the original import of the related tales. What we have already seen makes it clear that the persons and events in myths are believed in as real. They have a reality which is both transcendent and imperishable. When we were exploring the sense of the word *dema*, for example, it became quite apparent that the Marind-anim draw no distinction between the mythic and the supernatural worlds — supernature is for them even more real than nature. But even if we do recognize, as an undeniable fact, that the myths are *true* in the primitives' eyes, we still remain virtual strangers to the intensity of their conviction. They possess an insight which is unique and peculiar to themselves, but for us its quality seems no more than a dead letter. A few poets and artists may have some inkling of it, but they are exceptions.

There are certain aspects of the experience, however, which may in some sense be accessible to us. Perhaps if we make a short digression here it may bring us a little closer to an understanding of what is "real" in the mythic world. For instance, hardly any primitive society exists which does not include some more or less considerable number of individuals who differ from the rest through their ability to make contact with the unseen world. Medicine men, shamans, sorcerers, magicians, witch doctors, call them what you will, possess certain powers which common men have lost. As we realize, these persons are of various types and characters, some capable of causing harm, others of doing good. But these differences are not for the moment what concerns us. What is of interest at present is the special gift all of them, more or less equally, possess, of being able to relate directly to the supernatural powers. I will not here retrace what I have attempted to say elsewhere about sorcery;[26] it will be sufficient to point to the Australians and Papuans, and show what elements of the regard in which they hold their medicine-men are derived from their image of the unseen and supernatural powers — the mythic world.

Chapter XVI ("Various Forms of Magic") of the important work by Spencer and Gillen, *The Native Tribes of Central Australia*, describes in some detail how the Arunta medicine men are "made". They are of three kinds. The first are those who are "made" or initiated by the *Iruntarinia* ("spirit individuals, each one of whom is in reality the double of one of the ancestors of the tribe who lived in the Alcheringa"). These men undergo a series of ordeals, whose effect is to bring them into contact with the supernatural and mythical powers, and hence to confer on them powers which will enable them to carry out what we may speak of as the responsibilities of their profession. "In many Australian tribes," the authors add later, "the equivalent of the medicine man among the Arunta is the one individual who can hold intercourse with the spirits." But as this is now something well understood, there is no need to discuss it at length.[27]

The Marind-anim have beliefs concerning their medicine men (*mesav*) similar to those of the Australians: for example, their relationship with the *Dema*. If it is necessary to portray the *Dema* in some action, as in rituals and ceremonies,

> . . . the senior *mesav* lay down the lines. They give assurance that they are themselves in close touch with the *Dema* and are able to see them. They direct the performers how to prepare their masks and ornaments. An old *mesav* who was advising about the immensely complicated ornamentation required for the costume of a Coconut-palm *Dema*, and was in charge of the preparations generally, told me that one day in the bush he had been about to drink the liquid from a coconut when the Coconut *Dema* himself appeared to him. Just at the instant when, having opened the nut, he was lifting it to his lips, the *Dema* rushed out of it and leapt into his mouth.

In another place Wirz remarks,

> The *mesav* possesses the ability actually to perceive the *Dema*, who are invisible to everybody else, and enter into discussion with them. It may be that he sees them with his actual eyes and really converses with them; or possibly the *Dema* visit him in dreams. The *mesav* may even be able at will to become possessed by them. But this last is not within the capacity of every *mesav*; certain special preparations would seem to be necessary if he is to possess the art of putting himself into such a state of trance. – In this way the *mesav* act as direct intermediaries between the *Dema* and men. If there is something you want to know from the *Dema*, it is to the *mesav* you must apply.[28]

While the Marind recognize no personal divinity or any kind of systematic religious cult, the *mesav* occupy a position with them, and have a function much like priests, since they alone in the tribe can make contact with the unseen world, and they alone have the authority to teach the performers what they must do at rituals and ceremonies. In such performances the actors are expected to represent the unseen beings, and by doing so provide assurance that the unseen are really there. Though belief in the extraordinary powers of the *mesav* is not the same thing as belief in the myths, obviously the two are closely related. One could not exist without the other. No doubt there are also other heads under which the activities of the *mesav* might be examined. But in any case, as Wirz remarks, the *Dema* are everywhere; and just as in the mythic age they brought all things into existence – they were the creators – so there is scarcely any operation of magic today which does not, in the last analysis, owe its effectiveness to them; and in which, by the same token, myth does not have a determining part.

On the other hand the *mesav*, like the medicine men, the sorcerers or wise men in so many other tribes, presumably in virtue of the ordeals they have undergone in their novitiate and at the time of their initiation, all participate in the identity of the ancestors, culture heroes or *Dema*. Those mythic beings possessed, among other powers, two distinguishing faculties. They could at any instant take whatever form they chose for themselves, and they could also, in the world about them, effect whatever metamorphosis they desired upon the phenomena, without paying the slightest regard to the linkage of natural causes. Now these same two faculties still remain to a certain degree open to medicine men, sorcerers and wise men, not only in Australia and New Guinea, but in other parts of the world also. In all regions it is believed that such individuals have the ability to appear in any animal form they think fit (as crocodiles, lions, sharks, birds, etc.), whether simply to suit their own purposes or to carry out some plan of revenge with which they have been charged. Thus in Guiana the tiger *Kanaima* is never a real tiger; he is always a sorcerer transformed. In a number of different southern African regions no lion which attacks a man is ever thought to be an actual lion. Instances in this category are innumerable.

Sorcerers can also, if they wish, make themselves invisible. They have the skill, at need, to rise up in the air, fly to the moon, plunge to the bottom of the sea, or take themselves off to the region of the dead, then come back again. Nothing is easier for them than to bring about the death of an enemy who dwells at a distance and is altogether unsuspecting; all they need do is train all the battery of their magic on him; even a concentrated act of the will will suffice. Undoubtedly not all possess all these abilities; nor do all possess them in the same degree. But all are believed to be more or less well furnished with the talents, even though nobody is quite sure how far they extend. Uncertainty serves to enhance the terror the magic-men are able to inspire. However, all sorcerers are credited with some share, smaller or larger (it may be very small) of the two fundamental powers possessed by those multivalent and multifarious spirits of the mythic beginnings of the world, the *Dema*.

So it follows that two associated aspects of belief lend each other mutual support. The Australian Aborigine or the Papuan actually sees the medicine-men and the sorcerers of his tribe accomplish what he takes to be miracles; he will therefore feel no temptation to doubt the myths or think them merely fancies. For nothing that happens in them is any harder to believe than what he has actually seen happen. And conversely, since he has been accustomed since childhood to hearing stories which, by our lights, are completely improbable and unconvincing, but by him have always been accepted as true, he will not dream of questioning the powers the medicine-men and sorcerers claim to possess; for are they not comparable with those of the heroes and the *Dema*? Their minds thus float in an atmosphere of ready belief wholly directed towards the supernatural, and for that reason unquestioned. This is by no means to assert that all such minds are formed upon a strictly uniform pattern of intelligence, that all obey exactly the same tendencies, and all react equally to the same needs. A natural diversity of temperaments no doubt appears in the various communities, exactly as in ours. Among them there must arise, at least from time to time, individuals who have a disposition to be critical, to resist conformity, even to profess downright disbelief. But in general such tendencies, when they are present, are soon brought under control. To doubt what all the rest believe is at best a policy of some imprudence; to let it be seen, or openly to say so, is even more dangerous.

So long, therefore, as disturbing influences do not intervene, succeeding generations continue piously to hand down unchanged all traditional beliefs concerning, on the one hand, the mythic world, and on the other, the extraordinary powers of the medicine men and the sorcerers. It amounts to one and the same act of faith. All these beliefs have their common root in the idea primitives hold of nature, supernature, and all that relates to both. Perhaps we may agree that here we have one of the reasons supporting a fact often pointed out, without, certainly, pretending that it is in any sense a whole explanation: namely, the extraordinary importance placed upon their belief in sorcery by almost all of the tribes we have touched on, but especially in New Guinea; and the very powerful resistance the whites find themselves up against if and when they try to get rid of it. The natives do not feel themselves any more at liberty to abandon sorcery, than they feel free to give up believing in the myths.

A number of the myths we have been looking at compare a detail, event or custom of the present day with some precedent in the *alchera, ungud, bugari*, etc. These are "explained" (in the primitive sense) by applying what I have called the imitation-participation formula. This formula is also called upon to explain a great many magical practices, especially those of the kind called sympathetic; one could just as well, in most cases, call them imitation-magic. I mention an instance which may serve as a typical illustration; it comes from central Queensland, and is a ritual for breaking the drought. In this case recourse is not made simply to a single individual, the professional rain-maker; a large number of persons take an active part in the operation.

> On the Georgina River, at Roxburgh Downs, a piece of quartz-crystal, the rain-stone obtained from somewhere out in the ranges, is crushed and hammered to a powder. Some very straight-stemmed tree is chosen – generally a bloodwood with the butt for a long way up free from branches – and saplings, from 15 to 20 feet in length, are ranged all round it in the form of a bell-tent, forming a sort of shed. Outside, in front of this erection, a small piece of ground is cleared, a portion scooped out, and some water placed in it. The men, having been previously collected within the shed, now come out, and dancing and singing all around the artificial water-hole, break out with the sounds and imitate the antics of various aquatic birds and animals, e.g., ducks, frogs. All this time the women are camped at about 20 to 25 yards distant. The men next form themselves into a long string, Indian file one behind the other, and gradually encircle the gins, over whom they throw the crushed and pulverized stone: the women at the same time hold wooden troughs, shields, and pieces of bark over their heads, and pretend that they are protecting themselves from a heavy downpour of rain.[29]

The operation consists essentially of imitating what happens when it rains. A hole is filled with water, frogs croak, ducks and other birds flap their wings and squawk; the women protect themselves as best they can against the shower which leaves them soaked (the crystal powder the men throw over them). By means of this imitation of what normally accompanies it, rain is invited or coaxed to fall. – It is almost falling already; it surely will do so soon![30] This working-out of the circumstances that always accompany rain must, it is expected, act on it like a suggestion which, because of its magic, becomes irresistible.

Similarly, on certain days in the Indian north east frontier area, Nagas wend their way down the track from the rice paddies. They move slowly, with bent backs, as though bowed down under the burden of the harvest. By imitating what their gait will be if the harvest is good, they are persuading it to become so, and thus making sure of it. We are reminded again of the Kiwai Papuans, the New Caledonian Kanakas, and many other primitives who bury magic stones in their plantations in order to "teach" the yams and taro to grow to the same size.

The model thus put forward is expected to exercise a lucky influence on the plants' *dispositions*. We realize, of course, that we must not give this term a sense that is limitedly psychological. It suggests rather qualities that are partly physical, partly moral, present in every being, creature or object of whatever kind. In that uncertain moment when they commit themselves to any fresh enterprise, primitive people invariably judge it prudent to placate the dispositions of everything even minimally involved in it: men, animals, plants, tools, weapons, etc. When the hunting season begins they do all they can to render favourable all the various "dispositions" of the bushland. The procedures for obtaining rain, though they vary, almost always imply some hope of persuading the rain to come eagerly, and not to get off the track and water some lucky neighbour tribe's country instead. Great care is taken to get rid of, or conceal, anything that might frighten it off or put it in an unfriendly humour, or tempt it to take some other direction. In northern Queensland, Roth tells us further, "Rain is a person, and certain men or women who happen to be named after him can make him come".[31] At Dobu, the wind is a person. – What may these strong affirmations amount to in the minds of the natives? Can we form any adequate conception of it? Could we even, in any case, effectively express the idea in our own familiar idiom of thought?

The rational-animist theory is the first that comes to mind. It has had a long run of favour.[32] Sometimes, even, the natives themselves will be the first to propose it. So at least it might seem, if we are to believe certain observers. But the language of natives has so few exact equivalents with our western vocabulary that we should almost always distrust what it is asserted they have said. Words can be put into their mouths. For the Queensland Aborigines rain is a person; and it is also, as it is for us, an aqueous precipitation. How do they reconcile these two contentions? The problem has no solution — but then, it hardly is a problem. There is need for a reconciliation only if, for them as for us, the two ideas exist separately in the first place. Actually they do nothing of the sort. We have to concede that on a point like this the difference between their habit of mind and ours is a chasm well-nigh impossible to bridge.

Rain-makers exist among the Marind-anim also.

> In times of severe drought, when the water-supply is running low, the Dongam-anim (rain-maker) goes alone into the bush to bring down rain and storms by magic. No one else must be present, at the risk of causing the operation to fail. When he arrives at the spot he digs a hole about half a metre deep and puts in it a few water-loving plants — banana leaves, . . . taro stems, twigs of croton, and so on. Then he pours water over them and throws in a few clods of earth, which make a splash. After this the rain will not be long in coming. Next he sets fire to a small quantity of pork fat, or else holds it in a flame, and this causes it to crackle and splutter. This represents lightning and thunder.[33]

These Papuans go about the process in a different way from the Queensland Aborigines, but what they do is based upon and regulated by the same principle of imitation.

In other places imitation is reduced to a series of magic spells in which the effective principle is present only by implication, often as a mere allusion. That is to say the magic is cajoled and asserted in the same breath. That is enough to bring it off effectively. Here for example are some charms from New Mecklenburg, this time to cause the rain to stop:

> The crab walks backwards.
> *Rain, turn back!*

or

> The sea-slug glides backwards.
> *Rain, turn back!*

or

> The sea-urchin moves backwards.
> *Rain, turn back!*

or

> The shark bites through.
> *He bites off the rain!*

That is to say, "The shark will tear the rainclouds to pieces in his teeth, just as he tears men".[34]

There are also charms to make plants thrive:

> The shark twists,
> *The taros roll . . .*

That is, the taros are to become so round, they will roll as sharks do in the sea.

> The boar roots up earth.
> *The yams will root up earth.*

The yams must grow so large, they will cause the ground to break up as though wild pigs had been rooting in it. "Good yams grow to 50 or 80 centimetres in length, so that the earth over them heaves up high."[35]

A charm to send away sickness:

> The parrot flew away.
> The cuckoo flew away.
> The snipe flew away.
> *The sickness is gone!*

As he chants the verses the medicine man makes little passes over the sick person. The number and names of the birds and the order in which they are included are not necessarily always the same: "he chooses them to suit himself".[36]

The vital formula is here reduced to a bare minimum. It is able none the less to produce the effect desired, because words chanted aloud or sung are powers in themselves, especially if they take the form of magic verses and are pronounced by the medicine-man, who imbues them with his own special power. In view of this the charms function precisely as do the operations of the rain-makers. It is a mixture which defies analysis, of suggestion, command and wheedling imitation.

Koch-Grünberg has left us a lengthy description, detailed and precise, of magic practices for curing sickness in use with the Taulipang (in an upper area of the Orinoco). This is a particularly clear and revealing instance. The intimate bond between myth and the practice of magic is made to appear in a remarkably clear light, thanks to its *schema* of participation-imitation.

These Indians, like all primitives, do not believe any illness occurs naturally. When an illness has been implanted in somebody through magical machinations, it can be attacked and overcome by other procedures of a similar kind. When the medicine man is summoned to the sick person's side, he appeals first of all to the

patient's animals – that is, to certain mythic animals which for
each man have a function like that of familiar spirits.

> These animals . . . stand towards the malady in a known rela-
> tionship. For example, if the sickness is a suppurating sore, it is
> likely, the Indians believe, that the patient has been eating the
> flesh of one of the larger varieties of game, such as tapir, stag or
> wild boar. In that case certain kinds of jaguar will be invoked,
> since jaguars have the power to frighten away all kinds of
> abcesses, so the Indians believe. Jaguars prey on all these larger
> game beasts and never suffer from sores or ulcers after eating
> them. It follows therefore that they must possess a strong magical
> power, or know some special charm or spell that can protect them
> against the consequences of such a diet – in other words, one
> which, as we might say, confers an immunity.

Similarly as a cure for diarrhoea in infants the medicine man
appeals to the otter. This animal feeds on large fish, yet no harm
ever comes to its sucklings from its doing so. Against intestinal
worms his appeal is to a couple of dogs, for although dogs commonly suffer from worms the disease is never fatal to them.[37]

At this point we now see how mythology comes in. "The
animals which figure in the charms are for the most part the
same mystical beasts, or at any rate belong among them, as enter
into the medicine man's other conjurations."

There are moreover two Taulipang characters, known as the
"daughter" and the "son of the ancestors", otherwise "the Maid of
the Plains" and "The Young Man of the Earth", who are in some
sense the prototypes of the human race, the first of mankind.
They were the first to experience in their bodies all the human il-
lnesses. To them are opposed the "people", called also the
"children" of today; it is these who are obliged to make use of the
charms. (We recall in the myths of To Kabinana and To Karvuvu
how there is continual reference to their descendants, who will
all have to put up with the consequences of To Karvuvu's inep-
titude and misdoing.)

Koch-Grünberg goes on from this to demonstrate a large
number of charms and incantations which, being too long, cannot be quoted; but all follow closely after very much the same
model. The formal charm is quite regularly prefaced with a brief
but relevant mythical "precedent", then goes on repeating with
the same regularity what "the people of today, the children" –
meaning the modern descendants of those first ailing forefathers
– must do: they "must repeat the following magic phrases . . .".
The first of the listed examples is for use when "the children"

have enemies and are desirous of magically undermining their courage. The second is the mentioned cure for ulcers. It runs as follows:

> These foods which I ate, this wild game, tapir, stag, aguti, paca, venison, made me ill with suppurating sores. Now I send fear into the sores, I frighten them away with these peppers (five native varieties of pepper are named), so that they may never again be painful. I drive the pain away. Just as I suffered, so do the people of today, the children, now suffer from the same pain as I suffered. When the children suffer from these sores they must repeat this phrase and the pain will go away: *I am Wepemen!*

Wepemen is the name of a black jaguar, one of the mythical animals.[38]

The first listed cure is for "thorns in the face", or pimples. The introductory myth tells of a young woman who rejected all her suitors. In revenge they caused her to become ugly by cursing her with lumps all over the skin of her face.

> When others lay sicknesses upon them, the people of today, the children, must suffer from the same maladies as I did. The Daughter of the Ancestors was made to suffer these prickles when Makunaima and the other rejected suitors caused them to swell up. I send fear into these prickles so that she may never have to suffer them again. I make the pain go away. The people of today, the children, must speak these words. When someone has made them ill, they must call on our name and cry out, *I am Melatikatalima!*

(Melatikatalima is a kind of pepper which has the power to cure pimples just as the jaguar has power over ulcers.)

The other charms which follow are all very similar. The fourth, a cure for stomach ache, is called the dog's cure because it invokes a mystical spirit-dog. The fifth is for colds and sore throat. The sixth is for the sting of a ray, the seventh against snakebite.

> And then the Daughter said, I send the pain away. When the people of today are bitten by a snake, they must pronounce my name. If they suffer from snakebite and they say my name, the pain will go away.

After this there is a charm for the protection of new-born children, then another for promoting an easy birth, and so on.[39]

This hasty description, though it captures fairly faithfully the drift of the Indian's thoughts, displays little of the easy directness our civilized habit of thought has come to expect of a passage of exposition. We recognize in it, for all that, how in these charms the several crucial elements we have singled out earlier are blended together. First, in order to explain an event which takes place among "the people of today", the myth appeals to a precedent of the distant age beyond which enquiry cannot go. If modern people suffer from ulcers, worms or acne, or if they are bitten by snakes, etc., it is because in the ancestral period the same misfortune occurred to the prototypical young man or young woman from whom they are all descended. – Second, the verbal formula by whose aid the medicine man designs to drive away the sickness is rigidly required to begin by recapitulating the appropriate myth. The recapitulation in itself possesses a certain magical efficacy. (With the Cuna Indians, Nordenskiöld tells us, if the legend belonging to a remedy is left out, the cure will not work.) – Finally, if the charm does cure the sickness, it does so because the formula names the name of the powerful agency which, in the beginning of time, overcame the same malady: the mythic jaguar when it was festerings and abcesses, the dog when it was a stomach ache, and so on. And because in those days each one of the mythic animals was powerful in respect of one particular malady, just so today anyone who suffers from that disease need only repeat the appropriate charm and pronounce the mythical animal's name; the sickness and the pain will then vanish at once.

This mystical therapy, in which myth and magic are so closely bound together one might call them inseparable, brings final conviction to the conclusion which was already obvious from analogical beliefs observed earlier in Australia and Papua: the legitimate propriety and the practical efficacy of an action may often both be derived from one and the same myth. For it is the myth which establishes the precedent or lays down the model which the action imitates. In this way the outcome is sure to be successful because by this means it comes to participate in the power of the supernatural world.

Chapter VI

Persistence of the Mythic World

By now we have become sufficiently familiar with a number of Australian and Papuan myths, vitally important to the well-being, even to the continued existence of the tribes, to enable us to single out certain elements they have in common. Broadly speaking their content centres upon the activities and exploits of personages of half-human, half-animal identity, who are in almost all cases the ancestors of both human and animal descendants in the modern world. They deal with the movements of these personages across the face of the country, whose outlines (or at any rate the more salient landscape features) are of their creation. These, for the most part, were the places where they finally "went into the ground", taking the form of a rock or a tree, or something of the kind. All these myths are pitched in a period of time originating so far back that before it there was nothing at all. This period of antiquity hovers over, yet is always outside the range of time as we know it. In it all beings and objects existed in a perpetual condition of flux or fluidity. They possessed magic powers of which their modern descendants, with few exceptions, retain no more than a feeble residue. In that age the most extraordinary transformations could be instantaneously accomplished, without the slightest difficulty. Nothing was ever ruled out as impossible.

But we must now enquire further. The question is, does this matter of representing the mythic world – it might be better to refer to it as a particular assembly of beliefs, remarkably firm and stable in character, with its accompaniment of no less solidly established rites and practices (festivals, dances, ceremonies, secret cults) – belong properly to these Australian and Papuan primitives alone, as a possession peculiarly and exclusively theirs? Or may we find it also in other places, among tribes which, as far as our knowledge goes, never had any kind of contact with them? Even a quite quick glance at the facts may serve to throw some little fresh light on the course of development which myths follow, and in particular it may help to reveal the extent to which they enter into common cause with social institutions.

In the Andaman Islands, we are told by Radcliffe-Brown, "Among the ancestors who appear in the legends there are a few who bear names that are those of species of animals. In each case the ancestor is identified with the species that bears the same name." A later passage fills this out:

> Many of the actors in the legends bear the names of animals but at the same time are spoken of as though they were human beings. Many of the legends explain how some species of animal arose from some one of the ancestors who became an animal and the progenitor of the species. Thus, in the North Andaman, *Kolo* was one of the ancestors; he made wings for himself out of palm-leaves, and so was able to fly; he lived a solitary life in his home at the top of a tree, and was in the habit of stealing men's wives; in the end he became the sea-eagle, and this species still bears the name *kolo*.
>
> It is necessary to define exactly as possible what meaning these have to the natives. It is not simply that the legendary person is a man with the name and some of the characteristics of an animal; nor is it simply that the legendary person is the ancestor of the species of which he bears the name. We can only adequately express the thought of the Andamanese by saying that he regards the whole species as if it were a human being. When, in the legends, he speaks of "Sea-eagle" he is thereby personifying the species . . .; he is regarding the characteristics of the species as if they were characteristics or actions or results of actions of a person. Admittedly this is a vague description, but the vagueness is in the mental phenomenon described; the Andamanese do not, in this matter, think clearly and analyse their own thoughts.[1]

Neither are the natives of central and north west Australia, and the Papuans in New Guinea, in the habit of analyzing their thoughts. Wirz, as we have seen, makes this very clear. Therefore it would appear quite wrong-headed for us to try to differentiate the aspects of their representation of the mythic ancestors under which the human and the animal elements are fused together. Analysis is simply irrelevant. To persist is only destructive. For the moment all we need to note is that for the Andaman Islanders the fusion seems very similar to what we have seen in Australia and New Guinea.

If we leave the Indian Ocean altogether and come to the northern Pacific coast of America, we still find the same thing. These key factors in Australian and Papuan myth are precisely what Frank Boas has picked upon as distinguishing characteristics in the myths of many Red Indian tribes:

> The Tsimshian distinguish clearly between two types of stories – the myth (*ada-ox*) and the tale (*ma lesk*). The latter is essentially historical in character, although from our point of view it may contain supernatural elements. The incidents narrated in the former are believed to have happened during the time when animals appeared in the form of human beings . . .
> Similar distinctions are made by all other tribes of the North Pacific coast. I mention here only the terms of *nu yam* of the Kwakiutl, *ik!anam* of the Chinook and *spetakl* of the Thompson Indians, which designate myths in the sense here given as opposed to tales belonging to the present period. It should be remembered that in the mind of the Indian it is not the religious, ritualistic, or explanatory character of a tale that makes it a myth, but the fact that it pertains to a period when the world was different from what it is now. It seems to my mind advantageous to adopt this objective definition of myth as felt by natives, rather than any of the many definitions based on a subjective standpoint.[2]

Thus, those two elements always present in Australian and New Guinea sacred myths – the mixed, part-human, part-animal nature of the beings, and the notion of an original time-beyond-time in which they perform their exploits – reappear in a closely similar form among the Indians of the American north Pacific coast; they have an importance there which leads Boas to regard them as definitive. Leonard Adam in a study of the Wakash (another north west American Indian tribe) remarks quite independently, "Before there were men, they believe, there were animals on earth; but they represent them like men wearing animal skins, or animal masks. They only had to take off these skins or masks to appear in human form".[3] This is unquestionably another allusion to half-human, half-animal ancestors, like those of the Australians and Papuans. We have seen that, in order to become an animal, all a man endowed with the necessary magic has to do is put on its skin, or take it off if he wishes to become human again. We shall need to come back to this when we deal with *transformations*.

According to J.A. Teit, the Thompson River Indians say, "At one time, very long ago, the earth was very different from what it is at present. There were no trees, and many kinds of bushes and plants were wanting; neither was there any salmon or other fish, nor any berries. The people who lived during this age were called *spetakl*. They were mostly animals who, nevertheless, had human form. They were gifted in magic; and their children used to reach maturity in a few months."[4]

At no great distance from these, Teit has also collected very similar myths from the Salishan and Sahaptin tribes. Here, for example, is their myth of the earth, with what it brought to birth.

Old-One, or Chief, made the earth out of a woman, and said she would be the mother of all the people. Thus the earth was once a human being, and she is alive yet; but she has been transformed, and we cannot see her in the same way as we can see a person. Nevertheless she has legs, arms, head, heart, flesh, bones, and blood. The soil is her flesh; the trees and vegetation are her hair; the rocks, her bones; and the wind is her breath. She lies spread out, and we live on her. She shivers and contracts when cold, and expands and perspires when hot. When she moves, we have an earthquake. Old-One, after transforming her, took some of her flesh and rolled it into balls, as people do with mud or clay. These he transformed into the beings of the ancient world, who were people, and yet at the same time animals.

These beings had some of the characteristics that animals have now, and in some respects acted like animals. In form, some were like animals, while others more nearly resembled people. All had greater powers, and were more cunning, than either animals or people. They were not well balanced. Each had great powers in certain ways, but was weak and helpless in other ways. Thus each was exceedingly wise in some things, and exceedingly foolish in others. They all had the gift of speech. As a rule, they were selfish, and there was much trouble among them. Some were cannibals, and lived by eating one another . . . Some people lived on the earth at the same time. They had all the characteristics that Indians have now, but they were more ignorant. Deer also were on the earth at that time, and were real animals as now.[5]

For the most part, however, in these stories the present day inhabitants of the country do not make their appearance until later. Hence the Nez-Percés, according to R.L. Packard, believe that, "Once, before there were any people in the world, the different animals and trees lived and moved about and talked together just like human beings.[6]

In the rest of North America myths of this kind were no less widely current. In New England, we are told by F.G. Speck, among the Penobscot (who inhabited what is now the state of

Maine), "there are the regular mythical tales of every class in which the characters in the narrative transform themselves into animals on any occasion. It is as though this undifferentiated human-animal character were a normal condition in what may be fittingly termed the mythological age."[7] Here, then, right against the Atlantic coast, we find mythology defining itself again in precisely the same terms as Boas describes on the North Pacific side. And these terms are exactly the same as we have observed to be essential in the myths of Australia and New Guinea.

In lower latitudes, in south eastern North America, James Mooney made a searching study of the myths of the great Cherokee tribe:

> Cherokee myths may be roughly classified as sacred myths, animal stories, local legends, and historical traditions. To the first class belong the genesis stories, dealing with the creation of the world, the nature of the heavenly bodies and elemental forces, the origin of life and death, the spirit world and the invisible beings, the ancient monsters, and the hero-gods . . .
> The sacred myths were not for every one, but only those might hear who observed the proper form and ceremony . . .
> To the second class belong the shorter animal myths, which have lost whatever sacred character they may once have had, and are told now merely as humorous explanations of certain animal peculiarities. While the sacred myths have a constant bearing upon formulistic prayers and observances, it is only in rare instances that any rite or custom is based upon an animal myth. Moreover the sacred myths are known as a rule only to the professional priests or conjurors, while the shorter animal stories are more or less familiar to nearly everyone and are found in almost identical form among Cherokee, Creeks and other southern tribes.

As in Australia and New Guinea, myths also provide explanations for outstanding features of the landscape. "Almost every prominent rock and mountain, every deep bend in the river, in the old Cherokee country had its accompanying legend. It may be a little story that can be told in a paragraph to account for some natural feature, or it may be one chapter of a myth that has its sequel in a mountain a hundred miles away. As is usual when a people has lived for a long time in the same country, nearly every important myth is localized, thus assuming more definite character."[8]

On one last point, but a point of considerable significance, the resemblance between all these myths comes to appear even more striking.

In Cherokee mythology, as in that of Indian tribes generally, there is no essential difference between men and animals. In the primal genesis period they seem to have been completely undifferentiated, and we find all creatures alike living and working together in harmony and mutual helpfulness until man, by his aggressiveness and disregard for the rights of others, provokes their hostility, when insects, birds, fishes, reptiles, and four-footed beasts join forces against him.

Again:

The animals of the Cherokee myths, like the traditional hero-gods, were larger and of more perfect type than their present representatives. They had chiefs, councils and townhouses, mingled with human kind on terms of perfect equality and spoke the same language. In some unexplained way they finally left this lower world and ascended to Galŭñlati, the world above, where they still exist . . . The animals that we know, small in size and poor in intellect, came upon the earth later, and are not the descendants of the mythic animals, but only weak imitations . . . Trees and plants also were alive and could talk in the old days, and had their place in council, but do not figure prominently in the myths."[9]

It is a far fetch, as we are well aware, from the tribal culture of the Australians and Papuans to the level of civilization reached by the Cherokees, and this difference is necessarily reflected in their myths. But for that very reason it becomes so much the more interesting to see, as we so clearly do, that these relatively advanced Indians also hold several basic tenets concerning the mythic world which are among the most constant beliefs of the Australians and Papuans.

In Central and South America the sacred myths, as we have seen from Ehrenreich's reports, present the same essential characteristics as do the foregoing. This shows particularly clearly where ancestors and animal-human hero-figures are involved. A few specimen-examples will make the point plain. Among the Witoto, Preuss writes, "It is often impossible to tell, from the names alone, whether groups referred to under the names of plants or animals are human tribes or not, because there is nothing by which to distinguish animals or plants from men. The name will frequently be that of an ancestor. But it is only when at a given moment (that is in a mythic story) the characters act in certain ways that they reveal to which category they belong, or show their origin." It would be hard to find a more effective way to express their "undifferentiated human-animal character" (Speck's phrase, quoted a page or so back). As in the Australian and Papuan examples, the characters are *both* animal and human *simultaneously*. It is the same again with the Bakairi. "I can quite confidently affirm", declares von den Steinen, "that my informant was rock-solid in his conviction that the evil ancestor who makes his appearance in the myth *was* a jaguar, even though he hunted with a bow and arrows; it was not that he was merely *called* one . . . The name was never used merely symbolically . . . As no essential difference exists between men and animals, therefore there can be no difficulty in asserting that an ancestor was at the same time a jaguar and also a being in human form who shot with bow and arrow."[10]

Koch-Grünberg gathered similar conclusions in the region of the upper Orinoco: "While the story is being told the notions of man and beast constantly intertwine. The teller, in a sense, steps out of his role to assure the listeners solemnly that the wasps, stags, and so on, in his story were actually men, even though the legend treats them as animal characters. In the story the tribal ancestor, Homanikiko, stands for the whole race of Kobeua. He appears to be a great magician, transforming himself effortlessly, sometimes into animal-form, then back again to human."[11]

Koch-Grünberg insists frequently on the importance of animals in the myths. "The myths throw into high relief the large part that is played by animals in the life of the Indians. Animals are credited with having been the first to possess, even to discover, the amenities of civilized living: such innovations as fire, the cultivation of plants, the making of utensils, etc. It was the dog which gave to man the hammock, and introduced seeds of cotton."[12]

Von den Steinen reports to the same effect: it was the deer which first learned how to rid the manioc of its poison (this among the Bakairi). Antonio (von den Steinen's guide and informant) firmly believed that the deer, who knew what to do with the manioc root, taught it to Keri, the Sun-hero. It was from Keri that the Bakairi women learned the process.[13] Surely it is not taking anything for granted to assume that this dog and deer must have been magic beings of the mixed animal-human kind, since in many primitive tribes such beings were given a civilizing role and in particular were credited with being inventors and discoverers.

"Men and beasts", said Aua sagely — the Eskimo shaman whose intelligence Rasmussen valued so highly — "are much alike. And so it was our fathers believed that men could be animals for a time, then men again."[14] Indeed this belief, sometimes left implicit, but often carefully formulated, comes out in many Eskimo stories. There is for example among the Netsilik a myth which runs like this:

> In the very first times there was no light on earth. Everything was in darkness, the lands could not be seen, the animals could not be seen. And still, both people and animals lived on the earth, but there was no difference between them. They lived a mixed life; a person could become an animal, and an animal could become a human being. There were wolves, bears, and foxes but as soon as they turned into humans they were all the same. They may have had different habits, but all spoke the same tongue, lived in the same kind of house, and spoke and hunted in the same way.[15]

There is no difficulty in recognizing here the Australian and Papuan kind of half-human, half-animal beings. What now follows illustrates the fluidity of the same world and the extraordinary ease with which it effected its transformations.

> In all old legends the marvellous, the incredible, the supernatural plays an extremely important part, in fact it is the pivot of intrigue and action. At the time when they happened, great wonders were constantly being performed among mankind; and everything connected with their magic, and not least their amulets, had far greater power than nowadays. Now people are only people, and no longer are they master of their own fate to the same extent as then, when their amulets at the merest wish could turn them to anything they liked; a sea animal, a polar bear, a sparrow, an ermine, a fly, in fact to a mussel, a stone, or a piece of wood.[16]

The Caribou Eskimos believed that

> In the olden days things were very different from what they are now. Everything had a soul, everything was more alive. When a caribou had been eaten, the meat grew again on the bones. Only one had to be careful not to crush or break any of the bones. (We shall find their belief coming up again later in North American Indian folklore.) There were no sledges in those days. The houses were alive, and could be moved with everything in them, and the people as well, from one place to another . . . Snow shovels could go about by themselves, could move from one place to another without having to be carried. That is why now, when in solitary places, we never dare to stick a snow shovel into the snow. We are afraid lest it should come alive and go off on its own. So we always lay snow shovels down in the snow, so that they do not stand up.[17]

Though at a great distance from the Caribou, it is still the same with the Eskimos of Bering Strait. E.W. Nelson writes:

It is believed that in ancient times all animals had the power to change their forms at will. When they wanted to become people they merely pushed up the muzzle or beak in front of the head and changed at once into man-like beings. The muzzle of the animal then remained like a cap on top of the head, or it might be removed altogether, and in order to become an animal again it had only to pull it down. The belief referred to is well illustrated in raven tales, where the changes are repeatedly made by the characters. In this belief rests the foundation of the mask dances of the Eskimo.

Many of the masks are half-human, half-animal. Others are masks with shutters. When the shutters open, it can then be seen that there is a being of a different kind inside.[18]

In Siberia among the Samoyedes, a people who have had only slight contact with the Russians, there have lately been encountered some beliefs which appear characteristic and whose affinities with the foregoing can scarcely be denied. Kai Donner tells us,

> I was able to acquire a great many stories of the mythical heroes who had flourished in these regions. The magnificently beautiful lake, which, encircled by a no less lovely forest of cedars, lay in front of the Jurte, had according to the story they told sprung up in the footstep of the great Altep Khan, who fought a battle there. They believed the high peaks and the hills had arisen from the bodies of all the fallen heroes and that the little brooks had gushed up where their swords had struck the earth. Two of the hills were phantom ships which had turned to stone, etc. In short, every item had its story, and folksong and myth had brought the whole of nature to life for them.

Nor is there lacking a belief in animal ancestry.

> Along the Ket no pictures can be found of him (the tribal ancestor Kuoder-gup); here he is revered because he is a spirit, but so also is the animal species to which he belongs. For the remarkable fact is precisely this: he is always believed to be an animal, yet one endowed with human faculties. On the Upper Ket he is a bear; the tribe on that account call themselves the Bear People, because such was the animal from which they took their origin.[19]

Not to draw this matter our unduly, we shall refer here only very briefly to certain related beliefs, of which many are found among the lesser African tribes, notably the Bushmen. In spite of great differences between the people in physical type and social institutions, these Bushmen beliefs have at various times been put forward to support a comparison with the Australian Aborigines. "The most important figure in the mythology of the

Cape Bushmen", writes Schapera, "is the mantis, round whom a whole cycle of myths has been formed. Besides his own proper name, *kaggen*, he possesses several others, as does his wife, whose usual name, however, is . . . the rock rabbit (*hyrax capensis*)." They have three children, without counting an adopted daughter (the porcupine), herself married and with two children. "All these, the Bushmen say, were once men and women, people of the Early Race which preceded the Bushmen, but now they are animals."[20]

The Bushmen regard rain as a person. "The Rain or Water, *!khwa*, is also acknowledged by these Bushmen as a supernatural personage, and various beliefs and usages are directed towards it. It is often represented as an animal; in the form of a bull it carries off a young maiden, in the form of an eland it was shot by a man of the early race with disastrous effects. It is thought of most commonly, however, as an animal living in a waterhole, and it is believed that wherever this animal goes, rain will fall . . ." Again, "In the mythology the wind is represented as having formerly been a man, which now wears the form of a bird."[21]

Finally, among the Bantu (whose institutions, though somewhat uneven, are in a general way more advanced than those of the Bushmen), it is not difficult to discern the presence of mythical beliefs of the same kind as these last. To instance only one example, the Ila-speaking people of Northern Rhodesia, according to Smith and Dale, also refer to "the ancient time, when things were still fluid, before animals and men had assumed their final forms".[22]

With all these facts before us – and it would be very easy to find a great many more – we may take it that the answer to the question posed at the beginning of this chapter has been found. The Australian and Papuan Aborigines' attitude towards and representation of the mythic world, of which they supply so clear an evidence, does not belong to them either peculiarly or exclusively as their own. On the contrary, in a great many tribes from either hemisphere, of a more or less primitive character, we shall certainly discover if not every essential ingredient of it, at least the most important ones: the same belief in a time standing outside of time, or as we might call it, pre-temporal time, belonging to a world very different from the world we know; belief in the existence, during that age, of culture heroes who were at the same instant both animals and men, who were the ancestors of both human and animal species now living; belief in

the "fluidity" which then made possible all kinds of transformations without impedance from any obstacle in the laws of
physical nature or the fixed forms of the various species,
whereby all things became marvellously possible.

Are we then on this account bound to affirm that this picture
of the mythic world (along with all the emotional components,
rites, practices and ceremony that it implies) must reappear with
few differences in all other primitive tribal systems, no matter of
what diversity of circumstances and physical background? By no
means; that would be going far beyond what the evidence war-
rants. What the facts do bring home to us, however, is that we
ought always to take into separate account the formative conditions out of which each tribe (or group of tribes) has evolved, and
as far as may be possible, also its particular history. It is the
stated opinion of Mauss that it would have been well to reserve
the term *primitive* for the Australian Aborigines alone, since they
are the only tribes still surviving who carry on the life-traits of
Palaeolithic man; and as far as the rest are concerned, those who
are generally but inaccurately styled primitives, to keep a clear
distinction between those whose culture remains Neolithic and
others whose civilization is more recent and advanced.[23] If this
view is acceptable it will make plain the reason why in no other
part of the world (unless in parts as yet undiscovered) are we
likely to see displayed the whole gamut of truly primitive beliefs
and practices so clearly and definitively as in Australia and New
Guinea. Instances may certainly exist where analogies may be
found that are both startling and undeniable; but even in them
certain differences will force themselves on our attention.

To avoid entering upon a discussion of details which could
easily become too involved, we may content ourselves with
pointing out quite briefly those differences which are most
noteworthy. In the first place, secret and sacred myth-material
does not carry the same vital significance for the others as for the
Australian and Papuan tribes we have discussed. The periodic
increase of animal and vegetable species, indeed the very continuity of the human community itself, no longer depends before
all else upon the regular celebration of rituals which make it
possible for properly initiated men to attain communion with the
mythic ancestors.

What is more, the animal-ancestors themselves tend to change
their character and take on aspects of a more or less clearly
defined personal kind. In time they develop into "divinities".
Such divine persons do not all remain of one equal status, as do

for example the central Australian animal-ancestors described by Spencer and Gillen or by Strehlow. They settle into classes and sometimes form themselves into hierarchies, in which orders of priority are set up. At the same time a change comes over the former ceremonies. In the end they merge into a formal cult which entails an established priesthood. The priestly function is as a rule performed by the communal chief or king, who becomes the obligatory intermediary between the living society and those who have died; he is then the only member of the community qualified to approach the invisible powers and the "gods".

At a later stage sacrifices make their appearance and take up a position of great importance in the cult. To the Australian and Papuan Aborigines, however, sacrifices are unknown.[24]

I will therefore not go so far as to claim, as Durkheim does, that the Australian Aboriginal tribes set before us the earliest existing elements of *religious* experience, but would prefer to suggest that the complex of beliefs and rituals which is embodied in their mythology amounts to what I may call *pre-religion*. What I mean by coining this expression − which I do with suitable apologies − will be clear enough from what has been said in previous chapters in respect to the mythic world, animal-ancestors, rites and ceremonies, mystical experience, participation-imitation, and so on. The term has this advantage at least, namely that it places its emphasis upon the point wherein I venture to differ most decisively from the distinguished views of the founder of *L'Année sociologique*.[25] According to him, however diverse may appear the different forms which religious expression takes (whether it be the style seen in the Australian tribes, or those which we see in occidental or oriental or any other civilizations), the religious experience itself remains always of an essentially uniform, if not actually identical nature. My study of the facts has led me to a conclusion which is slightly different. To me it seems preferable not to apply to every instance a concept which is so narrowly defined. I shall therefore refrain from using the word religion to signify the body of beliefs and rituals which is given expression through the myths as I have described and analyzed them in the chapters hitherto. Only when certain strong elements within that body grow weak or fade entirely away, and new ones take their place and develop freshly, can it be said that religion in its true sense has become established.

But by drawing a distinction in this way between pre-religion and true (that is, civilized) religion, it is not intended to set the two at poles apart. That would be seriously to misconstrue the qualities they actually have in common, including everything that Durkheim has so discerningly pointed out. I have myself demonstrated why the emotions experienced by both actors and spectators during the ritual performances may rightfully be considered religious. The very expression *pre-religion*, though in itself it implies no imperatively consequent development, nevertheless signifies a stage of cultural life which might be capable at a later time of leading to religion in the fullest sense. Here, however, it seems proper to lay stress on the differences which are to be distinguished between pre-religion and religion proper, instead of dwelling, as we have done up to this point, on their bonds of resemblance. In this way one may put oneself on firm guard against serious error. There will be less risk of reading back into the primitive situation characteristics which belong only to the most advanced societies. While taking careful note of the quasi-religious facts we are able to discern in the pattern of tribal culture, we must not forget that these people constitute the most primitive communities we have so far had any opportunity to become acquainted with.

The present is not the proper occasion for an analysis of the changes which, sooner or later, may accompany the process of development from what I have called the pre-religious conditions to religions or religious cults properly so described. We need say no more than that such developments may take a wide variety of forms, and that the shift is never brought about by an orderly or controlled series of substitutions of one general revision of the system for another. Very often, indeed, beliefs and practices which are already well set for oblivion nevertheless somehow manage to cling on and become mingled with others which ought logically to have driven them out. And likewise some others which have already disappeared from plain sight, leave traces which hang on indefinitely, although what they stand for is no longer known.

But is it not a remarkable fact that, wherever one looks in the modern world, one becomes aware of evidences that indicate that every settled, formal religion of today has passed through an earlier period when it embraced divinities of a part anthropomorph, part zoomorph kind with close resemblances to the mythic ancestors we have been discussing? Quite a number of North American tribes possess a myth-cycle relating to a culture hero who is not only a transformer but also a trickster. This hero, who is one of the mythic beings endowed with special powers, is given an individual identity, one might almost call it a developed character, much more idiosyncratically personal than any found among the animal ancestors or mythic heroes of the Australians and Papuans. He is, none the less for that, known to all as Coyote, Crow, Eagle, Hare or Spider, etc. It is not merely that he is given an animal's name: he truly *is* the animal at the same time as he is man. He participates in both natures. Similarly in the antique world we recall the long ages in which there persisted a tradition of gods who were partly animal in form. It was so in the sacred legends of India and the Far East, just as it was in the Mediterranean world and in Egypt, Asia Minor, Crete, even Greece. In all these regions gods in the form of animals persisted, as late as in the classical age, in certain remote or backward areas like rural Arcadia. Others comparable may be located in Celtic, Germanic, Scandinavian, Slavic and other mythologies. In short it would appear that zoomorphism, at least of a partial sort, must for a very long period have prevailed almost universally among divinities.

Representations of the gods in plastic and pictorial art provide abundant testimony to this persistence. In all parts of the world images of the gods – in paintings, drawings, sculptures or rock carvings – have given expression to the duality of their nature in a vividly eloquent fashion: human bodies with animal heads or animal bodies with human faces; the upper part human, the lower animal, or the reverse. At times in a figure which is wholly human one limb only, or merely a single extremity, will be animal. A very tenacious tradition has perpetuated these composite appearances as the centuries passed. In many localities where, along with the myths, a belief in part-human, part-animal ancestors was long retained, the real meaning of the images was kept clear. But as pre-religion at last yielded, by slow degrees, to religious doctrines and practices properly so called, it gradually became obscured. Ultimately the figures came to be regarded only as curiosities, and to the eye of commonsense appeared merely comic or incongruous.

Much the same thing can be said of the animal masks, or those which were part-human, part-animal – often extraordinary, at times altogether fantastic – used in the dances and ceremonies of a great many tribes. For those who first made and wore them there was nothing grotesque about them. Their purpose was simply to translate into fact and substance the shapes and forms of beings which lived in the minds of the makers. For example, von den Steinen, when he was among the Bakairi noted certain dance masks of which the two handsomest were described as "piranha images". On the cheeks were painted red markings. The masks represented the great piranha species, a dangerous fish which inhabits the rivers of the region. "The most brilliant ornament on these two masks is made of splendid arara [that is, macaw] feathers, which are fixed in the elongated nasal septum and project for some distance on either side. They are fastened to a small bamboo stock which is ornamented with tassels. The Indians are so far from feeling any obligation to give the figure a physiognomy that is zoologically convincing that they pierce its nose just as they do their own, and embellish it with feathers similarly." Beyond the fish they see the man; beyond the man, the fish. The mask expresses, for the eyes of all to see, the unity of the double nature possessed by a being belonging to the mythic age. It may often happen that long after that twofold identity has dropped from sight – has ceased to be noticed or at all understood by the people – its image will still remain, perpetuated in a mask.

In a similar way among the Australian and Papuan tribes we have been considering, there is a very intimate correspondence between the animal ancestors and certain local sites. From these sites the ancestors are inseparable. These are the places where, at the proper season, it is obligatory to perform the sacred increase and fertility ceremonies. Eventually such local centres will come to lose their significance, in proportion as that of the ancestors themselves declines. But, like the ancestors, they never suffer a sudden and total eclipse. Just as in many surviving divinities there persists, if only in trace form, some continuity from the former animal-human existence, so also may a god-figure (even when it becomes the central focus of a cult that functions for a whole wide region – an entire tribe, even a group of tribes –) keep, notwithstanding, its association with a particular place. We find this to be the case quite frequently in the Mediterranean mythological area, as indeed elsewhere. Sometimes we discover a divinity who has affiliations with several locations at the same time – vestigial evidence, no doubt, of a former time when the same deity was accepted in several localties, either simultaneously or successively, where his rituals had been conducted. As time goes on it becomes hard to decide whether the site became sacred because a temple or altar was erected there originally, or whether it was sanctified at an earlier period and this was the reason why the temple was built on it.

When the sites we have called local totemic centres fell into disuse, so also, as we have seen, did the ceremonies and rituals associated with them. One ritual practice, however, did have a wide persistence. Certainly it was not one of the animal or vegetable increase ceremonies. But rites of initiation have survived even today among a large number of tribes still in a more or less primitive condition; they are dedicated to a purpose that is still seen as necessary and of vital importance. They constitute the sole means whereby the young men, as they arrive at puberty, can be effectively integrated with the tribe as adult members of it. That is to say, they give assurance of the full admission – in a form of social rebirth – of the novices into the life of the community and afford them in their turn the right to pass on to their own descendants the solemn secrets without which the tribe would perish. Such is no doubt the explanation of the extraordinary tenacity of the initiatory rituals. So also may the persistent element of mystery which attaches to the symbolism, and the ordeals through which initiation is attained, be accounted for. This secrecy is carried to such a point as, very often, to prevent whites who are in daily contact with the natives from knowing anything at all of what goes on in the ceremonies. "These mysterious rites", one observer remarks, "extend deeply into the socio-political life of the people as a whole. That is why they never slacken."[27] Missionaries, especially in Africa, have tried to suppress them. But they have met with stubborn resistance. Some, indeed, question whether, instead of repressing the practices, they might not more wisely encourage them to continue, while adapting them to the basic requirements of Christian morality. By this means they might possibily avoid delivering a mortal blow to the continuing life of the tribes.

With the passage of time, and in step with the establishment of modern religious beliefs, the secret and sacred primitive beliefs diminish. The same care is no longer taken to keep them jealously away from the uninitiated and from women and children. Gradually everyone gets to know them and so more and more they come to be regarded only as stories and legends, the common property of the whole tribe. While this is happening there is also a progressive weakening, to the point ultimately of actual disappearance, first of the kind of quasi-religious awe the myths originally inspired, then of the solemn emotions which clung to their repetition, and finally of the devoted vigilance of those who were entrusted with the preservation of the sacred artifacts. Once revered, the narratives collapse into the profane. Nevertheless their essential content remains much what it was: great deeds and exploits done by the animal ancestors and culture heroes, instantaneous and frequent transformations, beings endowed with miraculous powers, the general "fluid" potentiality of everything, and so on. This was the world of the myths; and it is still present to underlie and support the legends and stories. Native intelligences possess an ability to range from myth to folktale unblinkingly, with no sense at all of having changed direction. Thus we find the same tale collected by Wirz from the Marind-anim and by Landtman from the Kiwai Islanders, their near neighbours; but the one tribe now regards it still as a sacred myth, the other as no more than a popular tale.

That sacred myth, by shedding its sanctity, should so easily settle down into folklore or some other simple kind of narrative is not difficult to accept; it is explained by the natural character of the primitive mind itself. That is, by the way in which primitives regard both the worlds, the mythic and the common, and look upon the relationship between them. Certainly they see the mythic world as a form of supernature. But they visualize no hard barrier between it and this one. Nature and supernature do not set themselves up in opposition to represent two rival and hostile principles of reality. Beings of the mythic world differ greatly, naturally, from their corresponding forms in this. That is only to be expected, since the myths show them as possessing a great many magical powers which historical man has lost, though he too (in the mythic age) also possessed them in the highest degree; what remains to him now is no more than some few feeble remainders. The difference, however, is merely one of more and less. All living creatures in the modern world remain in essence the same, though on a severely diminished scale, as the supernaturals once were in their much grander way. We call back to mind the notions entertained by certain primitives about the faculty of growth possessed by various living beings, men, animals or plants. When these are of supernatural stock, mythic heroes, their growing up can be marvellously fast. A coconut shoots in a single night; next day the tree is mature and six nuts are ripe already. A child is no sooner born but he can eat and speak; in a matter of hours he has shot up and can perform heroic deeds, etc. This extraordinary rapidity is only the result of the amazingly powerful magic force which animate[28] such prodigious beings. Even in ordinary and everyday circumstances when a coconut palm springs up, or children grow into men, they by no means do so simply in consequence of certain physical laws taking their natural course; the native thinker has no concept of any such laws. As he sees it, everything comes about through the operation of some force of exactly the same miraculous kind, though of far less vigour, as what applies in the case of any prodigy.[29] Thus it follows that while the mythic world is acknowledged to be infinitely greater and grander than our own, the two are nevertheless of the same order. Any marvellous change which comes to light in the world about us must therefore of necessity be understood after the example of those that appeared upon the scene as daily commonplaces in the mythic age.

Hence it may now appear obvious how it happened that primitive man, confronted with so many marvellous interventions of the supernatural powers into the affairs of everyday life, could remain so calmly undisturbed by them. He merely took their advent as a matter of course. Such interventions did no violence to nature; they never embarrassed or contradicted the natural order. Indeed they provided him with a conveniently ready explanation for those phenomena which are the only ones for which explanation is really required: those mysterious, strange and unexpected events which can in no other way be accounted for. When we grasp this, we may by the same token begin to understand why it is that primitive minds will always be so eager to find satisfaction in a mythical story.

Chapter VII

The Mythic World and Folklore: I

The mythic world of the central and north western Australian and the Dutch New Guinea tribes we have examined is not, as we have realized, their own possession exclusively, nor does it appear indissolubly integral with their social and religious institutions. We have seen, not indeed all, but at least the most important elements of it in beliefs and practices belonging to other tribes quite different from them and, for that matter, equally different from one another. It would seem therefore that, for all these differences, there must be something contained in it of a very general character – one might go so far as to say, universal. To make this point conclusively clear it remains only to show that the same tribes in their common tales and legends, whether they have been non-sacred stories from their origin, or have lost their sacred character by slow attrition – still follow, by implication, the same traditional mythic patterns. It is not possible, of course, to examine the situation exhaustively, but fortunately a reasonably small number of select examples will suffice to furnish the proof that we need.

It makes sense to begin with the most primitive tribes. We recognize, of course, that the transition between sacred and profane is a very gradual, hardly noticeable one. The secular tales assuredly no longer insist upon any kind of Genesis-message in order to lay down the law about the original half-human, half-animal culture heroes, ancestors of both the tribes themselves and their associated animal species, founders of the tribal institutions, inventors of tribal work-skills, bringers of knowledge and custom, and so on. But still the world that appears in them remains "fluid"; there is no miraculous metamorphosis which cannot be accomplished in it in the mere twinkling of an eye. Incessantly we meet with characters who change from human to animal form, or the reverse, with a nonchalant ease that the nar-

rative takes wholly for granted. Myths and legends which unfold
against a background of such a fluid sense of reality are legion. A
few examples follow, taken from Marind-anim or Kiwai
folklore.

A certain hero, Teimbre, returns to his hut where he sees a
snake coiled round his bow. He tries, but without success, to
pull it off. He gives up and goes away. Meantime the snake
transforms itself into a beautiful girl. She tidies the house and
cooks the meal. "Who did this?" exclaims the warrior on his
return. "It couldn't have been my dog?" The snake is once again
coiled about the bow. He goes out again and this time takes the
dog with him. When he returns, arriving without any warning,
he catches the girl unawares. He takes her for his wife. Nothing
of the snake is left.[1]

Beings of this kind, who can at will take some other shape, are
called by the Marind *Dema* (the associated adjective is *dema*,
here uncapitalized). The term implies that they possess powers
of magic still derived from the mythic age. The legend will often
say so plainly. "The *ndik* (heron; a sort of *dema* heron is meant)
and the sea eagle (a *dema* eagle) had long been friends. Together
at Darir they went fishing every day in the marshes. But the people of the village did not realize that they were both *Dema*, for
they never changed into birds until they were alone and far
away from the village . . ." However the sea eagle's son somehow
discovered that his father was a *Dema* who could transform
himself into a bird, and he told his mother. When the eagle
learned of this, lest the woman should betray his secret, he persuaded his friend to kill her. – A girl saw a kangaroo by a spring
and tried to catch it . . . Next day, when she went to draw water,
a young man dressed with beautiful ornaments was there,
waiting for her. He was the kangaroo *Dema*. "Wouldn't you like
to come with me?" . . . the next day he carried her off. They looked everywhere for her; she was gone. At last Samanimb came
back out of the forest and told her mother that Jano was not an
ordinary man but a *Dema* who was able to change into a
kangaroo.[2]

Sometimes a *Dema* who possesses this ability to transform
himself abuses the power – it happens quite often in these
myths – and then his victims may take their revenge.

Nazr caught alive a little pig, which was really of human birth. He
planned to rear it, and gave it into the care of his two Nakairi (serving maids), Sangam and Samaz. But this pig was in fact a *Dema*

. . . Sometimes he took the form of a young man, sometimes of a pig. By day he seemed to be a pig with nothing strange about him. But at night, with Samaz and Sangam by, he turned into a young man and seduced them both. Nobody was in the least aware of his sly tricks until one day the girls' mother picked up in the hut a kind of leg-strap or puttee which could only belong to a man. It dawned on her that the pig was a *Dema*, and she told what she had discovered. The people deemed it must be killed. Nazr gave his consent.[3]

Dema individuals like this pig are commonly fearful of their part-human, part-animal identity becoming known. We have just seen an instance of a *Dema* bringing about the death of his wife for fear she should unmask him.

Another tale:

The (*dema*) crocodile and the (*dema*) eagle were brothers. They dwelt at the mouth of the Bian, on the left bank, near Walinau Island. The crocodile lived on the shore, the eagle in a tall tree beside the sea. One day the brothers saw two girls walking along the beach. The eagle-youth (he immediately changed into human form) called out to them, "Where are you going?" "We want to get across to Walinau, where there is a festival; but we can't find a way to get across." "Don't trouble about that!" replied the crocodile-youth and the eagle-youth with one voice, "we will carry you to the other side of the water!" One of the girls then sat on the crocodile-youth's back and the other on the back of the eagle-youth. At that moment both turned back into animal form. Quickly the crocodile slithered into the sea with his prey and the eagle flew up with his to his nest in the tree . . . he lived with her there. In the end she escaped.[4]

The girls talk to the young men, then suddenly they find they are in the power of a crocodile and an eagle. The change is instantaneous. How can something so extraordinary come to pass? The Papuan does not ask. It is enough to understand that they are *Dema*; that explains all. It simply does not enter the head of the native to question the likelihood of such happenings. A logician might explain that he concludes *ab actu ad posse*: it has to be possible, because it has occurred before. Von den Steinen also very appositely draws attention to this same primitive habit of mind. The Bakairi, for example, argue that their neighbours the Trumai lived at the bottom of the river. "But that's impossible — the Trumai aren't fish. They can't survive under water!" — The reasoning falls on deaf ears; their Bakairi confidence is not in the least shaken. As they see it, the thing is incontrovertible: the simple fact is that the Trumai live at the bottom of the river. They go there to sleep every night. How men can live under water is not for the Bakairi to explain; such knowledge is no concern of theirs. But as to the matter of the Trumai being at the same time human beings and water-creatures, that is no more difficult to credit than any number of other dualities met with in the myths. And who ever called those in question?[5]

Thus we see the "fluidity" of the myth-world reappearing in full force in the world of folklore. It even makes itself felt in practical life as soon as some individual of more than ordinary magical potency intrudes within it. According to one mythical story of the Marind-anim, "a (*dema*) bitch gave birth to a baby boy". This, the natives acknowledge, is not an everyday happening; but they do not hold, on that account, that it is impossible. They so far believe this that, aside from myth altogether, they contend that something of the sort might very well occur at any time and simply be considered exceptional. "Every so often," Wirz tells, "there will be some rumour running about that a child has been fathered by a dog, or else born to a bitch. In either case they are always convinced of the possibility of it."[6]

It is not very surprising, therefore, to find that Marind folklore is prodigal with metamorphoses even more fabulous than those we have instanced. But the Marind themselves do not find them incredible; since their whole picture of reality is "fluid". The external forms of things is — I use the phrase of Im Thurn, from *Among the Indians of Guiana*, cited earlier — merely "an accident".[7] Here follow two characteristic samples:

> Soon the sea carried away the wooden stake and the waves tossed it about. Suddenly, though nobody saw it happen, it had grown four legs. One end had changed into a head, the other into a tail. The piece of wood had become a crocodile. It began to crawl in the direction where the children were bathing, intending to carry them off. It snapped up one of them. An old woman saw it and called to the men, who came running with their bows and arrows. But they saw nothing; only a wooden stick being tossed hither and thither on the mudbank. "Wait a while!" said the old woman, "that stick will suddenly turn itself back into a crocodile if any of the children come near it." Indeed that is just what happened. They shot at the animal, but it disappeared; they had to go looking for it in the water. One boy, the bravest of them, dived in with a rope. But down there at the bottom of the sea was the crocodile's home; the heads of its victims were arranged all round it. It was no ordinary crocodile but a *Dema* . . . They killed it; out of its bones a sago palm grew.[8]

This myth invites an explanation of a psychological kind (and Wirz gives it), through the resemblance, which is quite striking, between a crocodile lying perfectly still at the edge of the water and a treetrunk. But all that the myth actually does say is that it was a *Dema* — as such it could change and rechange its form at will, and could return to life after being killed.

> Iagrivar had married an *Iwag* (a girl of the mythic world). One day, as they were on their way to their plantation, she saw him turn into a snake and break up the earth with his tail, so that the work would cost him less trouble, and he could get through it in less time. The girl ran back to the village and said to the people, "The young man I married is a *Dema*! he can change into a snake!" When Iagrivar went away from that country, he had to cross an arm of the sea and there was no canoe. "Don't worry, he said (to his wife), "I'll get you one." He at once stretched himself out, bent himself into a curve, and himself became a canoe . . . The next night, while all the people were celebrating a feast, Iagrivar once again turned himself into a snake and crept towards the village.[9]

In a world peopled with *Demas* like this, why should any metamorphosis at all be precluded, since no one is expected even to speculate on how it is to be carried out?

There are other mythical stories, however, which do supply a few hints on this last point, and give details of certain processes followed in passing from one shape to another. Thus in one Marind myth,

> Nobody was left in the village but the father and the uncle of the young man. The latter went into the forest. When he got there he carved out of wood some large beaks of a certain shape (like those of toucans), and got ready all sorts of ornaments made of feathers. Then, carrying all those things with him, he returned to the village where he had left his father and his uncle. He gave each of them a toucan's beak and a feather ornament. They fixed them to their shoulders like wings. Then they also fixed the beaks over their noses. "Come, now we will learn to fly," said the young man, and he led them back into the forest and to a place where he had constructed a trestle-work out of palm stems. All three climbed this and attempted to come down by flying. At first they jumped from a low height and then from higher and higher; finally they found they could fly. In this way they turned into real toucans. The women came out from their gardens and saw what had happened. Then they too transformed themselves into birds.[10]

This method of transforming oneself into a bird is believed by the Marind still to be in use by village sorcerers (in whom a few of the magical powers of the *Dema* survive).

Any experienced sorcerer will know a charm by which to transport himself invisibly through the air to some distant place. However he will not make use of this power, unless he has first eaten the fat of a certain bird which is a good flier; in addition, he will also have fasted for a certain time, to make himself light. He will then go to a kind of shelter he has built in the forest of palm fronds, and cover his upper and lower arms with decorations made out of long heron-feathers. Finally he must set fire to the little hut, but not leave it . . . the smoke and flame are expected to raise him up in the air. Then, like a bird, he will fly off towards the spot where he wishes to go . . . The fat he has eaten is designed to transfer to the sorcerer's body the ability to fly, which belonged to the bird. To bring off his plan the sorcerer thus has recourse to several different procedures. But like the feathering of his arms, all such processes as are seen in the myths owe their success to the magical power which he is privileged to enjoy.[11]

Landtman has collected a rich gathering of popular tales of the Kiwai Island area. This folklore, the animal tales in particular, closely resembles that of the Marind-anim; beings and objects have the same "fluidity", there is the same duality of human and animal nature. The same miraculous transformations are unhesitatingly accepted as true, the same magical procedures are followed to produce them. I can do no better to illustrate what these stories mean to the natives, than summarize a typical example. Regretfully, I must abridge the details.[12]

A certain Iasa boy had very bad ulcerated sores all over his body and always stayed in the house. No one lived at that place except the boy and some girls. Every day a few of the girls went to make sago and some others to catch crabs. Only one girl felt sorry for the sick boy, and she took a little piece of sago and threw it to him, without going close to him. The others did not trouble about him in the least . . . One day he went to the creek to swim and saw a *hawia* (white heron-like bird). He sat down on the beach and watched. The bird came and he drew his bow and broke its two legs. He ran and caught the bird. He brought the bird into the house and pulled out the tail feathers which he attached to his back and fastened some to each arm, making them into wings. He exchange his own eyes for those of the bird, and he also assumed its beak. When he rubbed his body, feathers came out all over it, and he also appropriated the bird's legs. He was no longer a man but a bird. Flapping his wings by way of trial he thought, "Oh, proper white pigeon (bird)". He walked about in the house in the shape of the bird ("inside proper man he stop, outside skin belong pigeon"). After a while he stripped off the skin of the bird and hid it, resuming his human form with his skin full of sores . . .

The one girl . . . had seen through the boy: "Eye belong boy he no belong sick man . . . I think he make fool of us". In the morning all got up as usual, some girls went to cut sago, and others to catch crabs. The boy remained alone. He took off his bad skin, which he rolled up and stowed away close to his bed. He looked at his face in the water, being really a fine boy, "skin, body belong him good, hair he fine, good, hair he light". He took the bird's skin from the place where it was hidden and putting it on flew up into the air. He went to Muba Iasa, the point where the girls were catching crabs. The girl who had been giving him food was walking along the beach and the bird followed her closely. When the bird came close to her, she concluded, "That man I been look out (look after) all time, I think that him". She left her fish and crabs and ran after the bird, anxious to catch it. The other girls said, "You think you can catch him? You go look out crab". The girl gave up chasing the bird. The heron flew up and returned to the house, where the boy took off and hid the skin of the bird, resuming that of the sick man . . .

These manoeuvres go on for some time. (The girls busy themselves in making a canoe.)

Once when the others went away in the canoe to catch crabs, she stayed behind, hiding herself in the bushes close to the house. She wanted to find out the secret of the bird, for looking at its eyes she had been thinking, "That good man inside that skin, I think he all time make fool you me." The man got up and looked around: "Nobody here!" and the girl, peeping into the house, saw him: "My word, he come now!" He stripped off the bad skin and the woman said, "Oh, he take out skin. He good man. Oh! my husband! Plenty woman no find him out, I find him now!" Seeing the bird's skin he was putting on, she said, "Oh, he take that white pigeon now! Oh, he fly now!" . . .

The girl went into the house and found the human skin full of sores. She thought, "I burn him, no good he take him put him on, gammon all time", and she put it into the fire. She brought her bed and placed it alongside that of the boy, made a fire and sat down to wait. She kept her digging stick close to her in case the others wanted to fight.

The bird flew back to the house where the girl was waiting. All unsuspecting he mounted the ladder, took off the bird's skin, and carrying it in his hand entered the house in his proper shape. The woman took hold of his hand and snatched away the feather dress, saying, "What name you all time stow away along bad skin? No good this place stop no man (= is without a man), you man belong me." The man, without saying anything, sat down on the floor with bent head: "He (= she) find me out now!" He look round:

"All cloth belong me he been burn now, that cloth belong pigeon he been pull out along hand."

The girl rolled up the bird's skin in a small mat and hid it in front of herself under her grass skirt . . .[13] The other girls arrived, and the eldest sister looked in first. All the other girls, too, looked at the boy: "Oh, good fellow man, I want that man". The man did not say a word and sat with his head down, for he was ashamed now that they had found him out. The little sister . . . waited for the others to speak first and thought, "Before you no been come sit alongside that man, you no been give him no kaikai, fish. What for you look body all time? I no been look body, I been look eye."

She took out the bird's skin and gave it to the man, who put it on and became a bird.[14]

Here at Kiwai Island as with the Marind-anim, a mythical character who desires to fly simply puts on wings — that is, he fixes feather ornaments to his arms and back. When he does this, thanks to his acquired magical powers, he can fly and is a bird; to return to human shape, he need only take the feathers off. This tale moreover throws a certain light on what the Papuans understand by "transformation". The young man whose story it relates appears in three forms. First he is the boy covered with sores, who takes no notice of the girls except the one who, through kindness of heart, shows some interest in him. Then he is the handsome youth, perfectly healthy, whom she expects to marry and about whom the other girls quarrel with her. Then again, he is a bird covered with feathers and provided with broad wings. Changing from one of these forms to either of the others consists merely, for him, in getting out of one skin ("cloth" = singular of "clothes") and putting on another. The alteration from handsome youth to bird is carried out exactly in the same way as that from sick to healthy and attractive man. In the latter case he takes off his diseased skin and puts it carefully away, so as to be able to put it on again when the time comes. Similarly when he wants to become a bird he puts on his feathered "cloth" and attaches his wings. To become a man again he only has to take them off.

In these circumstances we can scarcely give the word transformation its full dictionary sense. No doubt a change in form *does* take place, but it leaves the personal identity of the individual wholly intact. He who in the ordinary way appears a human being, now seems to be a bird; but he is still the same person. He has only changed his "cloth", or skin. Over his human body he has put on a feathered dress. Nevertheless as long as he goes on wearing it, although he remains himself perfectly, he is not then a man, but a bird. He can hover in the air and pass over great distances; he can fly high into the sky. So neither is it merely a matter of a change of vestment. The subjective identity continues, but none the less for that, the bird has taken the place of the man. If we are to understand what such a transformation really signifies (to the degree that we can understand it at all) we need to come back to the kind of unity-in-duality we have encountered earlier with men-kangaroos, men-wildcats, men-ducks, men-mice, and the like, in the myths reported by Spencer and Gillen and by Carl Strehlow. Such mixed beings are men and animals simultaneously. At any given moment, however, they can reveal themselves in only one aspect of the double form. If, for example, a being is for the moment manifesting himself as human, then the animal which he also is remains for the time being out of sight; subjacent, though potential. If at that instant it is in the animal form that he is seen, then it is the human identity that is invisible. Though apparently absent, the other aspect is nevertheless also present (a duality the Eskimos express very ingeniously with their shutter-masks). Tranformation in the myths and folktales therefore rests, generally speaking, upon some such quality of unity-in-duality as this. When the fox "becomes" a woman, concealed beneath the human form the fox is still present; while she is a vixen, beyond the fox-shape there is still a woman's spirit. Movement from one of these "forms" to the other is accomplished by a simple change of dress or skin.

This change it itself a transformation in primitive terms, because in primitive parlance "skin" and "body" are equivalent. In the story we have just summarized, in order to prevent the young man from turning himself back into an invalid the girl takes the diseased skin he had left at home and throws it into the fire; so that he may not turn himself back into a bird again, she snatches away the feathered dress he is holding in his hand. He then realizes that his metamorphoses are over and becomes resigned.[15]

To provide oneself with wings by attaching feathers to one's arms is the most usual method employed in folktale for turning oneself into a bird. But there are others. For example, in one tale from the Kiwai Islanders,

> Emobali's sister thought to herself, "What's way I do?" She took a bird-of-paradise feather, put it in her mouth and sucked it in. This made her turn into a bird-of-paradise, and the people tried to catch

her, but she flew away crying out in the fashion of these birds, *"Kou, kou, kou."* Perching in a large tree she took out the feather and once more became a girl; and she said to the people, "you fellow stop. Me and my brother, me two no belong man, me belong cassowary." Again she transformed herself into a bird and flew away for good.

In another tale, "Now the girl had a feather of a small bird called *girinienie*, this she put in her mouth and sucked it in, and at the same moment she became this bird . . . The girl flew to her mother, took out the feather from her mouth and resumed her human form." In other stories, instead of the feather being sucked in it is swallowed. "By swallowing the feather of a hornbill he turned himself into a bird of the same species and flew over to Tudu Island." – "They tried to strike Gurume, but he fled, throwing away his ornaments as he ran with the people in hot pursuit behind him. After a while he put a feather in his mouth and swallowed it, thus transforming himself into a bird, *kekesio* by name. In the shape of the bird he alighted on the head of one of his pursuers, and when a blow was directed at him he dodged it, and the man was hit instead and killed."[16]

Feathers are an *appurtenance* of birds; like its skin and body, they are effectively the bird itself. To put them on, suck one in or swallow one, amounts to participation with the bird; and that, if one possesses the necessary magic, is an assured way of becoming transformed into it. That is what mythic heroes do, and so also do characters in folktale, who, being of the *Dema* kind, possess the same ability. For this same reason feathers have particularly strong magic qualities. They are used to decorate arrows. They are frequently used for personal adornment. The first people to stick feathers in their hair no doubt hoped or expected thereby to acquire some of that magic for themselves.

In folktales, men of this kind who, like the Australian or Papuan theriomorphs, could turn at will into animals and back again into human form, sometimes marry human women, and these marriages are fruitful. Often, however, the wife may be ignorant of the husband's double identity. In a story from Kiwai Island, Tiburi sees a girl who has undressed to go fishing. He turns himself into a snake, swims to her under water and has intercourse with her without her knowing, since she is standing breast-deep in the water . . . He does so again on the following days and she has a child by him.

One night Tiburi was told in a dream of the birth of his son. He transformed himself into a snake, swallowed a great quantity of vegetable food and betook himself to Uame's place. On seeing the snake One first fled, but the reptile passed its tongue quickly out and in and beat the ground with its tail as if to say, "You no fright, that man (husband) belong you, me here." The snake licked the little baby, and on seeing this, One understood that he was her husband; "Oh, that man belong me here," she thought. "That thing been make him pickaninny."

Nivia grew up and was given a small bow and arrows. He asked who his father was, and One told him how she had conceived him . . . Tiburi again dreamed of his child and came to see him in his human shape wearing many beautiful ornaments.

The child and his mother both know that Tiburi is a snake man. The animal form he reassumes whenever he wishes does not deter them from recognizing in him their father and husband.[17]

Another Kiwai tale:

One day the two brothers caught two little female pigs alive and brought them home. There they kept them shut up within a fence. After a time the mother asked them to marry the two pigs, and they did so and arranged a feast . . . After a time the mother died. A little later the one pig bore a boy and the other a girl, and they were not pigs but men. When they had grown up the two married. On seeing their children married the two men said, "My God, pickaninny belong you-me (= us) he married good, he proper man. He-got no people here, that's why me been take that pig-woman. This time he-got people; what name (why) you-me stop?" The two men felt ashamed and one night ran away. They threw off their human skins and became pigs. Since that time there are many pigs in the bush. When we eat pig we are in fact eating human flesh, said the narrator.[18]

This tale is typical; it certainly produces a very different impression on the natives from its effect on us. The events belong to a world quite different from ours and are comparable with those of true formal myths, in which animals exist on a fully equal footing with human beings. All the personages are *Demas*. In effect the two brothers are pig-men, as becomes plain in the conclusion when they take off the skins which had given them their human form. There is nothing to wonder at, therefore, in their mother's telling them to marry the sow-women. These latter give birth to human offspring. This tale obviously belongs to the same category as the preceding.

Here is another in which it is the woman who has the human-animal identity.

Inside the Dibiri creek lived a snake-man, Aboma by name, with his daughter. Nearby on the shore lived a man by himself. One day the snake-girl thought, "No good I stop along water, more better I go shore along that man. That man he marry me." And she and the man were married. After a time . . . she gave birth to a boy. When the father and mother went to work (i.e., in the plantation) they had to leave the baby alone in the house, for there was no one to look after it. The mother was very anxious . . . She went to Aboma, her father, and said, "All time I go garden, no man he look out (after) my pickaninny. That's all my man he stop, no got no people." (only my husband is there, no one else). Aboma pitied her and the baby and the next day when his daughter and son-in-law went to work he came on shore and looked after the child. In the evening the woman returned home first and spoke to her father, giving him food, and he went back into the water. The husband did not know that a stranger had been there, and his wife had not told him anything about her father, for she felt ashamed because he was a snake.

In the tale of the pig-wives the two brothers feel "ashamed" after the marriage of their children has set up a society that is purely human. Hence there is now no longer any place for pig-men like themselves and they disappear. This feeling of insurmountable shame comes to light constantly as the dual identity of a man or woman is revealed or betrayed — as might happen inadvertently, for example, through some indiscretion. Their sense of injury is so great that they withdraw from the social group to which they do not truly belong. Nothing can stop them. And once they have gone, nothing will bring them back.

Inside a well in Kiwai there lived a snake who was also a man, and one day he dug some deep holes round the well, covering them with leaves. A number of girls came to draw water and fell into the holes, and the snake dragged them underneath the ground, and they became his wives. (Eventually the girls escape and return to the village; he follows.) In the night the snake-man appeared outside the house and called the girls to come out. One of them went out and said to him, "You no kaikai me (= do not eat me). You take out skin belong snake, you stand up all same man, father belong me want look you." The snake assumed his human form and was taken into the house, and the people said to him, "You leave him place belong you, come stop this place", which the snake did.

He contributed victoriously to the defence of the village. But he was also a seducer, and the husbands killed him.[19] Properly speaking there is no metamorphosis here. He is both man and snake, the one and the other, all at once, taking one form or the other as the whim sways him (that is, by wearing, or not wearing, the snake's skin). Thus we find in the Kiwai folklore an animal-human being who could hardly resemble more closely the animal ancestors, the men-kangaroos, and the rest, of both Arunta and Marind-anim sacred myth.

Stories of such mixed beings are beyond counting. Here is one last example: "On a hill in Mabuiag there lived a *hawia* (white heron) which was also a man. He married a female *hawia*, and they had a son, who was a well-shaped boy, not a bird." Sometimes the dual identity of the being is betrayed to visible effect by something in the physical body. "At Mao there lived a woman called Iare, who was like a pig, with two forelegs and two hind-legs. She took part in the dance of the people by sitting on the ground and moving her forelegs." – A being may even take more than two forms: "Sivagu is the 'master' of Augaromuba, a point between Mawata and Mabudavana. He is a kind of étengena (= spirit) . . . and at different times appears in the shape of a man, a snake or a hawk . . ."[20]

There is doubtless no need to say any more to demonstrate how the world of Kiwai folklore possesses the same "fluidity" as Australian and Papuan sacred myth. The beings who make their appearance in it present exactly the same duality of nature. Nevertheless in secular myths and tales like these, as in those which are purely and simply popular, no concern remains with ancestor-or hero-worship, or with creation-figures or original culture-builders as such. For that reason the personages of the narratives no longer inspire the same feeling of reverential awe as was accorded to those of the primal sacred myths.

The folklore gathered by missionaries in former German New Guinea is very similar to that of Kiwai. There is a Kai tale, for example, which tells:

A man had lost his wife. After the mourning was over he went hunting one day. A kangaroo was taken. The widower, seeing it was a female, wanted it to take his wife's place. He took her home and put on her a beautiful necklet of dog-teeth; then he showed her a pile of taro and said, as he went out again, "Cook those!" She did nothing about it. When he came back and found nothing done, he flew into a rage and hurled his axe at her. She dodged the blow and ran off into the bush. The loss of such a wife as this hardly troubled him, but she had gone off with his necklet of dog-teeth! So he went hunting again: in the end the kangaroo was found and

killed, and the man got his necklet back. Since this experiment
with a kangaroo-wife did not succeed, it was strictly forbidden
from that time forward for a man to take any wife but one who
was a human woman.[21]

Quite evidently this kangaroo was a half-human, half-animal
being of the same kind as the animal-ancestors of the Arunta or
the Marind-anim. There is no need even for a transformation to
be brought in; it can appear without it that the female kangaroo
is also a woman, and the woman a kangaroo.

> One day a mother left her two little boys to go to her garden and
> get food. The boys, finding time drag in the village, went down to
> the sea to shoot fish (i.e., with bow and arrows). They saw one that
> was particularly handsome. They aimed at it and smashed its head
> in; much blood gushed out. When they saw how much blood there
> was, they were appalled; they realized what they had done. They
> rushed back to the house and anxiously waited for their mother to
> come home. She in the meantime, on her way, had already
> become aware of the calamity her children had caused. She put
> down her burden, climbed up a hill and looked around. Her eyes
> fell on the stream of blood which was still flowing, and she
> understood at once that it was her husband's.[22]

The fish which had so much blood *was* a man. The children do
not question this for a moment; they are aghast. Their mother
too knows at once that they have killed her husband. No doubt
she was already aware that he was fish and man at the same
time.

Here is another tale of the same kind. Themes reappear in it
that we have met with more than once before:

> A fish, whose name was Marenelang, transformed himself into a
> man . . . Two girls saw him and became enamoured of him. They
> married him and each had a child. The children played at bows
> and arrows, and amused themselves by shooting at each other. By
> a clumsy slip they hit their great-grandfather and put out one of
> his eyes. He fell into a great rage. "Offspring of a fish!" he cried,
> "how dare you put out my eye." They burst into tears because he
> called them *offspring of a fish*.
>   Their parents were away working in their field. Suddenly the
> father had a presentiment. He said to his two wives, "I have a
> presentiment. You go on working and come home later; I shall go
> ahead." He found his two children weeping . . . He tossed them
> into the sea, where the other fish made them welcome; then he
> went with them to the bottom and explained to them, "This is my
> own village. Your mothers took me to theirs, but my own proper
> village is here."

When the mothers returned they could not find their children. They turned to their grandfather who told them what had happened. "Why," they answered, "did you speak so harshly to them? . . . They were living here as human beings. When you scolded them, they felt ashamed. That is why their father has taken them away with him."[23]

Here is yet another example of the insurmountable shame which prevents a half-human, half-animal being from going on living in a purely human society after the secret of his mixed identity has been exposed.

In the River Ngeng a crocodile gave birth to a little girl . . . She continued to live inside her mother's body . . . When she was grown up she used to go ashore to dance. She ate some bananas in a plantation belonging to a man who caught her and wished to take her away. "Let me go! Let me go! Don't let anybody see me. I am a crocodile daughter!"

But the young man did not let her go. Just as, hearing the girl's cries, the mother crocodile showed herself on the surface of the water, he called out to her, "Wait a moment, I will bring the bride-price at once!" He took the girl back to her mother, went to fetch a pig and some objects of value, and tossed them all into the crocodile's mouth. The crocodile disappeared. The girl then consented to stay with him.

They lived happily together and after some time the woman had a son . . . One day because of some mistake committed by the child the man became angry and said to him, "Your crocodile mother (grandmother), I suppose, ate what they call a coconut?"[24] The child up till then had known nothing of his mother's origin. He went straight back into the house, lay under his mat and wept bitterly. That is how his mother came upon him when she returned from the field. He asked her at once, "Mother, where did you come from?" She then told him that she was the daughter of a crocodile. But she resented the insult levelled at her son as though it had been at herself, and she resolved to put up with no more like it in the future. She swept the house, cooked the taro and put it in her husband's basket, and made up her bundle. Then the two, mother and son, left a footprint in the cinders (as a sign in farewell) and went down to the river. They called to her mother. At this moment the man came home. Seeing the house empty, and the footprints in the cinders, he understood at once that something had happened, and full of gloomy fears he ran to the river. He shouted to his wife; but all she did was turn round and show him her son, saying "Look on us now for the last time!" Then with her mother, who had arrived in the meantime, she recited magic spells over the child, who immediately transformed into a baby crocodile. She herself took that shape, and sank. In despair the man leaped into the water, diving after his wife and child. But they had disappeared.[25]

In this tale also, shame forbids a woman of animal origin to continue living in a human community after her secret has become known and her child has been subjected to insult. We notice, too, that dealing with such mixed beings is the same as dealing with ordinary humans. The man who wants to marry the girl offers the crocodile-mother the customary gifts. The regular bride-price is paid to her. She then holds herself satisfied, and the girl makes no more resistance. This mother-in-law is never seen except in the shape of a crocodile. Her future son-in-law, however, knows she is also a woman.

A final tale, taken from the Yabim, will illustrate how close the animals (being still animals) may come to being human:

> The sow Kobakobao had a litter, and among the offspring one was a human child . . . She brought him up with the others. When this child grew up, the daughter of a headman fell in love with him. He brought her to his family. Here at last she was found by her own people who had gone to search for her. She made her relatives welcome when they came upon a visit. But it was impossible to offer the visitors only taro for refreshment. Kobakobao consented, to save face for her son, that two of his own litter should be killed, cooked and eaten.
>
> After the young man and his wife had said their farewells to the parents-in-law, the husband returned to the beach, where he found old Kobakobao and her other children had rolled themselves mournfully in the sand. He sat down and wept with them. When they had mourned sufficiently the mother spoke to him of what he had done. "We were living together happily," she said, "until you brought this young woman to us, and made us miserable. Let us all now return to where we came from!" She then threw herself into the sea with her children, intending to go back to her own country. The man's eldest (pig) brother, however, stayed with him. The mother said, "If there isn't enough pork, he can come and fetch some of his nephews or nieces to kill."[26]

This last suggestion can probably be rationalized by recalling the belief, very widespread among primitives, that when animals die they do not cease to exist any more than men do; they simply pass on to some other place where they wait, as often as not, to be reborn. Among animals this generally occurs straight away. As a rule all that is needful to ensure this is that the animal's bones should be kept together after it dies. Whether or not their flesh is eaten, is a detail of no importance.

It would be easy to show that Australian Aboriginal folklore —
as much of it as we know — belongs to the same mental world
and presents the same characteristics as in New Guinea, whence
we have drawn these last few specimens. It has the same "fluidity", the same human-animal duality, the same transformations,
etc. One story will satisfy the need for an illustration. "An *erlia*
(that is, of the *emu* clan) man lived far away beyond Urapunga,
in the Western Macdonnells. He could change himself into an
emu (*erlia*) when he wanted to do so, or rather he could enclose
himself in an emu skin with emu legs and feet. This *atua alchera*
had two lubras . . . one man, two women . . ." After an absence
he returns to the camp, "but could not find the women because
another man had come and taken them away". He found and
followed their tracks.

> The man with the lubras saw him coming, hid the women behind
> boughs, and himself climbed a tree. The *erlia* man, who had put
> on his emu skin and feet, came running up and slashed at the
> trunk as he ran by, with his *ilia inka*, emu feet; . . . a piece of wood
> . . . he cut off. Then he turned round, ran back and took another
> slice off the other side; then he took another run . . . so that the
> tree fell. Then . . . with his foot and toes he stamped and cut the
> man to pieces. He sang out to his lubras, who came out of their
> hiding place, and took them back to his own emu country, where
> the three of them died . . .[27]

In what way are we to interpret this transformation which permits the being to be either emu or man? — From his birth he is
one and the other, both at once. When, as a man, he wants to
take emu form, he puts on emu skin and feet, and that suffices.
Then he *is* an emu, right up to the moment when he takes off the
skin and legs and becomes a man again. This is exactly the same
as what happens in the tales cited earlier, in which transformations are presented. The skin is so truly a dress or vestment that
the natives of Kiwai Island, who had never seen clothed bodies
before, called the clothes of the first white men they saw, their
"skin". The original Kiwai form of the word for "clothes" is *Oboro-
tama*, which literally means "skin (*tama*) of a spirit (*oboro*)". "For
on their first arrival in the country the white people were regarded as spirits returning from the abode of the dead, and their
clothes were believed to be a kind of skin."[28]
If now we leave the Australian and New Guinea tribes behind
for those which Koch-Grünberg and von den Steinen have
studied in South America — tribes which have acquired scarcely

any higher elevation in the scale of civilization — their folklore and particularly their animal tales will still carry us into the same kind of "fluid" world. For example there is an Arekuna tale in which

> . . . a medicine-man, in order to escape from his step-mother, transformed himself into a small bird. The daughter of the giant armadillo caught sight of him in her plantation, and heard him sing . . . She said to him, "Come down and perch on my arm! I would like you to be my own special bird . . ." He, observing that the girl was pretty, hopped on to her arm. She gave him a cage. Then every night she dreamed of the little bird as a handsome young man. She hung the cage from the end of her hammock. Then she told her mother, "I dreamed about him; he was a handsome young man." That same day she said to the bird, "Transform yourself into a man and marry me!" He did that the same night; he turned into a man and slept with her.[29]

A tale like this carries a number of implicit suggestions. There is no need for them to be formally stated; any Indian listener would be certain to catch every hint. The armadillo's daughter is herself at once human and animal, and, like a *Dema*, endowed with magical powers. Hence she is intuitively aware of the double nature of the little bird that she wants to keep all to herself. And anyhow, don't we all believe — risking bad luck if we deny it! — that what we dream about, especially if we dream it more than once, is surely bound to come to pass? So we naturally expect the bird will return to his human form and marry the maiden! — In any case we find plenty of examples in the tales of birds being also human at the same time. "One day the medicine-man saw a tree which had fallen over and died. All the small birds . . . were weeping over the tree, for it was their uncle. The medicine-man was about to shoot them with his blowpipe. But at that moment the birds all transformed themselves into people and cried out, 'Don't shoot!' . . ."[30]

On the subject of such metamorphoses a remark of Koch-Grünberg adds confirmation to what we have gathered already. Reliance on the magical properties of the *kumi* plant comes into the picture, doubtless, only at a relatively late stage. The original notion was that all that was necessary was to put on a feathered dress in order to become a bird. This is what is alluded to when in the tales it is said that birds dwelling in the upper sky-world, like king vultures, parrots, araras and ducks, take off their feathered garments when they come home, and are then human in form.[31]

This observation is borne out by a whole series of tales. In one, the daughter of the king vulture alighted upon the hero's breast. Just as she was about to tear at his flesh with her beak, he grasped her in his arms. The other carrion birds all flew away. He said to the king vulture's daughter, "Turn into a woman! I am quite alone here and have no one to help me." He took her with him into his lonely house. There he kept her like a tame bird. He said to her, "Now I shall go fishing. When I get back I hope to find you transformed into a woman." . . .

> She obeyed . . . and he married her. He brought her game. "You can eat it as you wish, raw or cooked!" Then he ate with her, and she quickly got accustomed to him. She loved him. He brought her much venison, and at night he slept with her.
> After some time she had a wish to see her family. He agreed. She reassumed her bird-form and flew off. Next day he saw her in a dream (as she had promised him), and soon after she arrived back with two of her brothers. They circled as they descended in wide sweeps, until they were quite close to him, over his head. His wife spoke to him: "These are my brothers. Do not be ashamed of me. I am not ashamed of you. You will find it just as easy to get along with them."
> He killed a stag and they ate it together. His brothers-in-law stayed two days. They had brought him a feather-garment of the king vulture species. The woman told them to put it on her husband. So he dressed himself in the garment and thus became transformed into a vulture. She chewed some *kumi* and breathed it over him. Then she said, "Now let us go. Have no fear!" . . . All four of them arrived in the sky at the dwelling of the king vultures . . . The father came to see his daughter's husband. He made him very welcome. There were many people present.[32]

The woman's brothers, vultures themselves, when they decided to bring their sister's husband to their dwelling place in the sky, were obliged to transform him for the time being into a bird to make the journey. How was it to be done? Nothing easier! They simply brought him one of their own feather-garments. He had to put it on: when he did, he was a vulture like them. When they arrived in the sky, what had they all to do, but take off these garments, to become human once again?

If now we turn to consider other communities more "advanced" than these, such as the Eskimo, the Pueblos of New Mexico, the North American Indians, most of the Bantu, etc., it will not be very surprising if we find a folklore that is rather different, at least in its detail, from this. Inevitably it must reflect the later-developed aspects of their religious, political and economic life – in short, the settled traditions of these societies, as also the greater complexity of their relations with their neighbours. The question which then arises is this. After taking all these differences into account, shall we nevertheless encounter here too, in their later characteristic vision of the world, the same basically "fluid" elements as we have found to be so remarkably widely prevalent in the secular tales, no less than in the sacred myths, of those more primitive peoples?

We can base our answer only on a necessarily limited number of examples. Nevertheless we need not hesitate to assert that the result will be valid, even if far from comprehensive, for all communities of this kind. This may seem a rash generalization, extrapolation rather; but provided we reserve an appropriate place for such exceptions as experience may reveal, the risk of error will not be so grave as at first might be thought. For the matter turns wholly upon only a very few essential elements which constitute the way the world is perceived. That is something very narrowly dependent on the relationship between the present outlook and the origins from which it has sprung. There are quite sound reasons for supposing the mental origins of all the tribes in question to have been very similar. In any case the closing pages of this book will provide an effective, if also indirect, confirmation of the views advanced in this present chapter.

Because of the powerful conditioning effects of environment, especially climate, Eskimo culture, in spite of the immense area of country it covers, nevertheless retains a sufficiently homogeneous general character for us to be able to speak of the folklore in broadly unified terms; it is not necessary always to specify the exact region where it has been collected. In it, theriomorphic beings of the kind found in the folklore we have already looked at make a constant appearance. From Cumberland Sound comes a story, reported by Rink and Boas, which tells how "an angakok and his son visited a house inhabited by ravens and gulls . . . We must imagine the birds sitting in this house – the bird-cliff – conversing and looking at the two men, who are seen to approach on the ice, coming shoreward, and who finally reach the entrance of the house". Evidently the birds are in all respects creatures of the half-human, half-animal, dual-natured kind, as the narrator goes on to add: "The angakok possessed the power to see the birds in their human forms". No doubt this implies that the angakok can

discern, underneath his feather-garment, the man who is wearing it.[33]

The same theme turns up frequently in the folklore of the
Caribou Eskimos. Rasmussen records these examples: "There
was once an *akla*, a land-bear, that lived in human form. It used
to go down to the dwellings of men and steal away dead bodies,
and sometimes it would also take live human beings . . ." "This is
what is told of the ravens and gulls, that lived in a human form,
and had dogs and dwelt in human dwellings." "There was once a
caribou that suddenly began to talk, when it came on its way to a
crossing of a river. It cried out, "Are there people there on the
other side?' . . ." One anecdote plainly harks back to the "fluidity"
of the mythic age: "This is something that has been borne in
mind from the time when animals were just as often human
beings as they were animals, and sometimes lived together, all
kinds of animals in one big house, which could suddenly turn
into a cave or the lair of a beast." "There were once two men who
went on a journey visiting. They set out and came to a place
where there lived wolves and wolverines in human form. The
wolves were having a great song festival . . ." "Then one day a
man and his wife came on a visit. They were wolves in human
form, and when they had been there some time, the wolf wanted
to change wives with the man for one night" (the host's wife was
a fox). Complications set in and in the end the vixen-wife runs
away. "On the following day her husband went after her, and
following up her tracks, he noticed that they were real human
tracks at first. Then suddenly one foot changed to that of a fox,
and close to the hole where it lived, both feet were those of a
fox."[34]

Together with the dual identity which marks these half-
human, half-animal beings, we once again find among the
Eskimos the metamorphoses with which they are so closely
associated. Here as previously, transformations are most frequently effected by a simple change of "skin" or vestment. In a
folktale of the Copper Eskimo reported by Diamond Jenness,

> A woman was travelling alone over the land, carrying a baby on
> her back. One day she came to a house. She went inside, and
> found only a woman with a wolf-skin stretched out alongside of
> her; all the men, she was told, had gone out hunting. After a time
> the hunters drew near, and this woman took her wolf-skin and
> went out to meet them. Her visitor, looking out, saw her change
> into a wolf, and wag her tail from side to side as she advanced to
> meet the hunters, who were also wolves. Presently they all chang-

ed to human beings again and entered the hut. They began to talk about their hunt . . ."[35]

To achieve this last transformation they *took off* their wolf-skins. The narrative does not actually say so, no doubt because it is obvious. These men who turn into wolves, these wolves who turn into men (they could equally well be described as either wolfmen or men-wolves) constitute a favourite theme in Eskimo folklore. What need is there to dwell on the resemblance to corresponding themes in more primitive folk legend, since they are so obvious?

Here is another instance, no less usual, involving the same kind of transformation. Stith Thompson reports:

A man who was walking, once upon a time, came to a pond, where there were a number of geese. These geese had taken off their garments and had become women, and were now swimming in the pond. The man came up to them without being seen, and seized their feather-garments. (The expression "feather-garments", we note, in passing, is the same as is used in the Taulipang folktale of the king vultures.) He gave them all back but two, whereupon the women put them on and flew away. Finally he gave one of the two remaining ones hers, whereupon she also flew off. The last woman, however, he kept with him, took to his house, and married. Soon she became pregnant and gave birth to two children. One day, while her husband had gone away, she found some wings, which she took into the house and hid behind the skin-coverings of the walls. When her husband again went away, she put these on herself and her two children, whereupon they turned to geese and flew away.[36]

In their feather-garments these women are geese; without them they are human.

The following tale from Alaska, reported by Jenness, is very reminiscent of another from New Guinea which we have already noted. A young hunter comes upon some girls playing at hide-and-seek. They are naked (that is to say, they have taken off their animal-robe or skin, for they are ducks). He catches the prettiest one, carries her off and makes her his wife. All seems well, but she will not eat meat; she lives on grass. One day her mother-in-law said to her, "What kind of girl are you that you are always eating grass? Are you a duck?" — Then the girl was very angry; she went inside, weeping, dressed her two children, and went out again with them. The husband set out in pursuit. Suddenly, looking at her tracks, he exclaimed, 'Why, one of her feet is webbed like a duck's! Perhaps I shall never find her now.'

In the end, he did. At first she did not recognize him. "No Eskimos ever come here," she said, "This is my country, the duck's country."[37] As in the New Guinea story, when she heard her mother-in-law's disparaging reference to her animal origin, she resented the insult and was ashamed. Life with the human community became impossible for her. She went away with no thought of ever returning, and took her children with her. It is interesting to see that when she leaves for the ducks' country, though she has taken her feather-garment, she still walks and does not fly.

Except for one last example, interesting because it gives certain details of the process of a transformation, I shall report no more tales based on this theme, since it is so commonplace. Jenness again reports how a wife, against the express command of her husband, listened to the talk of an old woman, who in leaving the house, turned into a red fox. (She had allowed this old woman to touch her head.) First she went to sleep, then awoke with a terrible headache and an irresistible desire to go out. When she put her hands to her head, she felt the bumps of horns beginning to grow. She went outside. Already her head had changed into the head of a caribou. She made a circle first, then went off straight to the mountains.

Her husband went to look for her and at last found her in a herd of caribou. Following the advice given him by a helpful bear, he had to skin her. "Take a rope . . . throw the rope over her horns – then throw her on her back and skin her. You must be very careful not to kill her, and when you are skinning her, mind you don't cut the flesh anywhere. Then when you have skinned the body, make a small incision in the belly and your wife will come out from within unharmed." He does so and all is well. These – one might call them realist – details still allow the idea of a transformation, like so many of the others we have encountered, to persist. Bewitched by the old woman who was really a red fox, the woman puts on a caribou skin, and thus transformed, goes off to live with the herd. In order to turn her back into a human being it is necessary to remove the skin, and therefore the husband is obliged to flay the caribou she has become.[38]

In another story from the same tribe there is a transformation of a kind which is much more easily accomplished.

One day Nakasunaluk went caribou hunting and saw a herd of five or six deer. He stalked close to them and was about to launch his arrow when one of the deer pushed back the hood from its head and changed into a man. It called Nakasunaluk, telling him to come near. Nakasunaluk went over, and the deer asked him if he would like to join them. He said he would, so the deer removed his clothes and turned him into a caribou like themselves; then they all moved off together . . . Thus he lived a long time with the deer, until one day they asked if he would like to go back home . . . 'Yes,' he said . . ."[39]

So at his request he was changed back to a man. He went back to his people and told them his story. This story seems to take us back to the mythic world pure and simple. Men and animals are placed together on a footing of full equality, and changed without effort from the one condition to the other. We have already met with a mention of the animal-hood, pushed back to reveal the man underneath, in a Papuan tale.

The folklore of North America is among the most extensively recorded and best documented we possess. The few examples we are now about to draw from it will introduce us to a world that is certainly no less "fluid" than that of the other folklore we have seen, and is equally populated with beings of a mixed human-animal nature. It is the scene of some quite extravagant transformations.

Among the tales of the Cochiti (New Mexico) Indians, many examples are found of animal characters which are really animal-men. Speaking about mountain lions and bears, Fr Noel Dumarest remarks, "These animals are thought to be human and to put on their animal skins at pleasure. Some of them are malevolent and classed with Navaho; others are *chaiani* and visit the pueblos to cure the sick." – In one such tale two girls, who are actually bear-children, bring a young man home. The parents arrive. The father bear flies into a rage, and so too, after a time, does the mother. Then after a while the bears remove their skins, and the youth perceives that they are really human beings.[40] Sometimes these mixed beings possess superhuman faculties like a *Dema*. In a Cochiti tale reported by Ruth Benedict, a little boy, one of six brothers, manages on his own to expose a witch. He is possessed of one great supernatural advantage: "On one side he was a bear and on the other he was a person." He becomes sleepy. "He lay down and slept. The one side that was a man was asleep, but the other side did not sleep. He had his eye open on one side."[41] The naive realism of this is intended to present a rational view of the dual identity of this unusual person. In an account offered as a variant of this tale, the bear-man becomes the lover of a woman who has a child by him. "It was half bear and half-human . . . they named it Sanosa."

Another tale shows men and animals on a footing of equality.[42] [A man goes hunting deer; he is away unexpectedly long and his wife goes to find him. She puts the baby down in what she thinks is a safe place, intending to return. She finds the husband and they return for the baby, but find it gone.]

> Then he searched for tracks around there. "Someone took away my child," said his father. Then he spoke thus, "Now there are deer tracks," said he. "A deer took away my child," said he. "I shall go after him," said he. Then thither northwestward he went. (He saw the child.) The baby was sitting on the deer's antlers. The deer took him to his house. He dwelt in a cave. Then the baby's father also entered. Far inside it was. There were many little deer, young ones, and among them was his child. "I come for my poor child whom you stole from me," said he to the deer. "There the little fawns are in a corral," said the deer. "If you recognize your child, then you shall take him off. Do you recognize him?" "No," said he, "they are all alike." (Proof by recognition is a frequent motif in all folklore).[43] [Now the most aged of the stags said to him,] "Now you may take him away. I give back to you your child." Then he took the child back.
>
> [But there was a condition:] ". . . You will make him enter inside. When four days are passed, you will take out your child, you and his mother. You will tell her she must not see her child (before that time). If she should see him, he will come back here," said the old deer. "When four days are passed, she will grind corn and make him wafer bread. Then she will see her son." But on the fourth day the mother could hold out no longer; she opened the door just a trifle and immediately the little deer escaped.

The deer, like so many other animals in the folktales, are no sooner at home than they take human form and live as men. What is no less remarkable is the fact that the child who is taken away is fully transformed into a fawn. His father is no more surprised at this, than to find himself conversing with the stag-kidnapper in the form of a man.

These same mixed beings occur also in the folktales of numerous other North American tribes. In a tale of the Menomini reported by Alanson Skinner a thunderbird addresses the hero thus: "When you return you shall carve my image upon a board and place it in the bundle, in order to please me. You must take two plain square blocks, and upon each of these outline my figure in sacred red paint, one shall represent me as a Great Powered Bird, and one shall represent me as a man with a flint-lock in my hand. I am of dual nature. I can change myself into either a bird or a man at will."[44] Another legend of the same people retold by Stith Thompson tells of the brother of Manabozho: "As he was alone the good *manidos* (*manitou*, equivalent to *dema*) gave him a twin brother. He was formed like a human being, but, being a *manido*, could assume the shape of a wolf, in which form he hunted for food."[45]

In a Nez-Percé tale reported by Spinden, "The old woman did not like the way she had been treated; so, after Raccoon had slipped outside, she put on the hide, and thus changed herself into a grizzly bear." Obviously this procedure of transformation is merely the ordinary one. Occasionally we will find the process described even very nonchalantly: ". . . He was among the eagle people in Eagle Land. The full grown people, like the full grown eagles, had white faces and heads, while those of the young people, like those of young eagles, were dark. Eagle skins were hanging about all over the village, and it amused him to watch some of the people put on the eagle skins and change to eagles, and after flying around, take them off and become human beings again."[46]

Sometimes the transformation works out in another way. A Cochiti tale (again Ruth Benedict) tells how a wife noticed that her husband preferred her younger sister, who returned his interest.

> The elder sister knew that they were together and she said, "I am going to die". She went into the inner room and placed a large basket in the center of the floor. She sat down in the basket crying. Her feet began to turn into the tail of a snake. She was crying and the tears were running down her cheeks. She was already a snake. The boy's mother came to look for her, but she could not find her. So she went into the inner room and found that her daughter-in-law had become a great snake. She took sacred meal in her hand and went to the chief of the Flint Society . . . He sang all the curing songs of the Flint Society but he could not restore her. She was a snake.
> They did everything possible but could not bring her back to human form.[47]

In the following tale reported by James A. Teit we are able to follow the course of a transformation stage by stage.

> A chief had many horses, and among them a stallion which his wife often rode. The woman grew careless of her household duties, and always wanted to look after the horses. When the people moved camp and the horses were brought in, it was notic-

ed that the stallion made right for the woman, and sniffed about her as stallions do with mares. After this she was watched. When her husband learned the truth, he shot the stallion. The woman cried, and would not go to bed. At daybreak she was gone, no one knew where. About a year after this it was discovered that she had gone off with some wild horses. One day when the people were travelling over a large open space, they saw a band of horses, and the woman among them. She had partly changed into a horse; her pubic hair had grown so long that it resembled a tail. She also had much hair on her body, and the hair of her head had grown to resemble a horse's mane. Her arms and legs had also changed considerably; but her face was still human, and bore some resemblance to her original self. The chief sent some young men to chase her. All the wild horses ran away; but she could not run so fast as they, and was run down and lassoed. She was brought into her husband's lodge; and the people watched her for some time trying to tame her, but she continued to act and whinny like a horse. At last they let her free. The following year they saw her again. She had become almost entirely horse, and had a colt by her side. She had many children afterwards.[48]

In this tale, however, true dual identity is not taken for granted; properly speaking we do not here see a mare-woman. In the first place she is wholly woman and, at any rate to judge by appearances, she transforms herself little by little into an animal, and in the end is wholly mare. The child she gives birth to is a foal. The metamorphosis demonstrates nevertheless that she must have been of a *dema*-like nature. Perhaps this explains, or supplies one of the reasons, why she is spared by her husband and by the tribe when they have her in their power.

Here is a last story, retold by Stith Thompson from the same tribe; but I reproduce only its indispensable details.[49] They are particularly instructive and vividly germane to our understanding — if we may flatter ourselves that we ever do understand it — of the *participation* which the Indian sees ("senses intuitively" might be a better term) as existing between an individual human being and some particular animal species.

"There was a man who was a great deer-hunter. He was constantly hunting, and was very successful. He thought continually of the deer, and dreamed of them. They were as friends to him. (The fact that they appear to him in dreams is an indication of their favourable *disposition* towards him.) Probably they were his *manitou* (his guardian-animal). He had two wives, one of whom had borne him no children, while the other had borne a male child."

One day he followed a doe. When he reached her, she was a woman. She persuaded him to go with her.[50] "As they went along, he thought, 'It is not well that I am acting thus. My wives and child are at home awaiting me.' The woman knew his thoughts at once, and said, 'You must not worry or think that you are doing wrong. You shall be my husband, and you will never regret it.'" He arrived with her in her (underground) country. "They found themselves in a large house full of people who were just like Indians . . . They were well dressed in clothes of dressed skin, and wore deer-skin robes. They seemed to be very amiable and happy . . . That night the woman said to the hunter, 'You are my husband and will sleep with me. You may embrace me, but you must not try to have intercourse with me. You must not do so before the rutting season. Then you may also go with my sisters.'"

The next day he was sent out to hunt. "Two young deer, his brothers-in-law, ran ahead and stood on a knoll. Presently the hunter saw them and killed both of them." (The bones are saved and thrown into the water; when that is done the killed deer come back to life.)[51] Thus these Deer people lived by hunting and killing each other and then reviving. The hunter lived with his wife and her people . . . He never failed to kill deer, for some of the young deer were always anxious to be killed for the benefit of the people.

"At last the rutting season came on, and the chief put the body (that is to say, the skin) of a large old buck on the hunter, and so transformed him into a buck." Other males attack and beat him and take his wife; he feels downcast. "The chief said, 'Do not feel sad. We shall give you ornaments tomorrow which will make you strong, and then nobody can take your wife away from you.' On the following morning he put large antlers on him, and gave him the body of a buck in its prime. That day the hunter beat off all the rival bucks and kept his wife and also all her sisters and cousins for himself. He hurt many of his brothers-in-law in fighting. The Deer people had shamans who healed the wounds of those hurt in battle, and they were busy throughout the rutting season . . . In due time his wife gave birth to a son."

With his wife and the child the hunter now goes back to visit his own [human] people. They provide a feast for everybody.[52] "The hunter stayed with his people for a considerable time. Whenever they wanted fresh meat, he gave his bows and arrows to his son and told him to hunt. The youth always took with him his half-brother, the son of his father by his Indian wife. They killed deer, for the deer were the boy's relatives and were willing to be killed. They threw their bones into the water and the deer came back to life."

After a time they returned to the country of the Deer people, and all the hunter's [Indian] tribe went with him. "The first day of the journey, the hunter said to his wife, 'Let us send our son out, and I will shoot him.' He hunted, and brought home a young deer, which the people ate. They missed the Deer-Boy and wondered where he had gone. At night the hunter threw the bones into the water, and the boy came to life. On the next day the hunter's wife went out, and he killed her and fed the people. They missed her, and wondered where she had gone. At night he threw the bones into the water, and she came to life."[53]

"After many days" they reached the Deer people's house and were well received, but the tribe decided to return and the Deer-Boy went with them. He "never returned. He became an Indian and a great hunter. From him the people learned how to treat deer. He said to them, 'When you kill deer, always see to it that the bones are not lost. Throw them into the water.[54] A hunter who does this pleases the deer. They have affection for him, are not afraid of him, and do not keep out of his way . . . The deer will always remain plentiful, because they are not really killed.' (That is, if proper care is taken the killed deer come back to life immediately.) . . .[55] The hunter never returned to the people. He became a deer."

Could imagination conceive a more lively presentation of beings in whom the two natures, human and animal, appear so intimately blended, it is impossible to tell them apart? When the doe is overtaken by the hunter, she is also at the same time a woman who takes the man for her husband. Nevertheless, woman as she is, she remains a deer and will accept the conjugal relationship with her husband only in the rutting season. Her family and her tribe are composed of deer; yet when they are in their own country they form a human society. They dwell in a great "house", and live in it as men. But in the rutting season they are deer once again and they fight for possession of the females. The hunter himself, once transformed into a vigorous buck (after putting on the skin of a mature male),[56] takes part in the battle. In their human form these deer require meat; they hunt, kill and eat their fellow-creatures, often their closest kin. So the hunter kills his doe-wife and his deer-boy son without hesitation or scruple. For provided the bones of the animal are carefully respected, preserved and cast into the water, they immediately revive. They were not really "killed". (The same notion is accepted, as we have seen, by the Eskimos with regard to seals.) The hunter's human tribe pays a visit to the deer-people and fraternizes with them. The hunter has two children, one the child of an Indian wife, the other of the doe-wife. The two boys are always together. The one who is a deer-boy goes to the country of the humans and stays there without any desire to go back. He becomes a true Indian and teaches the tribe the proper treatment of deer when the hunters kill them. In return the father remains with the deer-people where he went in order to live with his deer-wife; he ends by becoming a deer entirely. In short, the *participation* between the human and animal groups is so complete that a member of either one can pass freely into the other, and *vice versa*. More than that, as well as taking part in the life of one or the other group, the individual retains certain characteristics which belong to the group he began with. Thus the doe-wife, though in human form, only makes love at the same season as the other does.

This remarkable fragment of North American Indian folklore transports us into a world which has strong affinities with that of the Australian and New Guinea myths. These Indians have animal ancestors, who are at the same time human beings, and from whom, similarly, are descended both the human tribes and the animal species which bear the same name. It is true that in the Indian folktale of the deer nothing is said specifically of a mythic ancestor common to the human people and the deer-tribe alike. Nor is there any mention of tribal rituals or tabus of a totemic kind. Nevertheless it is pointed out that the deer are the *"manitou"* of the hunter, which comes to much the same thing as calling it his personal totem. The members of the tribe and the deer-people are not alien, not strangers to each other. Everything happens very much as though there did exist a bond between them entirely similar to the unique form of kinship we call totemism.

It would in any case be difficult to come across a story better calculated to render the idea of totemism so approachable – not to say comprehensible – for us as this one does. It does not, admittedly, make any precise affirmation as to the identification of the human group with the animal species. But the familiar details so simply and naturally presuppose it that there is no room for doubt. They enable us to probe to the quick, if one may put it like that, the truth and reality of the actions and feelings which are born of so intimate a community of nature. From the beginning to the end of this story one's sympathies are aroused just as naturally and spontaneously for the animal characters as for the human, for the animal doe as for the human hunter who is to become her husband. Animal or human, they are all, and in a fully factual sense, neither more nor less than beings of double nature. The doe is a woman from the very first, the hunter is already in full potential the animal he is about to become. And yet we are able, seemingly, to share fully in the feelings both experience, and can perfectly understand the course of action that those feelings lead them to.

And so it comes to pass that myths springing from the most primitive of communities and stories like this Indian one may illuminate one another with a precious light. The animal ancestors of primitive myth lend plausibility and conviction to the consubstantial interchange, the kinship principle, obviously of a totemic kind, which operates between the hunter and his tribe, and the deer people. And to reverse the prospect, his manner of living among them as with the closest of natural kin also brings us sensibly towards an understanding of what the Australian or Papuan Aborigine feels for the animal he regards totemically in the light of an elder brother or a forefather.

Chapter VIII

The Mythic World and Folklore: II

We are far from possessing a comprehensive corpus of the folklore of black Africa. But what we do know of it is enough to verify the assertion that in general its folktales and legendry grow out of the same mythic world as all the others. We find the same "fluidity" of nature, the same mixed half-animal, half-human beings, and the same prodigious transformations accomplished with ease in the twinkling of an eye.

Here to begin with are a few typical African examples of the belief in human-animal mixed beings. In the midst of a story whose principal figures are animals, one suddenly realizes they are men — or the other way round. The teller feels no need to give warning of this alteration, for whether in the one form or the other, the story is still about the same personages. In a Zulu folktale about pigeons, Henry Callaway remarks, "So here the progress of the tale shows that men and not pigeons are meant. They are unable to fly across a river." In Lamba folklore (Southern Africa) there is frequent mention of lions which appear in human form, marry wives and then attempt to devour them. This in the general way is regarded by the Lambas as sheer fancy. All the same, C.M. Doke tells us, if a stranger from outside comes to marry one of the village girls, they have a proverbial saying, "Ask him about his home and his ancestry; if you don't, you may find yourself marrying a lion, that will eventually devour you!"[1] A tale of the Mbaka (Angola), recounted by Heli Chatelain, tells of the leopard, who is travelling with his grandson. "Stopping on the road, they meet some women who are planting peanuts. The leopard says, 'Grandson, I come directly.' He goes to a thicket of the forest; he undoes his bundle, takes out a shirt, takes out drawers, takes out trousers, takes out a vest, takes out a coat; he dresses. Having finished dressing, cane in hand, he goes. He finds the girls. 'Good afternoon, ladies, are you well?' " Another story recorded by Chatelain tells how there was once a famine among the lions. The cattle of man were too well guarded; how were they to attack them? . . . A young lioness transforms herself into human form. They dress her elegantly and give her a charming coiffure. What she must do is explained to her. The owner of the cattle will request her hand in marriage. She will accept, and, at the propitious moment, will kill him. The young lioness agrees. She goes off at once, in the form of a girl. Everything happens according to plan — but the man is saved by his little boy, who refuses to leave him even at night.[2] In the world of this African folklore as in that of the myths, the external form of all beings is merely an "accident". Those who are of the *dema* kind have the power to change it to suit themselves.

Sometimes it is the man who becomes an animal. For example in this Tongaland story (southern Africa), according to H. Berthoud,

> A man named Babana lived in the Rikoto district. At night he used to transform himself into an elephant and went out to eat the pumpkins in people's gardens . . . They chased after him . . . But after a while they lost the elephant tracks, though they found traces of a man's, and there was some blood. Then they came upon the spot where he had discarded his tusks, in the form of two rods, which until then had been fixed in his mouth. At this the people turned back home, saying, "How could this elephant manage to look like an elephant when we tackled him, and yet afterwards turn into a man?" A suspicion dawned. They called all the men by name and Babana's absence was clear. "At the moment when we tackled the elephant," they asked, "where was Babana?" "Perhaps," some said, "he stayed at home; no doubt he is still there." They went to his hut to make sure. There he was in bed, nursing injuries obviously made by spears. "What's that?" they demanded — He replied, "I transformed myself into an elephant because I was longing for pumpkins." They made a comic song about him and it spread all over the country.[3]

What we remark in this blithe anecdote is the Tongalanders' immediate but cool suspicion, when they notice how human tracks suddenly take the place of elephant ones, that the elephant and the man may be the same individual. Such transformations are obviously familiar; there is nothing in them to cause amazement.

In East Africa the hyaena conceived the idea of marrying an A-Kamba wife, reports C.W. Hobley.

> The hyaena therefore started taking with him some cattle and goats to pay for his intended bride. During the day he assumed

human shape and walked on two legs, but when darkness came on he reverted to a hyaena and went on four legs. He arrived with his stock at a village where a certain damsel lived and stated his errand, and was received in a friendly way; he said his name was Mutili. Night came and he changed back to a hyaena, and feeling hungry he went to the hut of his prospective mother-in-law to eat. When he reached the hut, however, some sheep who were there smelt him, became frightened and rushed to and fro; the mother of the girl thereupon came to the door with a firebrand to see what was frightening the sheep, and called out, "Who is there?" In reply the hyaena gave vent to a loud howl. The woman, who had never heard the cry of a hyaena before, replied, "Well, whoever you are, go to sleep now and in the morning we will talk." So the hyaena got no supper and in the night he became very hungry, and seeing a sheep near by with a great fat tail, he bit off the tail and ate it. In the morning the villagers turned out the sheep and saw one with his tail missing. They were very surprised at this, and looking round for the cause saw the hyaena (now of course in the shape of a man again) and the fat from the tail hanging all round his mouth. Thereupon the villagers seized sticks and beat him severely, shouting out, "You are not *Mutili* but *Mbiti* because you eat meat raw." They drove him out of the village, and he fled away to the woods.[4]

Here the hyaena appears conventionally greedy and stupid, which the hearers take as a great joke. Nevertheless, as long as he seems to be human in form he can be accepted as a bona fide suitor, in a position to pay for the dowry, and the villagers are friendly to him. The suitor and the hyaena are however one and the same identity, and the tale acknowledges no obligation to explain how the sudden substitution of the one for the other is to be accounted for.

I shall dwell no further on stories of this kind, since there are many of them, with many variations; but will move straight on to some others which resemble them closely and yet are not precisely folk *tales*. On the contrary, they are offered as factual records of recent events, with eye-witnesses at hand to attest them. To us the clear distinction between fact and fiction is always vital. For the blacks, however, it is scarcely so at all. They are as ready to believe the one kind of story as the other. What happens in folktales is deemed no whit more improbable than certain things that actually do happen in their own neighbourhood.

The following account will adequately illustrate this attitude of mind. A.W. Cardinall reports that:

A certain clerk in Government employ at head-quarters had a bitch which had recently presented him with a litter of fine puppies. The family he allowed to sleep under his couch. One morning the clerk, who had passed a bad night through being disturbed by the bitch's growls and restlessness, searched about for the cause. He soon found a hyaena hidden under a settee in the next room. Naturally he shouted out for a gun, and to his surprise the hyaena asked him not to shoot as she was a woman and not a hyaena at all. Several people had by this time run up to see what all the noise was about and witnessed a hyaena-woman emerge from her hiding-place. She was a woman right down to her legs which were those of a hyaena.

Everyone was much alarmed at this unexpected sight and some constables were called in. The woman explained that she was from Kumbungu, that she had the power of turning at night time into a hyaena, and that having heard that the Clerk's bitch had given birth to a fine litter of fat puppies she had discarded her clothes and changed into a hyaena and had then loped along to the clerk's house. Here, however, she had been kept off by the mother dog's growling and had been afraid to seize the puppies lest the clerk might be awakened. She had hidden herself hoping for a chance later, but the dawn had arrived before this had come so that she had decided to resume her natural form. This she was in process of doing when a fly had settled on her and thus had prevented the metamorphosis from being completed, for it is believed that if a fly sits on these werewolves they cannot change back into their human forms until the following night.

Now that scene was witnessed by some thirty people, many of whom were educated and supposedly Christian. They one and all believed implicitly that they had seen a being half-hyaena and half-woman. The fact that a European who passed saw only a naked woman and nothing else detracted nothing from their faith. It merely showed that what the African sees is not the same as what the European can see. The woman was driven out of the town by the natives and returned to Kumbungu.[5]

Except that here the conviction of the witnesses appears so positive, might we not easily take this to be just another fanciful tale like that of the hyaena who set out to find a wife? In that story the hyaena could transform himself into a man, in this a woman can turn into a hyaena. Either of these changes is as easily believable as the other for the natives, and nothing could be more remote from their thoughts than to raise any doubt of their natural feasibility.

Here from South Africa is another story, reported by Andersson, which is no less characteristic.

During his journeyings in Great Namaqua-Land, Sir James Alexander was told by the natives that the Bush-women have it in their power to change their forms into lions, hyaenas, and other beasts of prey. The following legend illustrates this superstition: –

Once on a time, a certain Manaqua was travelling in company with a Bushwoman carrying a child on her back. They had proceeded some distance on their journey, when a troop of wild horses (zebras) appeared, and the man said to the woman, "I am hungry; and as I know you can turn yourself into a lion, do so now, and catch us a wild horse, that we may eat."

The woman answered, "You'll be afraid."

"No, no," said the man. "I am afraid of dying of hunger, but not of you."

Whilst he was speaking, hair began to appear at the back of the woman's neck, her nails assumed the appearance of claws, and her features altered. She set down the child.

The man, alarmed at the change, climbed a tree close by, while the woman glared at him fearfully; and, going to one side, she threw off her skin petticoat, when a perfect lion rushed out into the plain. It bounded and crept among the bushes towards the wild horses; and springing on one of them, it fell, and the lion lapped its blood. The lion then came back to where the child was crying, and the man called from the tree, "Enough! Enough! Don't hurt me. Put off your lion's shape. I'll never ask to see this again."

The lion looked at him and growled. "I'll remain here till I die," exclaimed the man, "if you don't become a woman again." The mane and tail began to disappear, the lion went towards the bush where the skin petticoat lay; it was slipped on, and the woman in her proper shape took up the child. The man descended, partook of the horse's flesh, but never again asked the woman to catch game for him.[6]

"Humbug!" says Andersson. Of course. But we have just encountered a very similar transformation in a story where it formed the central point and was reported as a recent actuality. The fact is, nobody doubts that such things can happen. This kind of belief is very widespread. Among the Bantu it is quite commonly believed that if a lion or a leopard attacks a man, it is not an actual lion but really a sorcerer who has transformed himself in order to gain his end. C.M. Doke tells us, "An *imfwiti* may accost his victim as he travels along a lonely section of the path, and ask him if he is travelling alone or whether others are behind. If he gets the answer, 'I am alone', he quickly goes behind an anthill and keeps quiet. When the man has gone on a little the *imfwiti* changes himself into a lion, pursues his victim, and eats him. After eating him he changes back once more into human form, picks up his axe and spear from behind the anthill, and goes his way." Alternatively lions may be metamorphosed chiefs. David Livingstone reported from the lower Zambezi:

> There are also a great many lions and hyaenas, and there is no check upon the increase of the former, for the people, believing that the souls of their chiefs enter into them, never attempt to kill them; they even believe that a chief may metamorphose himself into a lion, kill any one he chooses, and then return to the human form; therefore when they see one they commence clapping their hands, which is the usual method of salutation here. The consequence is, that lions are so abundant, that we see little huts made in trees, indicating the places where some of the inhabitants have slept when benighted in the fields.

Livingstone also records:

> Stopping one afternoon at a Kebrabasa village, a man, who pretended to be able to change himself into a lion, came to salute us. Smelling the gunpowder from a gun which had been discharged, he went on one side to get out of the wind of the piece, trembling in a most artistic manner, but quite overacting his part. The Makololo explained to us that he was a *pondoro*, or a man who can change his form at will, and added that he trembles when he smells gunpowder."[7]

A chief told Paul du Chaillu that a leopard had killed two of his men. – "Why did you not make a trap to catch the leopard?" – "Because it was not one that can be trapped; it was a man who changed himself into a leopard, and then, after he had been a leopard for some time, he changed himself into a man again." When du Chaillu remained incredulous, the chief tried to convince him with arguments, too long to be reported here in detail. On two successive days the leopard had claimed a victim. Convinced it must be a sorcerer in disguise, the chief sent for a great "doctor" who discovered, in a solemn seance of divination, that the leopard was no other than the chief's nephew and heir. They summoned him at once and arrested him; he made a complete confession! It was really he who had killed the two men. He remembered that on that day, as he was walking in the woods, he had suddenly turned into a leopard . . . etc. He was put to death by slow torture over fire (which was the usual method of dealing with sorcerers, to make sure of getting completely rid of them).[8]

This belief in transformation may also be seen in a slightly different form. The man who is turned into a murderous animal (lion, leopard, snake etc.) may not himself be the murderer, but only his instrument; he acts to carry out the will of another, or under his orders. Father Bösch tells us of the *Masumbano*, or lion-men, of the Banyamwesi:

> An ordinary lion never attacks a man, and yet every year a considerable number of people fall victim to this beast. Magic can explain this quite easily. It is not either lions or leopards the native fears, even though in the bush he will never venture to name them; what really terrify him are the *masumbano*, which is to say, men changed into lions or leopards. The art of changing a man into a lion or leopard is here called *kasumba shimba nolo ngwe, create* a lion or leopard . . . This act of creation is carried out according to strict and detailed rules.[9]

Lions and leopards of this particular kind, therefore, who are the instruments of sorcerers, are not simple animals like the rest, but are in a sense artificial ones, made for the purpose by those who use them. The meaning of the native expression recalled by Bösch is plain: they are *created* for the use which they serve.

A very similar belief is found in southern Africa, as for example among the Lambas. "All death in Lambaland is put down to witchcraft," Doke explains, "It matters not that a lion has devoured the unfortunate victim; it could not have been an ordinary lion, but one produced or induced by witchcraft."[10] And again along the margin of Lake Nyasa among the *ba-Konde*: according to Alexander Merensky, "The chief, Muaihojo, went to Missionary Bunk and told him a panther had killed a bullock and some sheep belonging to him. He requested the missionary to look in his Bible to find out which of his men had created this animal." Another similar story is told by Missionary Schumann:

> Some people came to me, and after their spokesman had sufficiently praised me to the skies as the preserver of law and order in the whole country, he at last came out with their request. Some lions had been breaking into their cattleyards, and I was to pronounce a prohibition on the man who had been sending them, and force him to stop. There exists here an unshakable belief that certain persons are able to create lions and let them loose on other men. Kabeta, in Buntali, is one of these lion-senders, and the men he persecutes bring him both cattle and young girls, hoping to persuade him to call the lions back. They credited me with power to do even better and tame the lion-tamer.

When Missionary Nauhaus told a native that Major von Wissmann was about to arrive on a lion hunt, the response was, "That's good. Show him all the lions and let him kill the lot." "You are thinking of lion-men," Nauhaus answered, "but I am talking about real ones." "That's as may be," the man reflected, "but then, who sends the lions to attack us? Who makes them?" – "God makes them; God is the Creator of all," Nauhaus replied. – "But there are so many!" – "Well, they breed like other animals." – "If God is their creator," the man retorted, "why do they kill us then? Are we not God's children?"[11]

Clearly the missionary and his questioner do not have the same notion of lions, or God, or creation. According to the native's belief there are two kinds of lion: ordinary ones, which never attack man or his cattle, and the artificial ones which certain individuals have the power to create, and can then send to destroy some man or his beasts. The verb *create* does not for them have the full and powerful significance which it does for Missionary Nauhaus. Lions "created" in this way are not sublimely evoked out of deep chaos; they are purely and simply the product of a transformation which a sorcerer is able to bring about. This is put in a clear light by another missionary, T.M. Thomas, who lived for a considerable time with the Matabele during the last century: "An accomplished wizard, finding the grave of a newly buried man, gave the corpse medicine and restored it to life; he transformed the man into a wolf, which he employed as his servant to go on errands, dig his garden, and do other works, such as catching game, destroying the gardens of the people, or their cattle, or themselves . . ." This is something that often happens, but there are occasions, nevertheless, when the wizards are unable to complete their evil design or curse, and thus they come to be found out. At such times the bodies they are resuscitating will remain in an unfinished state. Such are the idiots, of whom some few are to be seen the region.[12]

Thus by means of spells and charms and mumbo jumbo the sorcerer may turn a man, whether living or dead, into an animal which becomes his slave and instrument. Such metamorphoses of men – dead or alive – into animals come constantly into legends and tales. They are also accepted as facts of experience; we have just seen several examples. Is it surprising, then, to find sorcerers using them for their own advantage? There is a belief of a similar kind among the Bavenda (South Africa), reported by H.A. Stayt, that "A *muloi* (= witch-doctor) can, by rubbing medicine on to a climbing shrub, turn the branch into a snake which, at the order, 'Go to that man and let me know that he is dead', goes straight to the victim and bites him."[13]

From animals "created" in this fashion to those which are "made" (out of wood, snow, mud or what you will) with a generally murderous purpose in mind, the way is but short. We may as well consider both together; each notion is a reflection of the other.

In the folklore of the Australian and Papuan Aborigines we have already come across stories in which someone endowed with magical powers brings to life an animal he has fabricated. This is usually done with the idea of making use of it for some kind of vengeance. The following bird tale, reported by Roth from Central Queensland, is an instance.

> The bangapan or redbill is a very little chap, with white tail and red legs: the pigmy-goose, on the other hand, though comparatively small in itself, is a much bigger bird. Well, it happened one day that the redbill was hunting for lily-seed in a waterhole that actually belonged to him, when a pigmy-goose came flying by, drove him away, and gathered the seed himself. The redbill, being too small to act on the defensive, bethought him of a piece of bloodwood to make a crocodile of, but the log floated downstream when he threw it into the water. He next tried a piece of white gum, but it was also too light, so he finally threw in a huge block of ironwood. This sank to the bottom, and the redbill made a crocodile out of it. And on the very next occasion that the pigmy-goose came to get some lily-seeds the crocodile made a meal of him.[14]

Landtman collected a number of comparable tales at Kiwai Island. In one, a first wife, neglected by her husband for another who came after her, meditates revenge. She makes a model of a crocodile and puts it in the river Maubo-tiri, saying to it, "If Siváre come here, you catch him." She returns home and sits on the gable verandah to watch. "Siváre donned his war ornaments and seizing his weapons went on his way to another village. In the act of wading across the river he was caught by the crocodile, who pulled him under the water and took him into a hole in the bottom". Landtman explains further:

> In various ways, sorcerers can cause an enemy to be taken by a crocodile. One method is to make a model crocodile and place it in a river which the man is in a habit of frequenting; at the same time a formula is uttered in which the crocodile is asked to seize that man, but no one else. The model transforms itself into a real crocodile and does as it has been told; in certain cases it afterwards becomes a lifeless model again. The victim has occasionally been brought back to life when killed in such circumstances. Some sorcerers merely put a croton twig into a creek and utter a

spell requesting it to go and catch the enemy, whose name is mentioned. The twig turns into a crocodile, which seizes the man . . ."[15]

We recall the Bavenda sorcerer who could create a snake out of a wild vine and send it to bite the desired victim.

In another Kiwai tale recorded by Landtman, two men, Wée and Dobási, planned their revenge for a grievance against the other villagers. They decided to make two rats which would spoil the people's coconuts.

At first they made them of a kind of soft wood, but the teeth were not strong enough and broke off. Then they used the right kind of wood and succeeded better.

The people arranged a great feast . . . While the people were dancing, Wée and Dobási stole away to the coconut grove and passed into the two wooden rats. They gnawed a hole in every one of the coconuts which the people had stored in the bush, and when all were finished they went to the houses and did the same with the nuts which were kept there. Then they collected ants and put them into the holes, and the ants consumed all the meat which was left.

When the havoc was discovered, "The people flew into a rage, men and women seized their arms, surrounded Wee and Dobasi's house and forced the door open, meaning to attack the two men. But they had transformed themselves into rats and were on the look-out . . . The rats leapt upon the shoulders and head of one man and the others shot their arrows at them but hit the man instead, and from him the rats sprang upon another man, and he too was killed . . . The affray did not end until half of their number were killed.[16]

This story is more than usually suggestive. With its help we can grasp rather better than before what it is primitives have in mind when they talk about "created" and "made" animals. When the two Papuans decide to take revenge on the village, they *make* two wooden rats. But they do not bring the rats to life and then give them an order to go and gnaw the coconuts belonging to the village, and so ruin them. They themselves enter into the wooden bodies and set to work personally to render the nuts uneatable. They are still in this form when they escape the arrows of their attackers and turn them back upon the villagers who have launched them. In that case does the intervention of the sorcerers themselves in the execution of their baleful purpose introduce any new element?

No, not at all. Whether the mischief is caused by *created* rats — rats specially charged with the mission, brought to life only to do that one thing — or by the sorcerers themselves, acting *within* the rats they themselves have *made*, is, as the natives view the matter, neither here nor there. They are merely two methods of achieving the same object, variations, but identical in their effect. The native draws no distinction between them, he is not concerned to split hairs. In each case he knows that the single and only real cause of the trouble is the sorcerers themselves. That is all that matters; it is the only point which holds his attention. If the two sorcerers had not insinuated themselves into the wooden rat-models, but instead had brought the animals to life and sent them off to gnaw the coconuts in the same way as other sorcerers send off a crocodile they have themselves carved, with instructions to carry off their enemies (or as African sorcerers send out a "created" lion to devour a man or his cattle) — they would still be looked upon as the only true and responsible authors of the deed. The natives will not even stop at declaring, as we would, that these rats, the crocodile or the lion, have acted as the sorcerers' servants, agents or instruments to carry out the orders they had given. In the pattern of their thoughts the matter goes deeper. They think of these animals (whether "created" or "made") as extensions of the sorcerers' own personal identity. They are appurtenances of it; that is, integral parts of their personalities. This fact is made apparent in a positive manner, without complication, simply by the entry of the two sorcerers into the wooden rats.

Myths and stories of the same kind have been recorded in very diverse regions. P.E. Tattevin recounts a Pentecost Island tale which tells of two small boys who became angry with their grandmother when she refused to give them food.

> At last, tired (of asking), they went off and cut down a tree and chipped at it until it looked like a shark. Then they pulled it along after them, singing:
>> Shark, shark take her away!
>> Who? Why, our grandmother.
>> Why take her away?
>> Because she wouldn't give us our coconut.
> They continued singing as they dragged it along. When they reached the door they left it there. The shark rushed into the house, seized the grandmother and leapt into the sea. That is how sharks came to be man-eaters.[17]

In this folktale, which belongs to the class called etiological, the malice of the children comes to the same effect as the anger of the jealous wife in the Papuan tale. It casts a spell. Their irritable *disposition* acts by magic to transform the wooden shark into a living man-eater.

The Dayaks have a word, *pulong*, glossed by Hardeland as signifying little animals much about the size of a small mouse, "which certain *hantuen* (magic-men) carve from wood and then bring to life. They keep them in a wooden box and once a month give them eggs or chickens to eat. When he does not wish to go himself, the *hantuen* can send these *pulong* out to do someone an injury. They creep into the victim's body and cause him to suffer a fearful and unrelieved stomach-ache until in the end, it may be as much as a year later, he dies."[18]

Similarly, among the Netsilik Eskimos, Rasmussen records a tale of an old woman who, abandoned by the rest, fabricates a bear out of snow, which becomes a formidable animal. (I have had occasion to refer to a story very similar to this in an earlier work.)[19]

Stith Thompson relates a Quinault (North American Indian) tale which tells how "One day Grouse made a wooden seal, carving it out of cedar, and burning it until it was black. Then he talked to the seal, and told it what it was to do; and it dived down into the water and went out to sea."[20]

Animals thus fabricated and brought to life are not in all cases destined to wreak havoc. The Copper Eskimo, for example, as Rasmussen recalls, say that "There was once a man who could make all kinds of salmon of wood. He hewed them off with an axe, and, when he had finished them, threw them into a lake." For each different kind of salmon he used a wood that was the same colour as its flesh. "All woods, they say, are salmon. Sea scorpions are said to be made of a kind of willow that grows along the ground, and has a rough bark."[21]

A Mackenzie River Eskimo tale, according to Jenness, relates how

> There was once an old couple who had no children. They lived in a house apart from the other people, because these never gave them any meat when they caught seals. Once when they killed some polar bears, the old man, having nothing to eat, took some of the blood and put it into a wooden pot and made a polar bear of it. This, they say, was the first bear he made, but afterwards he took to making bigger ones. When this first bear grew up it went out and caught two seals, so that the two old people had plenty to eat. The same bear often brought them bearded seals also. But one day the old man told it to go and bring some polar bears. Next morning

the bear was sullen, but at last it went off and killed a number of bears and brought them in. Then it went away and never returned, and the old couple, when it failed to reappear, sang a magic song and wept and died.[22]

Here the artifically fabricated animal is completely at one with its natural species, and on an equal footing with them in exactly the same way as if it had been born as they were and the same blood ran in its veins. (Blood is indeed what it was made from.) By ordering him to kill his brothers, the old man and woman commit an unpardonable fault. He obeys, but immediately disappears. The old couple then know there is nothing left for them but to die.

Here is a last folktale of this kind, gathered by Dorsey from the Pawnee.

> There was a village, and in the village lived a poor boy. The poor boy's parents were poor, for they had no ponies. The boy was very fond of ponies and often sat upon the bank when the other boys watered theirs. One day the boy made up his mind that he would have ponies of his own. So he arose and crossed the creek, brought timber and made a corral for his ponies. He then dug a quantity of sticky mud, which he took to the corral. He also found a buffalo bladder, and with this carried water to the place where he had left the mud. He then poured water over the mud, which became sticky. Then he made two ponies of mud. He also got white clay, which he put upon one pony, so that it was bald-faced. Every day the boy went and watered his ponies. He would carry them down to the creek, then dip their noses in the water. He would take them back to the corral, get grass and green young cottonwood shoots, and place them before the ponies.

One day the boy went down to see his mud ponies and found only one standing, for the other had crumbled. The boy cried awhile and said, "I will take good care of the one I have left." The boy cried and and cried until he fell asleep. He had a dream. He thought he had a fine pony; but when he waked he saw none. Again he went to sleep, and in his dream he saw a bald-faced pony, which spoke to him and said, "My son, I know you are poor. The Mother-Earth has taken pity on you. I am part of the Mother-Earth. I am to belong to you. You must do as I say, and you will be a chief among your people." The boy woke up and it was broad daylight. So he went to the place where he had left his pony and there, in front of the little willow corral, stood a fine-looking bald-faced pony.

The pony says to him, "I am one of the mud-ponies you had in your corral." The boy eventually does become a chief as promised.[25]

In this tale, as in those preceding it, there is present by implication the idea that an emotional *disposition* may have the power to produce certain effects by magic. The intense longing which burns in the boy's breast when he sees the other young men watering their ponies, has a potency equal to the anger, revengefulness or envy (to which it is closely akin) which we have seen to have so much effect in the other tales. In a way that it is perhaps not possible to show clearly, yet which primitives, without any need to examine it in detail, know intuitively to be real, such *dispositions* – states of mind or feeling – are able to bring animals thus "made" to life, and cause them immediately to carry out the commands of their creators.

To what extent are such improbable stories as these actually given credence? Are they taken simply as tales of some easy plausibility, which it never occurs to anyone to think of as anything but fiction or fable? Or is there anyone at all who takes them for accounts of something that once really happened, and could at any time happen again? Put in these terms the question is one for which it is not possible to find a plain answer, not, at least, one which will cover every case. One has to bear in mind the difference between the various cultures, between the separate divisions inside any one group of tribes, or between the individuals of one and the same tribe. From time to time an observer will insist that the natives themselves habitually draw a very strict distinction between myths and rituals of the sacrosant and traditional kind as acts of faith, and other stories which they regard as simply pleasant or as merely amusing; but then someone else, speaking of the very same tribe, will affirm the direct contrary. We would need to be able to make certain in every case that we understood the exact sense in which the terms were used, and be sure we knew, also, what weight to give to the testimony offered. Quite obviously we are ourselves in no position to attempt such an ample evaluation. We must therefore limit our undertaking to merely indicating, with the help of the legends and tales before us, and from which it has been possible to make this meagre selection, the way in which the natives themselves, for the most part, see them.

Extraordinary as it may seem to us, the fact is that they look on them, with certain rare exceptions, as wholly true, or at any rate, credible. This is one of the points upon which the differences in orientation between the mentality of primitives and ourselves shine out with the most distinct clarity. The minds of primitives function in a world that is vastly more "fluid" than ours, which permits the unseen powers to intervene at all times to contradict or turn aside the expected phenomena of nature; no merely physical obstacle can obstruct their force. What possible reason, therefore, could occur to the primitive intelligence to doubt the veracity of the tales, in view of the ease with which events no less astonishing may be expected to come to pass at any time, and indeed frequently do? Did not some thirty witnesses see with their own eyes the hyaena woman in the story reported by A.W. Cardinall?

Not long ago on the Sepik River (former German New Guinea), E.A. Wisdom, the Administrator of the Mandated Territory, on a tour of inspection reported as follows:

> These natives are still only in the primitive stages of civilization, as is witnessed, for instance, by the examples of sorcery which is still prevalent in some of the villages. At the village of Krinjambi the *tul tul* (= government man, local headman) informed me that a crocodile had attacked and killed his little daughter, while she was seated in a canoe, only a few yards from the village. The *tul tul* complained that a native from a village a few miles further up the river practised sorcery, and, for the purpose of removing his daughter, had carved a piece of wood into the shape of a small crocodile. Placing the carving in the water he had instructed it to swim downsteam and attack the child. It was useless to try to dissuade the *tul tul* from his belief that the carving had changed into a real crocodile, and was the cause of his daughter's death. The District Officer was instructed to make a full enquiry . . .[24]

We may be sure the whole tribe held the same belief as the *tul tul*. We have seen plenty of equivalents in a number of other tribes where the people talk (and not only in myths and tales) of lions, crocodiles, snakes, etc., all artificially man-made and man-killing, exactly like this sinister crocodile of the Sepik River.

In more advanced communities stories like these continue to be told, but little by little they lose their literal credibility. Yet we occasionally do still encounter, in communities of relatively elevated culture, some beliefs that are like them, and certainly not less astonishing.[25]

That a piece of wood whittled into the shape of a crocodile should suddenly become a living creature which can swim away and carry off the prey it was created to attack, is a belief which will seem less remarkable if we recall that, for such minds as these we are speaking of, no metamorphosis must be ruled out simply because it appears impossible or absurd for some merely physical reason. We must also remember that no distinction is drawn between animate and inanimate things. To these intelligences the difference is insignificant. Objects which we look upon as lifeless participate, just as living beings do, in the universal life-force which penetrates all substance and is felt everywhere without exception; the degree of participation may vary, it is true, but it reaches everywhere and flows from one object to another. Miraculous powers like, for instance, that of growth are not restricted to animals and plants; stones and minerals also grow. The medicine-man pleads coaxingly with the amulet he is about to employ. The soothsayer talks intimately to the pig whose liver he will presently examine prophetically. This is all perfectly ordinary; why, therefore, should there be thought to be an unbridgeable distance between the wooden symbol and the living crocodile? What is to prevent the sorcerer's voodoo from changing the one into the other?

When natives speak of such transformations, quite different images spring into their minds from those that come into ours. From our point of view such changes go beyond anything that could reasonably be imagined. For the woody fibres which form the substance of the fabricated crocodile must − by some miracle − be substituted a countless multitude of living cells, fluids, veins, organs, etc. But the primitive imagination takes no account of the crocodile's interior at all, whether wooden or biological. The native looks only at the external appearance, what he can actually see.[26] Considered in this light there would seem to be no metamorphosis at all in the strict sense of the word, seeing that it is only a question of the wooden crocodile coming to life and behaving exactly as is expected of any crocodile. All that the transformation demonstrates is that the sorcerer possesses a power strong enough to cause the crocodile to pass from one state to another. Once its mission is accomplished, may it not just as easily be changed back into the stock-still wooden figure it was to begin with?

The very slight importance attached (in folklore) to a creature's viscera and their physiological functioning can be explained by their ordinary and habitual attitude towards causation generally. They know well enough that these organs are necessary to life and, if damaged or destroyed, will cause the death of any living animal in due and possibly rapid course. But that does not prevent them from believing at the same time that life also depends on something else: namely the presence in the body of a certain power, a vital sustaining principle, a kind of "soul" which, as often as not, is material in form (for example certain Australian Aborigines locate it in the fat around the kidneys).[27] So as long as that power remains intact in its location the individual will go on living. If it is removed or injured he will die, no matter how healthy the rest of his body. In other words, a man does not continue to live merely because his lungs, heart, liver, brain, and so on, function normally; they function in consequence of his being alive. So obviously if the sorcerer is one who possesses sufficient power to bring the wooden model of the animal to life, it goes without saying that the same power will be adequate to provide it with the necessary organs. When the creature's work is done and the sorcerer takes back the life he gave to it, the viscera also naturally disappear and nothing is left but a simple object made of wood. The life which the sorcerer has the power to give and take does not come to pass as a result of any series of second causes acting together in harmony; it is neither more nor less than a simple manifestation of the presence in the body of this mysterious principle. We may well observe, indeed, that for primitives like these (Australians or others), death never comes by natural causes; and to shift the perspective, neither does life. Both life and death are looked upon by them in a way that is different from ours.

What is true of life in general can be applied to any separate function of living beings. It is not just because we have eyes that we can see. Vision is a particular power, analogous to the magic ones. Animals possess this special power and the eyes are the medium through which they exercise it. The eyes are participators in this power and are the organs (that is, in the sense of instruments) by which it operates. Hence it is a reasonable thing to paint eyes on the prow of a fishing canoe, to help it to steer well towards the spots where fish will be found. In ways which the primitive mind feels no need to analyze, those eyes bring to the canoe itself something of the power called vision. Similarly it is not because birds have wings that they are able to fly; their rising into the air, staying up there, and passing through it, evidences the presence of a magical power that all birds possess. That magical power is put to work by means of their wings. It is the wings that are the participators in that power. For that reason the sorcerer or shaman who wants to fly, and has command of the necessary power, fastens wings on his shoulders and forearms, and thereby becomes himself a kind of bird. If the magical power were to fail, all the feathers in the world would not make up for it. Feathers are only the instruments in which the power is located; but that is the reason why they are so sought after and made use of.

The following instance, reported by P. te Wechtel, will serve to bring into some clarity the kind of light in which the primitive intelligence may regard organic functions.

> The Dayak can be more childishly simple in his animism that we often suppose. On one occasion I saw in a small tributary of the Barito a large prau lying. The owner had set up at its sternpost a water wheel made of four planks, which, without any mechanical power was expected to propel the prau through the water. The man, who as we passed through was just finishing off the job, had once seen a steamer of the *Paketvaart-Maatschappy* with its huge stern wheel steaming up the Bariot, and was now trying to discover whether his own vessel might not be able to go forward in a similar manner.[28]

The wheel corresponded to the wings, as did the ship to the body, of a bird. On the big Dutch steamer the wheel was the visible instrument of the magical power which sent it along: who could tell if another wheel set up at the stern of the native vessel might not also *participate* sufficiently in some magical power of the same kind and get it going?

A native teacher in Dahomey, Christian and very well educated, when asked to report how far his compatriots believed in the truth of the animal stories which were so abundant in their folklore, gave assurance that they were accepted unquestioningly. Notwithstanding the surprise evinced by his interlocutor, and the objections he raised, he remained firm in his answer. Various reliable observers – among them Rasmussen – have similarly confirmed what has been called the extreme credulity of primitive people. But for all that, when primitives declare that such animal stories are "true", we find it very difficult to give serious credence to what they say. And yet whence does this scepticism proceed, unless from a tendency, against which we find it hard to fight, to ascribe to them our own attitudes of mind, our own habits of thinking, and in general our own mental conditioning as a whole? Instead of making the effort to follow in the line of their kind of thinking, we laxly allow ourselves to take for granted, quite thoughtlessly, that they

are like we are ourselves today, constrained by various com-
punctions of logic and a critical spirit which have been
developed in us only in the course of long centuries of civilization. The consequences of this ill-founded postulate are not slow
to make their appearance. What the natives say, for example, as
to the truth of the animal stories, is something we find so
disconcerting that we can scarcely make anything at all of it,
unless to suppose they did not understand our questions, or that
they have not been honest in their answers. But let us make a
really energetic and persevering effort to enter genuinely into
their real thought-processes. Instead of forming our idea of the
way they think on the model of our own thinking, let us approach it with detachment and study it in the light of their self-
expression in words and actions. If we can actually achieve this,
their way of thinking will no longer appear so enigmatic and
unintelligible.

In a word, as I have had occasion to point out in earlier works,
their mental experience does not coincide exactly with ours
either in extent or depth. Wolves and bears and snakes, and so
on, which are also at the same time men, as we see whenever
they take off their skins – lions and leopards and crocodiles
"created" by enchanters to be dispatched to devour either their
victims or their victims' cattle – "artificial" creatures which
miraculously come to life – all that sort of thing, which to us appears to be fiction pure and simple, is for a great many
primitives the substance of veritable experience and received as
truth. (Remember the stand taken by the *tul-tul* in Papua, who
believed his little daughter had been carried off by a crocodile at
the instigation of an enemy; the hyaena-woman seen by so many
witnesses at the clerk's house in Togoland; and others.) These
happenings, and a great many more like them, are by almost all
of the native peoples concerned placed in the same category as
events of ordinary daily occurrence. That is not to suggest that
they themselves think of such things as commonplace. But they
reason that *extraordinary things are part and parcel of common life*.
Because of the mystical bent of their minds, and the habits of
thought to which their whole mental conditioning leads them, it
naturally follows that their lives are filled, to an infinitely
greater extent than our own, with first-impact impressions. As
we well know, they pay far more attention than we do to the
significance of dreams and presages, prophecy, premonitions,
presentiments or telepathy; in short; everything which when it
appears gives testimony of the activity of powers and influences
of the unseen world.

Hence their total experience, although over a great proportion of it there is little to distinguish it from our own, retains beyond that common range a great many insights which to a white man mean nothing and which only the native can grasp and respond to. And as to those aspects of experience which to our view seem simply chimerical, there is absolutely nothing in them to set his credulity at defiance.

On what grounds should it ever occur to him to doubt the objective truth of those things rather than of the rest? When a telegram announces there has been a fire in New York City which has caused vast damage, it would not for an instant occur to us to refuse to believe it; we have heard numerous times before about buildings being burnt down with everything in them. Just in the same way, when in a myth or tale a wolf takes off its skin and reveals himself to be a human being, any Eskimo will be familiar with that particular transformation: he has met with it time and again. So such a trifle will not hold him back for a moment. The question, "Is it really true?" will not even arise in his mind, because in his repertoire of possibilities this is something too ordinary to hold a challenge. If we raise the point with him, and supposing he understands what we are questioning, he will be as much surprised by our doubt as we are by his belief. He can't see the reason for it. For him to grasp what disturbs us, he would need to change his whole mental landscape; he would have brusquely and suddenly to abandon all that part of his own proper habitual understanding that he is most deeply attached to. He would have to give up his own picture of a world in which mystical forces govern everything and substitute for it an intellectualized European one. This is an enormous demand! – we are asking for a miracle. But the simple fact is, the native will merely regard the objection as irrelevant, even slightly absurd – a white man's fancy. His reply will be merely a polite affirmation that the stories are quite true.

If that part of his experience upon which the stories are based could only be seen as clearly distinct from the rest, the part he shares with ourselves – that is to say, if it did no more than give him an entry into a separate world where we are unable to go, one which we would be content to describe as imaginary – the incompatibility might seem less. But the plain fact is that no such line of distinction can be drawn. On the contrary, those supernatural powers by which the primitive feels himself to be surrounded on all sides intervene continually in the regular course of all common events so as to modify them. They are able to impose upon those events — that whole range of experience, no matter how commonplace, matter-of-fact and day-to-day — an appearance, a colour, which is no less disturbing to us than it is reassuring to the native. Out of this situation comes a constant stream of surprises. We make sudden discoveries that a certain being, or a certain commonplace object, is in his view something altogether different from what we had supposed. The notion he has of it is a thousand miles away from ours, even though it might never have occurred to us to imagine anybody could see it in any other way.

We may take as an illustrative example the way animals are portrayed, since they hold such a prominent place in the myths, in folklore, and also in common experience (broadly regarded) in the primitives' lives. When the natives suddenly and unexpectedly find themselves in the presence of an animal, no matter how little they may at that moment be expecting a supernatural encounter, but especially if the animal seen is one of a species endowed with mystical powers, they will never fail to remark (or possibly just imagine) that there is something unusual about the appearance or movements of the creature. At once they begin to wonder, "Is this a real animal? Or have I perhaps to reckon with an enchanter, or else some spirit which has put on this shape and means to do me harm?" This reaction is virtually instinctive, since the first sight of the creature brings into play the whole affective category of the supernatural.

Here follow just a few factual evidences (where many more could easily be found) which will leave the point in no doubt. Raymond Firth writes:

> Natives say that in Tikopia (Polynesia) all birds and animals are *ata* of various *atua* [see note 30] which appear in this form to mankind. To this general statement there are certain exceptions since a few kinds of bird are not regarded as serving *atua* as a vehicle for manifestation, and are eaten freely. The great majority of species, however, are associated with supernatural beings.
>
> But not all animals of the one kind are so characterized. Some may be acting as media or materializations of the spirits, fraught with religious interest and perhaps with peril, while others of the same species remain simple and harmless creatures. The problem then arises of how to distinguish the one type from the other — to separate the spirit in animal shape from the mere animal. This problem has had to be faced by the native and an attempt made at its solution, since while on the one hand it is impracticable for him to respect and give licence to every member of every animal

species which he encounters, it is imperative, from the point of view of religious belief, to observe a becoming reverence to such creatures as may be possessed by supernormal attributes. The broad test is based in a rational manner on the behaviour of the animal itself. If it behaves strangely in a manner not characteristic of its species then it is an *atua* in animal guise; if it acts in a normal fashion then it is an ordinary individual and may be treated as such. A native said to me . . . "You are going in the woods, look on an animal has run hither, that the spirit has entered in it, has stimulated it. There the same relation with the fish. The spirit has gone to seek the fish will come to it, to body to it."[29] The point of this statement is that if a person walking through the woods sees a startled bird fly away from him or a swamp hen run, then it is simply a creature in natural form; if, however, it comes towards him and exhibits none of the fear which is to be expected in the circumstances, or if it hovers near him and keeps up a continuous cry for no apparent reason, then it is held to be inhabited at the moment by a supernatural being. So also with fish, into which spirits also enter on occasion, and which betray their nature by abnormal conduct.

The same applies to the bat (*peka*) which is common in the island. Being a fruit-eater it is looked on by the people as a great pest, but probably as a reflex of the same circumstance, is regarded as a creature of the gods, in particular of the clan of Tafua. Sometimes when encountered it is a manifestation of the *atua*; more often it is merely the animal itself . . . When a man finds a bat eating fruit in his orchard or gnawing at a coconut, if he be a cautious person he does not endeavour to kill it, but merely scares it away, apostrophizing it under the name of *Pa* (Ancestor) as it flaps off, to go to other districts and obtain food. He treats it gently lest being an *atua* masquerading in animal guise, it resent harsh treatment and retaliate by returning again and again to his crops.[30]

The lizard is a real deity, not merely a common thing; the deity does not reside in it, but changes into it, and thenceforth it goes as a veritable deity. The ordinary animal which crawls about in the house is only a lizard, but when one appears with a glistering body as if oil had been poured over it, that is a true deity which has entered, whatever may be the errand on which he comes; he has appeared to look on us.[31]

Similarly in South America among the Taulipang, mentioned earlier. Koch-Grünberg tells us that over and above the mythic creatures who are understood by these people to have sometimes an animal, sometimes a human form, there are also numerous others,

... some ordinary, but others monstrous examples of their species, who stand out from the rest because they possess special supernatural powers. Even these are for the most part only men who have the ability to put on animal cloaks and so transform themselves into beasts . . . The jaguar himself is a man who for the time being clothes himself in an animal skin. By the same token an enchanter . . . can at a whim turn himself into a jaguar. In addition to the customary "land jaguar", which on account of this ability must certainly be reckoned among supernatural beasts, there also exist certain kinds of fabulous "water jaguars", but they doubtless are merely creations of the Indians' imagination.[32]

Finally, not to over-extend these examples, here are one or two from Africa. In East Africa among the Kikuyu, as we learn from C.W. Hobley, "If the owner of the village should meet a large caterpillar, called *thatu*, near the gate, he pours a little fat and milk in its path; if it turns back, all is well. If, on the other hand, it should walk round the spot where the fat, and so forth, was poured, and still come on towards the village, the people know that it is a spirit which has assumed the form of a caterpillar, and a ram is sacrificed in the village. If one of these caterpillars is found in a food hut, a ram is again sacrificed for the same reason." A.B. Ellis tells us that in West Africa among the Ewe-speaking people, "The native idea concerning the crocodile seems to be that it is the abode of a spirit . . . which, in default of a human tenement, has been obliged to use the body of a lower animal . . . Some natives say that it is not every crocodile who is thus tenanted by a malicious spirit, but that, as it is impossible to know beforehand which is and which is not, it is both wiser and safer to propitiate all."[33]

In the light of all this, one may well appreciate the consternation with which a primitive individual could greet the sudden appearance of certain animals. "This snake which looks as though it wants to come into the hut could well be my kinsman who died last week coming back to visit his relations," thinks the Kaffir; and the Lamba wonders, "Is that lion I see yonder a reincarnated chief, or an animal created by some sorcerer?" Just as the rice is maturing in the Malay Archipelago, flocks of small birds fly down to feed upon it. Attempts are made to shoo them away, but not without some uneasiness . . . might not there be among the marauders some few who are really ancestral spirits who have assumed that form simply in order to claim their just share of the harvest? All these animals (and there are also others of different kinds – not to mention the large class of animal sorcerers and bad-luck-bringers mentioned by Lebzelter[34] — which are not "true" animals but really men, dead or living, and spirits which have simply assumed animal forms) resemble very closely those which the myths, legends and tales of the folk bring so frequently before the eyes of the native. They belong one and all, and for exactly the same reasons, to the same order of experience which brings him into touch with the supernatural powers. This is also, moreover, the explanation why he finds it so easy to give credit to the metamorphosis of men into animals and animals into men, which is a feature of folklore no less frequently than of myth. So far from being considered incompatible with common experience, it is found to be a normal part of it. And to reverse the contention, all the prodigious legendary transformations which are familiar to him from childhood contribute to his unhesitating acceptance of such things in real life as a simple matter of course, because they are so similar.

But let us look further. The difference between "real" animals and the others, though primitives regard it as important, does not stand as categorical for them. Or rather, the view they take of plain and ordinary animals is not exactly like ours. It could be argued, and without any sense of paradox, that ordinary ("true") animals occupy a place in their minds that is much closer to those of myth and folklore than do animals as we know them. In our society people even of the least well informed kind have a notion of what any animal is, that we would without hesitation call zoological. Whether or not there may be any superstitious fancies tagged on,[35] the idea that we have of it, from the evidence of our senses, can always be rounded off with facts from some reliable source of objective information. They will give us the criteria to distinguish between vertebrates and insects, for example, and among vertebrates, between mammals, birds, fishes, and so on. The very language with which we name them already implies a system of classification.

But the way primitives see animals, even the most ordinary of them, is quite different. Their outward and visible form is something not inevitable but accidental; and even their most outstanding physical characteristics have little more real importance merely in themselves. What the native first wants to learn, and the consideration he puts before all others, is, what are the animal's *powers*, what does it *know* — in effect, to what extent does it *participate* in the world of supernatural force? Undoubtedly this all-important preoccupation does not in the least prevent him from observing with great pains and infinite patience the habits of those animals he needs for subsistence. He is practised in this study from a very early age and in time comes to acquire an almost infallible knowledge of their patterns of behaviour, their comings and goings, their growth, cries, territory, lairs and so on. A whole system of observed detail, positive and exact, forms itself in his mind into a general blend with all he has learned from the myths, which taken all together, give him the idea (even though it may in time have become vague or subconscious) that animals are, or at least once may have been, also human beings.

Traces of this last belief are retained in folklore almost everywhere. "Animals and birds were once blacks", the natives in Queensland told Walter Roth. According to Hardeland, the Dayaks, like many other primitive people, credit their riverine crocodiles with being quite other than what they superficially appear: "*Badjai* (that is, crocodiles) are slaves of the *Djata* (Water Gods). They have human form and only appear in the shape of crocodiles in the upper world."[36] In South Africa, as the Bushmen believe, there is scarcely any difference between baboons and men. "Baboons speak Bushman, speak sounding like Bushmen. When we hear them talking there, we are apt to think that other people are to be found there, though we did not know of them. When we catch sight of them, then we see that they were baboons talking like people . . ." "My grandfather . . . also told me that baboons speak Bushman. He also told me that baboons are not like other things, for they have their wives; they also resemble people . . . My father used to tell me, that if in the early morning I heard a baboon calling to me as I went past, I must not talk with the baboon . . . For the baboon is not a good person . . ."[37]

These beliefs were found among the Bushmen more than half a century ago and may perhaps have an air of being unrepresentative. Nevertheless there are other tribes like them, occupying a relatively low position in the scale of civilization, which also showed a marked tendency towards placing animals and men upon an equal footing. Look, for example, at two of the tribes studied by von den Steinen in central Brazil, the Trumai and the Bororo. If we wish to comprehend the idea these tribes have of animals, says von den Steinen, "we must completely set aside in our thoughts all of the barriers that stand between men and animals". The tribesman has no knowledge of any dividing gulf between himself and the animal world. "All he saw was that in the main all the creatures lived much as he did himself. They have their family life, they communicated with one another by means of sounds, they had their dwelling-places, they occasionally fought one another, they lived partly by hunting other game and partly on fruits; and in short, man regarded himself as *primus inter pares*, but not as superior to the animals." "He regards his myths and legends, which to us are nothing but fairytales and beast fables, with a seriousness comparable with our respect for Holy Writ and all it teaches. In them he countenances a mingling of human and animal subjects such that, were he to regard himself as created of a different substance from the rest of the creation, it could only make them all appear farcical and ridiculous."[38] Hose and McDougall tell us that the natives of Sarawak, in Borneo,

> . . . make, without questioning and in most cases without explicit statement even to themselves, the practical assumption that the mental processes of animals, their passions, desires and motives, and powers of reasoning are of the same order and in fact extremely similar to their own. That the Kenyahs entertain this belief in a very practical manner is shown in their conduct when preparing for a hunting or fishing excursion. If, for example, they are preparing to poison the fish of a section of the river with the *tuba* root, they always speak of the matter as little as possible and use the most indirect and fanciful modes of expression; thus they will say, "There are many leaves fallen here", meaning, "There are plenty of fish in this part of the river". And these elaborate precautions are taken lest the birds should overhear their remarks and inform the fish of their intentions, when of course the fish would not stay to be caught but would swim away to some other part of the river.[39]

It is the same with most North American Indians. "The Menomini", says Alanson Skinner, "believe that animals of all kinds are endowed with intelligence almost equal to that of human beings and that the only reason why men are able to take them is because they are more fortunate than the beasts." In the Coeur d'Alène tribe, according to James A. Teit, "Much respect was paid to bear and beaver, as these animals were thought to know, see and hear everything. They knew what people said and thought about them. If a man intended to hunt them they knew it. They allowed themselves to be killed only out of pity for the people." (We have seen that this last belief is in force among other Indian tribes, and also among the Eskimo.) Of the Eskimo of Bering Strait E.W. Nelson informs us,

It is also believed that many animals have supernatural powers of hearing, it being claimed that if they are being spoken of, although far away, they will know it. In this respect red and black bears are much feared, and it is said that if man makes sport of bears or calls them by any disrespectful nickname or epithet, no matter where he is, the bear will hear and will watch for and kill him the next time he enters the mountains. (For this reason a hunter who is going out for bears will speak of them with the greatest respect and announce that he is going for some other animal, so that they will be deceived and not expect him.) They never like to speak of what they intend to hunt for fear that the animals may hear and give them bad luck. On one occasion I was talking with my guide, who was going reindeer hunting, and spoke of his chances of success in securing deer; he appeared to be offended and reproved me for letting the deer know what he wished to do.[40]

With modification in different regions and again from tribe to tribe, intelligence and powers equal, if not superior, to those of men are attributed in various places to some particular animal. A survey of all these details could be endless, and we shall not attempt it. But we have seen earlier how much respect is paid to bears by Australian Aboriginal tribes.[41] The same prestige is accorded to bears in northern and arctic regions of Asia and America. In Siberia among the Ostyaks of the Yenisei, says a reviewer, "as with so many other tribes of north eastern Asia, bears are no mere ordinary animals but their souls are those of dead men." The honour given to bears by the Ainu is well known. The Cree (Plains Indians), as Skinner notes, have a phrase for the bear, they call him "the four-footed man", or "chief's son". James Mooney reports that with the Cherokee, "a reverence for the bear and a belief that it is half human is very general among the tribes, and is probably based in part upon the ability of the animal to stand upright and the resemblance of its tracks to human footprints". Perhaps we should also add to these preoccupations the fear that bears inspire.[42]

In other places the revered animal may be something quite different — the hare, the crocodile, the lion, the tiger, some particular snake or bird or even insect, to which human, or superhuman, powers are attributed. The infant assimilates these attitudes from the moment he first begins to realize what people around him are saying. He acquires the same respectful, reverential convictions about them as he does for the myths, and he will never for a moment dream of asking — exceptions may occur, but they will be rare — whether they are true. Before seeds of doubt can germinate and grow, a questioning attitude must needs be created, of a kind that is scarcely ever found in such tribes. If feelings of wonder are aroused, they are more likely to be brought admiringly to the contemplation of abnormal and unusual things such as the apparently supernatural powers with which certain animals (even plants) are endowed. These are envied; the native would like to have them for himself. In order to acquire them he may have recourse to various methods. One of the most usual is to eat the animal, or more specifically, that one of its organs which is believed to be the seat of the superior faculty it is desired to acquire. Thus (I limit myself to a single example), according to the Ainu, Batchelor says, "The water-ousel came down from heaven. He is of a black colour, and lives along the watercourses. His heart is exceedingly wise, and in speech he is most eloquent. When therefore he is killed he should be immediately torn open, and his heart wrenched out and swallowed. This should be done before it gets cold or damaged in any way. If a man swallows it at once, he will become very fluent and wise, and will also be able to overcome all his opponents in argument."[43]

An observation made by Westermann brings out very vividly the particular character of the attitude certain primitives adopt towards the mystical aspects of animals, and the bearing it has upon their totemic beliefs. Among the Kpelle, "virtually those animals alone are totemic, which possess characteristics man finds outstandingly desirable". In this there speaks the conviction that in certain respects a number of animals are superior to man, that is, they have greater strength, or speed, or cunning. Man thus does not feel himself to be elevated high above the animal creation, but closely related to them, and on that account never finds it beneath his dignity to enter into compacts with them and make use of them as friends and helpers in the battle for existence. This near and friendly relationship is borne out in folklore by the figure of the generously helpful or rescuing beast.

> The help offered by animals comes forward in the manner of one comrade helping another: the hunter elephant at his human master's command rounds up other elephants and thus assists the hunter to kill them. The leopard watches over his human friend's fields to keep away thieves, antelopes and wild pigs. Or else – and this is even more to the point – the animal helper conveys his valuable superior powers to his human devotee . . . the leopard gives him his strength, the dwarf antelope its quick awareness; similarly the banana gives him its fruitfulness and the wind its

velocity. The transfer is made easier by the fact that man has the power to transform himself into the animal of his totem and so assume identity with it.

This explanation of totemic system embraces both what the natives themselves believe of it, and what they express in their lives.[44]

In a recent article Captain Rattray draws attention to what he calls a symbiosis of men and animals – that is, the same intimate association between them (I would rather call it a participation) as we have already reviewed on a number of occasions. He adds some fresh instances. In one tribe belonging to northern Nigeria, a father, imparting the secrets of his clan to his son, who has just arrived at puberty, tells him that the leopard is his totem and that it is forbidden for him ever to kill it; and that he himself, the father, when he dies, and after all the funeral ceremonies are past, will reappear to him in leopard form. – At another place the members of a crocodile clan tell Captain Rattray,

> If we killed a crocodile we should become lepers. In Bojan every one has his or her crocodile; when a man is going to die his crocodile dies first. A crocodile comes out of the water to die. It is buried and we lament for it, and give it a small piece of white cloth and pour beer on its grave. To kill a crocodile is to kill a Bojan man. No crocodile would seize us without a very good reason. A crocodile resembles its human owner; if you are fat, your crocodile is fat; if you have a sore foot, your crocodile has one too.[45]

Facts of this kind are endless, and not only in West Africa. They bring evidence to confirm two points on which this present study has placed much stress: firstly, in all symbolic and tribal representations which primitives treat as having great importance, animals will be found to occupy a position of the highest significance; and secondly, in the way primitives look on animals, and this includes the most ordinary creatures, there is always present an element of the mystical. The most commonplace of "real" animals, even one whose animality is most brutal, still participates in some measure in the complex nature of a being which is theriomorphically both animal and man.

Not all the forces then, by which primitives are conscious of being surrounded, everywhere and at all times, are wholly invisible and intangible. There are certain powers which they are able to perceive in action and motion, to approach, touch or even evade. These are the animals. Some of them possess formidable natural weapons of attack and defence. Others have talents one can only wonder at, astonishing capabilities that man would be only too happy to borrow from them. Thus they belong at the same time to both regions of experience, the mundane and the marvellous, or the physical and the mystical. In virtue of either or both they are present in the mind of primitive man practically all the time. For, on the one hand, necessity obliges him, if he is not to die of hunger or cold, to make himself master over certain animals, yet at the same time to keep on favourable terms with them. On the other hand, the traditions of the tribe – that is to say, the myths, and from time to time, certain ceremonies and customs – bring home to him the part that is played even now by animals (who at the same time are also men), in the unseen world, and equally in day-to-day commerce between that world and visible reality.

Hence animals of the kind encountered every day, even when nothing at all is present to arouse any suspicion that they might not be "true beasts", do not in any essential particular differ from those which people the myths and folklore.

So where minds oriented in this way are concerned, let us not speak of anthropomorphism. Such minds are not given to regarding plants as "botany", or animals as "zoology".[46] At least, if among them any such classificatory impulse does exist, the idea is at once overridden by elements of a very different kind, for it can never free itself from the quasi-religious beliefs and attitudes implicit in the tribal institutions.

It is not until people have begun to set up a categorical distinction between animal and human nature, and the habit has formed of separating the two so pointedly that the one comes to be regarded as the direct opposite of the other, that any scope at all develops for what we call anthropomorphism. When the point is reached it then becomes possible to attribute to an animal, sometimes more and sometimes less seriously, this, that or the other quality or defect of a kind that properly belongs to man. People delight in this the more they regard it as a game, and the more they really perceive the distance between man and animals to be unbridgeable. By appearing to ignore this distinction, anthropomorphism has, indirectly, the effect of emphasizing it. But the primitive myths and tales that tell of men-animals and animal-men do not *pretend* to ignore the difference: they simply do not see it at all. Therefore the stories can owe nothing whatever to anthropomorphism. They are antecedent to it, and that by a long measure.

What then, it may perhaps be objected, are we to make of

those animal fables, plentiful among many primitives (like, for example, the Bantu), which they find so amusing, and in which the lightest of disguises reveals rather than conceals the human personality which underlies the animal? No one dares to laugh openly at a chief. But when the king of the animals – lion or elephant – is tricked, made a laughing-stock, hamstrung, and in the end falls headlong into the trap prepared for him by some small, cunning creature – when, in short, under the colour of the fiction, the spirit of satire is permitted to soothe for a moment the grievances of the weak and oppressed, are not the persons of the drama beasts dressed up in human characteristics? Is not this inexhaustibly resourceful folklore raised up upon an anthropomorphic base? – True enough. And it is also true that nobody mistakes these humans-in-disguise for real animals. We may as well concede, then, that there is a place in primitive folklore for such anecdotes of a satirical or moralistic tendency. But if we turn back to the genuine animal stories we were looking at in earlier chapters, myths and folktales in which no such satiric or grotesque tendency appears, we shall see at once that anthropomorphism played no part in those. Those stags, lions, vultures, and so on, whose nature was originally theriomorphically double, never were of the plain, merely categorical animal kind such as we conceive all beasts to be, with a cloak of human attributes thrown over them. Their innate natural identity, sometimes quite different from what we know categorically as animality, never had any need to be enhanced with a coat of human varnish.

With this we must be content; no good will come of setting up rigid and exclusive barriers of distinction and definition. There is no reason at all why animals, represented at first in the style we have just observed, should not later appear, in plenty of stories, travestied as men. For all that, such anthropomorphism is merely superficial – laid on, so to speak, with a trowel for the comic effect – and very often, underneath it, there persist more or less clear-cut traces of the primitive representation of animals in the manner we have seen in both myths and folklore.

We have seen how very closely similar the main patterns of primitive folklore, and of animal tales in particular, remain, even in places and among communities that otherwise have little in common. This broad conformity rarely falters. Almost everywhere in the world myths, legends and fairytales speak to us of the same mixed theriomorphic beings, capable of taking either form as they please. It is always the same "fluid" world that they put before us. On this score the Eskimo and the Ainu have nothing to learn from the Arunta or the Marind-anim, or the Bantu or any of the other black African tribes, or the Indians of North or South America.

In its turn, our own European folklore reveals a remarkably sympathetic correspondence with the primitives on just these points. Is it necessary to adduce proofs? All we need do, if we wish to be convinced, is open any book of popular stories; it makes no difference whether French, English, German, Italian, Spanish, Rumanian, Slavic, Greek, or any. Or it will be enough to turn to the fairytales of Perrault, stylized as they are. The wolf in *Little Red Riding Hood* is a theriomorph. When in wolf-form he thinks and speaks like a man; when he appears as the grandmother, his behaviour is that of a wild beast. *Puss in Boots* is an even clearer example. This animal-man is the most faithful of servants and the most astute of counsellors. Between his shrewd savoir-faire and his audacity he makes his master's fortune. We sometimes see him in the character of a man, sometimes as a quadruped. In the end he renounces the appearance of a cat altogether. However, not all of his double nature vanishes: "The cat became a great lord, and never afterwards hunted mice, *except for fun*". In *Cinderella* the world is entirely "fluid"; the fairy power never meets with the slightest resistance. The most incredible transformations are accomplished in a flash: a pumpkin becomes a carriage, mice are metamorphosed into dapple greys, a fat rat becomes a coachman and six lizards change into footmen. And then at the stroke of midnight all are suddenly back where they were before.

Popular tales like these, as is well known, have a very ancient origin, and they are by no means on the way to fading out. It would be very wrong of us not to recognize their deep significance, even if it were only for the way they link us with ages and civilizations in other respects so very different from our own. In so many aspects of life – religious belief, social structure, density of population, economic organization, foreign relations, the development of the arts and sciences, and many more – the disparity between our social patterns and those of the peoples we call primitive has never ceased to increase. But in spite of this, folklore remains everywhere much the same in all essentials. European fairytales present us with exactly the same picture of a "fluid" world as do the myths and legends of Australia and New Guinea.

To attempt an explanation of this fact would carry us very much further than this present work can hope to go. But we may at least give an indication of the path such an investigation would presumably need to follow. Given the close relationship between our own folklore and the myths and tales of primitives (and this would appear incontestable), clearly the same kind of mentality comes to expression in both. Each is marked in the same way, with the same essential characteristics. So it must follow that much of what, in earlier parts of this book, has been shown to be true of the mythology of tribes far removed from us, is also quite valid for the folklore (for the animal stories especially) of our own western culture. This leads to a clarification of all that is mysterious, fantastic and wildly extravagant in it; everything at last begins to make sense. All we have to do is refer it all back to the mentality in which it had its origin. We recognize its affinities with the primitive in its markedly mystical tendencies, and also in its indifference to contradiction at such times as the *participations* are taking effect.

With the Australians, and even with many other communities of a relatively advanced culture, myths and the greater part of all legends and tales of a folkloric character pass as records of truth. We have seen the reasons for this. According to the habit of thought among these primitives, the "fluid" world in which most of those events take place is undoubtedly kept distinct from the more stabilized one in which they live; nevertheless in the totality of their experience of the world, both ideas are included. As we habitually see the issues, on the contrary, the "fluid" image appears to be perfectly incompatible with reality as we know it, either from a logical or a physical point of view. Whether lay or learned, we all without exception perceive ourselves to be living in a world where nature has been intellectualized, within a framework of necessary laws and fixed forms all corresponding with our concepts. Among us, therefore, there is no one, outside the range of toddlers and babies, who can give real belief to fairytales. They have come to be classed typically as fabulous and unbelievable. But they are not any the less for that carried on from generation to generation; they survive as living vestiges of an ancient mental life which in all other respects has become very remote from us. These vestiges are perfectly harmless, because the world the tales carry us off to is today merely the realm of fantasy; it makes no pretence whatever to have any existence at all in terms of present reality.

Furthermore there are few among us who do not quickly respond to the charm of such stories. Grown-ups and children alike relish them. Perhaps we ought not to weigh them in the same balance with literary masterpieces, classic or modern. But what they bring us, one feels instinctively, is not to be looked for from any other source. Though as literature they may be nondescript, for all that there is a savour about them that is unique. What is the reason for this effect, so vital and also so universal? The answer is simple. It arises from the fact that they keep us in touch with the "fluid" world of basic, primitive thought. They carry us back into the company of marvellous beings who can survive in no other world but that.

Works of mature literary art (poems, novels, romances, dramas, farces and so on) scarcely ever sanction an excursion outside the frame of common experience — beyond the range of the actual, or at any rate the possible. A novel, for example, or a play, never shows us anything but men or women more or less like ourselves, in situations which seem more or less familiar to our idea of the world. What the characters say and do, even when they are the merest puppets, symbolic, heroic or exotic, always in the last analysis implies for both the writer and his public what we might call an *a priori* general notion of nature and the social community. Even if the author is not a realist, even if he does not in the least care to create convincing likenesses, he nevertheless needs to feel that in the long run his work "rings true". He will never consent to its flying in the face of psychological probability, or representing events that are manifestly absurd as though they were real. Always the facts must be such as *might* have been possible in the way he presents them; and the characters must be such as *could* have done the things we see happening. That is the first rule of the game; no author in his right mind would think of breaking it.

Folktales know no such scruples. They have but the slightest regard for the logical, or even the physical feasibility of the prodigies they relate, and very little more for psychology. In the fairytales we have been looking at, a cat who is at the same time a man becomes a great lord without really ceasing to be a cat. In less time than it takes to say so, a pumpkin turns into a coach, a fat rat into a coachman. The world in which this happens is no less "fluid" than that of the Australian and New Guinea myths — and is no less incongruous to our own idea of the laws of nature and the exigencies of reason. But we are not put off the stories on that account, nor do we reject them as childish. Quite the contrary, we find in them a perpetual interest. How can we explain this charm?

Our continuing delight will seem less strange if we bear in mind that, from time immemorial, such tales have been told from one end of the world to the other, and have always, apart from a very few exceptions, been *treated* as true – at any rate by primitives, who do not even entertain a sense of the impossible. Those tellers who pass them on today have all received them as "true" from their forefathers, and the young people who hear them now will pass them on in their turn, just as spontaneously. If we could only look far enough back into the past, we should surely see that our own ancestors were not exceptional on this point. So that what really needs explaining is not why, among so many more or less primitive cultures, such stories are for the most part perfectly naively "believed"; but on the contrary, why, in our own community, we have for so long ceased to believe them.

Without doubt it happened, either wholly or in part, because of the rational structure of the civilization developed in classical antiquity and passed on to us. From the sum of human experience, all regarded in primitive times as valid, certain items came gradually to be excluded. They were notions that would not answer to rational control or that refused to submit to rational verification – in effect, mystical beliefs and other evidences of supernatural contact. In other words, our presently prevailing concept of reality came, with a more and more exacting precision, to coincide with the view taken of nature, as also of the mind, as a fixed system of operational law. From that point forward whatever lay beyond these new frontiers, religious experience alone being excepted, must be rejected as impossible. This meant that, for intelligences which had broken with primitive habits of thinking in order to embrace rationality as the structural basis of thought, the mythical world, along with the world of folklore which is hardly at all to be distinguished from it, could no longer be accepted as forming any significant part of reality.

Even so, however, history reveals that this revised programme was not wholly welcomed by all men. It was adopted in certain communities only; in those, moreover, only after centuries of resistance. And even then its effect was far from universal, its establishment anything but unshakable. What we understand from this is nothing less than that its new and rational disciplines were felt as excessively demanding; and that as long as human nature continues to have any respect for those tendencies within it which have been inherent from the very beginning, it will not even under modern conditions be seriously put off by the transparent impossibilities that can be recognized in the mythic world, and will never even dream of excluding from what it considers to be reality those special insights which come to it directly from mystical sources.

Hence the denial of such mystical insights, however rationally justified (one might even suggest, *because* rationally justified) brings with it, even when it has become customary and automatic, an element of uneasiness, what in the modern jargon is called an inhibited feeling. Left to take their natural course those tendencies would lead the mind into a quite different pathway. In order to suppress them with no weakening, we have to guard the mind against every possible inclination to stray; and this is something we cannot do without some constant violation of our nature.

Here, then, is the reason, and it is a very deep-seated one, why folklore and fairytales continue to have such a magical attraction for us, and why their language has such seductive charm. The moment we begin to hear one being told, the feeling of inhibition vanishes, the oppressive sense of constraint is gone. Instantaneously our fettered nature leaps forward to reassert itself. While we listen we throw aside, as it were with a fierce abandonment, all our frenzied discontents; we decline to be hemmed in with repressions. It is not that we forget we shall have to take them up again presently. We have no desire to deny reason in perpetuity; if the necessity arose we would be quite ready to pick up the rational burden once again. But take it simply as it comes, the relaxation, for as long as it lasts, gratifies and enchants us to our depths. It gives us a sensation of becoming once again like the folk of long ago (who still have their counterparts in many places even today), when men looked upon the mystical part of their experience of the world, not as less, but as even more truly real than the empiric. Thus the tales amount to much more than mere entertainment. They offer a kind of respite. The enjoyment they bring is far richer that anything which merely distracts and amuses.

That is certainly the reason why folktales travel, as they do with so little essential alteration, from community to community and across so many centuries of time. We in particular respond to their appeal with a delight that is ever fresh; there is no risk at all of its ever falling away. As with the wave of an enchanter's wand (a gesture with which the fairies have never been niggardly) we are at once wafted back, without any sensation of change or alteration, into the world of our ancient forefathers. And there we find in the full flower of life, vividly before us, the mysterious, "fluid" world of the primal myths. No matter how far removed we thought we had been from the mentality which in the first place produced them, the spectacle captivates us at once and holds us fast —

> And as for me,
> When I but hear the Sleeping Beauty told,
> I am more pleased than with a crock of gold.[47]

Appendix on Animism

LB makes it clear at an early stage that he is in disagreement with the Animist thesis in anthropology. Animism, according to Sir Edward Burnett Tylor (who could be called the leader in his day of the English school of anthropologists, and whom LB constantly opposed), was "in fact the groundwork of the Philosophy of Religion, from that of savages up to that of civilized men". Defining it as "the doctrine of souls and other spiritual beings in general", Tylor also said it was "among those opinions which are produced by a little knowledge, to be dispelled by a little more".[1] With that sentiment no doubt LB would agree. Indeed his quarrel with "the followers of Tylor", including Andrew Lang and Sir James Frazer, would seem to be based more on their propensity for rationalizing their conclusions than on their concern with souls and spiritual beings in general. He complains that the English Animists make "philosophers" of primitives and introduce "logical postulates" into a mental world which is better served by explanations (of the mythic institutions) more conformable with his own "Affective Category of the Supernatural".

"Animism", said Tylor in 1871, "is not a new technical term, though now seldom used." He revived it in his influential study, *Primitive Culture*, a two-volume work of some one thousand pages, of which about three quarters is concerned with Animism in one aspect or another. In a shorter work, *Anthropology: an Introduction to the Study of Man and Civilization*, published ten years later, he restated his position. I take two passages from this work, not hoping to do real justice to Tylor himself, but to illustrate the sort of thing to which LB took exception. The first sets out the rational approach to anthropology, the second rationalizes a particular mythical example.

We know how strong our own desire is to account for everything. This desire is as strong among barbarians, and accordingly they devise such explanations as satisfy their minds. But they are apt to go a stage further, and their explanations turn into the form of stories with names of places and persons, thus becoming full-made myths. Educated men do not now consider it honest to make fictitious history in this way, but people of untrained mind, in what is called the myth-making stage, which has lasted on from the savage period and has not quite disappeared among ourselves, have no such scruples about converting their guesses as to what may have happened, into the most life-like stories of what they say did happen. Thus, when comparative anatomy was hardly known, the finding of huge fossil bones in the ground led people to think they were the remains of huge beasts, and enormous men, or giants, who formerly lived on earth. Modern science decides that they were right as to the beasts, which were ancient species of elephant, rhinoceros, etc., but wrong as to the giants, none of the great bones really belonging to any creature like man. But while the belief lasted that they were bones of giants, men's imagination worked in making stories about these giants and their terrific doings . . . So lately as the last century Dr Cotton Mather . . . sent to our Royal Society an account of the discovery of such bones in New England, which he argued were remains of antediluvian giants.

Clever writers are too apt to sit down and settle the mythic origin of any tale, as if this could be done by ingenious guessing. Even if it is nonsense and never was intended for anything else, the myth-interpreter can find a serious origin for it all the same. Thus a learned but rash mythologist declares that in our English nursery-rhyme, "the cow jumped over the moon", is a remnant of an old nature-myth, describing as a cow a cloud passing over the moon. What is really wanted in interpreting myths is something beyond simple guessing; there must be reasons why one particular guess is more probable than any other. It would have been rash to judge that *Prometheus* the fire-bringer is a personifaction of the wooden fire-drill, were it not known that the Sanskrit name of this instrument is *pramantha*; taken together, the correspondence of name and nature amounts to a high probability that we have got back to the real origin of the Prometheus-legend.[2]

Such argumentation goes a long way to account for LB's antipathy. It remains to suggest what aspects of Animism were acceptable to him (whether or not the word was), and why he placed so much importance on Wirz's examination of the Marind myth of the bow.

It is clear that he regards this myth as in some sense definitive (*un cas en quelque sorte privilégié, comme le serait une expérience cruciale*). In the case of the bow-*Dema* and the accepted "animation" (Wirz: *Beseelung*) of modern bows, we have, as Wirz makes clear, a fascinating example of not only an artifact, but also a legend that is visibly man-made. Moreover, unlike Tylor's nursery rhyme (rejected as irrational) or his Promethean rational "high probability", this myth was made "*auf spielerische Weise*", at least partly for a joke. Yet it commands a full degree of authority because it achieved the miracle of *participation*.

It may be useful here to include a somewhat more ample summary of Wirz's remarks than LB actually quotes. He deals with the myth in both part ii and part iii of *Die Marind-anim*; the latter is the fuller treatment, where Wirz is discussing aspects of tribal magic. (These translations are made directly from Wirz.)

> That an article of such constant use, which might almost be said to grow in the hand of the Marind, as the bow, should become the subject of so many myths and be given such an infinite number of names, is only what might be expected. The bow, moreoever, is regarded as being, more than any other article of common use, endowed with spiritual qualities, as descending from a *Dema* ancestor. Because of this it also follows that it possesses human form, since the *Dema* had it from the beginning . . . The animate vitality of the bow finds expression through various of its attributes, which advance it to a status and esteem far above what is accorded to other objects which do not command so much affection. Even though the bow is a human invention the Marind nevertheless sees in it the image of the bow-*Dema* considered as its creator. Through the processes of copying the original model, something of the primeval bow-*Dema*'s soul-substance or spirituality is in a certain sense transferred to the new weapon, just as any other reproduction of an object in nature recaptures within itself a quantum of the spiritual power which belongs to the original – depending upon the amount of force inherent in the ancestral prototype. The elasticity of the drawn bow and the strength that is in it to speed the arrow and so slay the enemy or bring down the game are, as the Marind sees them, testimony to the bow's spiritual liveliness. Such faculties and powers descend to it from the *Dema*. They reappear as a matter of course in every fresh bow which is constructed after the model of the *Dema* original, in exactly the same way as animals reproduce innate characteristics and tendencies inherited by every generation from their *Dema* ancestors. The Marind habitually say of such things, "That is something that has come down from the *Dema*", or "That is the way the *Dema* always did it". I remember very clearly, for example, how the people would shake their heads in imitation of the giant stork, and exclaim, "See, this was the *Dema*'s habit!"[3]

At this point Wirz discusses certain physical details of the bow, distinguishing between coastal and inland types. Both preserved the recognizable human form of the *Dema*. In the naming of various parts of the bow Wirz concedes certain affinities with the Animists (though not to the rationalist school) and clearly the passage is one which LB finds slightly embarrassing. It will be noticed that in his own text he handles Wirz's reference to Animism with gingerly care. There is, however, no basic disagreement between them. Wirz now continues:

> Let us now return to the names given to the different parts of the bow, which rest upon animistic associatione. Apart from the nose and foot of the weapon, the Marind distinguishes also other parts which he traces back to the *Dema* ancestor: i.e., the mouth (grooves running between the nodes), the eyes (small bosses above the intersections), and the beard (fine rootlike lines underneath them). The bow-*Dema*'s wife – that is, the bowstring – clings tight about his neck [she also, according to the myth, has a separate name of her own]. The lower or foot end of the bow demonstrates the act of copulation in which the *Dema* and his wife are joined. Thus all the various parts of the bow have separate names . . .
>
> That the Marind-anim should possess so extensive a range of names for the bow, their constant companion, is quite understandable. We ourselves have a similar familiar intimacy with guns and give names to the various parts. But in this case the reasons underlying the names are different. They all rest upon certain animistic indications and upon the reading into the bow of a human kind of personality – i.e., that of the bow-*Dema*. In view of this it may be quite proper to describe the naming process as animistic. But in and of themselves the names infer nothing at all of any indwelling ghostly identity or animating spirit. In the first place the names were invented from a playful impulse to attribute to the weapon and its parts features already recognizable in other objects. At any rate they provided a starting point for the myth, which could then develop. Once the myth was established the Marind amused themselves by carrying invention further. The resilience and potential energy of the bent bow, which the natives were perfectly capable of distinguishing from any animal psyche, were by this association brought into a relationship with the bow-*Dema*, and were thus in effect deemed to be derived from him as the bow's ancestor, very much as though, like the psychic functions of animals, its attributes had come down to it through many generations of heredity.[4]

Wirz again stresses the element of playfulness in the evolution of the bow myth:

Actually the naming process goes even further, as every part of the bow is given an individual or *Dema-* name to itself . . . but these names naturally are all purely regional and were bestowed in a jocular spirit. They are nevertheless in quite current use.[5]

Notes

In these notes Lévy-Bruhl is referred to shortly as LB. The notes incorporate but do not confine themselves to LB's original notes, which were mostly (with a number of exceptions) simply footnote textual references. Both quotations within the text and notes traced to their sources I have at times somewhat indulgently expanded; those which come from sources already translated are given in their English versions. Here only very brief textual identifications are given; fuller bibliographical information will be found in the bibliography.

Introduction

1. I have retained LB's use of the words Papua and Papuan as they appear in the text. The modern political divisions of New Guinea did not of course exist when he wrote, and it seemed pointless to insist on distinctions which could add nothing to his own usage.
2. LB's anxiety to avoid misinterpretation reflects a contemporary situation which has now lost heat.
3. LB is careful to maintain a distinction between the element of religiosity he perceives in primitive cultures and formal religion in modern times, which he usually designates "religion properly so-called".
4. An implied but critical allusion to a contemporary view, expressed for example by Emile Durkheim, who in the introduction to his *The Elementary Forms of the Religious Life* refers to the Australian Aboriginal mythology as "the most primitive and simple religion which is actually known", and again (p. 167) as "the most primitive . . . in all probability, that has ever existed". Marcel Mauss also expressed a similar view of Aboriginal antiquity; see chapter VI, p. 182.
5. LB implies a cosy western-type concept of family life that does not really fit the Aboriginal situation. Tribal seniority, related to initiation, is more important.
6. This is explained presently (see p. 12) in a passage quoted from T.G.H. Strehlow; LB clearly has Aranda myths in mind.

7. Gunnar Landtman, *The Kiwai Papuans of British New Guinea*, pp. 298-99. Landtman says the Kiwai Islanders have "no systematized ideas as to the supernatural world in which everybody believes, and no priests. No public cult exists; no prayers are said. The Kiwais lack any concept of a supreme deity. Creation is conceived as a series of unconnected occurrences. It seems to be characteristic of the natives' way of thinking that the idea of the entirety of things and phenomena is lacking; Nature is to them composed of independent units" (slightly condensed).

8. A.R. Radcliffe-Brown, *The Andaman Islanders*, p. 188.

9. Paul Wirz, *Die Marind-anim von Holländisch-Süd-Neu-Guinea*, I, ii, p. 21. R.F. Fortune, *Sorcerers of Dobu*, pp. 31, 95.

10. Knud Rasmussen, "Intellectual Culture of the Iglulik Eskimos", p. 69.

11. *Participation* or "mystical participation" is discussed at length in LB's *How Natives Think* (see especially chapter II of Part I).

12. Ibid., chapter III. On the question of LB's *prelogical* views, C. Lévi-Strauss (*The Scope of Anthropology*, p. 41) says that he chose at the outset "to relegate mythic representation to the antechamber of logic" and "rendered the separation irremediable when he later renounced the notion of prelogical thought. In doing so he was simply throwing out the baby with the bathwater: he denied to 'primitive mentality' the cognitive character which he had originally conceded to it, and cast it back entirely into the realm of affectivity." But if anything was changed it would seem to have been more the terminology than any fundamental idea. Jean Cazeneuve (*Lucien Lévy-Bruhl*, p. 14) remarks, "Briefly, what has been described to us under the name of primitive mentality is undoubtedly a permanent structure of the human mind, but in our society this structure is blurred by the supremacy of scientific thought, whereas it remains in the foreground among preliterate peoples."

13. Maurice Leenhardt, "Documents Néo-Calédoniens", pp. 114-15, note 70. But see also C. Lévi-Strauss, *The Savage Mind*, chapter I.

14. Mooney and Olbrechts, "The Swimmer Manuscript", pp. 89-90. Swimmer is the name of an Indian informant. This study, left unfinished by James Mooney, was after his death edited and extended by F.M. Olbrechts.

15. Ibid., p. 53.

16. See LB, *Primitives and the Supernatural*, introduction.
Under the term "representation" LB groups all attempts, especially of a ritual nature, to give formal expression to sacred and spiritual matters. The allusion is generally to some form of tribal image-making, e.g. heroic poetry or narrative, dance or related ceremonies, painting, drawing or other kinds of design. Such imagery is not "representational" in the modern sense but mostly refers to matters already known; its character is mainly mnemonic.

17. Compare J. Cazeneuve, *Lucien Lévy-Bruhl*, p. 14:

> Emotion and sentiment give primitive man a knowledge of reality other than that given to him by purely objective experience. Thus the category of the supernatural is of the affective order, and Lévy-Bruhl now introduces a new notion into his analysis — that of the *affective category of the supernatural* — to designate the element common to all mystical representations, what it is they all share. This is more felt than known and is not to be found at the level of ideas ... Primitive man does not need an intellectual act in order to recognize this special tonality when the *affective category of the supernatural* comes into play.

18. Few will wish to dispute what LB says here, but it is a point which invites ventilation. Early missionaries frequently sought to underline any possible correspondence between native religious ideas and Christianity, and this sometimes resulted in distorted parallels. (Compare Wirz, passage quoted p. 127: "No matter what questions are put to the natives, they invariably answer 'yes'.") Carl Strehlow was accused by Sir Baldwin Spencer of this failing. Strehlow says in the opening pages of his *Die Aranda- und Loritjastämme*, I, p. 2, that according to Aboriginal belief there was in the beginning a great, good Being who was eternal, who appeared as a tall, strong man of a ruddy complexion with long, bright (Strehlow's *helles* might imply blond) hair falling to his shoulders. This was the personal figure called Altjira. His dwelling was in *dem Himmel* (whether "in the sky" of "in heaven"), and he was *der gute Gott der Aranda*, the benevolent God of the Aranda. These appearances are not very characteristically Aboriginal and it is hinted that there could be some reminiscence of religious pictures seen at the mission. (Spencer's criticism forms Appendix D of *The Arunta*.) It has been generally agreed that the Australian Aborigines had no single Supreme Deity in the Christian sense, but in various tribes there were individual creator-figures of considerable importance. T.G.H. Strehlow, *Aranda Traditions*, p. 7. A.W. Howitt (Carl Strehlow's contemporary) examined the question at some length in *The Native Tribes of South East Australia*, pp. 493-94 ff., and concluded there was no validity in any Australian Aboriginal "Allfather" myth.
19. Bronislaw Malinoswki, *Myth in Primitive Psychology*, pp. 21, 78, 124.
20. A.P. Elkin, "The Secret Life of the Australian Aborigines", p. 120.
21. Ibid., p. 132.
22. Wirz, *Die Marind-anim*, II, iv, p. 1; II, iii, p. 2.
23. Marjorie and Ralph Piddington, "Report on Field Work in North Western Australia", p. 353.
24. T.G.H. Strehlow, "Ankotarinja, an Aranda Myth", pp. 198-99.
25. Landtman, *The Kiwai Papuans*, p. 421.
26. C. Keysser, "Aus dem Leben der Kai", p. 61.
    Carl Strehlow, *Die Aranda- und Loritjastämme*, I. p. 101.
    There is still no settled spelling of Australian Aboriginal words, but in respect of Central Australian tribes the precedent of either Spencer or the Strehlows is usually followed, if not rigidly. Spencer writes *Arunta*, the Strehlows *Aranda*, according to English or German phonology. Charles Chewings, whose MS vocabulary of the language is preserved in the Barr Smith Library, Adelaide, writes *Arrenda*, but this form is not in general use. Some useful couplings (Spencer's spelling first) follow; but it will usually not be difficult to distinguish them in any case: Arunta/Aranda; alchera/altjira; Luritcha/Loritja; churinga/tjurunga; achilpa/tjilpa.
27. Fortune, *Sorcerers of Dobu*, p. 95.
28. Bronislaw Malinowski, *Argonauts of the Western Pacific*, pp. 299-300.
29. Elkin, "The Secret Life of the Australian Aborigines", pp. 128-29.
30. M. and R. Piddington, "Report on Field Work in North Western Australia", p. 353.
31. *Ungud* – "also called *lalan*" (Elkin, "Secret Life of the Australian Aborigines" p. 464) – is an Ungarinyin equivalent to the other terms listed. The broad connotations of all are similar but there are regional differences.
32. LB notes: With what is said here may be compared the following from an article by E.W. Gifford. It shows that the Yuma Indians (California) acknowledge a close relationship between myth and dreaming.

I thought it would be of especial interest to record Joe Homer's dreams since the creation story which he related to Mr Harrington is reputed to have been dreamed in part, at least. As Kroeber points out (*Handbook of the Indians of California*, p. 857), myth dreaming is a common cultural feature of the Mohave and Yuma. Joe Homer, who was 56 years old in 1921, had become a Methodist . . . When I reminded Joe Homer that he no longer dreams about the Awikwame Mountain, the home of the gods, he replied that it was too big a place to dream about more than once. *You would not go to Washington every year*, he said. The potency of dreaming as a means to properly learning a myth was emphasized on one occasion by Joe Homer. An Akwa'ala informant from Lower California had related an imperfect origin tale. Joe said that the informant's not having dreamed it was the cause of the imperfections.

(E.W. Gifford, "Yuma Dreams and Omens", p. 58).

With this LB couples from Spencer and Gillen, *The Arunta*, I, p. 306: "It is also very significant to find that natives who can speak English, as many of them can now do with varying degrees of proficiency, when referring to a man's Alchera and everything associated with it in the far past mythical times, always call it 'his dreaming'." However, LB's rendering of "dreaming" as "ce qu'il rêve" is not wholly satisfactory if taken literally.

Although his translation may indicate that LB did not quite grasp the exact sense of the Aboriginal "dreaming", it is interesting to note that, had he gone directly to the article by Kroeber cited by Gifford, he would have found, not on p. 857 as he states, but on p. 783, a striking confirmation of his views: "The direct basis of all religion – tradition, ritual song, and shamanistic power – is individual dreaming, in the opinion of the Yuma. They hold to this belief as thoroughly and consistently as the Mohave." A quite remarkable "autobiographic statement by one of their medicine men" follows. The basis of Australian belief in "the dreaming", however, or even in what is referred to as a man's personal "dreaming", is not like this. Its orientations are mystically tribal.

33. LB, *Primitive Mentality*, chapter II.
34. See first note 31. The popular use in Australia of the terms "dreamtime" or "eternal dreamtime" is justifiable but open to gross sentimental distortion. What Elkin says (pp. 14-15) is plain enough: ". . . not mere phantasy, but spiritual reality. A man's 'dreaming' is his share of the secret myths and rites . . .". "And again," his statement continues, "over a vast area of Australia the term, or one term, for cult-totem, is this very term which denotes dreaming." In various languages the word implies a mystical remoteness like the imagery of dreams but it must not be supposed it implies mere fantasy. "Von eine Traumzeit als Zeitperiode weiss übrigens der Eingeborene nichts", declared Carl Strehlow: the native knows nothing of any "dreamtime" conceived as history. T.G.H. Strehlow (*Songs of Central Australia*, p. 614) is a little more explicit. There he says that although the term "dreamtime" has become popular through its sentimentality, it is never used by the natives themselves when they speak English: *dreaming* means *totem*, and that only. It is in fact a confused translation of two Aranda words, one of which (*altjira*) means "to dream" and the other (*altjiranga*) "from all eternity". These are clearly the originals of Spencer's "alchera" and "alcheringa". But he had already translated it in 1896, when he wrote to L. Fison (21 November 1896), see Spencer's *Scientific Correspondence*, p. 132): "The natives say, 'It was so in the dreamtimes . . .' ". Attractive as it is, because of its somewhat

unstable connotations most anthropologists nowadays tend to avoid the use of the term unless they are speaking merely picturesquely.

35. Wirz, *Die Marind-anim*, I, ii, p. 6. (This admirable work, published in Hamburg in 1922, may well be supplemented by J. van Baal, *Dema. Description and Analysis of Marind-anim Culture*, 1966. As Van Baal's work appears in an English version I have allowed it to influence my English spelling of Marind words, whether taken from Wirz's German or LB's French.) Note LB's careful distinction between *dema* and *Dema*. The word may become a plural without change of form.

36. Ibid., I, ii, p. 8.

37. LB notes: For the sake of comparison it may be of interest to place against the several senses of *dema* among the Marind-anim those of *mukuru* among the Herero (south west Africa), as reported by a missionary.

> When after the 1904 rising the Herero tribe was destroyed all our congregations were annihilated with them. Soon after the rebellion the wretched remainder of the tribe became christianized. They were for the most part people of sheerly heathen origin, since the civilized ones had fled across the border and taken the best part of our former congregations with them. Their ideas were primitive and their language no better. They made contact with the Missioner but, unlike earlier converts, did not use the mission idiom. Their way of expressing themselves was so different from the earlier Christians that an old mission worker was moved to assert that they spoke a separate dialect. The first of the Missioners to arrive looked round for a native word to translate the name of God into their language, and chose *Mukuru* (instead of *Ndjambi Kuranga*). But in the minds of the people this put God on the same level as one of the tribal forefathers, with the unfortunate result that He was reduced in their estimation to a mere mumbo-jumbo. On one occasion after a certain Missioner had preached the sermon, a visiting Christian asked a member of the mission's congregation, "Who was the Missioner who preached this morning? How did he come to be so easy with our language? He explained the Word of God to us in such a fashion, you would think he had a *mukuru* in his pocket, putting words into his hand for him to toss about!" One Missioner asked a man who had been baptized many years earlier if he had torn up his certificate. The man replied, "I wouldn't dare! Isn't it *mukuru*?" The term *mukuru* is used, not only for God, but for all that is connected with divinity, exactly as used to be done by the old-time heathen. As far as they were concerned, anything at all was *mukuru* which, as they supposed, had unseen spirits in it.
>
> – Missioner Kuhlmann (Omaruru) in a series of articles in the *Windhueker Zeitung*, 1917. Cited by Viktor Lebzelter, *Eingeborenen-kulturen in Süd-West und Süd-Afrika*, p. 182.

38. See note 11 above.

39. LB notes: In other passages Wirz remarks that the *kugi* are primarily identified with the spirits of the dead.

40. Paul Wirz, "Anthropologische und enthnologische Ergebnisse der Central Neu-Guinea Expedition", pp. 52-53, 59. Wirz continues, "The native speaks without more precise definition or distinction merely of *kugi*, in which term he includes supernatural, powerful and destructive forces which he envisages as beings more or less human in form."

41. Ibid.

42. Ibid., p. 60.

43. Ibid. As to LB's conjecture that the people were too primitive to have created proper myths, he seems to miss the point of Wirz's remark which follows the quoted passage: "Of the rainbow they say that it is the blood of a slain man spurting up to heaven. Neither is any association certain between *kugi* and the stars, but whether, for all that, no myths about stars are to be reported, naturally is more than I could find out because I was among the people for too short a time."

44. The kind of *churinga* here referred to must be a small object (of stone or wood) ritually decorated and having high totemic significance, guarded with great secrecy. It is a symbol of the individual possessor's eternal identity, and is of sacred mythic origin. Apart from such objects the word *churinga/tjurunga* has other and much more complex meanings (see T.G.H. Strehlow, *Aranda Traditions*, pp. 84-86).

45. W.E.H. Stanner, "The Daly River Tribes", p. 401.

46. Paul Wirz, "Beitrag zur Ethnologie der Sentanier (Holländisch Neu-Guinea)", pp. 300, 301.

47. Ibid., p. 341. The reference is to small stones of interesting shapes (*soimi* stones), which are regarded as having a powerful *dema* magic. Wirz adds, "although various scientific and other enquirers persist in trying to do so".

48. Ibid., pp. 304-5, partly paraphrased. The square-bracketed sentence before the quotation (not in LB) seems necessary to bridge a gap.

49. Ibid., pp. 305-9, with some paraphrase and several omissions (by LB). In an attempt to remain in line with both LB and his original, I have had to extend his quotation a little and again the bracketed sentence bridges a gap.

50. Ibid., p. 303.

51. (Sir) George Grey, *Journals of Two Expeditions* (in Western Australia, 1837-39). See I, pp. 201ff, 213-16, and plates facing pp. 202, 203, 214. Grey also describes, and includes a sketch of another intaglio, apparently unrelated, which has a strangely modern look about it but remains quite unaccounted for and seems to have excited little remark (facing p. 206). It is not in any sense a *wondjina* figure.

52. A.P. Elkin, "Rock-paintings of North West Australia", pp. 261, 263, 275, 279. The Kimberley District is the tribal country of three tribes called by Elkin Ungarinyin, Wurara and Unambal. He records his impressions of them very tentatively: "I spent about nine weeks in the country of the Ungarinyin tribe . . . not sufficient to enable me to study the mythology . . . this paper only a preliminary contribution . . ." J.R.B. Love's *Stone-Age Bushmen of Today* (published a year later than *Primitive Mythology*) refers to these tribes as Ngarinjin, Worora and Wunambal and describes several *Wondjuna* sites. Incidentally LB's description of the faces as "regarding intently" the animal figures represents a personal interpretation, which would also appear to be a somewhat bold rationalization.

53. Ibid., pp. 269, note 8, 263, 276, 279.
Oceania I (1930-31) contains several short contributions (see especially pp. 350-51) touching the rainbow serpent myth (". . . perhaps the most important nature-deity", says A.R. Radcliffe-Brown, p. 342). Although LB does not mention these, possibly they may have prompted his explanatory comment on the rainbow snake and rain (in brackets), which is not in Elkin's article.

LB's note also refers to Spencer, *Scientific Correspondence*, p. 132, partly quoted in note 34: "The natives say, 'It was so in the dream-times', just as a Fijian says, 'Our fathers said, or did, so'. When the enquirer gets to that point, he need not try to get any farther."

54. Ralph Piddington, "The Totemic System of the Karadjeri Tribe", p. 374.
55. LB quotes Jaime de Angulo, "La Psychologie des Achumawi", p. 161: "For the Achumawi Indian there are two kinds of reality. One is the reality of daily and common life, and he is very well able to apply to that the most rigorous logic. The other is the reality of a world that is mysterious, fearful, and in which anything is possible. Except for this the two worlds are the same; he is unable to say where one ends and the other begins." The Achumawi are Indians of Central California whom Dr Angulo regards as being still extremely primitive. Incidentally in this article Angulo defends LB against those of his critics who (in 1928) attacked his theory of participation. But he himself is critical of the term "prelogical" and would rather employ the expression "aesthetic thinking" (*la pensée esthétique*) which he regards as part of modern civilized mental experience.
56. Sir Edward Burnett Tylor (1832-1917), a leading English anthropologist of his day, best known for his influential *Primitive Culture* (London 1871, revised edition 1921), in which he develops at length his theory of animism. LB's antagonism to Tylor's approach accounts in part for the gingerly tone of his opening remarks in this present introductory chapter.
57. Wirz, "Anthropologische und ethnologische Ergebnisse", p. 59.
58. E.B. Tylor, *Primitive Culture*. Vol. I, chapter viii concerns mythology.
59. Wirz, *Die Marind-anim* I, ii, pp. 15-16.
60. See note 33 above. It is to be noted that in German, Wirz's language, nouns are normally written with an initial capital letter and adjectives not; this is essentially still the case in LB's French use of *Dema* and *dema* (which I follow), except for the fact that the capital *D* also in some measure personalizes the reference.
61. LB notes: C.H. de Goeje, in his study of the myths of the Amazonian Caribs, has arrived at a firm opinion which agrees with what is said here. The myths of these people imply the existence of a world which is different from that of common experience, a world to which the Carib medicine men are introduced through visions (as are the Australians through dream experience), and to which novices come by virtue of initiation. "The myths are narratives of visions which the initiated Indian experiences in a clairvoyant ecstasy" (p. 515). And again, "The Indians know that the other world, of which the myths speak, and to which the initiated have access, is the wellspring or immediate cause of the visible and tangible world" (p. 500). Finally, "One frequently forms the impression that for the Indians the other world is the true reality, while the material world, which to us appears the only convincing one, is no more than what Goethe's apothegm expresses: *Alles Vergängliche ist nur ein Gleichnis* (All transitory things are but a parable) (p. 503).
"Oudheden uit Suriname, of zock naar den Amazonen", *West-Indische Gids*, XIII, 10-11 (1932) (inaccessible for checking).

Chapter I: The Mythic World

1. W.B. Spencer and F.J. Gillen, *The Native Tribes of Central Australia*, p. 73. In this volume the form *alcheringa* is usual, but in the later *The Arunta* Spencer amends it to *alchera*. See Introduction, note 34.

Konrad Theodor Preuss, *Der religiöse Gehalt der Mythen*, p. 12. However, Carl Strehlow and others also speak of the *Urzeit*.

2. Bronislaw Malinowski, *Argonauts of the Western Pacific*, p. 300.

3. Ibid., p. 301-2. In the passage which connects the two quotations Malinowski remarks that in historical stories we have conventions for clarifying the distance of an event, and that when telling of Joan of Arc, Achilles, King Arthur, "we have to mention all sorts of conditions long since disappeared", whereas "the mythical personages in the Trobriand tradition are living the same type of life . . . as the present natives".

4. Ibid., p. 305.

5. Presumably referring to Orulo's remark, quoted earlier (Introduction, pp. 6-7).

6. R.F. Fortune, *Sorcerers of Dobu*, p. 99. LB omits the Dobuan names.

7. LB gives no reference for Vedder but V. Lebzelter, *Rassen und Kulturen in Sud-Afrika*, p. 168, quotes a story (how a Bergdama man fetched fire from the lion's hearth) by H. Vedder from *Journal of the South West Africa Scientific Society*, II (1926-27), p. 43.

8. LB notes: See H. Hubert and M. Mauss, "Etude sommaire de la représentation du temps dans la religion et la magie", *Mélanges d'histoire des religions*, p. 189 (unavailable for checking).

9. Carl Strehlow, *Die Aranda- und Loritjastämme*, I, p. 2. Strehlow notes that the Aranda language possesses four distinct terms corresponding to the German *ewig* (eternal), of which *ngamitjina* is one. He relates that the world, which is eternal (*ngambakala*) was in the beginning covered by water (German *Meer* = sea). Out of the measureless waters rose up various hills, on which dwelt certain beings who had godlike powers. These were the *altjirangamitjina* (*altjira* + *ngamitjina*, die ewigen Unerschaffenen, the eternal uncreated); they were also called *inkara* (*die Unsterblichen*, the immortals). Strehlow refers also to the *Begriff des Nicht-Gewordenen*, the idea of the Unbecome or Uncreated. It is in this context that he rebukes Spencer and Gillen for their use of the expression "dreamtime".
    A.P. Elkin, "The Secret Life of the Australian Aborigines", pp. 135-36.

10. Paul Wirz, *Die Marind-anim von Holländisch Süd-Neu-Guinea*, I, ii, p. 16.
    Bronislaw Malinowski, *Myth in Primitive Psychology*, p. 21.
    Preuss, *Der religiöse Gehalt der Mythen*, pp. 12, 23.

11. The question of the Australian Aborigines' understanding of conception has been the subject of much ignorant speculation. They do not discard the idea of physical paternity, but as each new life is seen as a re-entry into human life of an eternal spirit, sex can be considered only as a physical preparation for a mystical event. The subject is discussed at some length in T.G.H. Strehlow, *Aranda Traditions*, pp. 88ff.
    A.P. Elkin, "Studies in Australian Totemism", p. 116; L. Fison and A.W. Howitt, *Kamilaroi and Kurnai*, pp. 232-33.
    In the text following, LB is at pains to distinguish two senses of the French *ancêtre*. The distinction between (mythic) ancestors and (historical) forefathers or forebears gives less difficulty in English.

12. T.G.H. Strehlow, "Ankotarinja, an Aranda Myth", p. 187. It is of some interest to continue the quotation for a few sentences, if only to add a little to note 9 above. "He had been lying asleep in the bosom of the earth, and the white ants had eaten his body hollow while the soil rested on him like a coverlet. As he was lying on the ground a thought arose in his mind: 'Perhaps it would be pleasant to arise.' He lay there deep in thought. Then he arose, out of the soft soil of a little watercourse."

13. Although Carl Strehlow's repudiation of the Dreamtime as a historical period is valid, clearly the events of the creative time are seen as having some sort of a natural sequentiality. Nevertheless mythic ancestors and historical forefathers are not beings of the same kind and are envisaged as having a different sort of temporal context. Note that the white ants mentioned in note 12 have a different kind of permanence again: they are not (in this story) "created beings" so much as a simple part of universal nature.

14. T.F. Bride (ed.), *Letters from Victorian Pioneers*, p. 96. The encampment referred to is apparently an assembly of tribes of the region for some special ceremonial. On such occasions, which were infrequent, large numbers assembled in tribal groups, often coming from distant parts of the general area. The writer (probably W. Thomas) means that the Aborigines have a perfect notion of the country, not of the compass.

15. Spencer and Gillen, *The Arunta*, I, p. 12.

16. LB, *Primitive Mentality*, p. 446.

17. W.E. Roth, "Superstition, Magic and Medicine", p. 26.

18. Ibid., "Notes on Government, Morals and Crime", p. 8.

19. A.R. Radcliffe-Brown, "Three Tribes of Western Australia", p. 167.

20. A.R. Radcliffe-Brown, "The Social Organization of Australian Tribes", p. 210.

21. Elkin, "The Secret Life of the Australian Aborigines", pp. 128, 129.

22. Ibid., p. 130.

23. Raymond Firth, "Anthropology in Australia 1926-32 and After", p. 10. The text continues, ". . . he is depressed, he feels insecure, he lacks incentive, and by so much is his chance of survival weakened. The psychological factor in itself may not be a pure cause of decline in population, but as leading to decreased work and so to food deficiencies, to concentration in brooding, inactive groups and so to increased susceptibility to disease, it is surely not without its effect." Recent population figures are more stable but the question is complex. In the first 150 years of settlement white occupation of tribal lands (that is, all of the south and most of the rest of the country) was devastating. Tribal communities still survive in a few places and they are becoming more vocal, especially in respect of Land Rights, but their future remains uncertain.

24. Wirz, *Die Marind-anim*, I, ii, p. 14. LB's point here is participation only. But the passage itself becomes clearer if we include a few of the sentences which precede it: "Later, after their [creative] activities were completed, the *Dema* returned, provided, that is, that they had not already become metamorphosed [i.e., into fixed landscape-features]. They settled themselves in the earth and in the sea, where they continued to dwell as spirit-beings. For they never experienced death. Others were changed into constellations, or came to animate the air and the sky, and their powers are still active there now (personification of the forces of nature). The places to which they returned . . . etc." The sentence omitted half-way through LB's quotation contains clearly a reference to *soimi* stones: "The *Dema* also transformed themselves into stones and became concentrated in them."

25. Note the capital *D*; and see Introduction, note 60.

26. Wirz, *Die Marind-anim*, I, ii. pp. 15, 137.

27. Ibid., I, ii, p. 34.

28. Gunnar Landtman, "The Origins of Sacrifice as Illustrated by a Primitive People", p. 109.

29. Malinowski, *Argonauts of the Western Pacific*, p. 330.

30.   LB's word is *chef*, which, however, cannot in the Australian context properly be translated as *chief*, since the Aborigines had no chiefs as African or
American tribes did. Authority rested with the "old men" of the community,
or tribal elders. A reasonable general translation might be "elder" or "headman", according to circumstances. LB's "hardly five years ago" refers to the
date of the article in question (1933).

31.   In line with the above, an "old man porcupine" would be a porcupine of
tribal authority; but used loosely, the term will signify simply an old or large
animal of the species. In the present context no doubt LB's supposition is
well founded. Olive Pink herself had some difficulty with the expression.
"By 'old man'," she says, "I think they meant 'of the grandfather generation'.
But as I did not enquire it is not certain." In another place she guesses it may
signify "boss" or "headman of the porcupine people". There are no true por-
cupines in Australia but the animal in question, echidna or spiny anteater, is
often so called.

32.   Olive Pink, "Spirit Ancestors in a Northern Aranda Horde Country". The
passages quoted or referred to are on pp. 177, 178, 179, 186. On p. 176 there
is an allusion to "totem names" as equivalent to "Christian names"; used in
familiar address instead of full tribal names. LB shortens the third passage,
but without serious distortion. I have restored most of LB's minor omissions
in the last passage. The ritual referred to is described in Pink's article,
pp. 184-85.

33.   A.R. Radcliffe-Brown, *The Andaman Islanders*, p. 387.

34.   Maurice Leenhardt, "Documents Néo-Calédoniens", pp. 114-15 (note 70).
Reference is to the legend, "Les Deux Soeurs de Moaxa". The second quotation is from p. 392.

35.   A.P. Elkin, "Totemism in North Western Australia (the Kimberley
Division)", p. 462. I restore Elkin's text but not his use of phonetic script for
native words. For Love's spellings see Introduction, note 52.

36.   Preuss, *Der religiöse Gehalt der Mythen*, p. 46.

37.   Of the difference of views between Spencer and Carl Strehlow more will be
said later (see chapter II, note 33). At present we need only remind
ourselves that Spencer's *numbakulla* and Strehlow's *ngambakala* both represent the same native word. Spencer's account of a certain myth in *The
Native Tribes of Central Australia*, p. 388, explains the word (at this early
stage, 1898, he spells it *ungambikula*), and it may be quoted here for an interesting comparison with either of the two Strehlow creation myths
already noted (notes 9 and 12 above).

>   At this time there dwelt in the *alkira aldorla*, that is the western sky,
> two beings of whom it was said that they were *ungambikula*, a word
> which means "out of nothing", or "self-existing". From their elevated
> dwelling-place they could see, far away to the east, a number of *inapert-
> wa* creatures, that is rudimentary human beings or incomplete men,
> whom it was their mission to make into men and women. In those days
> there were no men and women, and the *inapertwa* were of various
> shapes and dwelt in groups along by the shores of the salt water. They
> had no distinct limbs or organs of sight, hearing or smell, and did not eat
> food, and presented the appearance of human beings all doubled up into
> a rounded mass, in which just the outline of the different parts of the
> body could be vaguely seen. Coming down from their home in the
> western sky with their *lalira* or great stone knives, the *ungambikula* took
> hold of the *inapertwa*, one after the other. First of all the arms were

released, then the fingers were added by making four clefts at the end of each arm; then legs and toes were added and the nostrils bored with the fingers. A cut with the knife made the mouth, which was pulled open several times to make it flexible. A slit on each side separated the upper and lower eyelids, hidden behind which the eyes were already present, another stroke or two completed the body, and thus, out of the *inapertwa*, men and women were formed.

38. Spencer and Gillen, *The Arunta*, I, p. 355.
39. Carl Strehlow, *Die Aranda- und Loritjastämme*, I, pp. 2-4 (already paraphrased, note 9 above), and II, pp. 2-3 (I translate Strehlow's text, which LB shortens).
40. A.C. Haddon, *Reports of the Cambridge Anthropological Expedition to Torres Straits*, VI, p. 314 (Chapter xiv, "Mythical Beings").
41. Wirz, *Die Marind-anim*, II, iv, p. 73; I, ii, p. 184; II, ii, p. 10.
42. Radcliffe-Brown, *The Andaman Islanders*, p. 383.
    Gunnar Landtman, *Folktales of the Kiwai Papuans*, p. 473. As the story is short and has a moral it may be reproduced:

> In former times the dogs were different to what they are now, for they were like people, except that they had four legs. They used to help their master to work in the gardens, and could speak as men do. One day their master had connection with his wife in the bush, and the dogs were looking on. In the evening when the people and dogs were sitting together in the house the latter suddenly began to laugh. "What's the matter you laugh?" the people asked them, and the dogs said, "Me laugh for father; father been *kobóri* (have connection with) mother". And their master was ashamed.
>
> The next day the same thing happened, and the dogs went to look on at what their master and his wife were doing in the bush, and on their return home they laughed ... Then the master seized a *kómuni* (firetongs of bamboo) and squeezed together the dogs' jaws. After that he tied a string tightly round the tongs and placed them on his shelf. In this way the dogs lost their faculty of speech.

43. Carl Strehlow, *Die Aranda- und Loritjastämme*, II, p. 20.
44. Wirz, *Die Marind-anim*, I, ii, p. 45. This is the passage leading up to Wirz's quotation:

> One day the *Dema* Mahu, with his two wives Len and Piakor, came to Geb ... [The meeting is described. Mahu being hungry, Geb looks on while the two wives prepare food.] As Geb watched Mahu's wives he became strongly erect. Mahu noticed this and said to Geb, "These are my wives". For as he saw how the sight of women made Geb grow erect, he realized that he had no wife. While Mahu was eating his roasted cuscus he said quietly to Piakor, so that Geb could not hear, "Go, get a little sago and give it to Geb". At first Piakor would not do it, but in the end she did, and as she handed him the sago he became even more turgid. Geb put the sago in the fire to cook while the two women prepared *wati* (*piper methysticum*) for the men, Len for Geb and Piakor for Mahu. "Where is your wife?" finally said Mahu to Geb, as though he did not already know that he had none. Geb replied innocently. "In the hut". Mahu took a sly peep into the hut to see Geb's wife, but all he saw was a piece of bamboo. Now Geb said that this bit of [hollow] bamboo was his wife. That night Mahu sent Piakor to Geb, explaining to him all he needed to learn

about coitus. Next day Mahu decided to move on. He loaded up his canoe and got into it with Len. He said to Geb, "Now Piakor is your wife and will stay with you. I will come and visit you from time to time." Then Mahu went off. "*Ngeis-a eh!*" called Geb in farewell.

45. Ibid., I, ii, pp. 70, 103, 126. The second quotation may be filled out a little. Yagil, a cassowary *Dema* (malevolent), after killing people in the village, is tracked by his footprints (one human, one bird imprint). The villagers capture and kill him. They cut up the (cassowary) meat, store it in areca-flowers to keep it fresh, and throw away the bones. During the night, however, while the villagers are asleep, the flesh transforms itself into *ake* nuts (similar to areca nuts), and there, "just where the blood of the cassowary had dripped . . . there sprang up a fruit tree . . .". The close of the story tells how later the mother and brothers of the *Dema* cassowary find his bones and with them conjure up a thunderstorm or cyclone which kills all the villagers.

46. Fortune, *Sorcerers of Dobu*, p. 95.

47. Ibid., pp. 98, 223.

48. Erland Nordenskiöld, "La Conception de l'âme chez les Indiens Cuna de l'Isthme de Panamà", p. 16. Nordenskiölds's article is preceded with the tribute, "A Monsieur Lévy-Bruhl, hommage respectueux". He was forced through illness to leave his work in Panama, and died not long after returning home, in July 1932. Hence LB's reference to him in the next as *regretté*, which I do not translate.

It is presumed that when a person is sick his soul (*purba*) has been carried away by evil spirits. The cure is effected by a medicine man who places under the patient's hammock a box of small carved wooden figures, human in shape but efficacious chiefly because they are believed to contain certain benevolently disposed tree spirits in the wood they are made of. The intention is to send these well-meaning spirits (*nuchus*) to the region of the evil ones to negotiate with their chief for the restoration of the sick soul. Smoke is raised from the burning of cocoa and sometimes tobacco on a brazier, this being gratifying to the spirits. But the first thing the medicine man must do is to meditate on the origin of the *nuchus*, "that is to say, on the manner in which God created them". If he does not know the answer to that, the chant will have no effect.

Nordenskiöld on the previous page remarks that "The Cuna Indians have an incantation in which is told how the *nuchus* were created by God, . . . but unhappily Perez [his informant] does not know it".

Chapter II: Mythical Beings, Half-Human, Half-Animal

1. LB's paraphrase. See Orulo's remark (Knud Rasmussen, "Intellectual Culture of the Iglulik Eskimos", p. 69): "You always want the supernatural things to make sense, but we do not bother about that. We are content to understand."

2. Carl Strehlow, *Die Aranda- und Loritjastämme*, I, p. 51, note 5. I follow Strehlow's text, including his bracketed explanation of *namatuna*, to which LB adds "a few centimetres long". The point, however, is not merely that the namatuna is itself a *tjurunga*, but that it is small. For a full discussion of the meaning of *tjurunga* see T.G.H. Strehlow, *Aranda Traditions*, pp. 16 and 84 ff. The kind of tjurunga envisaged here is a small stone or wooden object,

bearing sacred designs, normally kept carefully wrapped up and very secretly hidden in a place known only to the initiated. *Tjurungas* are ritual objects of totemistic importance and of highly personal relevance. T.G.H. Strehlow describes them as "life-containing" (p. 18). "The ancestors themselves are said to have used them and stored them away; they were indeed their only and most treasured possessions . . . The ancestor regards the *tjurunga* which he owns as portion of his own being." During a man's lifetime the *tjurunga* of his totemic ancestor passes into his proper possession and he becomes identified with it. After his death it remains as a symbol of his continued spiritual existence.

3. W.B. Spencer and Gillen, *The Arunta*, I, pp. 20-21.

4. Paul Wirz, *Die Marind-anim von Holländisch Süd-Neu-Guinea*, II, iv, p. 92.

5. LB, *How Natives Think*, pp. 167-80.

6. Chapters II and III of LB's *Primitives and the Supernatural* are concerned with *disposition*.

7. Rev. G. Taplin, in J.D. Woods, ed., *The Native Tribes of South Australia*, p. 220.

8. Bronislaw Malinowski, "Fishing in the Trobriand Islands", pp. 91-92.

9. Mrs. K. Langloh Parker (afterwards Stow), *The Euahlayi Tribe*, p. 113.

10. LB's term "l'Australie du Sud" confuses southern Australia generally with the state of South Australia. His reference is really to south east Australia and in particular the state of Victoria. See T.F. Bride, ed., *Letters from Victorian Pioneers*, Letter 14 (attributed to Wm. Thomas), p. 90.

 True bears do not occur among native Australian fauna; the animal once called a bear (by white settlers only, from its resemblance to a toy teddy bear) is a marsupial, now known as a koala. Formerly hunted for its fur, now in declining numbers and protected, it is a harmless, gentle creature, arboreal, feeding exclusively on eucalyptus leaves. It has absolutely no "bearish" qualities.

11. Bride, *Letters from Victorian Pioneers*, Letter 96 (attributed to Wm. Thomas), p. 90. Quoted directly from the original; LB's translation is slightly reduced. The allusion is to R. Brough Smyth, *The Aborigines of Victoria*, I, p. 447. But actually it would appear not to be "another witness", since Smyth also is quoting from "the late William Thomas's MS". Smyth, incidentally, adds a reference to Tylor and Blumenbach on bears, remarking, "But our beast is not a bear, and the natives, of course, never heard him so called until the white man came".

 The Yarra is the river on which the city of Melbourne, capital of Victoria, is situated.

13. If LB makes too much of this point, so also does Carl Strehlow, on whom he obviously draws. See *Die Aranda- und Loritjastämme*, III, Part, i, 53, note 4. The context is a passage of Aranda song about grass-parrots. The couplet in question, with Strehlow's German translation, runs:

Taraleral	*ilaraperama*
Lachend	sprechen miteinander
Njilkilikil	*ilaraperama*
Zischend	sprechen miteinander

In English,

Laughing	talk together
Whisper	talk together

The gist of this is that the birds laugh, whisper and chatter among themselves. Strehlow's note comments: "As the Aranda say, many birds laugh (*lachen*), for example, young grass parrots; others weep (*weinen*) and groan (*stöhnen*). Most of them talk to one another (*sagen, reden*). Of white men's animals, horses *lachen*, cows *weinen*, and sheep and poultry *sagen*." Even so small a fragment sparks a quick flash of insight into Aranda poetic diction.

14. LB notes (but I take the quotation itself directly from its English source): "In southern Africa the belief is quite frequently met with that lions converse among themselves:

> On another occasion, when Africaner [the writer's native guide] and an attendant were passing near the end of a hill, from which jutted out a smooth rock of ten or twelve feet high, he observed a number of zebras pressing round it, obliged to keep the path, beyond which it was precipitous. A lion was seen creeping up towards the path, to intercept the large stallion, which is always in the rear to defend or warn the troop. The lion missed his mark, and while the zebra rushed round the point, the lion knew full well if he could mount the rock at one leap, the next would be on the zebra's back, it being obliged to turn towards the hill. He fell short, with only his head over the stone, looking at the galloping zebra switching his tail in the air. He then tried a second and a third leap, till he succeeded.
>
> In the meantime two more lions came up, and seemed to talk and roar away about something, while the old lion led them round the rock, and round it again; then he made another great leap, to show them what he and they must do next time. Africaner added with the most perfect gravity, "They evidently talked to each other, but though loud enough, I could not understand a word they said, and, fearing lest we should be the next objects of their skill, we crept away and left them in council."

Robert Moffat, *Missionary Labours and Scenes in Southern Africa*, p. 138.
In this region lions are commonly taken to be reincarnations of chiefs who have died."

15. W.E. Roth, *North Queensland Ethnography*, Bulletin 5, p. 15 (item 61): "Animals and birds were once blacks . . .". Items 65 and 66 (p. 17) discuss aspects of the complex Aboriginal idea of the soul, both in the Tully River and (with differences) the Bloomfield River traditions. "Dogs are reckoned upon having thinking powers, etc., or *wau-wu* . . ." (item 65). "The Bloomfield River natives have an idea of 'something' being associated with the *breath* or *wau-wu*: that when a black dies, is unconscious or delirious, etc., his *wau-wu* – and in this expression they apparently include his will, and thinking-powers – leaves the body and travels about. After an individual's decease, apparitions of him may be seen by the survivors . . ." (item 66).
Gunnar Landtman, *The Kiwai Papuans of British New Guinea*, p. 441.

16. Spencer and Gillen, *The Arunta*, I, p. 39.

17. Taplin, *The Native Tribes of South Australia*, p. 68, note. Taplin treats the stories as jokes, confining them to a footnote. They belong to white rather than to black folklore.
LB gives no reference but the following was probably in his mind: "My companions managed to keep them [the blacks] in good humour by replying to their inquiries respecting our nature and intentions; among which one of the most singular was, whether the bullocks were not our gins . . .". (Ludwig

Leichhardt, *Journal of an Overland Expedition, 1844-45*, p. 246. Gin = Aboriginal woman or wife.)

Roth, *North Queensland Ethnography*, Bulletin 5, p. 16 (item 63).

Edward Jerningham Wakefield, *Adventures in New Zealand from 1839-1844*. (LB's reference not seen; checked in edn. Christchurch, NZ, 1908, p. 358.)

18. LB notes: To cite only one example among many, "When the first Missionaries Hahn and Kleinschmidt came to the Herero in 1843, on account of their long hair and beards they were taken for ghosts in lion form. The women fled before them, crying, 'Ongeama, ozongeama', i.e., 'Lions, oviruru, spooks!' They had never before in their lives seen white men." (Missionar) J. Irle, "Die Religion der Herero", p. 340. See also du Chaillu's account of the reaction of the Pygmies at their first encounter with white men, see Chapter VII post, where also a story is told concerning a man-leopard.)

W.H. Prescott, *Conquest of Mexico* (Book II, Chapter iv) refers to the astonishment of the Mexicans (who were scarcely utter savages) at the approach of Cortès's cavalry: "They supposed the rider and the horse . . . to be one and the same".

19. LB notes: Compare these reflections by le Père Van Wing:

> When visiting schools in the Congo it happened more than once that I came across sentences like these in schoolbooks: "The palm is a tree", "The scorpion is an animal". And the teacher showed them how to put that into Lingala or Kicongo. In many Bantu languages there are no words which match exactly the European vocable for "tree", "animal". For many of the Bantu "palms" exist as a class which does not form part of the category of woody vegetation Europeans call "trees". As to animals, the Bantu vocabulary can be quite baffling, notwithstanding any number of dictionaries offer equivalent names for the species, variety, or other divisions applied to fauna. Hence in sentences like these the teacher is using his authority to impose on the scholars conclusions which to their understanding must amount to flagrant contradictions.
> J. Van Wing, "Enfants noirs", pp. 180-81.

(Van Wing continues, "What may be the psychological and educational consequence of blunders like these, anyone may guess. In morality and religion these verbal confusions are evidently no less frequent and much more pernicious.")

20. W.E. Roth, *North Queensland Ethnography*, Bulletins 2 and 18. The text transcribed is from Bulletin 18, p. 106.

21. Ibid. This is paraphrased from Bulletin 2. Looking for a parallel, Roth adds, "In English, the only case I can call to mind is that of man and giant". Bulletin 2, p. 67, note 1.

22. LB notes:

> This led me to discover that, in Ashanti, animals were looked on either as dangerous or harmless. This may appear a very ordinary classification, but when we find that the buffalo (bush cow), a most savage animal, is placed by the Ashanti in the latter category, and that the little *adown*, antelope, is in the former, we begin to realize that the Ashanti classification does not take cognizance of physical dangers, but of spiritual. The Ashanti hunter divides all the animals he may encounter in his forests or rivers into two classes, those animals which have powerful *sasa*, and those whose *sasa* is of small account, or at any rate is not vindictive.

R.S. Rattray, *Religion and Art in Ashanti*, p. 183.
A list follows in Rattray's text of the principal animals in both the classes.

Some of the animals in Rattray's list are designated *sasa mmoa*, that is, those which have *sasa*, while others are simply *mmoa*, beasts. *Sasa* is defined as "the invisible spiritual power of a [deceased] person or animal, which disturbs the mind of the living, or works a spell or mischief upon them, so that they suffer in various ways". It is "essentially the bad, revengeful and hurtful element of a spirit . . . which at all costs must be laid".

23. R.F. Fortune, *Sorcerers of Dobu*, p. 109. *A propos* the native identification of white men with "ghosts", LB might have seen a striking instance in Grey, *Journals*, vol II p. 363, where in a court proceedings a native three times in one paragraph refers to his assailant (not an Englishman but probably a Malay or Indian sailor — at any rate a stranger) as "this one of the dead". Grey does not stay to explain the locution.

24. Rasmussen, "Intellectual Culture of the Iglulik Eskimos", p. 79. Reference is to a glossary of terms in the special shaman language; these are highly artificial terms somewhat resembling Anglo-Saxon kennings, e.g. "eyes" become "the disks of sight", the circumlocution for "white man" is "an almost human being".

25. Fortune, *Sorcerers of Dobu*, p. 101 (the parenthesis is LB's addition).

26. Ibid., pp. 107-8.

27. Ibid., p. 109.

28. Ibid., p. 119. The quotation is extended slightly.

29. Grandville was the pseudonym of Jean Ignace Isidore Gerard (1803-47), famous in France for his drawings portraying human characters with animal heads.

30. LB, *Primitives and the Supernatural*, pp. 65-112.

31. Erland Nordenskiöld, "La Conception de l'âme chez les Indiens Cuna", p. 12. The paragraph reads in full:

> "We and the animals are alike," Perez said to me one day. "The Cuna Indians do not believe there stands any great division between men and beasts, as Christians do. Animals not only possess a *purba* (soul), but their *purbas* are human. Speaking, for example, of the *purba* of a bird, one says *sikuidule*, which has the meaning of 'bird-man'. One never says that an animal has transformed itself into a man, because it already was a man, though in animal form."

32. Spencer and Gillen, *The Arunta*, I, pp. 73, 301. For the first two passages quoted, LB has split one quotation and reversed the order of the parts.

33. Carl Strehlow, *Die Aranda- und Loritjastämme*, I, p. 1. The point at issue in the present context is simply the duality of nature of ancestral beings. The emu-feet of the sacred Altjira ancestor illustrate it adequately. Reference has already been made to T.G.H. Strehlow's examination of the question of "The Great Father" in *Aranda Traditions* (p. 7 ff). T.G.H. Strehlow summarizes a Northern Aranda myth which centres upon what would appear to be a single (named) original ancestor, and no doubt many other tribal groups had similar stories. But there is little here to support any parallel with Christian concepts of monotheistic Divinity. Altjira must be thought of rather as "original" than "supreme", but the over-eagerness of the missionaries seems to have confused the issue and led to furious controversy about which even LB seems still slightly confused. Before publishing *The Arunta* (and long

after his collaborator Gillen's death, though his name is still attached to the work), Sir Baldwin Spencer made a last expedition to the Centre in 1926 to re-examine the matter and came back convinced of his former opinion, which he had expressed in a letter to Sir James Frazer as early as 10 March 1908 (Spencer's *Scientific Correspondence*, p. 109):

> I don't know what to do in regard to Strehlow [i.e. Carl Strehlow]. He is so uneducated that he can't write publishable German . . . For at least twenty years the Lutheran missions have been teaching the natives that Altjira means God, and that all their sacred ceremonies, in fact even their ordinary corroborees [i.e. non-sacred or entertainment ceremonials] are wicked things . . . Under these conditions it is not altogether surprising that when Strehlow questions the natives, he discovers that Altjira means God, and gets very doubtful information in regard to all sacred or secret matters . . .

This is testy criticism. In defence of Strehlow it might be urged that at least where missionary duty did not stand in his way he was a close, intimate and sympathetic observer of the people, beside whom Spencer's more precise, rational and scientific approach may often seem a little arid or lacking in warmth. The tone of his Appendix D in *The Arunta* is of course decorously polite, but his impatience with the missions is patent and Strehlow is still under subdued attack. "The differences between us", he says in the letter to Frazer, "are due to the fact that Strehlow is a missionary." T.G.H. Strehlow's *Journey to Horseshoe Bend*, which is the story of his father's last days and death, shows that in fact his sympathy for the blacks and his missionary zeal brought him much unhappy conflict, never resolved.

34. Ibid., I, pp. 48, 76. The first quotation is slightly shortened, and I complete Strehlow's sentence in the second. A *renina* is a snake, non-venomous, about 120 centimetres. *Iloara* is a saltpan. Birds' down was an important item of tribal trade; used in ceremonials for body decoration.

35. Wirz, *Die Marind-anim*, I, ii, pp. 102, 118, 144.

36. Ibid., I, ii, p. 178, II, iii, p. 96.

37. Possibly LB did not know or remember the singular dog-nanny in *Peter Pan*!

38. LB uses the term *marié*; but see Introduction, note 5. I add "socially responsible" because "married" alone is unconvincing.

39. Nothing like a full record of tribal epic from the Aranda is accessible even now, though T.G.H. Strehlow's *Songs of Central Australia* does something to redeem the lack. It is rather a study of style and substance than a collection of the songs, though it quotes extensively. In any case it appeared long after LB's death, as did also the translations of R.M. Berndt (see bibliography). One example of T.G.H. Strehlow's Aranda songs did, however, appear in time for LB to encounter it, "Ankotarinja, an Aranda Myth", in *Oceania* in 1933. Carl Strehlow's work on the Aranda and Loritja tribes (see bibliography) began in 1907 and was completed in 1920; it quotes many ceremonial songs, but for the most part somewhat fragmentarily, and is more valuable for descriptive detail than as a systematic survey. (No version in English is accessible, though one was made by Charles Chewings, and is held by the Barr-Smith Library, University of Adelaide.) Incidentially Spencer seems not to have been very interested in Aboriginal poetry or song. I feel reasonably certain that LB would have responded to both had the quite remarkable material been available to him, and for this reason I throw in the parenthetic phrase, "tribal epics", although perhaps LB was not

fully aware of their literary character and the phrase does not occur in his text.

40. LB writes, "les acteurs masqués", but Aranda/Arunta performers in the ceremonies were not masked, though some in New Guinea were. Among Australian tribes body decoration, however, had symbolic significance.

41. It is hard to resist an impression here that LB is reading certain European reactions into Australian Aboriginal situations. The underlying implications are however sound enough.

42. The rabbit figures extensively in North American mythology; he is often a trickster, for example Brer Rabbit.

43. Paul Ehrenreich, *Die Mythen und Legenden der Südamerikanischen Urvölker und ihre Beziehungen zu denen Nordamerikas und der alten Welt*, p. 24. Th. Koch-Grünberg, *Vom Roroima zum Orinoco*, II, p. 18 lists a number of benefits received from animals: "All mythologies abound with helpful beasts".

44. Spencer and Gillen's *The Native Tribes of Central Australia* reached print in 1898, *The Northern Tribes of Central Australia* in 1904. But it is true that the main impact of this material was not effectively felt until Spencer, fifteen years after Gillen's death, revised and republished their work as *The Arunta, A Study of a Stone Age People* in 1927. Although Carl Strehlow's publications were noticed abroad, few in Australia could read German, and his work remains a neglected monument. Works by other writers also appeared, but by and large it would be fair to suggest that in Australia itself there was little systematic reading of Australian anthropology before the appearance of *The Arunta*.

45. Ehrenreich, *Die Mythen und Legenden*, (see note 43), p. 40.

46. Ibid., p. 40. Ehrenreich's term is "die grossen Verwandler".

47. Ibid., p. 59.

48. Ibid., p. 68. The second paragraph, which I render at slightly greater length than LB, is still considerably shorter than Ehrenreich's original.

Chapter III: Myths, Totemism and Kinship

1. From an unsigned review in *Oceania* I (1930-31), p. 252. It refers to an article by A.R. Radcliffe-Brown, "Notes on Totemism in Eastern Australia". The reviewer dwells on Radcliffe-Brown's view that the *intichiuma* (initiation) ceremonies of the Arunta, "which have often been taken as a norm for Australia, are in reality a special and rather aberrant form of a more general kind of ritual." The words quoted in the text refer to this "more general" ritual.
   LB notes: "Association" here is what I would call *participation*.

2. See Introduction, note 4. For the relevance of Durkheim, see bibliography. N.B. subtitle of the French version of his book.

3. See Chapter II, note 44.

4. W.B. Spencer and F.J. Gillen, *The Arunta*, II, p. 58.

5. A general belief is that after death a person's spirit may linger for a time as a restless ghost, but after a short while will retire to the secret storehouse where his *churinga* is kept. It will remain there until rebirth. In the *churinga* is preserved the continuity of the spirit's existence and identity.

6. W.B. Spencer, "Totemism in Australia", *Presidential Address*, Australasian Association for the Advancement of Science, Section F, Ethnology and Anthropology, Dunedin, New Zealand (7 January 1904).

Karl von den Steinen, *Unter den Naturvölkern Zentral-Brasiliens*, p. 229: "The Bororo themselves boast that they are red araras. Not only are they transformed into araras when they die . . . not only are araras themselves Bororo and treated as equals; their attachment to the beautifully feathered bird is expressed so openly, that they even refer to themselves as araras, much as though a caterpillar should make pretension to being a butterfly . . ." Arara (macaw) feathers figure largely in Bororo decoration.

7. Carl Strehlow, *Die Aranda- und Loritjastämme*, II, p. 58. See also (a little later): "Anyone belonging to the Emu totem who spears an emu must carefully wipe away the blood so that it will not look so gruesome. Moreover he may eat nothing of the bird but the neck, the lungs and liver and some other less appetising parts. If he finds an emu's nest with eggs, he is allowed to eat only one of them." LB's "head and feet" is inaccurate. This, incidentally, is Loritja, not Aranda information.

8. Ibid., II, p. 74. The subject, however, is controversial and one is uneasy about LB's *amis du malin*, which represents Strehlow's *Freunde des Bösen*, friends of the Evil One. Such a phrase has no clear place in the native vocabulary and would seem to be of missionary origin. To translate with a word like "bedevilled" only skirts the difficulty. Perhaps the passage should be quoted for reference:

> Thus the marsupial mole, who is continually burrowing in the earth, comes to be regarded as the sorcerer of the animals; . . . the *eknata* worm when touched raises a troublesome itch and a swelling on the skin; the large ant is dreaded on account of its bite. Poisonous plants are rated 'devil's weeds' (*Pflanzen des Bösen*). Others among the excepted animals and plants are not eaten because they have a bad taste or are otherwise inedible, as for example tadpoles, various grasshoppers and beetles and the prickly *laga* creeper. That locusts should be disdained by the natives is somewhat strange, since the natives of other places eat them and they can scarcely taste worse than many of the creatures the Aranda and Loritja do use for food.

9. Spencer and Gillen, *The Arunta*, I, pp. 74-75.

10. A.W. Howitt, *The Native Tribes of South East Australia*, pp. 475, 486-87. Note that the Kurnai do not, like the Arunta (Aranda), ignore the pelican as a totemic bird.

11. After "Muk-rukut" Howitt continues, "The Kurnai say that the bird Leatherhead is appropriately placed among the Muk-rukut, because it is continually chattering".
Howitt adds a footnote after "totems": "Of course this does not include the sex totems".
Howitt's text continues after "level", following a comma, "while the tribal Allfather as represented by Mungan Ngaua belongs to a distinctly higher level of mental development". On the Allfather question, see introduction, note 18.

12. Ibid., p. 487.

13. Ibid., p. 506.

14. Ursula McConnel, "The Wik-Munkan Tribe", part 2, "Totemism", pp. 185, 187.

15. Paul Wirz, *Die Marind-anim von Holländisch Süd-Neu-Guinea*, I, ii, 31.

16. Ibid., I, ii, p. 16.

17. Ibid., I, ii, p. 43.

18. Ibid., II, iii, pp. 215-16.

19. Ibid., II, iii, p. 197.
20. LB continuously repeats his reminders of the distinction between *dema* and *Dema*. See especially the restatement in chapter V, p. 156.
21. Wirz, *Die Marind-anim*, II, iii, p. 103. As I did not succeed in locating the statement which follows this I have not translated it as a quotation, although LB presents it as one.
22. Ibid., I, ii, p. 11. The passage in Wirz continues:

> As time and the generations ran on they lost more and more of their unusual characteristics and became ordinary mortal men, animals and objects in nature. The change took place very gradually; by stages as the ancient past merged more closely into modern times, all the gradations of difference between the original *Dema* and the ordinary modern living creature were covered. Hence it is occasionally a doubtful matter to decide whether in particular instances an entity is properly to be regarded as a *Dema* or not.

23. Ibid., I, ii, pp. 160, 162. Wirz says here, "The bow wood, in which the Marind distinguishes between the forward or nose end, and a rear or foot end, represents the bow-*Dema* himself, while the bowstring (sinew), which with its two loops clings about his neck, represents his wife in the act of copulation." Wirz discusses the bow myth at length in more than one place of his study. See Appendix on Animism.
24. LB, *How Natives Think*, pp. 116-21; *The "Soul" of the Primitive*, pp. 156-57.
25. Extraction of the kidney fat is a frequent and malign motive in Australian Aboriginal sorcery. See A.P. Elkin, *Aboriginal Men of High Degree*, pp. 50, 52: "Operators . . . using this rope, wind it round their intended victim's body while he is asleep . . . they can extract his fat without leaving a mark. He revives, but later feels uneasy and ill, and suspects sorcery." In some cases the magic is performed, not on a person's physical body, but on his spirit-form.
26. Sir Everard Ferdinand Im Thurn, *Among the Indians of Guiana*, p. 350.

> . . . Man, whether he be Indian or other, naturally begins by thinking about himself; nor must the fact be understood to indicate that the Indian sees any sharp line of distinction, such as we see, between man and other animals, between one kind of animal and another, or between animals – man included – and inanimate objects. On the contrary, to the Indians, all objects, animate or inanimate, seem exactly of the same nature except that they differ in the accident of bodily form. Every object in the whole world is a being, consisting of a body and a spirit, and differs from every other object in no respect except that of bodily form.

27. D.F. Bleek, ed., "Beliefs and Customs of the !Xam Bushmen. From Material collected by Dr. W.H.I. Bleek and Miss C. Lloyd between 1870 and 1880. Bleek, Part 5, The Rain", pp. 308 ff.

> A story is told of how a man asked his grandfather to make rain. Rain is described as male or female, or "bull" and "cow", and certain anthropomorphic terms are used but apparently with a consciously picturesque or metaphorical application. The animals of the image are springboks. "His grandson says to him, 'you must not arouse a rain-bull, but you must make a she-rain, which is not angry, which rains gently, because it is a slow shower . . . for people are afraid of a he-rain, when they hear it thundering as it gets on its legs.' . . . The old man says to his grandson, 'You must not make a fire, for the bushes of our places are dry; you must wait quietly for the rain. I

will cut a she-rain which has milk, I will milk her, she will rain softly on the ground,' . . ." LB adds a further reference to Th. Koch-Grünberg, *Vom Roroima zum Orinoco*, pp. 190, 193; a Taulipang myth in which the rain, as a person, addresses defiance to a powerful mythic jaguar.

28. Wirz, *Die Marind-anim*, II, iii, p. 104. As Wirz plainly indicates, for the native imagination there is no conflict between the presence of human form in man-made artifacts and the view that the legends were developed after the artifacts were invented, nor would they deny that in the process of myth-making some part had been played by imaginative fancy or even a sense of humour. See notes 31 and 32, and the Appendix on Animism.

29. Ibid., I, ii, p. 34.

30. Ibid., I, ii, pp. 116, 166.

31. The "reasons of another nature" for which Wirz lays particular stress on the bow myth refer to another context, where he examines certain aspects of Marind magic, not here relevant. But LB here is concerned with some of the same details, such as the fact that the native and his bow are almost inseparable (Wirz calls the bow "ein so viel gebrauchtes und dem Marind gewissermassen in die Hand gewachsenes Gerät", and refers to it as a "beloved object"); the fact that it has become the subject of very many legends (some narrowly local); and the fact that it is given many and various names, both for itself and for its individual parts, a sign of the great intimacy with which it is regarded. Above all it is an outstanding instance of the way in which an artifact, although in the first place invented only for use, has acquired from its function a mythological importance, much extended, Wirz affirms, through the humour and imagination of the tribe. In its material aspect the bow is purely an article of utility; but in its spiritual it possesses an acquired yet undoubted participation with the mythic and supernatural sources of life. Because of its *Dema* identity it is necessary to accord it totemic status, but LB finds it a delicate subject to discuss, in case there should arise any entanglement with the Animist view of the origin of myths, which he opposes. See Appendix on Animism.

32. Wirz, *Die Marind-anim*, II, iii, pp. 105, 107. LB has here run together two separate passages, partly by paraphrase. Both will be found translated in the Appendix on Animism.

33. LB's note: *Primitive Mentality*, pp. 438-41
    However in relation to the mating of animals it is interesting to refer also to Spencer (*Scientific Correspondence*, p. 73). Writing to Sir James Frazer (23 July 1902), he remarks that in Australia "the natives do not believe that children are directly connected with intercourse, and therefore they are not likely to associate this with reproduction in the animal or plant kingdom". Traditions regarding human conception are discussed by T.G.H. Strehlow in *Aranda Traditions*, pp. 86 ff.

34. LB's note: *Primitives and the Supernatural*, pp. 109-12.

Chapter IV: The Power of Myth and its Effects

1. See introduction, note 5.

2. Moritz Freiherr von Leonhardi assembled and edited Carl Strehlow's papers for the Städisches Völkermuseum, Frankfurt-am-Main until the second *Abteilung* of *Teil* III (1911), when a notice of his death appears with an obituary comment by B. Hagen. A similar notice for Hagen appears in the last publication, *Teil V* (1920).

It needs to be pointed out that possession and guardianship of the (epic) songs are two different things; myths are *possessed* by individuals but the elders *guard* them (for instance, during the infancy of the possessor). See T.G.H. Strehlow, *Aranda Traditions*, pp. 119 ff. As to the linguistic, prosodic and archaic complexities of the texts, Strehlow explains them at some length in *Songs of Central Australia*, p. 58 ff, pointing out that in presenting what he calls the prose sense of the words in a patterned form adapted to the poetical and rhythmical requirements of epic song, certain changes are called for which alter the shape, arrangement and also the accentual stresses of the words to a considerable degree. Further (p. 208) these changes serve the ritual purpose in a particular and approved way, since they make it impossible for improper hearers – the unititiated and the unworthy – to comprehend them. Beyond this deliberate public obscurity there also remain in the songs a few words or phrases which nobody at all understands, probably archaisms whose meaning has simply been lost. No one knows how ancient (in a historical sense) the songs are. They are accepted unquestioningly as *tjurunga*, and the occasional poetical obscurities do not detract from their sacred character. All that is demanded is that the texts must be scrupulously preserved, and invariably sung without any change in the traditional language and form.

It should be pointed out that what both the Strehlows have to say about these "songs" refers to the formal and sacred epic. If the Aranda also had a non-serious song culture, occasional, trivial or spontaneous, it receives little attention from them. But there were fragments and snatches of the sacred songs which could be sung on secular occasions, or casually.

3. Ralph Piddington, "The Totemic System of the Karadjeri Tribe", pp. 393-94.

4. LB uses the word *réciter*, but Australian Aborigines (certainly not the Aranda) do not normally represent the myths by formal recitation. T.G.H. Strehlow refers (*Songs of Central Australia*, p. 97) to an instance of the declamation of verses, but points out that it is very rare. "Prose" versions exist but they are subordinate to sacred, formal ceremonial, which combines verse with music and mime or choreography (the word "dance" could fail to give the right impression).

5. Stefan Lehner, "Bukaua", in Richard Neuhauss, ed., *Deutsch Neu-Guinea*, III, pp. 478-79.

6. Paul Wirz, *Die Marind-anim von Holländisch Süd-Neu-Guinea*, II, iii, p. 112.

7. Erland Nordenskiöld, "La Conception de l'âme chez les Indiens Cuna", p. 6. The passage quoted is introduced by the remark, "In the imagination of the Cuna Indians stories about Creation play an enormous role", and is followed by the observation, "This is manifestly absurd" (an example is given) "and has to be explained symbolically". The quotations which follows are from pp. 14, 16 and 24.

8. Erland Nordenskiöld, "Faiseurs de miracles et voyants chez les Indiens Cuna", p. 468.

9. Ibid., p. 464.

10. A.C. Kruyt, "De Timoreezen", p. 480.

11. Note again LB's careful distinction between religion "properly so called" and primitive pre-religion.

12. Paul Wirz, *Die Marind-anim*, II, iv, p. 17. Wirz goes on, "This is not really the case, except in a few instances where the ceremonies refer directly to the secret cult." He appears himself to be the stranger referred to in his text, and in view of the fact that he was left unsatisfied in respect of several aspects of the *mayo* cult, it may not be improper to refer to a later study by J. Van Baal,

Dema: Description and Analysis of Marind-anim Culture (South New Guinea), (published in English in 1966). The Preface opens: "The first to present a comprehensive description of Marind-anim culture was the late Dr Paul Wirz . . . In spite of its obvious shortcomings the work is highly fascinating; it certainly fascinated me." There follows a generous survey of the obvious shortcomings; they include some notable gaps and incoherences in Wirz's interpretation of the *mayo* ceremonies. Of these LB could hardly be expected to be aware. The modern student will naturally turn to Van Baal, but not to the exclusion of Wirz, for whom Van Baal's admiration was well founded. We need to be reminded, in any case, that LB's interest does not lie in the detailed exposition of tribal material for its own sake, but in its broad contribution to his theories and speculations about primitive mentality in general. It is somewhat disconcerting to find LB has not a great deal to say about such dominant Marind concerns as sexual institutions or headhunting, but Wirz is not very informative on either, and they are hardly central to LB's theme.

13. Ibid., II, iii, p. 3. (LB mixes translation, paraphrase and summary here.)
14. Although Wirz's, and therefore LB's information is scrappy in respect of the *mayo* cult, the point of interest for LB lies in the "tribal education" of the novices, which he takes to be the principal emphasis of the rituals. The *mayo* festivals are properly initiation rituals, held about once in four years; they are of considerable duration, lasting several months. LB refers to the cult as a "fertility rite properly so called", which culminates in certain obscure sexual (and possibly, Wirz seems to suggest, cannibal) orgies. Van Baal discounts the latter·view as insufficiently informed, but confirms the sexual assumptions. The passage of Wirz which LB has in mind is clearly this (II, iii, p. 3):

> The essentials of the *mayo* rite are as follows. The as yet uninitiated youths, called the *mayo-anim*, must be isolated in the *mayo-mirav* (the *mayo* ceremonial terrain), a place set apart at some distance from their village, for some five months, and during that whole time they may not come into contact with any lay person. At the beginning of the ritual they are forbidden to eat anything, and all their ornaments and hair-adornments are taken away from them. All customary activities are restricted. They are not permitted to hunt or fish or prepare sago or cultivate any crop, and they are forbidden all sexual activity. They come to the *mayo-mirav* in a condition of complete ignorance, as though they were children new-born. They may wear nothing unless a covering of shredded palm-leaves. The first food that is offered to them will be inedible roots and the hard bark of certain trees. Not until someone comes, impersonating the mythic *Dema*, to give them instruction, and offers them samples to try, are they permitted to take, a little at a time, any of their ordinary food. At the same time the *Dema* instructs them in various customary arts and skills, for example the making of decorative ornaments, or the art of plaiting and dressing the hair; or the preparation of sago, and the activities of hunting and fishing, etc. In this way the novices gradually reassume their normal customs.
>
> In the first place they are given food of the least appetizing kind, and very little of it. Whatever it is, it is always mixed with sperm. If the novices were to swallow food unmixed with sperm they would become sick; the food would disagree with them. There is no obvious or conscious connection between the eating of sperm and any increase in fer-

tility; no sort of life-spirit is presumed to be liberated by the act. It is simply an opinion held universally by the natives that food prepared in this way is bland and easily digestible by the novices. If that were not the case they would become ill. If, for example, the *mayo-anim* were to drink water that had no semen in it (so an informant told me) their kidneys would swell up; if they ate bananas they would have bowel trouble; if sago, their feet would swell.

All this, according to Wirz, amounted to an argument for moral restraint; too much of the soft life was displeasing to the *Dema*.

But the information is incomplete. As Van Baal points out, the people were always reticent about the "great cults", especially the *mayo*, and since 1911 the rites were in any case forbidden by the Dutch authorities – which did not mean that they no longer took place (although perhaps less often), only that information became even more elusive. They are now mainly of historical interest. Some early photographs of ceremonial materials survive, but they are not easily traceable to their origins. See J. Van Baal, *Description and Analysis of Marind-anim Culture*, especially chapter X (pp. 471 ff), "The Great Cults.".

In general, as Van Baal points out, p. 471, "Every initiation postulates that there is a secret important enough to have it ceremoniously disclosed to the neophytes and jealously held back from the uninitiated. Accordingly, every initiation . . . has the character of a revelation."

The *mayo* rituals involve girls as well as boys. They are conducted in the adolescent years, at the entrance to adult life.

15. Carl Strehlow, *Die Aranda- und Loritjastämme*, III, Abt. i, p. 1.
16. Ibid., III, Abt. i, pp. 1-2 (continuous with the last). Where the quotation breaks, LB omits Strehlow's critical reference to Spencer, with whose use of the term "intichiuma" he is dissatisfied.
17. Ibid., II, p. 59, note.
18. Strehlow refers to the ceremony of the Schmeissfliege totem as one which must be performed even if reluctantly. LB's translation of this *unerwünschtes Tier* is *mouche bleu* or bluebottle; but the word every Australian will use is blowfly.
19. LB: *Le choeur récite ou chante les motifs essentiels:* it makes better Aboriginal sense to omit "recites", and perhaps "chorus" might better be replaced by a simple "group of performers". "Recitation" does not fit the Central Australian context. It may be apt enough elsewhere.
20. Carl Strehlow, *Die Aranda- und Loritjastämme*, III, Abt. i, p. 20. As quoted this *tjurunga*-song consists of thirteen couplets. The mimetic action accompanying the chanting imitates the mood and behaviour of the totem animal. At the end a cry is uttered which signifies the conclusion of the representation and the young men come running in.
21. Ibid., p. 34. Strehlow's description continues:

> After this he (the performer) draws his belly in rapidly a few times and pushes it out again as though exhausted from running. He looks suspiciously around in every direction, then kneels gingerly before the imaginary waterhole. He lifts his right leg a little and beats down with it a few times on the ground. Then he repeats the action with the left. Now he stretches his head forward and bends it over the pretended brink as though about to drink. When he has repeated this a few times someone comes out and embraces him and at this the performance is finished.

This song as recorded consists of ten couplets. After the performance the actor eats a piece of emu flesh. During the action "a group of old men knock stones together, which are of the size of emu eggs".

I think it proper to mention (though not to diminish his careful authority; and certainly LB will not be likely to have suspected this) that it is improbable that Carl Strehlow ever saw any actual sacred performances; his principles as a missionary would not allow him to appear to give countenance to non-Christian ceremonials by being seen to attend them. T.G.H. Strehlow mentions in *Journey to Horseshoe Bend* (p. 66) that not even old Loatjira, the "ceremonial chief" of Ntarea (a site near Hermannsburg, accepted by the younger Strehlow as his own "spiritual home"), was able to persuade his father to "witness one single Western Aranda ceremonial act". Loatjira had given him much of the traditional information which went into his books. It was the deeply sacred rituals he refused to look at. Whether his reluctance extended to the non-sacred performances we are not specifically told; they would have afforded some of the same mimetic and related skills. Nor was it that he did not wish to see them. What he feared was that his personal presence on one of the sacred occasions might have been "taken as tacit approval", which as a Christian pastor he could not concede. These motives seemed incomprehensible and led to an estrangement from Loatjira. No such inhibition restrained his son, though he retained a strict regard for essential tribal secrecy.

22. W.B. Spencer and F.J. Gillen, *The Arunta*, I, p. 187.

23. See note 16 concerning *intichiuma*; but the clash between Spencer and Strehlow carried more heat than light (see T.G.H. Strehlow, *Aranda Traditions*, p. 69).

    The two quotations are from one passage, but the order of the two parts is reversed. Spencer and Gillen, *The Arunta*, I, p. 147.

    LB here, I think, amiably fails to observe Spencer's sarcasm at the expense of Strehlow in this reference to the assistance of a Supernatural Being. Spencer's cynical rationalism shows in this context as he points out how the timing of the rainmaking ceremonies is always carefully related to weather conditions, and "if rain follows . . . then of course it is due to the influence of the [ceremony]; if it does not, then the non-success is attributed to the counter-evil influence of some, usually distant, body of men." The quoted fragment then follows: "Meanwhile it may be said that their performance . . ."

    Notwithstanding the controversy about an Aboriginal Supreme Being, it is interesting to note that while LB hedges at calling the ceremonies "religion proper", Spencer is less reluctant.

24. A.P. Elkin, "The Secret Life of the Australian Aborigines", p. 132.

    Talu rites and sites are the Kimberley District equivalent of the Arunta *intichiuma*.

    The second paragraph seems relevant and I therefore include it although it is omitted by LB. Elkin adds a footnote to remind us that while in general the Aboriginal cultural pattern is much the same everywhere, variations occur and in the more heavily white-occupied southern parts of Australia evidence is confused.

25. Ibid., p. 131. The term "reincarnation" occurs in a number of places in *The Arunta*, etc. See also (from a letter dated 1897, Spencer, *Scientific Correspondence*, p. 7):

Every human being has a spiritual double called *arumburinga nanja* (*sc.* sacred place where the mythic ancestor went into the ground). When a man dies his *ulthana* or spirit part goes to the sacred storehouse where his *churinga* is kept, and there lies in company with the spirit double. This is complicated, but we have to remember that the *ulthana* is exactly the same thing as the spirit part of the *alcheringa* ancestor, and each one of the latter has an *arumburinga* who goes on living unchanged, while the *ulthana* or spirit part of the *alcheringa* ancestor may be reincarnated time after time . . . The old men decide what *alcheringa* is reincarnated in every child born, and the child bears as its *churinga aritna* or sacred name, that of the *alcheringa* ancestor.

26. Piddington, "Totemic System of the Karadjeri Tribe", p. 377.
27. Ibid., pp. 380-81.

The bird which LB translates as *une espèce de moineau* (a kind of sparrow) is plainly stated by Piddington to be a bower bird. Varieties which frequent the area are the spotted and the great bower bird, which are similar. Ornithologists will be puzzled to see them associated with a fish diet, since they are not sea birds though found in some coastal areas, but feed mainly on seeds, fruits and insects. The explanation of the myth is no doubt "etiological". The male bird has an elaborate courtship technique. He builds himself an impressive "bower", perhaps in a small bush or in grass or rushes, making a sort of passage or runway through it. This is often extended beyond the bower itself with an arrangement of small stones. In this "theatre" (sometimes called a playground) he performs a kind of running dance, by which he attracts a female; but once the mating is achieved he gives not another thought to wife, nest or chick. The bird is a remarkable mimic of bush sounds (something the myth takes no account of), and is also remarkable as a collector of small *objets d'art*, with a propensity for gathering and placing in his bower brightly coloured fragments of anything that glitters. Most bower birds are fond of blue or yellow scraps, but the spotted and the great seem to have a preference for white. Hence the attractiveness of bleached cockleshells and fish scales, found on beaches. Since they do not eat fish as a rule (preferring *nalgoo*), the story of the two mythical *Djui* and their dying advice would appear interestingly plausible. An element of fantasy seems to connect the bird's habits (which it is impossible to suppose the natives were not accurately aware of) with, possibly, some other coastal legend with which this one has been assimilated. The only links between the bower bird and the avocation of fishing would appear to be the shells in the bower and the arrangement of stones at its entrance, which could be seen as resembling a fishtrap. I find it irresistible to add that, had LB looked a little more closely into one of his sources (Sir George Grey, *Journals of Two Expeditions in Western Australia*, I, p. 245), he would have found the bird and its bower described. But it could not have been recognized as "a kind of sparrow".

Nalgoo: Piddington, p. 391, refers to an increase ceremony for this fruit.

There is a centre for the increase of *nalgoo* (local *yarinyeri*) in the territory of the Wonguru horde near Cape Bossut. The ceremony is of an unusual type, being entirely carried out by the women, under the direction of men. At the increase centre are a number of pebbles which are said to represent *yarinyeri*. The women place the pebbles in their wooden dishes, and, holding the latter high in the air, allow the pebbles to fall in heaps on the ground, the dust being blown away from them by the wind as they fall. A number of heaps are made in this way. It should be noted that this ceremony must be performed when a westerly wind (*yaman*) is blowing, that the spirit *yarinyeri* may be disseminated over the land. If the ceremony were to be performed in a south-east wind (*pundur*), the *yarinyeri* would be blown out to sea and the performance of the ceremony be rendered futile.

A.P. Elkin, "Rock Paintings of North-West Australia", p. 262, refers to "the green, plum-like fruit called *nalgo*", which probably supplied LB with his description of it; he also refers to the appearance of the fruit in rock paintings.

28. Ibid., p. 385.
29. R.F. Fortune, *Sorcerers of Dobu*, p. 120.
30. Sir George Grey, *Journals of Two Expeditions in Western Australia*, I, pp. 201-6.
31. See introduction, note 51.
32. LB's footnote here refers to L. Frobenius, "Das Unbekannte Afrika", p. 54 (unavailable for checking; I translate the note from LB):

> It is interesting to place against this passage an observation by Dr. Frobenius cited by Maria Weyersberg [no location given]: "We must recognize a living relationship between the natives and the rock-paintings in this fact, namely that on the Senegal and in the Homburi hills the task is imposed on the young people during their period of retreat before initiation, of touching up the rock-paintings — whether with blood or with red pigment."

33. A.P. Elkin, "Rock-paintings of North-West Australia", p. 261. LB's quotation leaves out a good deal of Elkin's detail. The matter dealt with embraces three separate sites (none identical with Grey's). Elkin's major site, Beleguldo, is a very low cave about forty-five centimetres from floor to ceiling, but nine metres long. Its approaches are protected from the weather. The large *wondjina* described is on the ceiling and difficult to observe. The other sites mentioned are more accessible.
34. Ibid., p. 262. LB does not indicate clearly that this remark applies to a different site. See note 27 for *nalgo*.
35. Ibid., p. 276, note 22.
36. Elkin is being careful to point out that the subject of *wondjina* figures is at yet insufficiently researched. The age and origin of the figures remain indeterminate. "We cannot rule out the possibility that they were originally a copy of men in shirt and trousers." Visitors from Java could have provided models. He remarks (p. 274, note 19), "Whereas the female genital organs and breasts are in some instances clearly depicted, the male genital organ is never shown in any case known to me. Is this because clothes were worn by the male *wondjina*?" It is generally implied that although the modern tribes use the pictures they did not create them originally, hence their history is quite obscure, even tribally.
  Father P. Vertenten (M.S.C. in Okaba bei Merauke), "Zeichen- und Malkunst der Marindinesen", p. 157, discusses Marind drawings and painting.
37. Vertenten, p. 159, adds further to his description of the *gari*: "in addition to this the actor is laden with bundles of croton leaves and is required to beat a large drum". Van Baal also describes the *gari* (*Dema: Description and Analysis of Marind-anim Culture*, p. 356):

The *gari*, then, is a huge semi-circular ornament which is carried on the shoulders. There are two types of *gari*; the best known is the *gari* of the eastern Marind, an almost perfect semi-circle with a diameter of up to three or even four metres. The ornament is fan-shaped, made of the very light kernel of sago-leaf ribs. The thin, long strips, radially arranged, are lashed together and then painted in various colours, among which white predominates. The usual pattern shows a broad, dark-coloured semi-circular band round the centre, which is behind the bearer's head, a band often enclosed by another broad semi-circular band of a lighter colour. The main body is coloured white with lime, with the exception of a narrow outer border, which is given a dark colour. In one picture [he refers to Plate IX in his illustrations, early photographs not of his own collecting] I noticed a thin, phallus-like mannikin painted in the centre of the white field. The dimensions of these designs are relatively modest; it is the white field that dominates and not the ornaments. Sometimes the field is left blank (without any decoration at all).

Van Baal then proceeds to discuss the smaller *gari* of the western area, and then speaks at length of the function and symbolism of the apparatus.

38. Wirz, *Die Marind-anim*, I, ii, p. 124. The myth in question mentions a place called Karomnati, where at a certain stage of the story the *Dema* abandoned the *gari*. Wirz explains:

> The name of this place seems to have come about as follows. It most likely was originally called Karona-ti, which has the meaning of "much sperm"; for the large lime-washed surface of the *gari* is an open allusion to the sexual orgies which take place in the *mayo* ceremony (*yaba karona*, much sperm). Hence the whole Bragai clan uses the hunting cry, "*Yaba karona! yaba karona!*" or "*Yaba zomba! yaba zomba!*" (Much sperm! Much copulation or emission!)

LB quotes this explanation in a note, omitting, however, the last sentence. However, Van Baal calls the etymology false though he confirms the hunting cries. The symbolic importance of sperm among the Marind-anim is amply demonstrated by Van Baal (for example, p. 817), though he neither confirms nor denies Wirz's explanation of the symbolism of the white colour of the *gari*. He also makes plain a point not explicit in LB's reading of Wirz, namely that the Marind-anim are to a degree homosexually orientated. Nevertheless the sperm which is required in various ceremonies and procedures is normally produced by *otiv-bombari*, that is, the ritual orgies alluded to by Wirz and mentioned by LB. These are not, however, occasions of unbridled licentiousness or lasciviousness (Van Baal, pp. 164, 166, 493, 815 ff).

39. Ibid., pp. 120-21. From the myth of *Opeko-anim*, belonging to the Bragai-*ze*. The first of the two indicated omissions may be restored; it would suggest that Wirz was relying on Vertenten: "He often performs a dance, either alone or with a second performer, beating a large drum and stamping with alternate feet." Wirz here refers to the performer's elaborate dress and ornamentation, then continues: "The *gari* is made of thin strips of sago-leaf taken from the palm frond, which are stitched together and strengthened with rods arranged in a radial pattern. The *gari* is coloured almost all over with limewash, except at its inner and outer edges, which are respectively red and black. Designs appear on the white area, representing star, moon, crab, penis and snake, but these have no particular significance." Van Baal

confirms this descriptive detail (pp. 359 ff) but denies the last remark and is at pains to correct Wirz's assumptions (echoed by LB) as to the "real meaning" of the *gari*. He characterizes it positively as a sun symbol (see his Index and Glossary). Further, he disagrees with Wirz's interpretation of the Opeko-anim myth and specifically denies the assumption that the final orgies led to human sacrifice and cannibalism (p. 370). "We can hardly blame Wirz [whose work appeared 1922-25] for surmising that there was some secret final ceremony which nobody wanted to disclose anything about. Only he was on the wrong track when he thought of a cannibal feast" (p. 540). Missionary and government efforts to suppress Marind sexual promiscuity, whether homo- or heterosexual, especially after a virulent outbreak of syphilitic granuloma about 1907, would have been enough to account for the native reluctance to admit to the continuing practice of *otiv-bombari*. (See Van Baal, p. 492, describing an inspectorial visit to a community suspected of carrying out a *sosom* ceremonial involving the homosexual initiation of young boys.) Van Baal's explanation of the symbolism of the spear by which the *Mayo-iwag* is attached to the *Opeko-anim* also differs from Wirz's.

LB in his footnote also refers to a parallel with the myth of Yawima, another *Dema associated with the mayo* ceremonies. Like the Opeko man, Yawima has a *gari*, and also like him, abandons it at a certain stage of the myth. He also has an *iwag* or woman-companion. On his way to the *mayo* ceremony Yawima roughly violates her. She gives birth to a water snake, which bites Yawima in the ear, causing him great pain. At this he casts off both the *gari* and the *iwag* and, running off into the bush, disappears. (Wirz, II, ii, pp. 98-99; Van Baal, p. 289.)

However, interesting as these comparisons may be, it has to be admitted that as yet no satisfactory explanation of the Kimberley *wondjina* figures has been given.

40. Wirz, *Die Marind-anim*, I, ii, p. 130. The drawing by a native artist represents the storm-*Dema* Yorma. The figure wears a *gari*-like headdress and also carries a large drum. As LB points out, it resembles the Kimberley figures in being without a mouth. The myth relates that Yorma broke tribal decorum by masturbating in the sight of a woman and was punished accordingly. Normally the act is regarded as ridiculous rather than immoral; but see Van Baal, *Dema*, p. 382.

41. Gunnar Landtman, *Ethnographical Collection from the Kiwai District of British New Guinea*, p. 38, also Plate VIII. See also his *Folktales of the Kiwai Papuans*, p. 333, for references to and descriptions of *dori* and other headdresses.

42. An allusion to the fact that some of Grey's illustrations are coloured.

43. Paul Wirz, "Beitrag zur Ethnologie der Sentanier, (Holländisch Neu-Guinea)", p. 363.
     A.C. Haddon, ed., *Report of the Cambridge Anthropological Expedition to Torres Straits*. See vol IV, p. 39, "Personal Ornaments and Clothing". The article is illustrated with plates and drawings.
     The islands of Torres Straits are believed to be remnants of a former land bridge between New Guinea and Australia; some common elements remain in flora and fauna.

44. Such illustrations are found in all of Spencer and Gillen's books, the best in *The Arunta*. Most of the photographs relate to initiation (*engwura*) rather than increase (*intichiuma*) ceremonies, but the myth material is similar.

The important sacred artifacts used in ceremonies are the *waninga* and the *nurtunja*. These are sometimes small enough to fix in a headdress, but are mostly larger and either carried or fixed in the ground. A compact description of both, with a third object, *kauaua*, will be found in Spencer and Gillen, *The Native Tribes of Central Australia*, pp. 627-30. The resemblance of these objects to the *gari*, as LB rightly remarks, is slight.

45. Nevertheless the general pattern is strongly enough established for this to be taken for granted.

46. Salomon Reinach, French archaeologist, LB's contemporary and a pioneer in relating archaeology to anthropology.

47. No Tasmanians of a purely tribal status survive.

48. Emile Cartailhac and the Abbé Henri Breuil, *La Caverne d'Altamira à Santillane près Santander (Espangne)*, p. 146.

49. But Elkin is far from pretending that enough is known about the rock paintings or their origin.

50. See chapter II, note 22.

51. LB notes: In this cave M. le Comte Bégouen and the Abbé Breuil have recently described other drawings of the same kind ("De Quelques figures hybrides, mi-humaines et mi-animales, de la caverne des Trois Frères, Arriège", Comptes rendus de l'Acad. des Ins. et B.L. (1920), p. 303). See *Revue anthropologique*, XLVI (1934), pp. 115-19.

52. R. de Saint-Périer, "Gravures anthropomorphes de la grotte d'Isturitz", pp. 28-31.

53. Cartailhac and Breuil, *La Caverne d'Altamira*, pp. 242-43.

54. LB writes *acteurs masqués et costumés*. But in the Australian context neither masks nor (properly speaking) costumes are in use, though the performers are *decorated*, and certain symbolic objects might be said to be *worn*.

55. Saint-Périer, "Gravures anthropomorphes de la grotte d'Isturitz", pp. 28-31.

56. Cartailhac and Breuil, *La Caverne d'Altamira*, p. 242.

57. See T.G.H. Strehlow, *Aranda Traditions*, pp. 86 ff. With the Aranda the totem of the conceived child is not predetermined but depends upon the "conception site"; it may at times be a cause of confusion.

58. See chapter I, p. 57.

59. Alice Werner, *Myths and Legends of the Bantu*, pp. 208-9. The story concerns a giant who swallowed all the creatures which came in his way. He devoured a whole village but the woman escaped by hiding. Afterwards the heroic boy slays the monster, cuts up his body and lets out all the people and the cattle he has swallowed. The people make the boy their chief.

60. New Guinea notions of biological conception are not identical with Aboriginal Australian.

61. See the instructions given to the species it is desired to increase, p. 122 (quoted passage from Piddington).

Chapter V: Participation-Imitation in the Myths

1. Paul Wirz, *Die Marind-anim von Holländisch Süd-Neu-Guinea*, I, ii, p. 54.

2. Ibid., II, iii, p. 91. On the erotic aspects of the *mayo*, see chapter IV, especially notes 14, 38.

3. F.E. Williams (Australian Government Anthropologist, Territory of Papua), "Trading Voyages from the Gulf of Papua", pp. 139-66. Williams' text continues, "and one can too often detect by the sidelong glances of an informant

and the garbled nature of his story that he has reached and is endeavouring to steer clear of such a passage" (p. 158).

4. Ibid. The ten totems are named in a footnote. They are not animal totems. The *bevaia* is a composite form of canoe. The basic structure is that of a *lakatoi* ("a unique vessel, which is really a large raft of dugout canoes, and which carries the famous crab-claw sail"). The *bevaia* consists of "a double canoe, masted and fitted with bulwarks", adapted for oars as well as sail. It is used on trading voyages. The *bevaia haera* is the initiator of the voyage and the man of authority on board, but Williams discards the term "captain" as unfitting. He refers to him as "the *bevaia* man": "His business is to know the magic and carry it out and therefore to make the *bevaia* go fast and escape rough weather". Among several *tabus* laid upon the *bevaia* man he is forbidden to have any sex as it might make him become heavy and so endanger the ship. Nor is he allowed to wash.

Williams continues, "Above all he must have at his command the secret and potent names . . . The generalization, as framed by one informant, stands thus: 'Magic, to be effective, must employ the names of long-ago people, born in the beginning' " (pp. 157-58).

5. Ibid. Since it is tantalizing not to have the story in mind as a whole, I append a precis: Evarapu so far had been unable to find a wife, but one day two young men came to him and recommended he should approach their sister Aviara, who lived at Lavau. Evarapu sent his younger brother Iriri as an envoy, and to provide for his journey to so distant a place made for him a *ruru*, or model bird. When Iriri reached Lavau, Aviara offered herself to him; but he refused, as sexual intercourse might make him heavy (see note 4) and endanger his return home. He informed her that Evarapu would eventually call for her in a large canoe. Evarapu then made the canoe. In due course he arrived and carried Aviara away. They were pursued and met with delays and difficulties, but eventually arrived at Evarapu's home.

It is slightly surprising to find, in this context of models and precedents, that LB does not allude further to the model bird in this myth. Williams mentions it as a decoration or charm commonly carried at sea. The bird, which seems to symbolize flight and speed, has carved betel nuts fastened under its wings. The *bevaia haera* is described as performing a bird imitation. For a description of canoe-making and the associated tabus, compare pp. 68-69.

Williams's use of the word *precedent* here is a little awkward as he seems inclined to mean *precept*, in the sense of rule or tabu, warning. LB is apparently a little uneasy about this, as he is concerned with pure precedents and accompanies the reference with a remark (which I do not translate), "he referred to them just now as *models*".

6. Ibid. Williams's text makes it clear that as well as being the mythical hero's name, *aori* is also the name of a "little bird". The *love* of Iviri corresponds with the bird's crest or topknot. "Iviri is the name of a hill on the Kerema River, but in the story she is wholly human except that she was born with a *love*, or sprig of feathers growing in her hair" (p. 160). The story, which resembles the other, is as follows (pp. 160-61): "It tells how Aori went to the Kerema river to bring home as his bride the woman Iviri . . . He first goes in quest of her in a *ruru*, representing the little bird *aori*, and having found her he plucks out this *love*, tells her he will call for her later in a canoe, then flies home to make his preparations. The canoe completed and given the name *Heava*, he travels again to the Kerema River and returns home with his bride." After pursuit, separation and reunion, all is eventually well.

7. Ibid., pp. 164-65. The myth relates the story of Kivavia, who was told in a dream to go fishing with a bow and two ancestors would come to him in the form of decorated arrows with magical powers. (The story of the fisherman is slightly paraphrased in LB's version.)

8. Also compare K. Th. Preuss, *Der religiöse Gehalt der Mythen*, pp. 20, 31, 38, especially where, following P.E. Goddard, he refers to the Hupa Indians of California (P.E. Goddard, "Life and Culture of the Hupa", pp. 33-34).

9. John P. Harrington, "Tobacco among the Karuk Indians of California", pp. 8-9, 85.

10. Joseph Meier, "Mythen und Erzählungen der Küstenbewohner der Gazelle-Halbinsel (Neu Pommern)", p. 107.

11. Wirz, *Die Marind-anim*, I, ii, p. 69.

12. Meier, *Mythen und Erzählungen der Küstenbewohner der Gazelle- Halbinsel*, pp. 37-39. Meier's text continues, "Thus the snake changes its skin. To Kabinana was furious with To Karvuvu for frustrating man's power to change his skin, and causing snakes to do so instead . . . Originally we men were intended to slough our skins and so become bodily youthful once again."

13. Ibid., p. 16. The question is one of tabu tribal relationships.
"In the myths of the Shasta (north west North America) it is said similarly that if from time to time (though it is rare) incest occurs in the tribe, it is because there were ancestors or heroes in the mythic age who also committed it" (LB's note).

14. Ibid., pp. 61, 63-65.
The story of the sea-eagle and the frigate bird is worth a brief summary. To Kabinana and To Karvuvu have made two fishes and two birds. The frigate bird indicates where fish are found. But the sea eagle swoops and eats them. So To Kabinana exclaims, "What sort of a bird is this that you have made? It flew down and attacked a small tuna. Did you see that? Your bird is a thief. You have brought misery to our mortal race. What a worthless wretch you are! If I weren't fond of you I'd strike you down without a qualm!"
The last story quoted from "Pork and Bananas" is also very typical. They have food and To Kabinana says, "Let's keep it for this evening". When To Karvuvu sees some "sunset birds" he concludes it is time. He brings out the food and the birds eat it. To Kabinana says he should have waited until the birds had gone to roost. "You are certainly a clot. I sent you the food so that we could have it after dark, when the moon rose. But you decided it must be when the birds flew in. What a prize fool! Now we shall go hungry, and all our descendants in after times will know hunger also."

15. G.A. Dorsey, "Traditions of the Skidi Pawnee", pp. xxii, and 355, note 249.

16. Ibid., pp. 170, 304-6. The story of the stolen corn is "The Eagle Boy", which, beyond the incident related, becomes a more or less elaborate account of the boy's eagle-nature and his transformations. The brother and sister are separated but after various trials and adventures are eventually reunited.
The second story is "The Girl Who Grieved for her Brother". An orphan boy is lured away by a fawn to the abode of the Spider Woman. He loses his memory. His sister, who is under the protection of the chief of the Eagles, blows abroad eagle-feathers, which the boy sees. He recovers his wits and returns.
The story continues: the season is now winter. The girl blows with her breath, which becomes a snow storm (repeating the symbolism of the

feathers). The blizzard causes the Spider Woman to freeze. "These children lived on happily. In the spring they planted their crops again and their field looked green. So they were happy . . ." (p. 306).

17. Herbert J. Spinden, "Coyote of the Lower Country", from "Nez-Percé Tales", pp. 191-92.

18. Graebner, Fr. *Das Weltbild der Primitiven*, p. 21, cited by E. Cassirer, *The Philosophy of Symbolic Forms*,   p. 105: "Red spots in the plumage of the black cockatoo and of a certain hawk originated in a great fire, the spout-hole of the whale is a spear-thrust which he once – while still a man – received in the back of his head. The sandpiper came by his strange gait – abruptly running and standing still – when he attempted to follow the guardian of the waters and was compelled to stand still each time the guardian turned round."

19. A.R. Radcliffe-Brown, *The Andaman Islanders: A Study in Social Anthropology*, pp. 204, 342. See Bronislaw Malinowski, *Myth in Primitive Psychology*, p. 104.

20. R.F. Fortune, *Sorcerers of Dobu*, p. 262. See also Preuss, *Der religiöse Gehalt der Mythen*, p. 20 ("We see that with primitives it is not explanation, but belief that really counts") and Malinowski, *Myth in Primitive Psychology*, p. 121 ("Myth serves principally to establish a sociological charter, or a retrospective moral pattern of behaviour, or the primeval supreme miracle of magic . . . it becomes clear that elements both of explanation and of interest in nature must be found in sacred legends. For a precedent accounts for subsequent cases").

21. R.S. Rattray, *Ashanti Proverbs*, p. 41. Rattray adds a parenthetic comment: "As a matter of fact no case is known of a change from patrilineal to matrilineal descent".

22. C.G. and Brenda Z. Seligman, *Pagan Tribes of the Nilotic Sudan*, p. 143:

> Most of the Dinka clans whose *kwar* is an animal derive their origin from a man born as one of twins, his fellow-twin being an animal of the species that is the totem of the clan. Sometimes the association is not quite so close, in which case the totem animal usually lays certain commands upon one of the members of the clan, offering in return certain privileges. Commands and privileges alike show the close relationship existing between the animal and the man who is traditionally looked upon as the ancestor of the clan.

23. Karl yon den Steinen, *Unter den Naturvölkern Zentral Brasiliens*, p. 356. This is not quite what Fortune said: his phrase was, "some five generations ago when existence first came into being and natural history began" (already quoted, chapter I, p. 35).

24. LB's scrupulous distinction between (modern) religion "properly so called" and primitive pre-religion has appeared more than once before. Von den Steinen, on the contrary, says plainly, "Their myths and legends to us appear mere tales and animal fables, but by them are taken as seriously as we take the sacred scriptures and their teachings." (Ibid., Johnson reprint, p. 201.)

25. Fortune, *Sorcerers of Dobu*, p. 263.

26. LB, *Primitives and the Supernatural*, chapter VI.

27. W.B. Spencer and F.J. Gillen, *The Native Tribes of Central Australia*, pp. 522 ff, 523, 530. LB mentions only one of the three kinds. Initiation by the *Iruntarinia* (*alcheringa* spirits) is shown as the most prestigious, as it is also the

most painful, involving the boring of a hole through the tongue, other mutilations and a period of insanity. The second kind, carried out by *Oruncha* men, is similar but less severe; and the third, *Nungara*, is carried out by other medicine men and is the least of the three.

28. Wirz, *Die Marind-anim*, II, iv, p. 41, II, iii, pp. 79-81. Wirz adds after the first quotation: "The natives are very ready to believe stories like this. The more fantastic a *mesav*'s stories, the higher his prestige."

29. W.E. Roth, "Superstition, Magic and Medicine", p. 10. Item 19 is "Imitating Falling Rain, and the Antics of Aquatic Animals".

30. LB adds a note: It is tempting to recall the analysis by Renouvier of the effects of vertigo. A man finds himself at the edge of a cliff, and has a feeling of falling over it; his imagination pictures the fall so vividly that it becomes a fact. He leans closer and closer towards the abyss as though drawn to it, until in the end the imagined fall becomes actual.

31. Roth, "Superstition, Magic and Medicine", p. 9.

32. See Appendix on Animism.

33. Wirz, *Die Marind-anim*, II, iii, p. 74.

34. P.G. Peekel, *Religion und Zauberei auf dem Mittleren Neu-Mecklenburg, Bismarck Archipel, Südsee*, pp. 119-20.

35. Ibid., pp. 91-93. And compare: "Before the hunting foray they address a petition to certain crabs. Just as with their claws the crabs pull the fish and other creatures out of their holes in the coral, so they are to employ their talents to reach the game in the forest, and the pigs will be fetched out of their haunts so that they may be sighted and shot." (P.H. Meyer, "Wunekau, oder Sonnenverehrung in Neuguinea", p. 43).

36. Peekel, *Religion und Zauberei auf dem Mittleren Neu-Mecklenburg*, pp. 104, 106.

37. Th. Koch-Grunberg, *Vom Roroima zum Orinoco*, III, p. 220.

38. Ibid., III, pp. 223, 225. See also Preuss, *Der religiöse Gehalt der Mythen*, p. 34.

39. Ibid., III, pp. 230-70.

Chapter VI: Persistence of the Mythic World

1. A.R. Radcliffe-Brown, *The Andaman Islanders*, pp. 201, 387-88. The passage concludes, "However, we can help ourselves to understand their thoughts by recalling the tales that amused us as children, in which the fox or the rabbit was an embodiment of the whole species."

2. Franz Boas, "Tsimshian Mythology", p. 565.

3. Leonhard Adam, "Stammesorganization und Häuptlingstum der Wakashstämme", p. 260 (inaccessible for checking).

4. J.A. Teit, "Traditions of the Thompson River Indians of British Columbia", p. 19. Teit adds to the passage quoted, "There are among them many cannibal, and many mysterious persons".

5. Franz Boas, ed., "Folk Tales of Salishan and Sahaptin Tribes", collected by James A. Teit; see "Okanagon Tales", by J.A. Teit, pp. 80-81. The text here quoted is Teit's, which LB slightly condenses. LB's concluding sentence is "At that time a few men and animals like those of today did exist, but the number was small". This is not precisely what Teit says. However, as Teit remarks later, the story has some modern (that is, Christian) intrusions and modifications.

6. R.L. Packard, "Notes on the Mythology and Religion of the Nez-Percés", p. 327. The context is a legend, "How the Beaver Stole Fire from the Pines".
7. Frank G. Speck, "Penobscot Shamanism", p. 255.
8. James Mooney, "Myths of the Cherokee", pp. 229-31 (Johnson Reprint, 1970).
9. Ibid., pp. 261, 231. The second omitted sentence runs, "In one or two special cases, however, the present creature is the descendant of a former monster."
10. Konrad Theodor Preuss, *Religion und Mythologie der Uitoto*, p. 38.
    Karl Von den Steinen, *Unter den Naturvölkern Zentral-Brasiliens*, p. 353. This work appeared in Berlin, 1894. The Johnson reprint reproduces it but LB's page references do not correspond.
11. Theodor Koch-Grunberg, *Zwei Jahre bei den Indianern Nordwest-Brasiliens*, LB's reference, pp. 160-62 (inaccessible for checking).
12. Koch-Grunberg *Vom Roroima zum Orinoco*, II, pp. 18-19; LB's reference (inaccessible for checking).
13. Von den Steinen, *Unter den Naturvölkern Zentral-Brasiliens*, pp. 381-82. The story of Keri and the Manioc is interesting enough to include in summary. Von den Steinen's informant Antonio told him, "Keri received the manioc from the deer (*cervus simplicornus*), but first we need to know how the deer got it. It belonged to the *bagadu* fish . . . also known as *pirarara*, a fish we often catch but do not like to eat because it is too greasy . . ." The deer found this fish out of water, gasping, and rescued it. In gratitude it took the deer to its underwater dwelling and entertained him. It gave the deer some manioc slips. The deer planted them and they grew. One day Keri came across the deer and asked him for some. The deer refused. Keri in anger struck the deer and blew breath upon him. Suddenly horns grew out of the deer's head. Keri was amused and cried out, "See what the lord of the manioc looks like!" He ran off, taking the manioc with him. He offered it to the Bakairi women and showed them, as he had discovered from the deer, how to cure it of its poison. The deer still wears the horns and his diet is leaves and bark, which he chews from the branches of trees. "Antonio was completely convinced that the deer knew what to do . . . and showed Keri; but it was from Keri that the women learned the art."
14. LB's reference is to Knud Rasmussen, *Thulefahrt*, p. 61 (inaccessible). But the passage also occurs in *Across Arctic America*, p. 25. See also "Intellectual Culture of the Iglulik Eskimos", pp. 59-60.
15. Rasmussen, "The Netsilik Eskimos: Social Life and Spiritual Culture", p. 208.
16. Ibid., p. 267.
17. Rasmussen, "Observations on the Intellectual Culture of the Caribou Eskimos", pp. 82-83. LB omits three sentences: "They rose up with a rushing noise into the air and flew to the spot where the people wanted to go. In those days also newly drifted snow would burn. There was life in all things." He likewise omits the last three sentences of the quotation, but I include them because they continue his thought.
18. E.W. Nelson, "The Eskimos about Bering Strait", p. 425. See also the following passage, p. 395:

    Masks may also represent totemic animals, and the wearers during the festivals are believed actually to become the creature represented, or at least to be endowed with its spiritual essence. Some of the masks of the lower Yukon and the adjacent territory to the Kuskokwim are made with double faces. This is done by having the muzzle of the animal fitted over and concealing the *inua* below, the outer mask being held in place by pegs so arranged that it can be removed quickly at a certain time in the ceremony, thus symbolizing the transformation.

(*Inua* = shade, spirit. Nelson reports causing alarm when he captured the people's *shades* with his camera.)

19. Kai Donner, *Bei den Samojeden in Sibirien*, pp. 82, 100. These two quotations are taken untrimmed from his text, which LB abbreviates.
20. Isaac Schapera, *The Khoisan Peoples of South Africa, Bushmen and Hottentots*, pp. 177-78.
21. Ibid., pp. 179, 180.
22. E.W. Smith and A.M. Dale, *The Ila Speaking Peoples of Northern Rhodesia*, II, p. 337.
23. Marcel Mauss, *Société Française de Philosophie, Bulletin*, 23e année (1926), p. 26 (inaccessible for checking).
24. In histories of religion a good deal of stress is placed on sacrifice (e.g., Old Testament). It has a dominant role in Aztec religion. Sacrifice plays no part in Australian Aboriginal custom but there is (or was) some (generally ritual) cannibalism and in various initiation practices mutilations and pain have an important part. See T.G.H. Strehlow, *Aranda Traditions*, p. 38 ("the primitive lust for blood").
25. Presumably the work referred to is Émile Durkheim, *The Elementary Forms of the Religious Life*, subtitled in the French version only, "The Totemic System in Australia". Durkheim founded *L'Année sociologique* in 1896.
26. Von den Steinen, *Unter den Naturvölkern Zentral-Brasiliens* (Johnson reprint, p. 305) describes and illustrates one of the two masks. The cheek designs are large red triangles with points which come together under the nose. The eyes are mussel shells with holes bored in them.
27. The observer is not identified.
28. LB's word is *anime* (animates). It is presumably chosen deliberately.
29. See the story reported by Alice Werner (chapter IV, p. 140).

Chapter VII: The Mythic World and Folklore: I

1. Paul Wirz, *Die Marind-anim von Holländisch Süd-Neu-Guinea*, I, ii, p. 105.
2. Ibid., I, ii, pp. 113, 107-8.
3. Ibid., I, ii, p. 171.
4. Ibid., I, ii, pp. 133-34.
5. Karl Von den Steinen, *Unter den Naturvölkern Zentral-Brasiliens*, p. 229.
6. Wirz, *Die Marind-anim*, I, ii, pp. 149, 164.
7. See chapter III, note 26.
8. Wirz, *Die Marind-anim*, I, ii, pp. 122-23.
9. Ibid., I, ii, p. 75.
10. Ibid., I, ii, p. 74.
11. Ibid., II, iii, p. 74.
12. Gunnar Landtman, "Folktales of the Kiwai Papuans", pp. 492-96. The text quoted is a little fuller than LB's, though still much curtailed. The dialogue and asides in this and other quotations from Landtman follow the pidgin idiom of his informants.
13. LB omits the rest of Landtman's paragraph, but as it will illustrate the point made earlier about "etiological" myths (for example, how the crow became

black), I retain it: "Ever since the women of her kin have hair growing in that place [the same word is used for hair and feather and also for leaf]; the women belonging to another kin have no hair there. The same is the case with the men. Similarly the hair of some men and women turns white like the feathers of the heron, while it does not with other people ('all same split him two side')." See note 14.

14. The end of this story is more complex than LB's presentation might suggest. It has been possible here, in English, to follow Landtman's text a little more fully than LB could do in French, especially the racy little touches of pidgin, but the whole is too long to quote without reduction. As the story continues the young man escapes and is pursued by *all* the girls. At a new place a fresh settlement is made. Magic and symbolism become more dominant as the story advances. Eventually he escapes again. This story seems to vacillate between myth and legend.

15. At a late stage of the story the bird-skin is given back to the young man (Landtman, "Folktales of the Kiwai Papuans", p. 496). He "put it on and became a bird".

16. Ibid., pp. 213, 239, 271, 281. See p. 506: "Túbo . . . swallowed a feather and transformed himself into a certain bird called *bádu* which cries out his name, '*Túbo singi singi*'."

17. Ibid., pp. 502. Landtman also records a variant of the story (p. 503), which runs in part, "Tiburi saw the girl fishing in a swamp, his passion was excited and his penis created a wave in the water which reached the girl and caused her to become pregnant. One day Tiburi turned himself into a large snake and brought a great quantity of food to the two women. The mother and the daughter were at first very frightened, but at length . . . at their request he resumed human shape." Incidentally this story makes it appear that the New Guinea view of conception is not the same as the Australian.

18. Ibid., p. 293.

19. Ibid., p. 460. Much truncated from Landtman's text, which concludes the story thus: "At night the snake used to kill pigs and cassowaries which he swallowed and brought home, and then he gave them to the people and resumed his human shape. And when enemies came to attack the Kiwais they were all killed by the snake who had a mouth at both ends of his body and ten pairs of arms. One day, however, when the snake had 'stolen' a number of Kiwai women the men enticed him to go with them into the bush, and there they killed him." The account continues, telling how his spirit passed into a turtle, and afterwards into a bird, both poisonous, or at any rate avoided as food.

20. Ibid., pp. 416, 167, 198. An explanation of *étengena* is given (p. 192): "The *étengena* and *samé* . . . live in large trees, wells, etc.; some of them guard the people's plantations. The Kiwais call them *ororarora*, which word is also used of mysterious things in general. At times the *étengena* appear as men and at times in the form of snakes, birds, etc."

21. Richard Neuhauss, *Deutsch Neu-Guinea*, III (Keysser, "Aus dem Leben der Kai"), p. 185.

22. Ibid., III (Stolz, "Die Umgebung von Kap Konig Wilhelm"), p. 262.

23. Ibid., pp. 274-75. See also p. 278.

24. LB's concern to compress has here lost him a little of the charm of this story, which is best taken directly from Bamler's at this point.

Not long afterwards the people of the village added a sail to their new canoe and the owner decided to reward them with a feast. The little boy was full of eagerness and tried hard to be helpful. But he made mistakes about the coconuts and brought the wrong kind. The owner of the nuts became irritable and said to the child, "Did your crocodile (grand) mother, as they say, swallow a coconut?" (Deine Krokodilmutter (Grossmutter) hat wohl so etwas, was Kokosnuss heisst, gegessen?). As yet the child knew nothing of his mother's origin, but went back to the house at once, lay down under a mat and wept bitterly. His mother found him there when she came from the field. His first question was, "Mother, what was your parentage?" So the mother told him she was the daughter of the crocodile; but she felt the insult offered to her child as though it had been meant for herself . . .

25. Neuhauss, *Deutsch Neu-Guinea*, III (Bamler, "Tami"), pp. 564-66.
26. Ibid., III (Zahn, "Die Jabim"), pp. 356-60. See also Bamler, "Tami", p. 552.
27. W.B. Spencer and F.J. Gillen, *The Arunta*, I, pp. 325-26. The passage quoted is shortened by leaving out Arunta phrases included in the text. NB, "where they died" means only that they settled there permanently, remaining until their deaths. Spencer's sentence concludes, ". . . leaving their *churinga* in the *pertalchera* [= secret deposit] and thus formed an emu *knanikilla* [= local centre]".
28. Gunnar Landtman, *The Kiwai Papuans of British New Guinea*, p. 461.
29. Th. Koch-Grünberg, *Vom Roroima zum Orinoco*, II, pp. 112-13 (shortened).
30. Ibid., II, p. 98. The original text names the tree and all the birds.
31. Ibid., II, p. 24.
32. Ibid., II, pp. 82-87 (much reduced).
33. H.J. Rink and F. Boas, "Eskimo Tales and Songs", see "Raven and Gull (Greenland)", p. 128.
34. Knud Rasmussen, "Observations on the Intellectual Culture of the Caribou Eskimos", ii, pp. 2, 89, 90, 92, 91, 93-94. The tale, "The Man that Married a Vixen", is worth summarizing a little more fully. A hunter finds when he returns home each day that his meal has been prepared. Eventually he discovers that a fox (who has left her "tunic" outside the house) has been cooking for him. He seizes the tunic and gives it back only on condition that the vixen will be his wife. Then the wolf people arrive on a visit and the customary exchange of wives is requested (Eskimo hospitality). But when the wolf-man smells fox, the fox runs away and resumes animal form. The husband follows to the foxhole but cannot get it. He cries, "I want my wife back", and various animals answer. First the hare offers herself, then a wolf, then "they all came out, all the animals on earth". But the husband will have none of them. He begs the wolverine to dig out the hole, and when the price (a bladder filled with blubber) is paid, the man and fox are reunited and "afterwards they lived happily together".
35. Diamond Jenness, "Myths and Traditions from North Alaska . . .", from "Eskimo Folklore", p. 76A.
36. Stith Thompson, *Tales of the North American Indians*, p. 198. The parenthesized observation is LB's.
37. Jenness, "Myths and Traditions from North Alaska . . .", pp. 49A-52A.
38. Ibid., p. 57A. Note the similarity between the footprints of the escaping caribou wife ("Outside he found her footsteps and noticed how they suddenly changed to a caribou's") and those of the escaping fox and duck wives. LB does not stay to include the interview with the bear.
39. Ibid., p. 58A.
40. Father Noel Dumarest, "Notes on Cochiti, New Mexico", p. 199, note 5, pp. 234-36 (Chaiani = good spirits).

41. Ruth Benedict, "Tales of the Cochiti Indians", LB's *sorcière* is merely "an old woman" in Ruth Benedict's text, but that she is a "witch" may be taken for granted. This story is accompanied by a "variant" which includes the following preliminary material. A man and his wife are childless. In the mountains the hunter meets a bear to whom he confides his wish for a child. The bear suggests a plan: the man is to remain in the mountains while the bear goes to the house. He advises the man to go on asking for a child, and comes back to the house whenever the husband is away. At last a child is born that is half bear and half human. The boy grows up and asks who his father was – the hunter having disappeared from the scene. He is told about the bear and goes to seek him. At this point the story merges into the version already told.

42. Ibid., pp. 73-75. The story which now follows is longish and represents a compromise. In translation LB prunes it hard, but it is atmospheric in English and most readers will prefer to have a little more of Ruth Benedict's text. I use square brackets to summarize the beginning and at other places in order to follow the text just a little more fully. The interpolations in round brackets are LB's.

43. At this point Ruth Benedict draws attention to a lacuna in the narrative, apparently disregarded by the informant.

44. Alanson Skinner, "Social Life and Ceremonial Bundles of the Menomini Indians", p. 99. The ceremonial bundles of these Indians are bundles of symbolic or magic artifacts, carried on the warpath as charms.

45. Thompson, *Tales of the North American Indians*, p. 10.

46. Herbert J. Spinden, "Nez Percé Tales", p. 197.

47. Benedict, "Tales of the Cochiti Indians", p. 95.

48. James A. Teit, "Thompson Tales", p. 53.

49. Thompson, *Tales of the North American Indians*, pp. 167-73. LB adds a reference to p. 348, note 254, which lists a number of other tales in which marriage with animals is a motif, but does not detail them. The original folktale is long, rambling and might have some claim to be considered romantic.

50. LB's precis seems here and there a little unnecessarily bare, and I fill it out slightly. Thompson tells how, one day while hunting, the deer-hunter "came on the fresh tracks of a doe and fawn . . . they led to a knoll on which he saw a young woman and a child sitting. He was surprised and asked the woman if she had seen any deer pass. She answered 'No'." Sure that she must have seen them, he returns and asks her again. "The woman laughed, and said, 'You need not trouble yourself about the tracks. For a long time I have loved you and longed for you. Now you shall go with me to my house.'" He is uneasy (but not for long), and does so. For the rest, LB's "indispensable" details are adequate to underline the folkloric characteristics.

51. Thompson's text runs here, "The chief had told him in the morning to be careful not to throw away any part of the game. Now the people ate and were glad. They saved up all the bones . . . the chief sent a man to throw them into the water. . . . When the man returned . . . the two brothers-in-law and another man were with him. They had all come to life when their bones were thrown into the water."

52. Thompson specifies various magical procedures whereby all the people are feasted and satisfied.

53. "She told her husband it would be better not to continue to do this, because

people were becoming suspicious . . . She said, "After this kill your brothers-in-law.' The people travelled slowly . . . The hunter killed deer for them every day." The degree of rationalization added to the story, here and elsewhere (and in other stories also), no doubt is a sign of advancing sophistication in the culture.

54. LB (more freely in French): "Take care of the bones, do not lose any, and be careful not to crush them, but throw them into the water."

55. LB omits: "If it is impossible to throw the bones into water, then burn them. Then the deer will really die, but they will not find fault with you. If a man throws deer-bones about, and takes no care of them, if he lets dogs eat them, then the deer will be offended and will help him no more."

56. LB insists on the "skin", but what Thompson actually says is that the chief put the *body* of a buck on the hunter, and so transformed him into a buck. He afterwards adds antlers. Beyond that, no information is given as to how the transformation is effected.

Chapter VIII: The Mythic World and Folklore: II

1. Henry Callaway, *Nursery Tales, Traditions and Histories of the Zulus*, pp. 79-80, note 7.
    Clement M. Doke, *The Lambas of Northern Rhodesia: A Study of their Customs and Beliefs*, p. 304.

2. Heli Chatelain, *Folk-Tales of Angola*, pp. 163, 145-49. Apart from LB's immediate point one may remark that the drift of the first story seems amusingly cynical. The leopard is a type of smart fellow whose manners and tactics contrast with his inept grandson's. The behaviour of both seems openly anthropomorphic (see p. 250). With the lion story, Chatelain's text includes more detail. It makes plain that the ruse is for the lioness to marry the man and kill him in the bride-house. But the man has a young son who watches her and warns him. The house is burned down with the lioness in it.

3. H. Berthoud, "Weitere Thonga-Märchen", pp. 73-74.

4. C.W. Hobley, *Ethnology of A-Kamba and other East African Tribes*, pp. 109-10. In Hobley's text the story is introduced thus: "The hyaena, the hare and the lion agreed they would each go off and try to find a wife. The hare went off to marry the daughter of the jackal, the lion went off to find the daughter of another animal, but the hyaena thought he would go and try to marry the daughter of a Mkamba."

5. A.W. Cardinall, *Tales Told in Togoland*, pp. 13-14. The quoted text follows Cardinall. The last sentence (not included by LB) raises the interesting speculation, in what shape was the woman driven away?

6. C.J. Andersson, *The Lion and the Elephant*, pp. 113-14.

7. Doke, *The Lambas of Northern Rhodesia*, p. 303. Doke explains *imfwiti*: "A man does not have to become possessed by a spirit of witchcraft or by a demon to become an *imfwiti*; the profession is one of choice. A man becomes an *imfwiti* merely by buying from some *imfwiti* whom he gets to know the necessary *ubwanga bwakulowa* (witchcraft medicine) . . ."
    David Livingstone, *Missionary Travels and Researches in South Africa* (1857), p. 527, and *Narrative of an Expedition on the Zambesi and its Tributaries*, p. 159.
    It is of some interest to extend the quotation a little further:

"Do you not see how he is trembling now?" We told them to ask him to change himself at once into a lion, and we would give him a cloth for the performance. "Oh, no," replied they; "if we tell him so, he may change himself and come when we are asleep and kill us." Having similar superstitions at home, they became as firm believers in the Pondoro as the natives of the village. We were told that he assumes the form of a lion and remains in the woods for days, and is sometimes absent for a whole month. His considerate wife has built him a hut or den, in which she places food and beer for her transformed lord, whose metamorphosis does not impair his human appetite.

[The wife takes a certain medicine to the forest which enables him to change back again to a man. He sends her to the forest to bring away the game he has killed.]

We saw the Pondoro of another village dressed in a fantastic style, with numerous charms hung around him, and followed by a troop of boys who were honouring him with rounds of shrill cheering.

And still further, p. 160:

It is believed also that the souls of departed Chiefs enter into lions and render them sacred. On one occasion, when we had shot a buffalo in the path beyond the Kafue, a hungry lion, attracted probably by the smell of the meat, came close to our camp, and roused up all hands by his roaring. Tuba Makoro, imbued with the popular belief that the beast was a Chief in disguise, scolded him roundly during his brief intervals of silence. "You a Chief, eh? You call yourself a Chief, do you? What kind of a Chief are you to come sneaking about in the dark, trying to steal our buffalo meat. Are you not ashamed of yourself? A pretty Chief, truly; you are like the scavenger beetle, and think of yourself only. You have not the heart of a Chief; why don't you kill your own beef? You must have a stone in your chest, and no heart at all, indeed!" Tuba Makoro producing no impression on the transformed Chief, one of the men, the most sedate of the party, who seldom spoke, took up the matter, and tried the lion in another strain. In his slow, quiet way he expostulated with him on the impropriety of such conduct to strangers, who had never injured him. "We were travelling peaceably through the country back to our own Chief. We never killed people, nor stole anything. The buffalo meat was ours, not his, and it did not become a great Chief like him to be prowling round in the dark, trying, like a hyaena, to steal the meat of strangers. He might go and hunt for himself, as there was plenty of meat in the forest." The Pondoro, being deaf to reason, and only roaring the louder, the men became angry and threatened to send a ball through him if he did not go away. They snatched up their guns to shoot him, but he prudently kept in the dark, outside of the luminous circle made by our camp fires, and there they did not like to venture. A little strychnine was put into a piece of meat, and throw to him, when he soon departed, and we heard no more of the majestic sneaker.

8. Paul du Chaillu, *The Country of the Dwarfs*. LB's reference is to pp. 77-79, but he names no edition, and there were many. Recorded editions begin in 1871, but the only one I could find was a popular edition of unstated date (probably 1875), issued in London by James Blackwood. Although a genuine record, du Chaillu's account of his African adventures and discovery of the pygmies reads like a boys' adventure novel. The events recorded belong to the year 1863. LB's summary quotation, though adequate, fails to

give much of the flavour of the original. I make no apology for including a longer extract, pp. 59-60 in the Blackwood edition.

In the evening, as Akondogo and I were seated together, the good fellow, smoking his huge pipe, said to me, "Chally, I have had a great deal of trouble since I have seen you. A leopard has killed two of my people, and I have had a great many palavers with their families on account of their death."

I said, "Akondogo, you could not help it; you are not chief over the leopards. But after the first man had been killed, why did you not make a trap to catch the leopard?"

"The leopard I mean," said he, "is not one that can be trapped; it was a man who had changed himself into a leopard, and then, after he had been a leopard for some time, he changed himself into a man again."

I said, "Akondogo, why do you talk to me in that way? You know I do not believe that men are turned into beasts, and afterward into men again. It is stupid for people to believe so, but I cannot shake that belief in you alombe (black men)."

Poor Akondogo said, "Chally, I assure you that there are men who change into leopards, and from leopards into men again."

Not wishing to argue the question, I said, "Never mind; tell me the story of your trouble." Then Akondogo once more filled his pipe with tobacco, gave three or four big puffs of smoke, which rose high in the air, and thus began:

"My people and myself had been in the woods several days collecting India-rubber. One day a man disappeared, and nothing could be found of him but a pool of blood. The next day another man disappeared, and in searching for him more blood was found. We all got alarmed, and I sent for a great doctor; he came and drank the *mboundou*, so that he might be able to say how these two deaths came about. After the *ouganga* (doctor) had drunk the *mboundou*, and as all the people stood round him asking him what had killed these two men, and just as we were waiting with breathless silence for what he was going to say, he spoke to me and said, 'Akondogo, your own child [his nephew Akosho] killed the two men.' Immediately Akosho was sent for and seized, and he answered that it was true that he had killed the two men, but that he could not help it; he remembered well that that day, as he was walking in the woods, he suddenly became a leopard; that his heart longed for blood, and that he had killed the two men, and then, after each murder, he became a man again.

"There was a great uproar in the village; the people shouted, 'Death to the *aniemba* Akosha!'

"But," said Akondogo, "I loved my boy so much that I said to the people, 'Let us not believe Akosha; he must have become a *kende* (idiot, fool).' But Akosho kept saying he had killed the men, and took us into the woods where lay the two bodies, one with the head cut off, and the other with the belly torn open.

"Upon this," said Akondogo, "I ordered Akosho to be bound with cords, and tied in a horizontal position to a post, and to have a fire lighted at his feet, and be burned slowly to death, all which was done, the people standing by until he expired."

The end of the story was so horrid that I shuddered. It was a case of monomania. Akosho believed that he had been turned into a leopard, and committed two murders, the penalty of which he paid with his life. Here, in our country, he would have been sent to the insane asylum.

["in our country": du Chaillu was a French American.]

9. Rev. Père F. Bösch, *Les Banyamwesi, Peuple de l'Afrique Orientale*, pp. 241-42.

10. Doke, *The Lambas of Northern Rhodesia*, p. 176. LB does not quote the first statement, but as it coincides interestingly with instances he has alluded to, I transcribe it.

11. Alexander Merensky, *Deutsche Arbeit am Njasza, Deutsch Ostafrika*, p. 119.

12. Thomas Morgan Thomas, *Eleven Years in Central South Africa*, p. 293. This "quotation" is partly paraphrase; it seems worth while to restore the original text:

> The following tradition professes to account for the magicians' use of the wolf: − An accomplished wizard finding the grave of a newly buried man, gave the corpse medicine, restored life, and transformed it into a wolf, which he employed as his servant to go on errands, dig his garden, and do other works, such as catching game, destroying the gardens of the people, their cattle, or themselves. The way this strange wolf is said to do his work is this: − Coming within hearing distance of the town or house doomed to suffer, it cries out, "*maye! maye!*" (woe! woe!). When the people hear this dreaded voice, they must not stir from the spot, but remain perfectly quiet, or else the calamity will be still worse than it was originally intended. Sometimes, perhaps, the wizard himself rides the wolf into the centre of the town for the sake of giving more effect to his evil design or curse, and thus occasionally he is found out. When the first man had been dug up and converted into the black wolf by the great wizard, it is said that other wizards followed the example, and hence the transformatory process became common. Some cases having been interrupted, however, − the wizards caught in the very act − the risen bodies have remained in an incomplete state, and these constitute the few idiots seen in the land.

13. Hugh A. Stayt, *The Bavenda*, p. 277.

14. W.E. Roth, "Games, Sports and Pastimes", p. 7.

15. Gunnar Landtman, "Folktales of the Kiwai Papuans", pp. 144, 323-24. In this tale Siváre is not killed by the crocodile but is later restored by the first wife and an amicable settlement is reached.

16. Ibid., p. 322. It may be well to add the information given by Landtman, that when the coconuts first came, Wée and Dobási were away fishing and so were not given any. This was the grievance for which they took their revenge. The conclusion of the tale makes an etiological point. The two rats run into a hole, but one peeps out and says to the people, "All time I humbug coconut belong you-fellow. All rat follow me-two, I beginning now." (I will always attack your coconuts. From now on all rats will do the same as we did.)

17. P.E. Tattevin, "Mythes et légendes du sud de l'île Pentecôte", pp. 872-73. The beginning of the story is as follows.

> A man and his wife, going to the plantation to work, left their two sons in the care of their grandmother, giving her a coconut for them to eat. The two children played at lizard-hunting, then became hungry. They asked their grandmother for food. "In good time," said the grandmother, "your parents have only just left." So they hunted more lizards and then

asked again. "In good time," she said again, 'your parents have scarcely started working yet." A third time they asked and she refused again. So, tired of waiting, they went off . . .

18. A Hardeland, *Dayacksch-Deutsch Wörterbuch*, p. 445.
19. Knud Rasmussen, "The Netsilik Eskimos: Social Life and Spiritual Culture", pp. 288-90.
    LB, *The "Soul" of the Primitive*, 1928. LB refers to the original issue (1925), p. 220.
20. Stith Thompson, *Tales of the North American Indians*, p. 93.
21. Knud Rasmussen, "Intellectual Culture of the Copper Eskimos", p. 198. Rasmussen records (but LB with delicacy refrains from repeating) that "It is said of the salmon-maker that he is open all the way from mouth to backside".
22. D. Jenness, "Myths and Traditions from North Alaska", p. 42A. LB's reference is to *deux vieillards* (two elderly persons) but Jenness's English text says plainly they were "an old couple who had no children".
23. George Amos Dorsey, "Traditions of the Skidi Pawnee", pp. 152-53. Dorsey's story is interesting but inconveniently long. I transcribe a little more of it than LB does. The story continues to relate in some detail how the boy and the pony go together to find the boy's parents, who have disappeared. The pony continues to talk to the boy. The chief admires and covets the pony. The pony advises the boy to accept the chief's challenge and an exchange is made. But in a buffalo hunt the pony's feet become dislocated and the chief reverses the exchange. The pony recovers and thereafter the boy refuses to part with him. In a battle the pony helps the boy to victory; he is now recognized as a brave and is made a chief. In the meantime the pony sires a colt. After this the pony returns to the earth but the colt remains. "So the boy went home and told his people that the pony had turned to mud."
24. Commonwealth of Australia, *Parliamentary Papers* (1929-30-31), vol. iv, "Report to the Council of the League of Nations on the Administration of the Territory of New Guinea" (by the Administrator, Evan A. Wisdom), p. 120.
25. LB notes:

> A Lama from Kumbum (Tibet) told Father Huc, who reports the incident not without irony, "You know that a good many travellers find themselves, from time to time, on rugged, toilsome roads. Some of these travellers are holy lamas on a pilgrimage . . . We aid them by sending horses to them . . . What we send to the travellers are paper horses." And therewith he ran off to his cell . . . (and) returned, his hands filled with bits of paper, on each of which was printed the figure of a horse, saddled and bridled and going at full gallop . . . "Tomorrow we shall ascend a high mountain, thirty *li* from the lamasery, and there we shall pass the day, saying prayers and sending off horses." – "How do you send them to the travellers?" – "Oh! the means are very easy. After a certain form of prayer, we take a packet of horses which we throw up into the air, the wind carries them away, and by the power of Buddha they are then changed into real horses, which offer themselves to the travellers. [Here LB's note ends.]

The source of this is le Père Évariste-Régis Huc, *Souvenirs d'un voyage dans la Tartarie, le Thibet et la Chine*. This was translated into English by William Hazlitt as *Huc and Gabet, Travels in Tartary, Thibet and China*. I follow

Hazlitt's text, taken from the edition ed. Professor Paul Pelliot (1928), II,
p. 73. Since LB uses the phrase "not without irony", it is difficult to resist
quoting a remark by Pelliot, who points out that Huc's "ardent imagination"
led him "on occasion to invent what he supposed himself to be merely
reporting; he had the artist's instinct . . . he cannot be trusted in details".
Nevertheless in a folkloric sense the paper horses might remind us of
another oriental custom he might have come across: the paper money
which is burnt by Chinese mourners to ease the financial needs of departed
souls. The name of le Père Gabet is customarily coupled with that of Huc
but he was a travelling companion only and not a co-author of the *Travels*.

26. To suggest a Greek comparison, who has not speculated with idle wonder
     about the internal economy, for example, of centaurs?

27. See chapter III, note 25.

28. P. te Wechtel, "Erinnerungen aus den Ost- und West-Dusun-Ländern
     (Borneo)", p. 126.

29. Fortunately the author immediately interprets this gibberish.

30. Raymond Firth, "Totemism in Polynesia", pp. 305-8. Firth explains *ata* as
     the relationship of a supernatural being to the animal which is its
     manifested form. It could be its shadow, its reflection or a (ghost) image.
     Atua is the supernatural spirit itself. It may enter animal bodies, or even
     trees or stones. (The first of the two paragraphs referring to bats is included
     only for the light it throws on the second; LB does not use it.)

31. Ibid., p. 318. Firth records this information in the native language with
     piecemeal English interpolations; here only the English is taken.

32. Th. Koch-Grünberg, *Vom Roroima zum Orinoco*, III, pp. 187-88. It clarifies
     the passage somewhat to begin the paragraph at its beginning, thus: "*Super-
     natural animals*: the distinction between man and beast is quite clouded in
     the native mind. This appears plainly in their myths, which are simply a
     precipitate of their beliefs. *Keyeme Rato* and other water monsters are seen
     sometimes as men, sometimes as animals. But these are true spirits; they
     are also numerous animal creatures . . ." Where the text is interrupted a
     number of examples (birds of prey, jaguars) follow. Connections with
     magical practices are also touched on.

33. Hobley, *Ethnology of A-Kamba and other East African Tribes*, p. 51.
     A.B. Ellis, *The Ewe-Speaking Peoples of the Slave Coast of West Africa*,
     pp. 73-74.

34. Viktor Lebzelter, *Eingeborenen Kulturen in Südwest und Süd-afrika*, p. 167.
     LB's note, which follows, is partly translation, partly summary.

     Among the Bergdama (South Africa), the body of a dead lion is burnt,
     because it is not an ordinary animal and they fear that otherwise it might
     return to life. (For precisely the same reason the corpses of sorcerers are
     cremated. The lion is an animal-sorcerer.) If any animal stops motionless
     in the middle of one's path, and when one picks up a stone to throw at it,
     some power within one arrests one's hand, it will be a spirit-animal.
     (That is, it will be a dead person in animal form.) If a man hunts an
     animal and it shows no timidity as animals normally do, he will pay no
     further attention to it. That animal was no common beast, but a ghost.
     As the spirits of the dead can transform themselves into any object, so
     one can never tell whether a fruit is a true part of vegetable nature or a
     transformed ghost. If one eats the sweet resin of a certain tree and then
     becomes ill, it will be immediately concluded that it was not a real resin
     but a ghost. Supposing an animal comes into one's hut, be it a harmless

frog, a small beetle, or a venomous snake, one dare do nothing to it. No more may one hunt any of the larger game animals once it runs across the place where people live and work. While I was at Windhoek two badgers, which are highly valued as epicure food, paid a visit to the native quarter and ensconced themselves in an empty hut. All the huts in the area were immediately vacated and only after some days was anyone bold enough to come back anywhere near it.

35. E.g., black cats are lucky; three magpies are a portent, etc.
36. Hardeland, *Dayacksch Deutsch Wörterbuch*, pp. 24-25. LB quotes half of Hardeland's description only. It continues, "Sacrifices are made to them and the natives only dare to kill them, with the aid of magicians, when a blood revenge is called for after one of them has killed a near kinsman."
37. D.F. Bleek, ed., *Beliefs and Customs of the !Xam Bushmen*, p. 167.
38. Karl von den Steinen, *Unter den Naturvölken Zentral-Brasiliens* (Johnson reprint), pp. 201 and 351 (the quotation draws on both).
39. Charles Hose and W. McDougall, "The Relations between Men and Animals", p. 205.
40. Alanson Skinner, "Social Life and Ceremonial Bundles of the Menomini Indians", p. 132. LB quotes the first part only of Skinner's statement.
    James A. Teit. From a section on the Coeur d'Alène in "The Salishan Tribes of the Western Plateaus", 184. Teit goes on to detail the ceremonial respect paid to the slaughtered bear.
    E.W. Nelson, "The Eskimo about Bering Strait", p. 438. LB omits the bracketed sentence.
41. See chapter II, p. 71 and notes.
42. The first quotation is from a review by W.A. Unkrieg of Dr Hans Findersen, *Reisen und Forschungen in Nord Sibirien*, in *Zeitschrift für Ethnologie* LXII (1930), p. 377.
    Rev. J. Batchelor, *The Ainu and their Folklore*. Various references: e.g. p. 8, "This animal is certainly looked on as the great totem god of the whole race". A scrap of folklore follows, in line with the same human-animal ancestor-traditions as LB points out elsewhere.
    Skinner, "Political and Ceremonial Organization of the Plains-Ojibway", p. 541.
    James Mooney, "Myths of the Cherokee", pp. 29 ff. P. 231 has: "each animal had his appointed station and duty. Thus, the Walasi frog was the marshall and leader in the council, while the Rabbit was the messenger . . . he was also the great trickster and mischief maker. The bear figures as having been originally a man, with human form and nature."
43. Batchelor, *The Ainu and their Folklore*, pp. 337-38. Batchelor also mentions the inducement that the swallower will become rich.
44. Diedrich Westermann, *Die Kpelle, ein Negerstamm in Liberia*, p. 219. Inaccessible for checking. LB's punctuation leaves it uncertain where the first quotation ends. The last sentence of the second, given as Westermann's, could equally well be LB's own text.
45. R.S. Rattray, "The African Child in Proverb, Folklore and Fact", p. 469.
46. See chapter II, pp. 65-66 (intimate native knowledge, without science, of the natural world).
47. The quoted verses are from La Fontaine, possibly as LB found them cited by

P. Saintyves in his commentary on "Peau d'Âne", *Les Contes de Perrault*
(Paris, 1823), p. 187:
   et moi-même,
   Si Peau-d'Âne m'était conté,
   J'y prendrais un plaisir extrême.
As *Peau d'Âne* is not very familiar to English-speaking children I have
substituted a reference, still to Perrault, that they would be more likely to
recognize.

Appendix

1. E.B. Tylor, *Primitive Culture*, I, pp. 426, 23, 273.
2. Tylor, *Anthropology, An Introduction to the Study of Man and Civilization,*
   p. 388.
   Ibid., p. 396.
3. Paul Wirz, *Die Marind-anim von Holländisch Süd-Neu-Guinea*, II, iii, p. 105.
4. Ibid., p. 107.
5. Ibid.

Bibliography

The following list represents works which have been used or referred to by Lévy-Bruhl, and in addition some few which have been referred to in the notes. Where English language versions were known and accessible they have been preferred whenever possible. In some instances of books not available to the translator in Australia, reference has been made by means of xeroxed passages provided by overseas libraries. Where it has not been possible to sight the work at all, the entry is marked n.s. (not seen).

Adam, Leonhard. "Stammesorganization und Häuptlingstum der Wakashstämme". *Zeitschrift fur vergleichende Rechtswissenschaft,* XXXV. N.s. and untraced.

Andersson, Charles John (Karl Johan). *The Lion and the Elephant.* Ed. L. Lloyd. London: Hurst & Blackett, 1873.

Bamler, G. See Neuhauss, R. *Deutsch Neu-Guinea.*

Batchelor, Rev. John. *The Ainu and their Folk-Lore.* London: The Religious Tract Society, 1901.

Bégouen, Le comte, and Breuil, l'Abbé H. "De quelques figures hybrides (mi-humaines et mi-animales) de la caverne des Trois-Frères", (Arriège). *Revue Anthropologique* XLVI (1934). University of Paris, Institut d'ethnologie.

Benedict, Ruth. "Tales of the Cochiti Indians". *Bulletin* 98 (1931). Smithsonian Institution. Bureau of American Ethnology.

Berndt, Ronald Murray. *Djanggawul: an Aboriginal religious cult of north-eastern Arnhem Land.* London: Routledge and Kegan Paul, 1952 and Melbourne: F.W. Cheshire, 1952.

_____. and Berndt, Catherine. *The World of the First Australians.* Sydney: Ure Smith, 1952, 1964, etc.

_____. *Kunapipi, a study of an Australian religious cult.* Melbourne: F.W.C. Cheshire, 1951.

_____. *Love Songs of Arnhem Land.* The same texts also issued as *Three*

Faces of Love: traditional Aboriginal song-poetry. Melbourne: Nelson, 1976.

Berthoud, H. "Weitere Thonga-Märchen". *Zeitschrift für eingeborene Sprachen (Africa und Übersee)*, Jahrgang XXI (1930-31). Berlin: D. Reimer. Reprint. New York: H.P. Kraus, 1966.

Bleek, D.F., ed. "Beliefs and Customs of the !Xam Bushmen. From material collected by Dr W.H. Bleek and Miss L.C. Lloyd, between 1870 and 1880, Part V, The Rain." *Bantu Studies* VII (1933). Johannesburg: University of the Witwatersrand.

Boas, Franz, and Rink, H.J. "Eskimo Tales and Songs". *Journal of American Folk-Lore* II (1889). Boston, Mass.: American Folk-Lore Society. Reprint. New York: H.P. Kraus, 1963.

_____. "Folk Tales of Salishan and Sahaptin Tribes, collected by James A. Teit, Livingston Farrand, Marian K. Gould, Harold J. Spinden. Ed. Franz Boas." *Memoirs* XI (1917). Boston, Mass.: American Folk-Lore Society. Reprint. New York: H.P. Kraus, 1969.

_____. "Tsimshian Mythology". *Report* 31 (1916). Washington: Smithsonian Institution, Bureau of American Ethnology.

Bösch, Père F. (des Pères Blancs). *Les Banyamwezi, peuple de l'Afrique Orientale.* Münster: Anthropos Bibliothek, Aschendorff, 1930.

Breuil, l'Abbé H. See Bégouen, Le comte; also, Cartailhac, E.

Bride, T.F., ed. *Letters from Victorian Pioneers.* Melbourne: Govt. Printer, 1898. See also Thomas, Wm.

Callaway, Henry (Missionary Bishop of Kaffraria). *Nursery Tales, Traditions and Histories of the Zulus.* Natal (Springvale): J.A. Blair, 1868.

Cardinall, Sir Allan Wolsey. *Tales Told in Togoland. To which is added the Mythical and Traditional History of Dagomba.* Ed. E.F. Tamakloe. London: O.U.P., 1931.

Cartailhac, Émile, and Breuil, l'Abbé H. *La Caverne d'Altamira à Santillane*, près Santander (*Espagne*). Monaco: Impr. de Monaco, 1906.

Cassirer, Ernst. *The Philosophy of Symbolic Forms.* Translated by R. Manheim. New Haven, Conn.: Yale U.P., 1955. *Philosophie der symbolischen Formen.* Berlin, 1925.

Cazeneuve, Jean. *Lucien Lévy-Bruhl, sa vie, son oeuvre, avec un exposé de sa philosophie.* Paris: Presses Universitaires de France, 1963. *Lucien Lévy-Bruhl.* Translated Peter Rivière. New York: Harper and Row, 1972.

Chatelain, Heli. *Folk-Tales of Angola.* Fifty tales, with Ki-Mbundu text, literal English translation, Introduction and notes. Collected and edited by Heli Chatelain. Boston and New York: American Folk-Lore Society, 1894.

Chewings, Charles. A vocabulary of the Arrenda language and dialects, as spoken between Oodnadatta and Tennant Creek. Unpublished MS. Accessible (1) in working sheets (Barr Smith Library, University of Adelaide) and (2) in notebook form S.A. Museum Library, Adelaide, South Australia.

Dale, A.M. See Smith, E.W.

De Angulo, Jaime. "La Psychologie religieuse des Achumawi". *Anthropos* (Ephemeris) XXIII (1928). Salzburg.

De Goeje, C.H. "Oudheden uit Suriname, of zoek naar den Amazonen". *West-Indische Gids* III (1932). N.s. and untraced.

Doke, Clement M. *The Lambas of Northern Rhodesia. A study of their customs and beliefs.* London: G. Harrap, 1931.

Donner, Kai (Karl Reinhold). *Bei den Samojeden in Sibirien.* Translated from the Swedish W.H. von der Mülbe. Stuttgart: Strecker & Schröder, 1926.

Dorsey, George Amos. "Traditions of the Skidi Pawnee". *Memoirs* VIII (1904). Boston, Mass.: American Folk-Lore Society.

Du Chaillu, Paul. *The Country of the Dwarfs.* London: Blackwood, n.d. (1875?). Various editions, New York and London, from 1871.

Dumarest, Father Noel. "Notes on Cochiti, New Mexico". *Memoirs* VI (1919). Menasha, Wis.: American Anthropological Association.

Durkheim, Émile. *The Elementary Forms of the Religious Life. A study in Religious Sociology.* Translated by J.W. Swain. London: Geo. Allen & Unwin, 1915. *Les Formes élémentaires de la vie religieuse; le Système totémique en Australie.* Paris: Press Universitaires de France, 1912.

Ehrenreich, Paul. "Die Mythen und Legenden der Südamerikanischen Urvölker und ihre Beziehungen zu denen Nordamerikas und der alten Welt". *Zeitschrift für Ethnologie* Supplement (1905). Berlin: Berliner Gesellschaft für Anthropologie.

Elkin, A.P. *Aboriginal Men of High Degree.* 2nd ed. St. Lucia: University of Queensland Press, 1977.

———. "Rock-paintings of North-West-Australia". *Oceania* I (1930-31). Melbourne: Macmillan. Published for the Australian National Research Council.

———. "The Secret Life of the Australian Aborigines". *Oceania* III (1932-33).

———. "Totemism in North-Western Australia". *Oceania* III (1932-33).

Ellis, Alfred Burdon. *The Ewe-speaking Peoples of the Slave Coast of West Africa, their Religion, Manners, Customs, Laws, Languages,* London: Chapman & Hall, 1890. Reprint. Oosterhout, Netherlands: Anthropological Publications, 1966.

Evans-Pritchard, E.E. *Theory of Primitive Religion.* Oxford: Clarendon Press, 1965. (Chapter IV is on Lévy-Bruhl.)

Findersen, Dr Hans. *Reisen und Forschungen in Nord Sibirien.* Berlin, 1929. Reviewed by W.A. Unkrieg in *Zeitschrift für Ethnologie* LXII (1930), p. 377.

Firth, Raymond. "Anthropology in Australia, 1926-32 and After". *Oceania* III (1932-33).

———. "Totemism in Polynesia". *Oceania* I (1930-31).

Fison, Rev. Lorimer, and Howitt, A.W. *Kamilaroi and Kurnai. Group marriage and relationship, and marriage by elopement, drawn chiefly from the usage of the Australian Aborigines; also the Kurnai tribe, their customs in peace and war.* Introduction L. Morgan. Melbourne: Geo. Robertson, 1880.

Fortune, R.F. *Sorcerers of Dobu. The Social Anthropology of the Dobu Islanders of the Western Pacific.* Introduction M. Malinowski. London: Routledge, 1932.

Frobenius, L. "Das unbekannte Afrika". *Journal of the South-West Africa Scientific Society* V (1931), p. 54. N.s. and untraced.

Gifford, Edward Winslow. "Yuma Dreams and Omens". *Journal of American Folk-Lore* XXXIX (1926). Boston, Mass.: the American Folk-Lore Society.

Gillen, F.J. See Spencer, Sir Walter Baldwin.

Goddard, Pliny Earle. "Life and Culture of the Hupa". Berkeley: *University of California Publications in American Archaeology and Ethnology,* 1903.

Graebner, Fr. *Das Weltbild der Primitiven.* Cited by Ernst Cassirer.

Grey, Sir George. *Journals of Two Expeditions of Discovery in North West and Western Australia during the years 1837, 1838 and 1839. With observations of the moral and physical character of the Aboriginal inhabitants.* 2 vols. London: T. & W. Boone, 1841.

Haddon, Alfred Cort, ed. Cambridge Anthropological Expedition to Torres Straits. *Report.* 6 vols. Cambridge: Cambridge University Press, 1901-35.

———. "Mythical Beings". *Report,* vol. VI, pp. 314-16.

———. "Personal Ornaments and Clothing". *Report,* vol. IV, pp. 33-62.

Hardeland, A. *Dayacksch-Deutsch Wörterbuch.* Amsterdam: F. Muller, 1859.

Harrington, J.P. "Tobacco among the Karuk Indians of California". *Bulletin* 94, 1932. Washington: Smithsonian Institution, Bureau of American Ethnology.

Healy, John J. *Literature and the Aborigine in Australia 1770–1975.* St Lucia: University of Queensland Press, 1978.

Hobley, Charles William. *Ethnology of A-Kamba and Other East African Tribes.* Cambridge: Cambridge University Press, 1910.

Hose, Charles (Resident of the Baram District), and McDougall, W. "The Relations between Men and Animals". *Journal* XXXI (1901). London: The Royal Anthropological Institute of Great Britain and Ireland.

Howitt, Alfred W., and Fison, L. *Kamilaroi and Kurnai.* See Fison, L.

———. *The Native Tribes of South East Australia.* London: Macmillan, 1904.

Hubert, H. See Mauss, E.

Huc, le Père Évariste-Régis. *Souvenirs d'un voyage dans la Tartarie, le Thibet et la Chine, pendant les années 1844, 1845 et 1846.* Paris: Le Clère, 1850. Translated by Wm. Hazlitt, 1853. Hazlitt's version reprint. (ed. P. Pelliot), London: Routledge, 1928. Joseph Gabet, whose name is commonly associated with that of Huc, was Huc's travelling companion but not a co-author.

Im Thurn, Sir Everard Ferdinand. *Among the Indians of Guiana; being sketches, chiefly anthropologic, from the interior of British Guiana,* etc. London: Kegan, Paul, Trench & Co., 1883.

Irle, J. "Die Religion der Herero", *Archiv für Anthropologie,* New Series XV (43rd issue). Braunschweig: F. Vieweg, 1917.

Jenness, Diamond. "Eskimo Folk-Lore". Canadian Arctic Expedition 1913-18, *Report XIII,* Ottawa, 1928. Part A: "Myths and Traditions from Northern Alaska, the Mackenzie River and Coronation Gulf"; Part B: "Eskimo String Figures".

Junod, Henri A. *The Life of a South African Tribe* (Thonga tribe). 2 vols. London: D. Nutt, 1912 and 1913. N.s. This is probably the work referred to by LB.

Keysser, C. "Aus dem Leben der Kai". See Neuhauss, R. *Deutsch Neu-Guinea.*

Koch-Grünberg, Theodor. *Vom Roroima zum Orinoco. Ergebnisse einer Reise in Nord-Brasilien und Venezuela, in den Jahren 1911-1913, unternommen und hrsg. im Auftrage und mit Mitteln des Baesler-instituts in Berlin.* Berlin: D. Reimer, 1916-1917. 5 vols. I: *Schilderung der Reise;* II: *Mythen und Legenden der Tulipang und Arekuna-Indianer;* III: *Ethnographie;* IV: *Sprachen;* V: *Typen-Atlas.* Vols. II-V have imprint, Stuttgart: Strecker und Schröder.

———. *Zwei Jahre unter den Indianern, Reisen in Nordwest-Brasilien 1903-1905.* Stuttgart: Strecker und Schröder, 1909. Later editions entitled *Zwei Jahre bei den Indianern* etc. Revised 1923. N.s.

Kroeber, Alfred Louis. "Handbook of the Indians of California". *Bulletin 78* (1925). Washington: Smithsonian Institution, Bureau of American Ethnology. Reprint. Berkeley: California Book Co., 1953.

Kruyt, A.C. "De Timoreezen". *Bijdragen tot de taal-, en volkenkunde van Nederlands-Indie uitgegeven door het Koninglijk Instituut voor de taal,* etc., Deel 79. 's-Gravenhage: Martinus Nijhoff, 1923.

Landtman, Gunnar. *Ethnological Collection from the Kiwai Districts of British New Guinea in the National Museum of Finland.* Helsingfors: Commission of the Antell Collection, 1933.

———. "Folk-tales of the Kiwai Papuans". *Acta Societatis Scientiarum Fennicae.* Tom. XLVII (1917). Helsingfors: Finnish Society of Literature, 1917.

———. *The Kiwai Papuans of British New Guinea. A native-born instance of Rousseau's ideal community.* Introduction A.C. Haddon. London: Macmillan, 1927.

———. "The Origins of Sacrifice". In *Essays Presented to C.G. Seligman,* ed. L.E. Evans-Pritchard, Raymond Firth, Bronislaw Malinowski and Isaac Schapera. London: Kegan, Paul, Trench, Trubner & Co., 1934.

Lang, Andrew. *Custom and Myth.* London: Longmans, Green & Co., 1884. (In Chapter III Lang gives instructions how to make a bullroarer, adding a warning of danger.)

_____. *The Secret of the Totem*, London: Longmans, Green & Co., 1905.

_____. *Myth, Ritual and Religion*, London: Longmans, Green & Co., 1887. (NB Vol. II, Ch. xii.)

Lebzelter, Victor. *Rassen und Kulturen in Südafrika*. Vol. I, *Die Vorgeschichte von Süd- und Südwest Afrika*. Vol. II, *Eingeborenenkulturen in Südwest und Süd-Afrika*. Leipzig: K.W. Hiersemann, 1930.

Leenhardt, Maurice. "Documents Néo-Calédoniens". *Travaux et Memoires*, 1932. University of Paris, l'Institut d'Ethnologie. (Published under the direction of L. Lévy-Bruhl.)

Lehner, Stefan. See Neuhauss, R. *Deutsch Neu-Guinea*.

Leichhardt, Ludwig. *Journal of an Overland Expedition in Australia from Moreton Bay to Port Essington . . . during the years 1844-45*. London: T. and W. Boone, 1847.

Leonhardi, Freiherr von. See Strehlow, Carl.

Lévi-Strauss, Claude. *The Savage Mind*. London: Weidenfeld & Nicolson, 1966. *La Pensée sauvage*. Paris: Plon, 1962.

_____. *The Scope of Anthropology*. London: Cape, 1977. *Leçon inaugurale*. Paris: Collège de France, Jan. 5 1960.

Lévy-Bruhl, Lucien. The principal works of Lévy-Bruhl with a bearing on *Primitive Mythology* are given in the order of their original appearance.
Les Fonctions mentales dans les sociétés inférieures. Paris: Alcan, 1910. *How Natives Think*. Translated Lilian A. Clare. London: Geo. Allen & Unwin, 1926.

_____. *La Mentalité primitive*. Paris: Alcan, 1922. *Primitive Mentality*. Translated L.A. Clare. London: Geo. Allen & Unwin, 1923.

_____. *L'Âme primitive*. Paris: Alcan, 1925. *The "Soul" of the Primitive*. Translated L.A. Clare. London: Geo. Allen & Unwin, 1928.

_____. *Le Surnaturel et la nature dans la mentalité primitive*. Paris: Alcan, 1931. *Primitives and the Supernatural*. Translated L.A. Clare. London: Geo. Allen & Unwin, 1935.

_____. *La Mythologie primitive*. Paris: Alcan, 1935.

_____. *L'Expérience mystique et les symboles chez les primitifs*. Paris: Alcan, 1938.

_____. *Les Carnets de Lévy-Bruhl*. Paris: Presses Universitaires de France, 1949. *Lucien Lévy-Bruhl: The Notebooks on Primitive Mentality*. Translated Peter Rivière, Oxford: Blackwell, 1975.

See also Cazeneuve, J. and Evans Pritchard, E.E.

Livingstone, D. *Missionary Travels and Researches in South Africa*. London, 1857.

_____. and Livingstone, Charles. *Narrative of an Expedition to the Zambesi and its Tributaries; and of the Discovery of the lakes Shirwa and Nyassa, 1858-1864*. London: J. Murray, 1865.

_____. *A Popular Account of Dr Livingstone's Expedition to the Zambesi etc. Abridged from the larger work*. London: J. Murray, 1887.

Lloyd, L.C. See Bleek, D.F.

Love, J.R.B. *Stone-Age Bushmen of Today: Life and Adventures among a Tribe of Savages in North Western Australia*. London: Blackie, 1936.

McConnel, Ursula. "The Wik-Munkan Tribe". *Oceania* I (1930-31).

McDougall, W. See Hose, C.

Malinowski, Bronislaw. *Argonauts of the Western Pacific, Native Enterprise and Adventure in . . . Melanesia and New Guinea* etc. London: Routledge, 1922.

_____. "Fishing in the Trobriand Islands". *Man, A Monthly Record of Anthropological Science* XVIII, 1918. London: Royal Anthropological Institute of Great Britain and Ireland.

_____. *Myth in Primitive Psychology*, London: Paul, Trench, Trubner and Co. (Psyche Miniatures), 1926.

Mauss, Marcel. Quoted from Société Française de Philosophie, *Bulletin*, 23e année, 1926. N.s.

_____. and Hubert, H. "De Quelques résultats de la sociologie religieuse, le sacrifice, l'origine des pouvoirs magiques, la représentation du temps". In *Travaux de l'Année sociologique*. Ed. E. Durkheim. Paris: University of Paris, 1909.

Meier, Joseph. *Mythen und Erzählungen der Küstenbewohner der Gazelle-Halbinsel (Neu- Pommern). Im Urtext aufgezeichnet und ins Deutsch übertragen von P. Jos. Meier, M.S.C.* Münster: Anthropos Bibliothek, vol. I, part I. Aschendorff, 1909.

Merensky, Alexander. *Deutsche Arbeit am Njasza, Deutsch Ostafrika.* Berlin: Buchhandlung der Berliner Evangelistischen Missionsgesellschaft, 1894.

Meyer, P.H. "Wunekau, oder Sonnenverehrung in Neuguinea". Part iii, *Anthropos* (Ephemeris) XXVIII (1933). Salzburg.

Moffat, Robert. *Missionary Labours in Southern Africa*. London: John Snow & Co., 1842. Reprint. New York: Johnson, 1969.

Mooney, James. "Myths of the Cherokee". *Report* 19, part I (1900). Washington: Smithsonian Institution, Bureau of American Ethnology. Reprint. New York: Johnson, 1970.

_____. and Olbrechts, F.M. "The Swimmer Manuscript, Cherokee Sacred Formulas and Medical Prescriptions, by James Mooney; revised, completed and edited by Frans M. Olbrechts". *Bulletin* 99 (1932). Washington: Smithsonian Institution, Bureau of American Ethnology. (A portrait of Swimmer is reproduced in "Myths of the Cherokee", p. 277.)

Nelson, Edward William. "The Eskimos about Bering Strait". *Report* 18, part i (1899). Washington: Smithsonian Institution, Bureau of American Ethnology.

Neuhauss, Richard. *Deutsch Neu-Guinea*. 3 vols. Berlin: D. Reimer, 1911. Vol i is a general survey by Neuhauss. Vol ii is a *Völkeratlas* (photographs of representative types). Vol iii consists of reports contributed by missionary observers: (1) Ch. Keysser, "Aus dem Leben der Kai". (2) Stolz (no initial), "Die Umgebung von Kap Konig Wilhelm". (3) Heinrich Zahn, "Die Jabim". (4) Stefan Lehner, "Bukaua". (5) G. Bamler, "Tami".

Nordenskiöld, Erland. "La Conception de l'âme chez les Indiens Cuna de l'isthme de Panamà (la signification de trois mots cuna, *purba, niga* et *kuigin*)". *Journal*, New style XXIV (1932). Paris: la Société des Americanistes.

———. "Faiseurs de miracles, et voyants chez les Indiens Cuna". *Revista* (1932). Tucuman (Argentina): Universidad nacional de Tucuman, Instituto de Etnología.

Olbrechts, Frans M. See Mooney, James. "The Swimmer Manuscript".

Packer, R.L. "Notes on the Mythology and Religion of the Nez Percés". *Journal of American Folk-Lore* IV (1891). Boston, Mass.: American Folk-Lore Society.

Parker, Mrs. K. Langloh (nee Catherine Somerville Field, afterwards Stow). *The Euahlayi Tribe*. London: Constable, 1905.

Peekel, P.G. (Missionar in Namatanai, Neu-Mecklenburg.) *Auf dem mittleren Neu-Mecklenburg, Bismarck-Archipel, Südsee*. Münster: Anthropos Bibliothek I. iii, Aschendorff, 1910.

Perrault, Charles. See Saintyves, P.

Piddington, Ralph, "The Totemic System of the Karadjeri Tribe." *Oceania* II (1931-32).

———. and Marjorie Piddington. "Report of Fieldwork in North Western Australia". *Oceania* II (1931-32).

———. "The Totemic System of the Karadjeri Tribe". *Oceania* II (1931-32).

Pink, Olive. "Spirit Ancestors in a Northern Aranda Horde Country". *Oceania* IV (1933-34).

Prescott, W.H. *Conquest of Mexico* (first appeared 1843).

Preuss, Konrad Theodor. *Der religiöse Gehalt der Mythen*. Tübingen: J.C.B. Mohr, 1933.

———. *Religion und Mythologie der Uitoto*. Göttingen: Vandenhoeck and Ruprecht, 1921.

Radcliffe-Brown, A.R. *The Andaman Islanders*. A Study in Social Anthropology. Cambridge: Cambridge University Press, 1922.

———. "Notes on Totemism in Eastern Australia". *Journal* of the Royal Anthropological Institute, London (July-Dec. 1929), pp. 399-415. Noticed and reviewed in *Oceania* I (1930-31), p. 252 (unsigned).

———. "Three Tribes of Western Australia". *Journal* XLIII (1913). London: The Royal Anthropological Institute of Great Britain and Ireland.

———. "The Social Organization of Australian Tribes". *Oceania* I (1930-31).

Rasmussen, Knud. *Across Arctic America. Narrative of the Fifth Thule Expedition*. New York: Putnam, 1927. Abridged translation of *Fra Grønland til Stillehavet*. Copenhagen: Gyldendal, 1925.

———. *Thulefahrt*. 2 Jahre im Schlitten durch unerforschtes Eskimoland. Frankfurt a. M.: Frankfürter Societäts-Druecke, 1926. N.s.

———. Report. *Fifth Thule Expedition 1921-24. The Danish Expedition to*

Arctic North America in charge of Knud Rasmussen. 16 vols. Copenhagen: Gyldendalske Boghandel, 1927-1932. Danish and English versions. The relevant parts of the *Report* are: Vol. VII, part i, "Intellectual Culture of the Iglulik Eskimos"; part ii, "Observations on the Intellectual Culture of the Caribou Eskimos"; part iii, "Iglulik and Caribou Eskimo texts" (1929-30); Vol. VIII, "The Netsilik Eskimos, Social Life and Spiritual Culture" (1931); and Vol. IX, "Intellectual Culture of the Copper Eskimos" (1932).

Rattray, Capt. R.S. "The African Child in Proverb, Folklore and Fact". *Africa* VI (1933). Oxford: Oxford University Press

_____. *Ashanti Proverbs.* Oxford: Clarendon Press, 1916.

_____. *Religion and Art in Ashanti.* Oxford: Clarendon Press, 1927.

Rink, Heinrich Johannes. See Boas, F.

Roth, Walter E. *North Queensland Ethnography.* Brisbane: Government Printer. *Bulletin* 2, "The Structure of the Koko-Yimidir Language" (1901).

Bulletin 4, "Games, sports and Pastimes" (1902).

Bulletin 5, "Superstition, Magic and Medicine" (1903).

Bulletin 8, "Notes on Government, Morals and Crime" (1906).

Bulletin 18, "Social and Individual Nomenclature" (published with *Records of the Australian Museum,* Sydney, 1910 (*Records,* vol VIII, Sydney, 1910-13).

Saint-Périer, René de. "Gravures anthropomorphes de la grotte d'Isturitz". *L'Anthropologie* 44 (1934). Paris.

Saintyves, P. (Pseud. of E. Nourry). *Les Contes de Perrault et les récits parallèles, leurs origines, coûtumes primitives et liturgies populaires.* Paris: E. Nourry, 1923.

Schapera, Isaac. *The Khoisan Peoples of South Africa, Bushmen and Hottentots.* London: Routledge, 1930.

Seligman, C.G. and Seligman, Brenda Z. *Pagan Tribes of the Nilotic Sudan.* London: Routledge, 1932.

Skinner, Alanson. "Political Organization, Cults and Ceremonies of the Plains-Ojibway and Plains-Cree Indians". American Museum of Natural History. *Anthropological Papers* XI, part VI. New York: the Trustees, 1914.

_____. "Social Life and Ceremonial Bundles of the Menomini Indians". American Museum of Natural History, *Anthropological Papers* XIII, part I. New York: the Trustees, 1913.

Smith, Edwin W. and Dale, Andrew Murray. *The Ila Speaking Peoples of Northern Rhodesia.* London: Macmillan, 1920.

Smyth, R. Brough. *The Aborigines of Victoria. With notes relating to the habits of the natives of other parts of Australia and Tasmania.* Melbourne: J. Ferres (Govt. Printer), 1878.

Speck, Frank G. "Penobscot Shamanism". *Memoirs* VI (1919). New York: The American Anthropological Association.

Spencer, Sir Walter Baldwin. "Totemism in Australia". *Presidential Address,* Australian Association for the Advancement of Science,

Section F (Ethnology and Anthropology), Dunedin, New Zealand, 7 January 1904).

_____. *Native Tribes of the Northern Territory of Australia*. London: Macmillan, 1914.

_____., ed. *Report on the Work of the Horn Scientific Expedition to Central Australia*. London, 1896.

_____ and Frazer, Sir J.G. and others. *Scientific Correspondence*. Ed. R.R. Marett and T.K. Penniman. Oxford: Clarendon Press, 1932.

_____ and Gillen, Frances, J. *The Native Tribes of Central Australia*. London: Macmillan, 1899.

_____. and Gillen, F.J. *The Arunta: a Study of a Stone Age People*. London: Macmillan, 1927. (F.J. Gillen died in 1912.)

Spinden, Herbert J. "Nez-Percé Tales". In "Folk Tales of Salishan and Sahaptin Tribes". See Boas, F., ed.

Stanner, W.E.H. "The Daly River Tribes". *Oceania* III (1932-33).

Stayt, Hugh A. *The Bavenda*. Published for the International Institute of African Studies. London: Humphrey Milford, 1931.

Stolz, -. "Die Umgebung von Kap Konig Wilhelm". See Neuhauss, R.

Strehlow, Carl. *Die Aranda- und Loritjastämme in Zentral-Australien*. This monumental work, the publication of which by the Stätischer Völkermuseum, Frankfurt am Main, was interrupted by the 1914–18 war, was edited until his death in 1910 by Moritz, Freiherr von Leonhardi, and thereafter by Bernhardt Hagen, whose death also is noted in the final volume. The work was issued as follows:

Vol I, *Mythen, Sagen und Märchen des Arandastammes*. Gesammelt von Carl Strehlow, Missionar in Hermannsburg, Süd-Australien. Bearbeitet von Moritz, Freiherr von Leonhardi. Frankfurt a. M., 1907.

Vol II, *Mythen, Sagen and Märchen des Loritjastammes*. Die totemistischen Vorstellungen und die Tjurunga der Aranda und Loritja. Gesammelt und dargestellt von Carl Strehlow, etc., 1908.

Vol. III, *Die totemistischen Kulte der Aranda- und Lorijastämme*. Part 1, *Allgemeine Einleitung* und *Die totemistischen Kulte des Arandastammes*, 1910; Part 2, Die totemistischen Kulte des Loritjastammes, 1911;

Vol. IV, *Das soziale Leben der Aranda- und Loritjastämme*. Part 1, 1913; Part 2, 1915.

Vol. V, *Die materielle Kultur der Aranda- und Loritjastämme*. Mit einem Anhang: *Erklärung der Eingeborenen-Namen*, 1920.

Strehlow, Theodor Georg Heinrich. "Ankotarinja, an Aranda Myth". *Oceania* IV (1933-34).

_____. *Aranda Traditions*. Carlton: Melbourne University Press, 1947.

_____. *Journey to Horseshoe Bend*. Sydney: Angus & Robertson, 1969.

_____. *Songs of Central Australia*. Sydney: Angus & Robertson, 1970.

Taplin, Rev. George. *The Narrinyeri*. Adelaide: J.T. Shawyer, 1874. Also included in J.D. Woods, ed., *The Native Tribes of South Australia*. Adelaide: Wigg, 1879.

Tattevin, P.E. "Mythes et Légendes du sud de l'Île Pentecôte". *Anthropos* (Ephemeris) XXVI (1931). Salzburg.

Teit, James A. "Okanagon Tales" and "Thompson Tales", see Boas, F. ed., "Folk Tales of Salishan and Sahaptin Tribes".

———. "Traditions of the Thompson River Indians. Collected and edited by James A. Teit". *Memoirs* VI (1898). Boston, Mass.: American Folk-Lore Society.

———. "The Salishan Tribes of the Western Plateaus". *Report* 45 (1927-28). Washington: the Smithsonian Institution, Bureau of American Ethonology.

Te Wechtel, P. "Erinnerungen aus den Ost- und West-Dusun-Ländern, In besonderem Hinblick auf die animistische Lebensauffassung der Dayak". Von P. te Wechtel, Kapitan der Infanterie der Nederl. Indischen Armee. *International Archives of Ethnography*, XXIII. Leiden: E.J. Brill, 1915.

Thomas, Thomas Morgan. *Eleven Years in Central South Africa. A journey into the Interior, Sketch of recently discovered diamond and gold fields – Umzilikazi, his country and people – a brief history of the Zambesi missions*. London: J. Snow, 1872.

Thomas, William. See Bride, T.F.

Thompson, Stith. *Tales of the North American Indians*. Bloomington and London: Indiana University Press, 1967. First issued 1929.

Tylor, Sir Edward Burnett. *Anthropology. An introduction to the study of Man and Civilisation*. London: Macmillan, 1881.

———. *Primitive Culture*. London: John Murray, 1871. Revised ed., 1921.

Van Baal, J. *Dema*. Description and analysis of Marind-anim culture (South New Guinea). With the collaboration of Father J. Verschueren, M.S.C. Translation series, Koninglijk Instituut voor Taal-, Land- en Volkenkunde, The Hague, 1966.

Van der Kroef, Justus M. "Some Headhunting Traditions of Southern New Guinea". *The American Anthropologist* LIV (1952), pp. 221-35. Menasha, Wis. A brief account of an aspect of Marind-anim life not included by Lévy-Bruhl. Bibliography refers to articles by Van Baal, P. Vertenten, P. Wirz, etc.

Van Wing, le P.J., S.J. "Enfants noirs". *Congo, Revue genérale de la colonie belge* III, 1930. Brussels.

Vedder, H. See Lebzelter, V. "Die Bergdama des Mittellandes", in *Rassen und Kulturen in Südafrika*, vol ii, p. 168.

Vertenten, P. (Missionar in Okaba bei Merauke.) "Zeichen und Malkunst der Marindinesen (Bewohner von Niederländisch Süd-Neu-Guinea". *International Archives of Ethnography* vol xxii. Leiden: E.J. Brill, 1915.

Von den Steinen, Karl. *Unter den Naturvölkern Zentral-Brasiliens*, Reiseschilderung und Ergebnisse der Zweiten Schingù-Expedition 1887-1888. Berlin: D. Reimer, 1894. Reprint. New York: Johnson, 1968.

Wakefield, Edward Jerningham. *Adventure in New Zealand from 1839-1844.* London: John Murray, 1845.

Werner, Alice. *Myths and Legends of the Bantu.* London: G. Harrap, 1933.

Westermann, Diedrich. *Die Kpelle, ein Negerstamm in Liberia.* Göttingen: Vandenhoeck and Ruprecht, 1921. Leipzig: Hinrichs, 1921.

Williams, F.E. "Trading Voyages from the Gulf of Papua". *Oceania* III (1932-33).

Wirz, Paul. "Anthropologische und ethnologische Ergebnisse der Central Neu- Guinea Expedition 1921-1922". *Nova Guinea* XVI (1928). Maatschappij ter bevordering van het naturkundig Onderzoek der Nederlandsche Kolonien, Amsterdam.

_____. "Beitrag zur Ethnologie der Sentanier (Holländisch Neu-Guinea)". *Nova Guinea* XVI (1928).

_____. *Die Marind-anim von Holländisch-Süd-Neu-Guinea.* Hamburg: L. Friederichsen and Co. 1922. This work is in two volumes but four parts, separately paginated: Vol 1, Part i, "Die materielle Kultur der Marind-anim"; Part ii, "Die religiösen Vorstellungen und die Mythen der Marind-anim, sowie die Herausbildung der totemistisch-sozialen Gruppierungen"; and Vol 2, Part iii, "Das soziale Leben der Marind-anim"; Part iv, "Die Marind-anim in ihren Festen, ihrer Kunst und ihren Kentnissen und Eigenschaften".

Wisdom, Evan A. *Report to the Council of the League of Nations on the Administration of the Territory of New Guinea from 1 July 1928 to 30 June 1930.* Commonwealth of Australia, *Parliamentary Papers, Papers Ordered to be Printed,* 4 (1929-30-31).

Index

Figures in brackets following a page reference refer to matter of main or supplementary interest to be found in a note, numbered as it occurs in the relevant text.